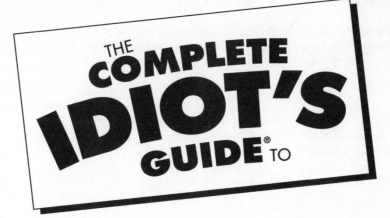

THE COMPLETE IDIOT'S GUIDE® TO

Starting Your Own Business

Fifth Edition

by Edward Paulson

ALPHA

A member of Penguin Group (USA) Inc.

This book is dedicated to the hundreds of thousands of prior readers, seminar attendees, clients, and university students who have inspired me and others by taking concrete steps to start their own successful business, and to you, who are yet to come along.

ALPHA BOOKS

Published by the Penguin Group

Penguin Group (USA) Inc., 375 Hudson Street, New York, New York 10014, U.S.A.

Penguin Group (Canada), 10 Alcorn Avenue, Toronto, Ontario, Canada M4V 3B2 (a division of Pearson Penguin Canada Inc.)

Penguin Books Ltd, 80 Strand, London WC2R 0RL, England

Penguin Ireland, 25 St Stephen's Green, Dublin 2, Ireland (a division of Penguin Books Ltd)

Penguin Group (Australia), 250 Camberwell Road, Camberwell, Victoria 3124, Australia (a division of Pearson Australia Group Pty Ltd)

Penguin Books India Pvt Ltd, 11 Community Centre, Panchsheel Park, New Delhi—110 017, India

Penguin Group (NZ), cnr Airborne and Rosedale Roads, Albany, Auckland 1310, New Zealand (a division of Pearson New Zealand Ltd)

Penguin Books (South Africa) (Pty) Ltd, 24 Sturdee Avenue, Rosebank, Johannesburg 2196, South Africa

Penguin Books Ltd, Registered Offices: 80 Strand, London WC2R 0RL, England

International Standard Book Number: 978-1-59257-584-8
Library of Congress Catalog Card Number: 2006930733

09   8   7   6   5   4

Interpretation of the printing code: The rightmost number of the first series of numbers is the year of the book's printing; the rightmost number of the second series of numbers is the number of the book's printing. For example, a printing code of 07-1 shows that the first printing occurred in 2007.

Printed in the United States of America

Note: This publication contains the opinions and ideas of its author. It is intended to provide helpful and informative material on the subject matter covered. It is sold with the understanding that the author and publisher are not engaged in rendering professional services in the book. If the reader requires personal assistance or advice, a competent professional should be consulted.

The author and publisher specifically disclaim any responsibility for any liability, loss, or risk, personal or otherwise, which is incurred as a consequence, directly or indirectly, of the use and application of any of the contents of this book.

Most Alpha books are available at special quantity discounts for bulk purchases for sales promotions, premiums, fund-raising, or educational use. Special books, or book excerpts, can also be created to fit specific needs.

For details, write: Special Markets, Alpha Books, 375 Hudson Street, New York, NY 10014.

Publisher: *Marie Butler-Knight*
Editorial Director: *Mike Sanders*
Managing Editor: *Billy Fields*
Acquisitions Editor: *Tom Stevens*
Development Editor: *Michael Thomas*
Production Editor: *Megan Douglass*
Copy Editor: *Ross Patty*

Cartoonist: *Chris Eliopoulos*
Cover Designer: *Bill Thomas*
Book Designers: *Trina Wurst/Kurt Owens*
Indexer: *Tonya Heard*
Layout: *Chad Dressler*
Proofreader: *Aaron Black*

Contents at a Glance

On the CD: Bonus Chapters

Contents

Introduction

Why not make your next job your own business? My guess is that you have had that thought or you would not be holding this book. Well, I say, "Why *not*?" Tens of millions of people have already started and successfully run their own businesses and there is a very real possibility that you can, too.

Let's face it—lifelong employment is a myth; you will most likely not be working for your current employer in just a few years. When you are an employee you always remain employed based on the whim of your boss. You could lose your job tomorrow and for no fault of yours. You could wind up unemployed simply because management had a change of heart and decided that your position was no longer needed. Poof! Gone! They generally aren't bad people, although there are some really rotten eggs. Change is simply the nature of business today, and it is up to you to change with the times.

Hundreds of thousands of people have purchased the four earlier editions of this book, and many have let me know how the book has contributed to their startup success. It is gratifying to know that the guidance provided in these chapters helped people take control of their business future by starting their own successful businesses.

In this edition, however, I push you one level further. I push you to understand (and hopefully believe) that work can be more than something you do to make money. Work can be something you do as an expression of who you are and what you are passionate about. That's right! I contend that you can not only have fun working at something you love, but also that you will make more money working at something you love when it is your own business.

Picture this if your corporate-trained mind will let you: you look forward to going to work, you feel that what you do makes a difference, you enjoy working with customers, you are making more money than you have ever made, and you control your own destiny. All of these are possible when you own the right business for *you*.

My overall goals in this book are for you to (1) assess yourself as a business owner; (2) pick the type of business that is right for you; (3) create a plan that simulates whether your idea makes business sense or not; and (4) successfully get your new business up and running. If you love your business idea and believe it can make you a decent living, then you would probably give it a try. After you complete the processes outlined in this book, you will have a more realistic assessment about the risks and rewards of "taking the plunge."

To help you accomplish all of these goals, I have revised the prior edition's content to make it even more valuable.

- The content was completely reorganized, updated, and revised.

- Several new, important chapters were added on small business benefits, buying a franchise, buying an existing business, dealing with China, and other important topics.

- A fabulous CD was included with editable versions of most of the business legal forms you will need. The CD alone is worth the price of the book in what it can save you in legal fees.

- Special emphasis was placed on not only writing a great business plan but also on preparing you for its presentation to possible investors.

- Important sections are included to help those of you in the corporate world successfully make the transition to business ownership.

- In addition to several Bonus Chapters, the CD also contains supplemental information to that already included in the printed book chapters. This extra material makes valuable reading for those of you looking to find that extra edge.

This was all done with one special end goal in mind: to help you succeed!

Every attempt has been made to include all of the information that I and other business owners regretted not having when we started our own businesses. I continually learn from my clients, students, and readers, and these important and sometimes painful lessons are included here for you to understand and avoid. This isn't reality television. This is the real world and being a business owner is often much different from what most people believe.

I have been in one form or another of entrepreneurship for over 25 years at this point, and I can tell you without question that there is nothing more exciting than seeing your idea become a thriving reality—and there are few things more painful than seeing it die. You don't have to go through a windshield to learn to wear a seat belt. I and my colleagues have already been through several business "windshields." Treat the thoughts and ideas in this book as your seat belt. Take them to heart and apply them where appropriate to avoid having an accident in the first place.

You are on the verge of a wonderful roller-coaster ride where you decide the direction of the track and the speed of the cart. Use this book to pick the optimal track layout, and then apply the tools to successfully steer the cart.

A simulation of your business idea will unfold as you work your way through this book, and as that idea develops, you will feel it become more "real." Letting uncertainty about the future stop you from taking control of your professional destiny may be doing yourself the biggest disservice of your life.

If you are diligent and lucky, you will put your plan to work and never have to worry about financial freedom again. It will be yours in abundance, and well deserved. There is nothing idiotic about that, is there?

How to Use This Book

The book is divided into three parts. The sequence is designed to lead you through the business plan writing, business formation, and startup management process step by step:

Part 1, "Starting the Right Business," is designed to help you get off on the right foot in creating your plan and starting your business. Chapter 1 helps you evaluate the strengths that you bring to the company and to also know where you will likely need help in the future. In this way, you can be on the lookout for the right people from the start. It also helps those of you in corporate jobs understand why you have not yet started your own business and provides an approach to becoming your own boss. Chapter 2 spells out the details related to the business plan writing process, which sets your expectations for what is involved in turning your idea into a credible business plan. Chapter 3 is the hub around which much of the rest of the book revolves. It presents the sections that your business plan must include and then points you to the particular chapters in Part 2 that are designed to help you write the sections of the plan. Chapter 4 is a special chapter that helps you determine your funding needs and determine ways of presenting your idea to potential investors in the least risky way. Chapter 5 presents the various benefits and drawbacks associated with buying into a franchise operation. Chapter 6 takes a little different spin and presents what is involved in buying an existing business instead of starting one from scratch. Chapter 7 introduces various legal business structures, such as sole proprietorships, partnerships, and corporations. It's kind of dry but critically important. (If you plan to start a corporation, make sure to check out the special CD Bonus Chapter 24)

Part 2, "Writing a Successful Plan," adds the meat to the business plan sections presented in Chapter 3. The chapter sequence in Part 2 corresponds to the business plan section sequence designated in Chapter 3. Starting with Chapter 8 you can, chapter by chapter, write your way through your plan. By the time you get to Chapter 16, you will have defined your market opportunity, assessed your competition, set up your marketing and sales approach, laid out your production plan, learned how to handle employees and payroll taxes, and understood financial statements along with their usefulness. There is a lot of content in these chapters, and when you add the accounting information from Chapter 15 to your plan, you should be just about done with the plan-writing process.

Part 3, "Running a Successful Business," presents all that stuff that nobody ever tells you about running a successful business. This section assumes that you will be successful in not only writing your plan but also in getting it funded and started. It teaches you how to manage your cash flow, set up for credit card sales, make sure your customers pay on time, deal with your banker, and handle international opportunities. Knowing the information in this section will help you make that transition from startup to survivor. Read this section when writing your plan to make sure that you include important forward-thinking thoughts into the proper sections. But also keep Part 3 next to your desk so that you can refer to it as you run your business. The lessons included in these chapters were costly for those who went through them.

Bonus Chapters Included on the Companion CD

Five chapters of additional information are included on the companion CD. This information is important and I strongly suggest that you take the time to review them as well as the chapters printed as part of the main book. These chapters cover ways for starting an Internet business, techniques for selecting your office location, ways to make your office efficient (and maybe even virtual) through effective use of telephone and computer technology, details about keeping your corporation legal, and proven ways for offering credit to customers while making sure you get paid. Like I said, this is important stuff that is worth your while to read.

In the Appendixes

At the very back, I included several appendixes to give you further sources of insight and information. Appendix A gives you definitions for oodles of terms used not only in this book, but in the industry as well. Appendix B contains a complete business plan for an idea called Kwik Chek that I wrote but never used because it didn't meet my personal objectives. Appendix C gives you resources that you can use if you want more information than is provided in this book. Appendix D gives you a listing of books and other printed matter you can use to further round out your background.

More About the Kwik Chek Business Plan

Almost anything is easier to do when you have a picture of how it's supposed to look when it's done. It's kind of like trying to assemble a model or toy without the picture of what it's supposed to look like all put together. It's one thing to read about how a business plan is created, but something completely different to see or read an actual plan.

For this reason, I included an actual business plan in Appendix B. This plan is one I wrote for a used-car evaluation service business I called Kwik Chek. When I wrote this business plan many years ago, I did it so that I could find out whether the idea would fly or whether I should go back to the drawing board. My original intent was to franchise the business nationwide, and I created the plan to see if I could meet that goal.

The Kwik Chek business concept didn't work for me because I wanted to be an absentee owner and franchise the concept rather than be an owner-operator. Fortunately, by going through the process of writing the business plan, I could see that this business wasn't going to help me achieve my goals. The idea still seems sound, but it's just not right for me.

Should you decide to pursue the idea using this business plan, good luck! If you succeed with the idea, please let me know; send me a dozen free car inspection certificates, and buy me dinner some time when you're passing through the Chicagoland area. Or a new Porsche would be nice!

You might, early on, want to read through the Kwik Chek plan to give you an idea about where your plan is going. Although the format I used in preparing the Kwik Chek plan is not the only one that works, it provides a starting place and a guide for you to follow when you start to write your own plan.

Extras

To guide you through the minefields of starting your own business, this book also provides additional tips and bits of information from those who have been there.

For starters, each chapter begins with a little story. Read these stories because they not only help you understand what the chapter talks about but also because every one of them is based on something that really happened. You can learn a lot from the stories alone.

You'll also find words of street wisdom, cautions, terminology, and helpful tips in these additional boxes:

On the CD

This box lets you know that the companion CD has a legal form or additional chapters and content on it that directly apply to the topic under discussion. Don't leave the CD in the sleeve. Pull it out and put it to work. This information is invaluable and can save you hours of frustration and potentially loads of money in professional fees.

Ed's Lessons Learned

This box gives you perspectives from business people who have gone through the same decision-making process you're going through now. Use their advice to help you make the right decisions.

Watch Out!

This box provides warnings to let you know about major, potentially business-threatening pitfalls along the way.

def•i•ni•tion

This sidebar defines technical business terms for you. These are usually also included in the Glossary.

Street Smarts

This box shows you street-smart information, shortcuts, and helpful advice.

Acknowledgments

There are numerous people to acknowledge and thank for their contributions to prior editions as well as this fifth edition. Up front, let me thank all those who contributed to the earlier editions. The following people provided vision, comment, inspiration, talent, and information that made this book more than it would have been.

Thank you, Alpha Books and Penguin Group (USA) Inc., for your success with the *Complete Idiot's Guide* series and for your strong commitment to this fifth edition. Thank you to Marie Butler-Knight for keeping this book available as a valuable tool for our readers, to Tom Stevens for his professionalism and vision, to Michael Thomas for making this book better from his constructive development editing, to Ross Patty for keeping it all readable, to Megan Douglass for taking the words and making them into the final book, and to the other members of the production staff for adding the final touches that make this product special. Thank you, Marcia Layton, for your input on the first and second editions. A huge thank you is included here to Steve Maple for his creation and providing of the incredibly valuable legal content included on the CD. Thank you, Oprah, for opening my eyes to the great potential of women as entrepreneurs and business owners. I hope this book helps them actualize themselves personally while simultaneously taking control of their professional and financial destinies.

There is a lifetime of experience and thank yous that go out to everyone whom I have worked with over the years. It is very possible that one of your stories is included in these chapters. This is only a partial listing of the contributors: Uday Om Pabrai, Mike Borch, Dan McManus, Mark Hallam for thinking like a banker, Frank Warner, Kate Clevenger for credit card processing information, Bill Cartmill and Henry Wong for continual updates on life in Silicon Valley, my students from DePaul University for detailed feedback, and my consulting clients who taught lessons but will remain nameless. War stories were provided by Dave Kalstrom, Jeff Kolling, Jim Herlinger, Ted Keane, Al Shugart, John Chambers, Michael Dell, and Dr. An Wang, among others. A very special thank you is offered here to my wife, Loree, who not only tolerated me but also scheduled around me during the writing phase, and to my mother, Jean, who once again put her professional secretary skills to work.

How-to-do, and not-do, insight was provided by various people from GenRad, Plantronics, Seagate, NuTech Testing Services, DAVID Systems (DSI ExpressNet), Telenova, IBM, Wang Laboratories, AT&T, and hundreds of clients and customers. If you are not mentioned here, please accept my apologies along with a thank you for the contribution you know that you made.

Special Thanks to the Technical Reviewer

The Complete Idiot's Guide to Starting Your Own Business, Fifth Edition was reviewed by an expert who double-checked the accuracy of what you'll learn here, to help us ensure that this book gives you everything you need to know about starting your own business. Special thanks are extended to Stephen Maple.

Stephen Maple is the Fitzwater Chair of Business for the University of Indianapolis School of Business, where he has taught since 1975. He is a graduate of the Indiana University School of Law and the Southern Methodist University School of Law. A member of the American Bar Association and a member of the Indiana bar since 1969, he is the author of *The Complete Idiot's Guide to Law for Small Business Owners* and *The Complete Idiot's Guide to Wills and Estates.*

Trademarks

All terms mentioned in this book that are known to be or are suspected of being trademarks or service marks have been appropriately capitalized. Alpha Books and Penguin Group (USA) Inc. cannot attest to the accuracy of this information. Use of a term in this book should not be regarded as affecting the validity of any trademark or service mark.

Part 1

Starting the Right Business for You

The first part of this book is important because it lays a framework that you will use for your business plan. Read, learn, and determine what feels true for you.

You will learn how to find the right business for you and discover ways to determine if your business idea is a good one. This section is set up to walk you through the typical decision process that I have seen my clients and students experience.

It explains what is involved in writing a startup business plan and helps you to understand the realities associated with owning a franchised business or buying a business that is already in operation. You will also learn about the different types of legal business forms such as partnerships and corporations.

Part 1 starts you on the road to business success. Let's get started.

You *Are* Your New Business

In This Chapter

- Learn why you may be better off with your own business
- Understand the relationship between you and your company
- Do you have what it takes to start a business?
- A look at your personal goals
- A look at your financial goals
- Transitioning from corporate employee to business owner

"Aren't you supposed to go into the office today?" asked Judy's husband Mike, nudging her shoulder from his side of the bed.

"Just let me sleep a little while longer. It's Saturday and I've had a long week," grumbled Judy.

Mike sat for a moment waiting to see if she would say more. She didn't.

"Okay. What's up? You have a big contract proposal due on Monday, and I think you said that it will take you all day to prepare it. So what's the deal?"

Judy rolled over to face him. He was right, and she knew it. But she just wanted a day off, even if it was a Saturday. On the other hand, she stood a reasonable shot at winning this proposal, and it would set her up for at least three months of work. Not a bad deal in a slow economy.

"I'm just missing being home with you and the kids," she said. "I get tired of working alone all the time and the thought of working all day on a weekend by myself while you guys are off playing bums me out."

Mike had seen her like this before and had a proposal for her.

"Tell you what. You get your butt out of bed and head into the office for the morning. Get as much done as you can by 1 o'clock and the kids and I will bring you in some sandwiches. We'll do a picnic at work on that little lawn area."

Judy looked resolute in her lethargy so Mike pulled out the big negotiation guns. He knew that once she started she would finish.

"Okay. I'll sweeten the pot a little. If you win this job, we'll plan a vacation to spend some of the money you'll earn. How does a week in Paris sound?"

Judy brightened up with the thought of a vacation. It had been well over a year since they took some time off, and she would need it if she won this project.

"Throw in lunch today with Paris and you have a deal," she replied, already heading toward the shower.

Every journey has its beginning, and your journey to becoming a successful small business owner starts with this chapter and *you*. Here we discuss your interests, your personality traits, and your goals as they relate to starting your own business. Simply stated, it is silly to invest time, money, and energy into starting a business that provides you with a job you don't want.

Believe it or not, not everyone is meant to run their own business. There are plenty of people who prefer working for someone else. (In fact, some people are better off working for someone else.) Understanding your own motivations is critical to deciding whether starting your own business will bring you happiness or grief.

You'll learn that it's really easy to start a business. All you have to do is sell something or fill out a few forms, and you're in business. However, starting a business that generates adequate and consistent income while providing personal reward is more difficult. This chapter will help you make decisions that will enable you to create a profitable *and* fulfilling business.

Lifelong Employment Is a Myth

If you think that you will work for the same company for your entire career, wake up! That might have been true in your parents' or grandparents' day, but it is just not true today. The world has changed, and you have to change with it.

Companies have shown that they generally have limited loyalty to their employees; employees have learned that they can count on their employer to keep laying people off until the company becomes profitable or for any number of other reasons. It may just be a matter of time until you are one of those caught in the "right sizing."

So you should be doing what any solid professional would be doing in this position—constantly looking for your next opportunity. Hopefully you picked up this book to see if owning your own business *is* that next opportunity.

Much of the uncertainty that comes with being an employee goes away when you are the business owner.

◆ You will know before anyone else if your company is having trouble.

◆ You will control your own benefits such as health insurance, life insurance, and pension.

◆ If the company does well you will have an opportunity to make more money from the success.

◆ If you are having problems with your boss, you can always have a heart-to-heart to get the problem resolved.

The benefits associated with running your own successful business are great, and the rate at which new businesses are being created indicates that many have already figured that out. Now it is your turn.

Does it make sense to leave your professional destiny, and the financial security of your family, in the hands of someone who has shown minimal allegiance to employees?

Cut Yourself Some Slack

You may be thinking that if things are so bad, why haven't you already left where you are and gone off on your own? The answer is tied directly into risk and your ability to withstand the risks associated with starting your own business. And there are risks, make no mistake.

If you are fresh out of school with no debts and nothing to lose, then it is pretty easy to take a risk and try a new idea, product, or company. But if you are a parent with children, a house, debts, and medical and other benefits along with a solid professional history, you have more to give up. Whether you know it or not, you are always performing a risk analysis in your head, and it is highly likely that you have not started your own business because you are not certain if you will make enough to warrant giving up what you already have.

So, if you are giving yourself a hard time because you have not shown the willingness to "risk it all," cut yourself some slack. I call that being responsible.

Here is the question to ask yourself: "If I knew for sure that I could make exactly the same amount of money in my own company as I am making now (including benefits), would I start my own company?" If the answer is "yes," then keep reading. If the answer is "no," then I think you need to keep your resume polished for your next employee position. No disrespect is meant. All I mean is that starting your own business involves risk, and the scenario I presented is about as low risk as it comes. If it wasn't enough enticement for you to take the plunge, then starting your own business may not be right for you.

On the other hand, if you said "yes" and would even take a cut in pay to run your own show, then you are right on target with potentially starting your own business. Now you need to determine, to a high enough degree of certainty, if your business idea can make you the money you need. That is the purpose of a business and ultimately the purpose of this book.

Your Business Starts with You

Perhaps the one characteristic that differentiates a small business from all others is the dramatic impact that the founders/owners have on the operation of the company. There is simply no way to separate the owners from the company in the early stages. Customers write checks to the company name but they think of themselves as doing business with the founder/owner. After all, when a company is small, there is really only one major decision maker: the owner. Owners set the ethics, quality, and value standards of their company, and those who think otherwise are kidding themselves. You create the public reputation and operational standards by which your future, larger, company will function. Make your standards ones that not only make you money but are also those that you can personally live with.

Startups are usually cash poor and must make do with as few employees as possible to stretch out the initial funding as long as possible. Keeping the employee overhead low is best accomplished with the founders doing as much of the work as possible until the cash flow becomes predictable enough to justify adding employees along with their associated expenses.

Street Smarts

The founders should have a clear handle on their own personality strengths and weaknesses along with a comprehensive inventory of each founder's specific skills. In this way, they can use themselves to best advantage keeping employee expenses low. As the company grows, founders struggle to learn another difficult skill: letting go of all of those things they did when the company was small.

Do You Have What It Takes?

There is a lot of folklore out there about startups and their founders. It is often difficult to separate fact from fantasy when evaluating founders, their startups, and their successes or failures.

Here are a few things that I have learned from entrepreneurs, about entrepreneurs:

◆ Most have started multiple businesses with the first few not really doing very well. Many have gone bankrupt multiple times and keep coming back to try again. Check out Donald Trump's background if you don't believe me.

◆ Most resent bureaucracy and tend to fall behind in maintaining the administrative sides of their businesses.

◆ Most get restless when things are going smoothly and are always looking for that next growth opportunity.

◆ They have a difficult time balancing the need for personal control with the need to trust employees to act on their behalf. Holding on too tightly to the reins often limits their business's growth opportunities.

◆ Most treat the business like it is a child at first and later as a family member. Don't laugh. It will likely happen to you as well. Think about it: you will likely spend more time with your business than with your family, all the while working to improve your family's financial security.

◆ Most will complain about the level of personal risk they live with and then risk it all again on what they believe is their next great idea.

◆ Most earn a decent income but very few earn the Bill Gates billions that make such great publicity.

◆ Most are normal people with a strong work ethic and commitment to providing the best quality to their customers.

◆ Most enjoy the freedom that comes with running their own show and paying their own bills, and are willing to accept the responsibilities that come with having that freedom.

◆ Many run their own businesses for a few years and then return to work as employees, no longer wanting to have the headaches associated with running their own shops. These people often make great employees as they have a more senior-level perspective of what is required to make a business run.

◆ A lot of them are women tired of working for "The Man." Heads up, guys—your next boss could very well be a woman.

If many of these points ring true for you, then you might have the right stuff for becoming a successful entrepreneur. Now it is time to see if you have the personality traits and skills needed to turn your business passion and idea into a profitable reality.

What Makes a Great Entrepreneur?

Whether an *entrepreneur* is born or made is a topic for scholars and philosophers. Suffice it to say that entrepreneurs come in all shapes, sizes, races, genders, and nationalities and that they have a few common characteristics that tend to differentiate them from those who work as employees. These differences are not themselves a criteria for success. They are required to deal with the typical demands of the entrepreneurial life.

To effectively deal with typical startup situations, entrepreneurs must …

◆ Have the ability to move forward in the face of large uncertainty.

◆ Be willing to start—to get going when others might wait.

◆ Be highly self-motivated.

def•i•ni•tion

An **entrepreneur** is an individual who starts and runs his or her own business rather than remains an employee of someone else's company. You can start an antique store and be an entrepreneur.

◆ Be willing to adapt along the way as things change from the expected.

◆ Believe in their ability to do what must be done to fulfill their customer commitments and business obligations.

◆ Make the image of success secondary to functioning on a financial shoestring.

◆ Have faith in their idea when others are not sure, while also not holding on too long to a bad idea that jeopardizes the financial health of the company.

◆ Be able to sell their products or services to prospective customers—be perceptive enough to determine how to create a fit between the customer's needs and their company's offering.

Street Smarts _____

I have entrepreneurs come in to speak to my university classes. The students regularly tell me that they acquire a higher level of respect for entrepreneurs after learning the daily realities that come with starting your own business. Some feel that entrepreneurship is not for them after better understanding the realities that come with opportunities and return more happily to their normal "day job."

◆ Be able to quickly understand the important aspects of a situation and then act appropriately to those important aspects. You may think that all the cool technical features of your new product are what prospective customers care about, but if the customer is primarily interested in the color you have to be perceptive enough to see that and talk about the color. This is particularly necessary in the early selling phase of the company, when reputation is limited and customer-perceived risk is at an all-time high.

What Are Your Strengths and Abilities?

You may now be wondering how you personally size up against the traits exhibited by successful entrepreneurs. The following quick assessment should not be treated as an absolute barometer of a "good" or "bad" entrepreneur, but it will give you an objective measure of yourself.

Answer the following questions as honestly as possible by placing a number between 1 and 10 in the blank. Use a 1 when you feel that the statement *least* applies to you and a 10 when it *very strongly* applies to you.

This is important: don't look at the paragraphs following this table *before* completing the personal assessment. Make it as honest as you can.

Personal Assessment Procedure

Assessment	Statement
	(1 = LOW 10 = HIGH)
_____	I am comfortable with moving forward and making decisions when I don't have all the answers to important questions.
_____	I am typically the one initiating things for my family, friends, or at work.
_____	I can keep myself on track even when nobody else is watching or monitoring my performance or activities.
_____	I can adapt my thinking and focus along the way as events change.
_____	I trust my current capability level and also believe that I can learn what is needed to meet future demands.
_____	I care more about getting the job done than how good I look doing that job. Performance is more important than image.
_____	I trust my business judgment and am willing to move forward on what I believe to be a good business idea even if others are not supportive of that idea.
_____	I trust my sales ability and know that I can sell my business along with its products and/or services as well as anyone.
_____	I tend to see the truth of a situation before others and can take the most effective actions for a given situation.
_____	I have enough money in savings, or access to enough money, to pay my personal and business bills for at least 6 months.
_____	Sum Total of All Rows (Totals between 10 and 100)

Make sure that you add up the total of all the table rows and write that total in the space allocated.

No doubt you will be higher in some areas and lower in others. That is normal for all people, including entrepreneurs. This process gives you a general guideline as to where you fit on the overall successful entrepreneurship scale and also tells you something about your areas of strength and areas where you could use some improvement.

If you scored less than 50, you may not be ready today for starting your own business. You may be better suited as an employee for now instead of being the person responsible for all of the pressure and uncertainty of running your own show. If you believe your answers and you still start your own business, then you need to surround yourself with people who are strong in the areas where you scored lower.

If you scored between 51 and 70, you show some entrepreneurship tendencies but might be better off first working for a small business for a while. This is the transition group.

If you scored over 70, you are likely champing at the bit to get started on your own business. You are probably beyond thinking about whether you should or shouldn't and are on to when, how, how many, and for how much. This will be particularly true for those who score higher and have fairly routine jobs with little excitement or uncertainty. This group should beware jumping on the first idea that comes along and should definitely spend the time finishing this book and writing a plan.

No simple test like this can possibly evaluate all of the skill and personality aspects that make you who you are. And no generalization could possibly tell you *with absolute certainty* whether you will or won't make it starting your own business. Ultimately, the decision is yours.

Stop by my website (www.edpaulson.com) and sign up for my electronic newsletter to get regular updates on this assessment and other interesting topics.

Do yourself a favor. Don't skimp or delude yourself on this portion of your evaluation process. All small business entrepreneurs quickly learn that they are their company's most important assets. They also learn that they will spend an immense amount of time doing what is required to make their businesses succeed. Doing what you enjoy improves your chances of success because you will likely be better at something you enjoy than at something you do "for the money." Doing what you like also improves the quality of your life and gives customers a reason to use you over someone else. Not ensuring a match in both of these important areas plants the seeds of failure before you even start. Before you commit money, energy, and time to your venture, make sure that it is something you really want to do.

Ed's Lessons Learned
From time to time, all business owners fantasize about giving up the administrative hassles of running a business. I'll even admit to fantasizing about taking a job counting screws in a hardware store every once in a while! A few years ago, when things were on a downturn with my business, I was talking with a fellow entrepreneur. When she asked how things were going, I said, "They are pretty bad right now, and I think some radical changes are due." She asked, "Are you thinking of getting a job?" I smiled and said, "No," to which she replied, "Then things aren't that bad."

What Are Your Needs?

When determining the viability of a startup *business* idea, you must consider the complement between the business you plan to start and how well it fits with your financial, family, and personal (spiritual) requirements. Otherwise, a few years down the road, you may find yourself resenting the company right at the point where it is poised to become the financial success you intended it to be. If your company does not make any money, it is a *hobby*. It helps to know how much you need to make ends meet.

def•i•ni•tion

Wealth comes from consistently having money left over after you pay all of your bills. A **hobby** is something you do for the fun of it. A **business** exists to make money.

This section prompts you to evaluate your own needs so that you can later map them against the requirements of your intended business. The overall intention is to best ensure that what your intended business will ask of you will be just what you are willing to give. Now that is business success if I ever heard it.

Financial Needs and Goals

How much money do you *want* to make, and how much money do you *need* to make? Understand that these two amounts are not the same. I've never met anyone who made as much money as they wanted, but most people make as much money as they need. It all comes down to how well they manage the money they make.

Wealth is a relative term. If you make $100,000 per year and spend $110,000, you are living beyond your means. Most people would consider you poor. However, if you make $65,000 and spend $50,000, then you're saving or investing $15,000 a year. Over the course of just a few years, you would be considered wealthy.

In short, don't just calculate how much money you want to bring in; look also at what it costs to live your current lifestyle. Calculate how much money you need to cover all your living expenses. You'll also have to account for the expenses associated with your business—federal taxes, state taxes, health insurance, life insurance, tuition assistance programs, vacation time, and so on. Don't guess at these amounts. Find out what you spent in each area over the last 12 months and use that as your baseline measurement for monthly financial survival. Let's face this issue head on—if your business idea does not have a reasonable chance of making this required amount of money in a short period of time, you should likely not start the business. You simply cannot support yourself for a long period of time if the business cannot pay you enough salary to cover your monthly living expenses.

The total of your minimum living costs and fixed business expenses is the amount you need to earn to live as comfortably as you are living now. You have to make at least this amount of money, or one of the following three things must happen:

1. You decrease your expenses.

2. You figure out a way to make more money from your venture.

3. You stay with your current job until your savings is high and your debt low.

Look at your finances both on a short-term (12 months) and long-term (2 to 5 years) basis. Remember, you need to get through the short term to make it to the long term. If you do not have the money to support yourself for at least 12 months (some say 18 to 24 months), then you should hold off starting your venture until you have the needed savings. Or you can look for outside sources to provide the money you need, such as family members, friends, or banks and government agencies. (See Chapter 4 for more details.) You need to be able to support yourself during those initial lean months when your business probably will not be making enough to pay your rent or your mortgage. So start saving those quarters now.

You should also consider how much money you're willing to spend before you pull the plug on a struggling business that is a cash drain. You may go to Las Vegas determined to stop gambling after you lose $500. Likewise, you should set a limit on how much you're willing to invest in a new business before it must pay for itself. Your odds of success at entrepreneurship are much better than at the gambling tables, but it is still a risk and must be treated as such.

Setting your limits in writing up front can help you make the decision to shut your business down if and when the time comes. That is one reason for writing a business plan. It's hard to set limits, but doing it up front can save you a lot of time and money. The Funding Needs section of your business plan should detail these up-front needs with a high degree of confidence, or you have done yourself a *huge* disservice.

Street Smarts

Most people dream of running their own businesses because they believe that it's the only way they'll become wealthy. In truth, most of the extremely wealthy members of our society obtained their money by owning a business. In many cases, they saw an opportunity to introduce a new product or service to the market and jumped in quickly. Some have succeeded and made millions—even billions. How about Larry Ellison of Oracle, Debbie Fields of Mrs. Fields' cookies, or even Henry Ford?

Not everyone who starts a business becomes wealthy, however. Statistics suggest that only 20 percent of all new businesses will be around in five years. When a business fails, the owner rarely makes a lot of money on the deal. Some statistics indicate that the average salary of a business owner after five years is around $65,000 and that it might go up to around $100,000 after 10 years or so. And they might work 80 hours a week for the privilege. Remember that this is an average, meaning some are higher and some lower. Because most of these businesses are privately owned, getting accurate data in this area is hard to do.

def•i•ni•tion

Cumulative cash requirement is the sum of all cash put into a company including the initial investment plus all payments to cover monthly net losses until the company becomes profitable. The largest projected negative value represents the total amount of cash needed to fund the startup phase of your business. (See Chapter 17 for more important details.)

Ed's Lessons Learned

People often don't understand that your startup business is like your boss. You might have to work after hours in a "normal" job. Why should you not need to do the same for your own business? You will have to, and your family must understand that this is true. Working for yourself doesn't mean that you take off whenever you, or they, like.

That may not sound bad to some of you, but take a look at the number of hours entrepreneurs have to put in to make that money. It's hard work! If you are already making that amount of money at a job you like, why would you take the chance? Many won't.

Also look at the total amount of money you will need to invest in order to get the business up and running. That total investment includes not only the amount of *cumulative cash requirement* of the business, but also the high likelihood that you may have to work for a period of time without taking a personal salary. If you reach the point where your projected cash supply is spent and you still can't afford to pay yourself a reasonable wage, it's time to decide whether this particular business is right for you. Your enthusiasm might be channeled behind the wrong business idea. Shifting your focus to a new business may be the key that opens the door to your financial success! Many successful small business owners struggle or fail at their first few attempts.

Family Motivations and Goals

If you are the type of person who cannot leave your family alone for the evening or weekend without having intense feelings of guilt, then you should examine your startup intentions and your family's needs before you begin a new business venture.

There will be times when you will need to work at night, on weekends, and on holidays. At these times, you will have to choose between family involvement and business commitments. Your family needs to accept your commitment to your business without being hurt or angry. They need to understand that it is in *all* of their best interests for the business to succeed.

Communicate openly with your spouse, children, parents, and friends about what you want to do and what kind of a time and energy commitment it will take. If you sense from initial discussions that your family may resent your directing attention away from them and toward a business, think about ways that you can involve them in the company. Instead of thinking that you have to choose between business and family, talk with them about what you can all do together to run a business. Putting your children on the payroll may be a savvy tax strategy to consider, as long as they are actually doing something productive for the business. Making your spouse an employee may enable you to pay for your family's health insurance through a company group plan. The more they have invested in the success of the business, the more they will support you to do the work needed to make it succeed.

Many divorces have resulted from the feeling that the business is more important than everything else in the business owner's life. Be sure your family knows that this is not the case. Typically, just telling them won't do it; you have to show them by setting aside time to be with them.

Spend the time to get your family involved from the beginning. Set their expectations properly to best avoid having recurring ugly scenes later. Your family can become a source of strength if they understand the importance of their support in your and the business's success. Nobody is an island, and you may end up alone snuggling with your checkbook if you don't handle your family situation with respect.

What Are Your Spiritual Goals?

Spirituality in the context of this chapter has more to do with what makes us feel good as human beings than with a formal religion. For some of us, a business helps us achieve spiritual goals through the belief that by providing a valued service to our clients, we are improving their lives. Spiritual goals can also be reached by creating an organization to perform social service work, such as a food kitchen or a halfway house. Some entrepreneurs want to create an organization where their employees can realize their full potential. In a world of compromised corporate ethics, some people start their own business to ensure that they can always work in an ethical environment of their own creation. This is motivation enough for them.

One of my clients is determined to start her own business, but not for any of the personal financial reasons we've discussed so far. She has enough money to support herself and has started businesses before. But she now wants to start one to bring new attention to the plight of people in recovery for alcohol or substance abuse. Her belief is that by creating products to better meet the needs of this group, she can draw attention to and help support them, donating the bulk of the profits to related charities and human service agencies. Like many other entrepreneurs, she is dedicated to her business idea; she just happens to be doing it for spiritual reasons.

In essence, don't neglect the nonbusiness side of your soul when deciding to start your own business. In fact, there are many people who believe that you should look here first.

Escaping the Big House—Leaving Corporate America

This section is for those of you who are now working for someone else and are interested in branching off into your own business. It may be that you have seen many of your fellow employees be "right sized," and you are wondering when your turn will come. It may be that you now don't trust corporate life as the secure lifetime investment you previously assumed it to be and want to have more control over your employment destiny.

I contend that employees are really contract workers in today's work environment. I don't mean that from a legal perspective but more from a practical perspective. Very few people I talk to today believe that they will still be working for their current employer when they retire.

Employees work for their employer by choice. If a better job offer comes along, many will likely take it. Most publicly held companies have now shown themselves prone to laying people off if needed, even if the company has enough cash on hand to suffer a downturn. This is the essence of a contracting relationship: the contractor chooses the client and the client selects the contractor, both knowing that the relationship will end at some future date. They negotiate the financial and responsibility details that apply during the contracting period, but both know that the relationship is temporary and not one for life.

Once you realize that you are essentially a contractor, your approach to work changes. You start to manage your time differently, always looking over your shoulder for your next engagement, knowing that the steady paycheck will at some point come to an end. You start to increase your savings, knowing that you might have a period of no income between engagements. You start to set up your medical and other personal benefits so that you, and not an employer, has primary control over them.

I speak quite often on this topic and provide the following advice to those aspiring entrepreneurs who are currently employed:

◆ Start building your savings so that you have the financial resources to weather an unexpected job termination. This should be a minimum of 6 months of living expenses (12 months preferred), but don't stop there—keep saving. It will always pay off.

◆ Start the personal evaluation and business planning process while you are still employed. This way, you already have a running start should you be terminated.

◆ Knowing that you have someplace else to go (your own business) may make you more effective in your current job. You lose nothing by planning out your personal business while still employed.

◆ You may come to appreciate your current job more as you realize what is involved in going it alone. It will likely give you a more mature look at what happens at your employer, letting you treat work as a "lab" of sorts. Consider going to night school to take business-oriented classes. They will make you a better manager for your employer and for your own business, and your employer may pay the tuition to boot!

◆ Keep it to yourself that you are planning to go off on your own. You may never take the entrepreneurship plunge, and nothing is gained in letting your employer know about your aspirations early in the planning process.

◆ Keep your entrepreneur's eye open at work for opportunities that could make your employer your first startup customer. But don't bring it up at work until you really are ready to go it alone since they may fire you on the spot if they know you are planning to leave. You just never know. Have a lot of your plan finished, and proven viable, before talking about it in public.

◆ Don't set yourself up to resent your current job if it is one that allows you to do what you enjoy, to do what you are good at, to make a good income with solid benefits, and provides a sense of personal satisfaction. If you are already happy with what you are doing, there may be little motivation to change jobs; but it is always a good idea to have a contingency plan in place should your job suddenly disappear.

Street Smarts

Just as you might occasionally envy the entrepreneurial lifestyle, the entrepreneur occasionally envies people who love their job working for someone else. More than one entrepreneur has returned to corporate life after selling their own business simply to not have the headaches that come with that "enviable" entrepreneurial lifestyle.

If you already have a job, great! If it is a job you love, even better! There is little in professional life more satisfying than working within a group of dedicated people doing what they love while making a positive difference in the world. Larger companies can provide this opportunity where, by contrast, starting your own business is usually a very solitary experience, especially in the early days. Just know that a shifting of the economic environment at your company could cost you your job through no fault of your own. At that point, you want to have taken the steps outlined in this section to make sure that you are ready for the change, perhaps using it as a starting point for becoming a successful entrepreneur.

What Is Your Personal Bottom Line?

Ultimately, it all comes down to you. What do you want, and why do you want it? Do you think that running your own business will give you the fulfillment that's been missing in your current job? Are you willing to earn less money for a while as you try to establish your company? How far are you willing to go to make your business work? Are you willing to get up and go to work even when nobody is going to yell at you if you stay home and watch soap operas?

If you like the stability of working 9 to 5, wake up! Owning your own business means that you don't have set hours because you'll be working long hours in the early stages. If this paragraph alone is enough to talk you out of pursuing your own business, then send me a thank you card. You are not ready yet to make that kind of commitment. It doesn't mean that you never will, just that right now is not your time.

On the other hand, if after reading this chapter you not only feel that starting your own business is the right thing to do but also have a better idea of what you personally bring to its success, then congratulations! You have just crossed the first major hurdle toward not only thinking and acting like an entrepreneur but also trusting that you are the right person to start your business. Some feel that these may be the most important decisions you will ever make in creating a successful business.

On the CD

When you start your own business, you *are* the business. People might think that they are working with a "company," but underneath it all, they know that they are working with a person: you. Take a few minutes to read the special bonus section I put on the CD entitled "Your Ethics and Your Business." Make sure you keep this very important issue in the front of your thinking. You can usually recover from a mistake, but it is really difficult to recover from a breach of integrity.

The Least You Need to Know

- Start to understand that lifelong employment is a myth and that it is up to you to protect your working future.

- Understanding your personal needs, goals, skills, and personality before you start your own business is critical to later success.

- Setting a limit on your losses and time investment is a valuable step before you start your own business and one important reason for writing a business plan.

- Make sure you have enough money saved to support yourself for at least 6 months in addition to the money needed to fund and establish your new business.

- Getting your family's support and acceptance before starting a business is a necessary step, or you might find yourself choosing between the two, which is a no-win for everyone.

- Planning to start your own business while still employed is a good move that protects you and your family from an unexpected job termination.

Navigating the Critical Planning Process

In This Chapter

- ◆ Why you should create a business plan
- ◆ Understanding how your plan will get written
- ◆ Finding the right information
- ◆ Planning to survive the short term for long term success

"You look about as glum as I have ever seen you," remarked Peter as he looked across the table at his friend Bill.

"No doubt," said Bill shaking his head. "I've gotten myself and my company into a huge mess, and I'm not sure what to do to get out of it."

"What happened?"

"Remember when I decided to take on the large distribution contract for South America earlier this year? Well, I just found out that our major customer in Argentina is going under and taking a chunk of my receivables with them. They

fell behind on their payments and we kept shipping believing—perhaps more accurately, hoping—that they were good for it. Now, I'm not sure that I can make payroll since those receivables were used to secure my line of credit with the bank."

"Ouch! That really hurts."

"Not as bad as knowing that I could have avoided the whole thing by staying with my original business plan instead of being seduced by the prospect of making 'big money' in a short period of time. We never planned to go to South America in the first place and had no initial interest in carrying those products. I just got greedy and now have put the entire company and a year's worth of work in serious jeopardy. When will I learn to listen to my own advice?"

There are so many little decisions that need to be made and so many factors to consider on your way to becoming a business owner that you may become overwhelmed before you even start. But if you take it step by step, you can carefully weigh all your options—and there are a lot of them. A *business plan* helps you to make sure that you take all of the right steps that lead to the same successful conclusion—your successful business.

Chapter 3 presents all of the details you need to know about creating the plan itself. This chapter is designed to help you understand the plan-writing process, which can turn into a pretty major project. Any project has a higher likelihood of success if you appreciate the magnitude of the undertaking and are clear about where you are starting, where you want to end up, and why it is worth doing in the first place.

def•i•ni•tion

A **business plan** is a document that can be as small as 10 pages or long enough to fill a book, with a reasonably detailed plan usually running 30 to 50 pages. (See Chapter 3 for the section details.)

Taking a few minutes to read and absorb the information presented in this chapter will keep you motivated to write your plan and keep you from having to rewrite portions of it. The time spent here will save you time later on.

Why Prepare a Business Plan?

Although you might have heard that you only need a business plan if you are trying to get financing to start a company, this is not true. In addition to using a business plan to secure funding from others, there are several other reasons to write one:

- ◆ Putting your goals and ideas down on paper helps to organize your thinking.

- ◆ Writing down your plans and goals demonstrates your commitment to your business, which impresses potential investors, suppliers, and employees.

- ◆ Once you have your plan down on paper, you have a guide to achieving your goals that you can refer to regularly to measure your progress.

- ◆ Not only do you have a guide that helps keep you on track, it also ensures that all your employees understand where you plan to take the business.

- ◆ Your plan helps focus your organization on its mission, reducing the chance that the business becomes sidetracked by other less important activities.

- ◆ As your own ultimate investor, you deserve to prove to yourself that your business idea is a good one. And if you are funding yourself, it is even *more* important that you write the plan because there is no outside investor check on your idea and approach.

Let's face it: others do not believe in your idea nearly as much as you do. Part of the reason is that they probably don't know as much about your business, your product, and your plans as you do. For everyone else to believe in your idea, they need to see what you intend to do. In this way, the plan is also a sales document; those who read it will be sold on your idea, vision, and approach. There will probably be many different people who want to see your business plan, each for different reasons, including some of the following:

- ◆ Banks and other funding sources will use your plan to determine whether you are truly capable of starting and running the business.

- ◆ The Small Business Administration (SBA) will review your plan to make sure it will be profitable so that you won't have any problem repaying their guaranteed loan (if you opt to apply for one).

- ◆ Your board of directors (if you create one) or management team will want to review your plan to understand the future direction of the company.

- ◆ Employees will want to see sections of the business plan to understand whether the company has long-term career opportunities for them and to understand what is expected of them. This is optional but it can be a good idea for key employees.

- ◆ Strategic partners or joint venture participants will want to know portions of your plan to determine whether your overall direction is in alignment with their plans and mission.

As a result of the planning process, you will learn more about your business idea than you ever thought possible. Treat it as a learning experience, and watch where it takes you. The plan will start quickly to take on a life of its own.

Think of It as a Simulation

A business plan is just a simulation. It is a way of predicting the future success of a business idea before you ever get started. Will the plan be correct? Perhaps, but the only way you will know if you were right with your predictions is after you have already taken the plunge and implemented the plan.

Large companies may spend hundreds of millions of dollars preparing a business plan because the levels of money involved with introducing a product on a national, or even international, scale are very large. Small business people rarely have this large planning and funding luxury; as a result, they produce less comprehensive plans and have to be quick enough to adapt to unexpected things that occur after they actually get started. But don't forget that the money and time you will invest in a business idea will be important to you and making some type of planning process good protection. (See Chapter 4 for more information on venture capital and other types of funding.)

My point here is that the business-planning process produces more than simply a written document. It produces a simulation of how you expect your startup business to function. It produces a way for you to determine, as best you can without actually doing it, whether the business idea stands a reasonable chance of success. It forces you to think through the numerous details involved with the daily creation of your business. It increases your likelihood of being successful. You are much better served spending a few extra days up front adding "meat" to the business simulation (a.k.a. plan) than spending weeks or years and hundreds of thousands of dollars "experiment-ing" in the real world. Experiment and find mistakes on paper and then use your scarce time and money to make your planned idea a reality.

The Overall Plan-Writing Process

Many people plan more extensively for a vacation than they do for a new business. "Oh, I've been in business for a long time. I can wing it." Big mistake! Don't quit your day job until you research the type of business you want to start and feel confident that you can succeed. Unless you are pretty sure that over a reasonable amount of time you can at least earn your current salary with your own business, why risk what you have? The planning process helps to decrease your uncertainty about your business idea and increase your confidence in your business income projections.

The plan is a representation of your level of professionalism, so make sure that it is …

- easily understood and without spelling or basic grammar errors.

- printed on white paper using laser jet or comparable print quality.

- laid out to be easily read, using page numbers and minimum 1-inch margins so readers can make notes as they go through it.

- double-spaced using a standard 12-point typeface such as Times, Helvetica, or Courier.

- nicely bound in such a way that the sheets don't fall on the floor when being read.

- written with the intent of creating reader understanding as its primary goal instead of assuming that the reader knows as much about your company and its offering as you do. Don't laugh. This is a common mistake for novice and experienced business people alike.

Some sections of the plan can remain confidential (such as financial information, new technology overviews, or client data); you won't typically share them with outsiders until they have earned that right. However, you should assume that many sections of the plan will become public because you'll be sharing it with many different audiences. Those less-sensitive sections might include information about your personnel, existing products and services, industry analyses, and any other company background information that normally appears in marketing literature. Taking a modular approach to your plan writing lets you mix and match the sections as appropriate to the intended reader.

Being Honest

If you want to show your business plan to potential investors, include the assumptions you made when writing the plan, potential risks and rewards, and any important milestones to ensure that the investors understand the whole picture. Making your situation appear too "rosy" will make investors skeptical, but making it appear too risky might scare them off. By simply being honest about what you see as the strengths and weaknesses of your situation, you allow investors to make up their own minds based on as much information as you have and your personal interpretation that the idea has merit.

Being up front with potential investors helps you avoid problems down the road if things don't go as well as you planned. Given the right opportunity, you can lead professional investors into a minefield, as long as you first tell them that there is a minefield. However, if they feel you misrepresented your company and the potential rewards they can expect, you will seriously damage your working relationship or even get into legal trouble.

Street Smarts _____

Don't worry about hitting your business projections exactly; experienced investors know that things can go "off plan" as a project unfolds and that these figures are your best guess. But hitting or exceeding your projections is always a good thing. Investors simply want to minimize the likelihood of losing their investment due to mistakes or poor management on your part. The business plan provides a framework for working out the details of your relationship with investors, sort of like a trial run. If you can't work together on the plan, you will likely not work well together in the business.

You want to be honest with yourself as well even if you do not intend to show the plan to a third party. Favorably skewing your sales and expense projections so that your plan shows, on paper, you making the income level you want does you no good at all if reality is substantially less cooperative. This is usually the case. Remember you are investing your time and money in this venture, and you want your plan to represent as accurately as possible your likelihood of making money on that investment.

This is really important to understand: you are investing twice in your new business—once when you put time and money into the business and again for what you don't earn on that money and time doing something else. If you give up an existing job paying you $40,000 per year to start your business and put $40,000 into the business to get it started, it is actually costing you $80,000 if you don't at least earn from the business the $40,000 you would have made working at your current job.

Getting Help

You are not alone when you prepare your plan, even though it might feel that way. Organizations out there have a vested interest in helping you succeed at starting your own business. These include the local Chamber of Commerce, entrepreneurial associations, and the federal government. Here are a few resources that can help:

- ◆ The Small Business Administration (SBA at www.sba.gov) works with a group of retired executives called SCORE (Service Corps of Retired Executives at www. score.org) to help you create a business plan and acquire funding. These are people who have already been where you plan to go; they can help you assemble the plan. Better yet, their services are free! Simply contact your local SBA office and ask for the phone number of the local SCORE office.

◆ Small Business Development Centers (SBDCs), which are collaborative programs developed by the SBA and local colleges and universities, also provide free counseling to people starting a business. There are more than 1,100 SBDC service locations in existence to assist you. You can find a local office by going to www.sba.gov/sbdc.

◆ The Online Women's Business Center is also sponsored by the Small Business Administration and is dedicated to helping women start their own businesses. More information is available at www.sba.gov/onlinewbc.

◆ Women- and minority-owned companies can also turn to Minority Business Development Agency (MBDA) for referral to one of the local Minority Business Development Centers. The MBDA is a part of the Department of Commerce and it provides low-cost assistance in writing a business plan, developing a marketing campaign, and pursuing government contracts.

See Appendix B for contact information for these and other resources.

You'll Never Have All the Information You Need

Of one thing you can be sure: you will never have all of the information you need to take all of the risk out of your venture. Even the large companies, who spend millions of dollars on research, cannot take all of the risk out of a new product launch.

At some point, you are going to have to say "enough is enough." Assume that the information you have is solid enough and the analysis comprehensive enough to determine if you should pursue or walk away from your idea. The plan may not seem a simulation at this point, and may actually feel real. That is good, and it means you have done your homework.

This can be a scary time because you always know more about a plan's flaws after you have been working on it for awhile. You know what the assumptions are and where the hidden traps are located. Don't beat yourself up about that. Nobody is perfect, and neither is your plan. You can only get it as close to ready as possible and then decide to move forward with implementation or drop the idea and move on to your next startup opportunity.

Experience tells many entrepreneurs when that time is right and the analysis is as reasonably complete as it is going to be. If you do not have that level of experience, then I suggest that you hire someone who does have it so that your plan can be evaluated in an objective way but with a seasoned eye. Many people contact me at this stage to have me critique their plan.

If you don't have the experience and cannot afford a seasoned veteran to review your plan, then I suggest that you follow your gut instinct. If you have excitement butterflies, don't let them keep you from moving forward. But if you have a queasy, uncertain feeling that something is wrong, then likely there *is* something wrong. It might be something that you forgot. Or something of a critical nature that requires more detailed research. Or simply that the pieces of the plan don't tie together as neatly as you would like.

In any of these cases, I suggest that you look to the source of this concern and determine its origin. You may look at the source of the uneasiness and dismiss it as simply paranoia. Or you may realize that this fear is well founded and more work is required. Just be honest with yourself about the concern, address it, and then take action. Only time will tell if you made the right decision.

The Minimum That Your Plan Must Cover

Few people who read your plan will remember everything that it contains. They will walk away from the reading remembering only a few basic points—usually those that are of the most importance to their particular interests.

Here are a few basic points that your plan must cover to adequately serve you as the writer/manager/owner and other likely readers:

◆ A detailed definition of the proposed business idea and why it is a good one in light of the market conditions

◆ How much money is required to get the business up and running on a solid financial footing

◆ When the business will not only recover the initial investment but also begin to show a reasonable profit (return on investment) for investors

◆ Why this business, run by you, stands a reasonable chance of succeeding

◆ A listing of the major challenges that this business faces in becoming successful and how they will be addressed

- Details of how sales are going to be generated through marketing, sales, and promotion activities

Your plan will include tons of information that you are responsible for researching, analyzing, and presenting. The ultimate goal of the presentation (the plan) is to answer the preceding points. Remember that you are simply trying, through your simulation, to remove as much perceived risk as possible from the prospect of investing in your company. If your plan accomplishes that goal with integrity, then it is a success.

Street Smarts

Busy people, which includes most investors, won't take the time to read a plan that is too long. They also won't figure out what you're talking about if you haven't been crystal clear. A small plan that clearly and concisely addresses all the major points of interest will be better received than a lengthy one that drones on about irrelevant information for pages and pages. You need to do the work for them; spell out your information in plain, well-written English. Lead your readers through the plan, step by step, explaining your idea and how you intend to make money doing it. Present the information succinctly and professionally.

Dealing with a Bad Business Idea

What a drag! You perform the entire analysis to discover the idea does not hold financial water. Now what? Be thankful! You have just saved yourself from a nasty experience.

If you had pursued the venture based on what you thought true in the beginning, you would be either personally bankrupt after investing all your hard-earned savings, or apologizing to your angry investors. Take heart! A negative outcome on this round does not negate the entire venture. You can now consider a different, potentially more successful approach to the same or similar idea.

Take a look at your approach to the business to see if modifying it can provide a better, and more profitable, strategy:

- Is the problem with the idea itself or simply how it is presented?

- Are you the right person to shepherd the idea to success, or should you be looking for others to round out other critical positions? Should you look at merging your talents with another, more established firm?

◆ Do you need more money to buy you additional time to achieve the needed market recognition?

◆ Should you initially offer a product or service that is more readily acceptable and then convert your customers over to your new product or service line once they are already familiar with you and your company?

◆ Are your sales estimates too low? What could you do to increase the sales faster, and what would be the additional cost?

◆ Are there things you can do to minimize the level of perceived risk?

Keep your chin up and remember: creating a successful business plan is a lot like solving a mystery. You have many stray facts that need to fit together properly before the venture makes sense on all levels. Take the time to learn the facts and keep looking for a viable solution.

Short- and Long-Term Planning

Nothing happens in the long term without *short-term* actions that move you toward your desired outcome. Short-term actions cannot help achieve any particular goal if no goals have been set or no plan has been developed. You have to know where you're going before you can figure out a route to get there, right?

def•i•ni•tion

Short-term goals refer to those goals you set for up to one year. Long-term goals refer to goals you hope to meet from one to five years in the future.

Taking the time to determine your own goals and your company's *long-term* mission and objectives will guide your daily actions. Without this framework, you and your employees may be busy, but the business will not move forward because everyone is pulling in separate directions. Making sure everyone knows and understands the goals and objectives of the company will make life a lot easier—for you as well as your employees. Defining the company's goals will minimize employee frustration because they will know what they're working toward. You can minimize confusion by identifying and eliminating activities that don't directly support the goals of the company. (Remember the story at the beginning of this chapter.)

It all starts with you. Take the time to learn more about yourself, your personal motivations, and your long-term goals to ensure that you take the company in the proper direction for you and your investors. For example, if you like the idea of working alone from a home office, make sure that you're not setting your business up to grow to a point where you have to hire employees or get an office outside your home. If your business starts to grow in a direction or at a speed that makes you uncomfortable, you may start to resent the business and eventually unravel what is otherwise a good thing. You can avoid this by simply deciding up front what kind of business you want to have, both short term and long term. Once you decide, you can move ahead to make it happen.

You should review and revise your plan every year to make sure that you are headed where you intended and also that any new information acquired along the way is added. In this way you keep on track while also ensuring that you and your company don't get stale.

The Least You Need to Know

- ◆ Knowing and aligning your goals helps you to define the actions needed today to help you reach those goals.

- ◆ A plan analysis that shows an idea isn't viable saves you time, money, and headaches. Review the plan from a new perspective to see if it is salvageable when approached differently.

- ◆ Your business plan isn't only for other people to read. It is for you to read and use as well.

- ◆ Your initial startup plan will only cover the early stages of your company's development. Future annual plan revisions will address the new circumstances and keep your plan current.

- ◆ Honesty is the best policy. Keep your plan accurate, and don't make claims you cannot back up without stating them as your best guess.

Your Recipe for a Professional Business Plan

In This Chapter

- ◆ Defining your mission statement
- ◆ Describing your business idea
- ◆ Understanding the plan sections and their contents
- ◆ Using the plan to sell investors on your business

"Why the special staff meeting?" asked Jake, the sales manager. "Not sure," was the reply from his colleague, who was responsible for production.

The company started out as a small beverage manufacturer; it now sold millions of dollars a year in fruit-drink products. At the president's insistence, the company had recently introduced two new lines of frozen fast foods. The products hadn't initially sold very well but sales were slowly improving.

Jake had worked with a top management team last year to create a business plan that everyone had signed off on. The company's real moneymaker, the main beverage product line, was doing well and supporting the new fast food products, but Jake had reservations about how long the company could last without the new frozen food lines carrying their respective part of the profits (which was just starting to happen). The planning team agreed that it was time to maintain the status quo, but the company president (who was also the founder) liked new projects. Jake didn't think the company could stand another product introduction so soon after the frozen food line's near-fiasco.

"Thanks for coming," said the president. "Now that I have more free time, I have been experimenting with new methods of food preparation. I think the American people will pay for fresh, vegetable-based foods that taste good and are easy to prepare. As a result, I want to introduce three new, fresh vegetable side-dish lines that will open up new markets for the company and take us into new retail outlets. I expect the full support of management in taking these products to market."

Jake mustered his courage and asked, "Sir, don't you think we should wait a little while before moving into new markets? Our frozen food lines are just now being accepted, and I have a concern that diffusing our efforts with fresh vegetable lines may be too much for us now. Why don't you take some time and perfect the recipes and give our distribution channel a chance to settle down?"

As the president and founder, what would you do? Would you make Jake sell rice noodles in Iceland for not supporting your plan? Would you take his advice? Would you thank him for his input and do what you want anyway? How do you determine what the proper business response should be?

Many managers use the business plan as their touchstone when making major impact decisions like the one presented in the opening scenario. It is the business plan that presents an approach, which, at the time of the plan writing, was considered the best possible option. Deviating substantially from that plan may indeed be a solid idea, but there should also be some type of justification as to why the new approach is better than the one presented in the plan. The carefully reasoned approach of the original plan contains a rationale that I believe requires an alternate set of reasoning if it is to be substantially changed. In short, the plan is the play book for your startup business's success. Staying with the play book at all costs may not be a great idea, but neither is disregarding the play book without valid reason. It confuses management, employees, customers, and, in particular, investors, who invested with a set of plan-created expectations and have every reason for concern if future actions do not lead to fulfilling those expectations.

This chapter presents the details associated with writing the business plan and is designed to be used in conjunction with later chapters that deal with specific sections of the plan.

Briefly Describing Your Business Idea

Describing your business idea sounds like a simple thing to do, but it is often quite difficult as it requires you to reduce the various complexities of your business idea into just a few sentences. Once you can present your idea in a few sentences, you are well on your road to understanding the essential aspects of your business. This description should be no longer than two paragraphs of around four sentences each, and once someone has read these two paragraphs he or she should know this about your business: (1) what your business does, (2) why it does these things, (3) what makes it unique when compared to other similar businesses, and (4) why the reader should care about your business in the first place. Getting all of this into a few sentences is a great exercise, and you will likely find yourself rewriting these few sentences many times as you work your way through the business plan writing process, so don't get discouraged.

Your Mission: Why Does Your Company Exist?

The mission statement covers, in just a few sentences, the reason for your company's existence. It provides the overall umbrella under which all other goals and actions fall. It says what your company does and who it does it for.

A typical *mission statement* for a clothing retailer, for example, might be the following:

> To provide trendy, natural-fiber clothing to health-conscious women between 18 and 35 years old, at reasonable prices in an environment where buying is fun.

> Or for another example: to be the number one or number two market share provider in every market in which we participate within 18 months of market entry.

Notice that the mission statement is brief and to the point, determining the overall direction of the company. It also sets limits. If a vendor tempts you with a hot men's clothing line, you can see that men's clothing would clearly be in violation of the mission statement. Either the company's prescribed mission statement needs to be changed, or the idea to add men's clothing needs to be dropped so that the company can stay focused on its core mission.

def•i•ni•tion

A **mission statement** is a written description that explains why you're in business. Usually only two paragraphs long at most, it explains to employees and customers why the company exists, such as to provide excellent customer service, the lowest prices, and a fun work environment.

Notice that the second mission statement, dealing with market share, requires that the company only pursue offerings that have tremendous sales potential, which virtually eliminates the consideration of niche market products or services.

When you create your company's mission statement, consider the following:

♦ What do you plan to do? For example, "We will sell second-hand office equipment."

♦ Who do you plan to do it for? For example, "We will focus on price-sensitive customers within a 20-minute drive of our shop."

♦ What best ensures success? For example, "We will target sale prices of products to be at 60 percent of new retail price for comparable products."

You can embellish these simple objectives with more specific points that add more details to the mission statement frame. Additional items might include the following:

♦ How your company will deal with changes in the marketplace (such as technology advancement or new competition), for example, by investing in new equipment or hiring more staff.

♦ The *benefits* (not the *features*) of your product or service, which will persuade customers to buy from you (such as a high customer-convenience purchasing approach). By focusing on benefits, rather than features, you will concentrate on the true value of your offering to the customer.

♦ How following the mission statement will contribute to the company's short- and long-term success, such as by keeping the company focused on a high-growth market or keeping expenses down.

def•i•ni•tion

Features are the different characteristics of a product or service. For example, the features of a drill bit may include its size, length, and the type of material it is made of.

Benefits are what the customer gains by using your product or service. One benefit of the drill bit is that it makes holes of a specific size. Customers buy something to obtain the benefits associated with using it. The features get them the benefits.

It may take you days to write these simple sentences. But these sentences define everything else that occurs within the plan and ultimately within the company, so defining them clearly is time well spent.

After defining your company's mission statement, you can define the company's overall *objectives*, or *goals*. These are projects that comply with the mission statement and have specific time frames and measurable results. A typical objective may be to "add three new products to the line over the next 12 months."

You can then break these goals down into *tasks* that you assign to individuals, to be completed within specified time frames. All these tasks contribute to the fulfillment of a particular objective. A task in our scenario may be "review the new product lines for 15 potential vendors within the next six months with the intention of selecting three as our primary vendors."

Tasks give rise to *action plans* that literally define who is doing what on which day. For example, "Visit XYZ Dress Company on Tuesday from 1 to 3 P.M.," would be a typical action item that helps complete a particular task. Completing the task moves the company closer to achieving its objectives and continues to support its mission.

def•i•ni•tion

Objectives or **goals** are large projects that affect your company and involve several people. Objectives help the company grow and become more successful. They are usually rather involved and may take several months to reach.

Tasks are individual assignments given to people to help the company reach its objective. Each task is broken down into action plans.

Action plans are the specific detailed activities you do to help the company achieve its goals. These include meetings, proposals, visits, or creations.

Action plans, tasks, and objectives are related to each other. Actions lead to larger task completion, which leads to the achievement of major objectives. The following figure shows how they all stack up.

Once you've got your business up and running, you should periodically take a look at the specific actions you are performing (say, within the last week) and then read your mission statement. Do your actions support that mission statement and further its overall intent? If so, congratulate yourself on your focus. If not, then you should evaluate how you spend your time. Have you gotten yourself into areas that do not correspond with your initial intentions? Does your initial mission statement need modification, or does how you spend your day need modification?

Ed's Lessons Learned

Always keep these important investor-related points in mind as you prepare your plan: investors are primarily interested in making as much money as possible, as quickly as possible, with as little risk as possible. They may have a passion for a particular industry, technology, or entrepreneur but ultimately their investment decision will be based on business realities. Your mission, goals, and actions must show them that you are passionate about helping them reach their financial objectives as well as your own.

All actions ultimately support the mission statement by achieving short-term (one year or less) and long-term (one to three years) goals.

The Pieces of Your Plan
=======================

Effective business planning is a lot like assembling a jigsaw puzzle. All these stray pieces need to be put together in a logical order for the puzzle to work. As you become more familiar with the pieces, the proper fit reveals itself, and there is only one way to assemble the puzzle that makes any sense.

I tend to look at a startup business plan as initially a sales document and secondarily, and very importantly, an operational document. The particular flow of the plan presented here is designed to enhance the sales document aspect of the plan, assuming that you have minimal background in your particular industry or with your particular idea. The operational component is intrinsic to the plan and will generally require that only particular sections be shared as opposed to sharing the entire plan at once as is done with investors.

The business plan is a document that is broken into sections. Each section deals with an important aspect of your business idea and its investment prospects. Your business plan should contain the following basic elements:

I. Cover Sheet	VII. Marketing Strategy
II. Table of Contents	VIII. Operations Plan
III. Executive Summary	IX. The Management Team
IV. Business Description	X. Financial Overview and Funding Needs
V. Market and Industry Analysis	XI. Summary and Conclusions
VI. The Competition	XII. Appendixes or Supplementary Materials

The next few sections of this chapter take a more detailed look at each part of the business plan. Refer to the Kwik Chek business plan included in Appendix A for a sample of how these parts were implemented in an actual business plan.

Street Smarts

One of my early sales managers described an effective sales presentation in this way: first, tell them what you are going to tell them (Executive Summary). Next, tell them what you want to tell them (the detail sections). Finally, tell them what you told them (Summary and Conclusions). A business plan is ultimately a sales document that explains your business idea in a similar way.

Cover Sheet

This is your plan's first impression, so make it a good one. The layout of the cover sheet should be uncluttered, professional looking, and easy to read. At a minimum, it should contain your company's name, the type of company it is (e.g., corporation, sole proprietorship), home state of operation (e.g., Illinois), address and phone/fax information, URL, primary contact person, and date. It is also a good idea to include a statement that this plan is for investment analysis purposes only, is a confidential document, and that it may not be copied or shared without your written permission. Adding a copyright statement and symbol is not a bad idea.

Some people also number their plans and keep track of who the plans were given to as some way of maintaining a level of confidentiality control. In these cases, a special "Number" and "Presented To" section is included on the cover sheet. Some people recommend sending a copy of the plan to yourself using registered mail and then not opening it. In this way, you have an envelope date-stamped by the post office that verifies when the contents were mailed. Make sure you attach a copy of the plan to the outside of the envelope so that you don't forget what is inside. Don't laugh. It happens.

Table of Contents

The Table of Contents is not a major element of your business plan, but it helps show readers what information can be found in the coming pages while also helping them refer to it more easily. Because tables of contents are generally found in well-organized documents, you will make a good impression by including one. It can't hurt you as long as you make sure that the section titles and page numbers shown in the Table of Contents match those actually in the plan. If you use the headings provided by your word processing software when writing your plan, you may be able to create the Table of Contents automatically.

Executive Summary

It may seem odd, but you will write this section last. I cannot overemphasize the importance of the Executive Summary. Write one paragraph (at most) to describe each section of the plan. Finish the Executive Summary by listing the amount of money required, the projected return on investment, the major advantages your company will have over the competition, and why this is an excellent investment opportunity.

The Executive Summary should be one or two pages long (at most) and is often the only section a potential investor will read. Based on these few paragraphs, the investor will decide whether to read the rest of the plan. If the investor doesn't proceed to read the rest of your plan after reading this summary, you've just lost a potential investor. For this reason, your summary needs to catch and hold the reader's attention. The summary is written last because you will learn things as you write the plan, and that wisdom should be included in the final version of the Executive Summary.

Business Description

The Business Description part of the plan explains your product or service idea and how it meets the needs of your market. Describe exactly what it is you will be selling and why people, or businesses, will buy it. How is it different from similar items already on the market? If it is a revolutionary concept, explain why the world needs it.

Don't get sidetracked into talking about all of the great things that you believe about your company in this section. This is, to an investor, like hearing proud parents talk about how their child rolled over by himself last night. Instead, make sure you focus on the benefits of this opportunity for the investor. You can include all of those other details as an appendix if you still feel the need.

Start by describing your product or service. For instance, is it a new kind of vehicle, a tasty new type of cookie, or a better housecleaning service? Explain what the product or service does for the user—what the benefits are and why customers will buy it. If there are similar products or services already on the market, briefly compare them to what you are offering and explain how yours is better. If your new product or service is unlike anything currently available, convince the reader that it is needed. Remember that there is a plan section dedicated to competitors, so only provide the highlights here. They can get the details from the competition chapter.

You may also want to include a History subsection here where you'll briefly touch on how your company has been organized, such as whether it has been structured as a corporation, partnership, or sole proprietorship, whether any stock has been issued, and who invested any money to start it and how much. (See Chapters 8 and 9 for help on determining the right legal structure for your business.) If you intend to use your plan for financing, these questions will come up immediately as you start to talk with investors, so you may as well take care of some of the questions right away. If your company is already in operation and looking for money to fund expansion, make sure to include a company success history as well, as that definitely helps minimize the perceived risk on the part of the investor. It might even be a good idea to start with this information so the reader knows that this is an existing business and not one in the idea stage.

Market and Industry Analysis

The Market and Industry Analysis section presents information describing the market need for your product or service. This is where you detail all the information you gathered regarding the size of your market, the number of potential customers for your product or service, and the growth rate for your market or for the industry as a whole (which can mean worldwide). This section not only relies heavily on the results of your research, but also on your ability to compile the information into a simple, concise, logical, and easy-to-read format. (See Chapters 10 and 12 for information on creating market estimates.)

The Competition

Who are the established companies already selling products and services similar to yours? How will they react to your company? Depending upon your idea and how long your product or service has been available, your competition might consist of other new and aggressive companies just like yours or established companies from whom you intend to take business. We all think our business idea is unique, but the customer might think it's like dozens of others. Rely more on the market data you've collected rather than your opinion about whether there is a similar idea already in existence. Better yet, ask prospective customers if what you offer is really that unique.

> **Watch Out!**
>
> Anyone who believes that they have no competition is in for a rude awakening, even if he or she has a totally revolutionary product. There is always someone out there willing and anxious to challenge companies with new and profitable ideas.

There is no reason to be afraid of competition. In fact, if you pretend that you have none or suggest that that's the case to others, no one will take you seriously. Accept that you have competitors and take every opportunity to learn from them. What are they doing right, and what can you do better? It is okay to mimic things your competition does well and to learn from their mistakes as long as you don't infringe on any trademarks or copyrights they may have in place. Generally, this means that you can copy certain ways of doing business, such as offering free delivery with your service or guaranteeing your work, but not their advertising or designs. I tell you more about dealing with the competition in Chapter 11.

> **Street Smarts**
>
> Don't make the mistake of thinking that your product is so wonderful that customers can't help but buy from you. This assumption will almost certainly push away the investor who reads your plan and will eventually cost you your company as well.

At this point, it's a good idea to provide a list of the other major players in the marketplace to show that you know exactly who your competition is. You should also indicate your impression of their strengths, weaknesses, and overall success in the market. By learning about your competition, the reader of your plan can better understand how you will succeed: either by going after a market opportunity that no existing competitor is addressing or by doing what everyone else is doing, but with a twist.

Marketing Strategy

If nobody buys your product or service, you're out of business. Period! Nothing ends a business faster than no customers. In this section of your business plan, you need to explain to the reader what you intend to do to get customers.

As part of your marketing strategy, you should describe how you intend to let the public know that you're in business. You should also explain your sales approach, such as selling by direct sales representatives, with a mail-order catalog, or through a retail storefront. You'll find a detailed discussion of all the different ways you can market your business in Chapter 12, but start to think now about how you'll describe your ideas to the reader of your business plan.

Notice that the Marketing Strategy section is included after you have already presented your business idea, detailed the market conditions, and covered competitive information. This section flow makes a lot of sense if you realize that the whole point of a marketing strategy is to obtain sales. Sales successes are dependent on market economic conditions, industry purchasing norms, and competitive offerings. Customers who must buy will do so either from your company or from one of your competitors, so you have to consider competitive pressures when developing your marketing strategy.

Operations Plan

This section describes operational procedures, manufacturing equipment, the level of production required, locations, international arrangements, licensing arrangements, and any other aspects related to providing the product or service defined in the idea section. (See Chapter 14 for a detailed manufacturing and production discussion.)

For those of you who are starting service businesses, this section might be short because service providers (such as management consultants, accountants, and attorneys) sell their time and experience. They don't use big machines to crank out words of wisdom, so production capacity is less of an issue. Assumptions should still explain how many hours per month you expect to spend on client-related work that you'll be paid for.

The Management Team

One of the most important elements of your business plan is the section telling the reader why you and your partners are the most qualified group to start and run this business. Investors give their money to people, not companies or product ideas. Investors want to feel confident that you have experience in the type of business you're starting and that other members of your management team complement your skills.

The management team is incredibly important to any new business and should take center stage in your thinking, explanations, and analyses. Your company has no historical track record. Investors cannot look to past company performance as a gauge of future performance, so they must assess the future based on the management team leading the company into that future: you and the other managers. When times are uncertain and your risk is large, you always want to be involved with people of high caliber. So do the investors. A great idea with the wrong team will not get funded. A great management team with a solid idea almost always will.

In this section, you need to briefly describe the backgrounds and experience of your management team to show the reader that you know what you're doing. If you have an associate with 25 years of experience in the business who's going to be working with you, be sure to mention it; it makes your company much more credible.

If you have advisers or consultants who have been working with you and giving you advice, mention them if they are fairly well-known or if they have a lot of experience. If you've set up a board of directors, briefly mention the members. You want to show the reader that you recognize you don't know everything and rely on professionals in those instances. Many business owners think they know everything and don't need advice from other people. These are usually the ones who don't last very long. (See Chapter 9 for more information about setting up a board of directors.)

Financial Overview and Funding Needs

Now it's down to the bottom line. Everything else up to this point was presented as the foundation for the financial analysis. This section spells out the actual investment required, how that invested money will be spent, and when the business will start making money. You define the amount of initial investment and how much you will need in the future based on certain sales and operations projections. The investors really want to know how much money will be invested, how much they can expect to make, and the time frame in which they'll make it. Everything else is simply a teaser to whet their appetite for the financial feast that follows. You should also include a *break-even analysis* that covers the volume required to push the company from a deficit to a profitable operation.

You should include an *income statement, balance sheet,* and *cash flow analysis* that project the first three years of operations. The first year is shown in months with the second and third years showing annual totals. These reports are called pro forma financial statements. Pro forma just means that the numbers are projections, or estimates, of future sales and expenses. (You'll learn more about preparing these reports in Chapter 17.)

def•i•ni•tion

A **break-even analysis** determines the sales level (break-even point) at which you are paying your overhead expenses but still not making a net income. You are living at a subsistence level, with just enough money to pay the rent and put food on the table, but nothing extra for movies and popcorn. The **income statement** reflects all income and expenses for a particular period of time (usually a year). The **balance sheet** shows your total assets and liabilities. The **cash flow analysis** shows exactly how much cash you received and how much you spent on a monthly basis.

The initial capital required to start the business, as indicated by the maximum negative cumulative cash flow, the funding sources, and how it will be spent is summarized in the Funds Needed and Their Uses portion of this section. (See Chapter 17 for a detailed discussion about projecting and managing cash flow, a critical talent that you will definitely have to master at some point if your business will survive.)

Summary and Conclusions

Some people don't include a Summary in their plans, but I think it's a good idea. It reiterates much of what was presented in the Executive Summary but now adds additional insight based on the reader being far more informed on the idea, the market, the competition, and the financial requirements. In this section, you can tie up the plan in a neat package and ensure that readers understand your view of the overall opportunity instead of letting them drift off on their own. They may not agree with what you present in this section, but they at least will have a concise summary of what the plan was about and the conclusions you would like them to draw.

Street Smarts

I sometimes include a special section titled Risks and Opportunities before the Summary and Conclusions section. The purpose of the Risks and Opportunities section is to spell out for the reader what I believe to be the major risks to the success of this venture and also the special opportunities associated with it. More than likely, readers will see many of these for themselves, but I want to make sure they know that I really am aware of the risks while also ensuring that they completely understand the special attractive nature of the opportunities presented.

Appendixes or Supplementary Materials

The appendixes and supplementary materials are often referred to throughout the plan but appear as detailed references at the end. Included are the charts, graphs, extrapolations, resumés, and pieces of literature needed to convince the investor that you have done your homework. Including this information at the end instead of within the plan keeps the plan flowing along without getting bogged down with too much detail. You want a plan that moves the big-picture reader along while still fulfilling the information cravings of the analytical investor. Just list these materials in your Table of Contents so interested readers can find them.

Ethics and Your Plan

Nobody gives money to people they don't trust. If you take liberties with your facts in preparing your plan, your exaggeration may be interpreted as lying. This is a problem if you want people to give you money.

Tempting as it is to present your idea with the brightest of projections, you must steer clear of stating conjecture as fact. If the reader finds out you have done this (which is likely when he or she checks out your plan in detail), you may not be able to recover the required level of trust needed between an investor and the startup management.

If your idea is a good one, then it will get funded. Trust that to be true and prepare the best possible business plan you can.

The Least You Need to Know

- The clearer you are about your business idea's benefits to investors, the more clearly you can convey those benefits in your plan.

- Your business plan is first a sales document to investors and then an operational plan that you use to keep your business on track.

- All of the plan sections need some level of attention since investors will likely have questions regarding all of these various topics.

- It is your responsibility to make the plan easy for the reader to understand. It is not the reader's job to decode your plan in the hope of discovering the investment opportunity.

Chapter 4

Finding the Money You Will Need

In This Chapter

- Understand the relationship between risk and reward
- Match funding risk with company stage
- Understand different funding methods
- Differentiate debt and equity funding
- Determine how much money you will need

Frank tossed his presentation materials on the front seat of his car, got in, and slammed the door. Taking a deep breath, he let back the seat and closed his eyes. A moment later his phone rang. Caller ID showed that it was his friend, Milton, a stock broker.

"So how did the presentation go?" asked Milton.

"Not well. They were polite, but I could tell they really didn't get the idea and I'll be stunned if they buy in."

"Sorry. Did they give you any feedback on what they did or didn't like about the plan? I, for one, like the product's second generation build-on idea a lot. What did they say about that?"

"Nothing," replied Frank with a slight pause. "I didn't tell them about it." He waited.

"Hmm. That was a good idea," sighed Milton with sarcasm in his voice. "Isn't that where you really expect your sales to increase and ramp you up enough to be a viable acquisition target?"

"Sure. It is. But it's also the most unique part of the plan, and I'm afraid someone will steal it if I'm not careful. Until I know they're interested, I'm not going to tell them about it."

Frank could imagine Milton shaking his head on the other end of the phone. "Look, Frank. Your plan just isn't very attractive without revealing that second development stage. No credible investor will give you money if they don't see that part. Sorry to be the one to break the bad news."

"So what you're telling me is I won't get the money if I don't reveal the second stage details. And my fear of revealing it may keep us from getting funded at all. Is that right?"

"Exactamundo," replied Milton enthusiastically. "If they can't see a way to make money off of their investment, why would they invest?"

Hard to believe that people aren't lining up to give this great idea of yours money, isn't it? Be honest. Why are they being so negative about your company's prospects? You know your idea will work. You can feel it in your bones, and all you need is a few hundred thousand dollars to turn it into reality. Sound familiar? Or am I the only person who has ever had the experience of asking people for money to fund my business only to walk away confused and a little disheartened by their response?

It might not be them. Sorry. Perhaps you have unrealistic expectations about how they should react given your specific situation. Perhaps they are reacting more objectively to the risk inherent in your venture than you are. Perhaps they're telling you something that is worth knowing about where your idea or plan falls short. Or, perhaps, they simply didn't understand the real financial, and possibly personal, benefit to them of getting involved.

This chapter helps you to sort through these points before you make those important investor presentations. It helps you anticipate the concerns that your investors may have so that you are better prepared to address them. The more credibly you can address their concerns, while infusing them with a strong dose of your own belief in the idea, the more likely you are to get the funding you are looking for.

Risk and Reward Are Intimately Linked

There is an unbreakable link between the level of *risk* that an investor sees in an investment and the amount of *reward* that he or she expects. Understanding the investor mindset is critical to making the right pitch.

def•i•ni•tion

Risk is the possibility that an investment will not produce as good a reward as expected. The higher the risk associated with an investment, the higher the expected return on investment because the investor is taking a bigger chance. **Reward** is what an investor expects to receive for having made the investment. This is usually some form of payment to the investor within a specified time frame.

Investors Give Money to Get Something Back

If you want a gift, go to your wealthy Aunt Sally. Oh, don't have a wealthy aunt or uncle? Hmm. That is a little bit of a problem. Now we have to deal with people who have no personal interest in us at all and who will get involved as an investor only if the investment makes financial sense. Let's take a look at what "financial sense" means to a realistic investor.

People with money are always looking for ways for it to make more money while best ensuring that they don't lose the money along the way. Anyone who has lost money in a stock market decline (which is probably all of us) knows that there is no such thing as "a sure bet."

So why put your money in the stock market? Simple. Assume that your bank savings account is now offering an annual interest rate of just under 1 percent. Assume also that you can tie up your money in a Certificate of Deposit (CD) for several years and perhaps get around 4.5 percent. Finally, assume that the stock market, on average over the past few decades, has shown annual returns of around 10 percent. Let's look at what this means: no-risk (savings) provides 1 percent. The CD is essentially risk free, but it ties up your money for a few years, which involves the risk that you might unexpectedly need it and have to pay a penalty to pull it out of the CD. For just a little more risk, the CD pays 4.5 percent, which is 3.5 percent more than the savings account. The stock market, which we all know is highly volatile and may require tying up your money for years to get a decent return that might or might not happen, is estimated to pay 10 percent on a prospective average basis.

Are you starting to see a pattern here? Why would you put money into something that is riskier than a savings account if you get the same percentage rate of return, 1 percent for the example here? You can get 1 percent from the bank without taking any risk at all, so if you are taking the stock market risk of losing part or all of your money, then you are going to want to be compensated for taking that risk. How much more compensation? Therein lies the art of financial negotiations.

The Greater the Perceived Risk, the Greater the Required Return

These next two bullet points will explain the basic friction that exists in the investor/borrower conversation:

- Investors are ideally looking for huge returns on their investment, within a short period of time and with no risk.

- Borrowers ideally want to borrow as much money as possible for as long as they need it, to pay nothing to the lender for the use of that money, and have no obligation to repay it if the money is lost.

Disconnect! Notice that investors and borrowers come at the transaction from completely different points of view. The more seasoned you get at lending or borrowing, the better you get at resolving the friction points. There are also industry "norms" that help provide some ballpark within which typical financial transaction terms should fall. But, realize that there is a huge gap between how investors and borrowers look at the lending/borrowing transaction.

Every investor has some level of risk tolerance. This means there is an investment risk level above which the investor will not provide money. Some have a higher level of risk tolerance (venture capitalists) and others a lower risk tolerance (bankers). To go to a banker with a high risk investment, like your new startup company, is asking a low risk tolerance investor to invest outside of his or her comfort zone. It is likely not going to happen, and if it does, she will constantly be uncomfortable with having taken the risk and, likely, make you uncomfortable along with her. Plus, banks have legal constraints within which they must work to maintain their insurance and other protections that define the circumstances under which they can lend money.

You should now see that there is a fuzzy balancing act you must perform between assessing an investment's level of perceived risk, the risk tolerance of the lender or investor, and the rate of investment return that this investor will require. Keep reading, and you will learn methods for assessing and presenting the risk level while also making sure that you are talking to the right type of investor for your situation.

Don't Treat Investments Personally

Try to address investment discussions on a business—not a personal—basis. Investments can become sticky when they become personally based. Most experienced investors will avoid these situations since they are no longer ruled by financial risk and reward but become entangled with personal issues. If you try to make an investment personal, you are likely going to lose the investor.

Remember that investors are always looking for all those hidden or obvious risks to their investment—where they could lose all or part of their money or simply not make on the investment what they could have made if they had put the money elsewhere.

Remember also that your new company has no track record of its own on which to stand. Its only track record is your track record and that of the other founder/owners.

For these two reasons, you must also know that at this early stage, investors are going to be checking you out, personally, as well as your business idea. Actually, they may be checking you out more than your business idea. The idea won't be using their money—you will be.

Street Smarts

Once you make an investment decision personal for either you or the investor, you run the very high risk of turning a business relationship into a battle of personalities and egos. Keep it business all the way when talking money with investors, and it will work out better for both you and them. You may sometimes need to play the "personal" card, but know that it has risks, and you can only play it so often before it not only gets "old" but starts to work against you.

Keep your personal finances as clean as possible and try not to commit them if you don't have to. Just be aware that the early round of investors may want a piece of your personal wealth as protection for their investment. Notice that the more you guarantee, the lower the risk becomes to the investor, which should also lower their return on investment requirements. If someone wants high returns and a 100 percent guarantee of their funds within the agreed upon timeframe, then they also have unrealistic expectations. Explain this in a business-like manner, without making it personal, and you might be able to educate them along the way. You can't blame them for asking for the sky, can you?

Comparing Debt and Equity Funding

Investors come in two flavors: those who provide *debt funding* and those who provide *equity funding*. Debt funding is funding that must be repaid and is usually a loan of some type. Equity funding means that an investor gave you money in exchange for stock (equity) in your company. Equity funding is usually paid back when the investor sells his stock either to the company, on the public market, or to another investor.

Notice that debt funding has risk associated with it in that the loan may not be paid back. But debt funding usually has required payments along the way that reduce the level of risk to the debt investor every month. Plus, it is reasonable to assume that you might have had to *personally guarantee* the debt to get it in the first place. As a result of your personal commitment, the interest rate on the debt is likely reasonable for the current lending market since the risk associated with your not repaying the loan is small.

def•i•ni•tion

Debt funding is funding that must be repaid and is usually a loan of some type. **Equity funding** means that an investor gave you money in exchange for stock (equity) in your company. A **personal guarantee** is often required by lenders of all types as a way for them to go after you personally for debt repayment should the business cease to exist and default on a debt payment.

Equity, on the other hand, is a completely different story. An investor gives you his or her money today in exchange for a percentage of the outstanding shares of stock in your company. More than likely, the investor will not see a dime on that money until the stock is sold, unless your company pays a dividend, which is unusual for a small startup company since cash is always at a premium. If your company is an S corporation, it is even possible that the investor may have to pay tax on income passed to him or her through the Schedule K-1 but not actually receive any cash. By the way, if the company goes under, the equity investment is lost, and the investor gets nothing in return for the initial risk. Now that is a sweet deal for an investor, isn't it? See Chapter 8 for a detailed discussion about the various business legal forms and their benefits.

For these reasons, equity investors will likely only give you money if they can see (and believe) that a relatively large return on their investment will come their way within a few years. This "relatively large" return is usually anywhere from between 5 and 50 times their investment per share. For example, if she pays you $1 per share of stock today, she will likely want to have a reasonable (not risk free) chance of receiving $5 or more in a few years or so. Venture capitalists will generally want to see a chance of 30 times or more from their investment within three to five years before they will take the plunge.

Equity investors will generally only invest in a startup with money that they can afford to lose since they know the risk level is that much higher. It is not quite like gambling, but it is close. If you have someone close to you who intends to invest his or her total savings as an equity investment, make sure that person completely understands the risk associated with the investment and that they may never get it back. More than one friendship has been strained or lost when friends equity invest, thinking that it is a loan to be repaid, and then lose all their money when the company goes under.

Company Stages and Funding

The *perceived risk* level associated with you and your company will change over time. In the early stages, the risk level is high since there is no historical track record, which creates uncertainty about the future performance. As that track record gets established, the perceived level of risk decreases, assuming that you create a good track record. This is why companies like IBM are perceived as less risky than your startup. This section tracks the various stages that your company will go through and that stage's relationship to funding requirements and risk.

def•i•ni•tion

Perceived risk is the risk assessment as seen through the eyes of the investor. You always want to be working to minimize the level of perceived risk.

Seed Stage

As the name of this stage implies, your company is a kernel of an idea waiting to sprout. You have an idea and might have scratched a few notes on the back of a cocktail napkin, but that is really it. You may now need some money to free you up from your "day job" so that you can write a great business plan using the recommended steps outlined in this book. Those looking to develop a product-based business will likely create some type of prototype of the product at this stage. This could mean a mock-up of a website or a plastic model, or bread board, of a more complicated electronic product.

The risk level here is high, but the funding needs are likely pretty low. Many people fund this out of their own pockets or treat it as a part-time job, without pay, while they keep their regular job. This approach is particularly applicable to those looking to eventually break out of the "big house" of corporate America.

Startup Stage

Plan and prototype in hand, you are now ready to start making your company a reality. You start to hire key people, set up an office, and create preproduction prototypes as opposed to the mockups from the seed stage. You have likely also beta tested your idea to see if actual customers are interested in what you have to offer. All of this information helps to convince investors that your idea and company are worth some more money. This is a time when some venture capital firms may be interested in getting involved. Know that funding at this stage is critical, and it may take quite some time to find, so planning ahead is a good idea.

The risk is still high, although not as high as with the seed stage, and the financing requirements are still relatively modest although much greater than the seed stage. Many unknowns still exist that can squash the entire deal, but you now have some management success that works in your favor. Keep the faith and keep asking for that money. If the idea and your team are as solid as you think, someone will buy into your idea. Make sure that you conserve money as much as possible at this stage since it is a waiting game in that you have to last, financially, until you get your startup funding.

First Stage

By this stage, you have a real company, with a real product and real customers. You have bumped your head a few times, had some wins, and learned a lot along the way. Your plan has been adjusted from what you initially thought in the seed stage, and you are rapidly moving forward.

Ed's Lessons Learned

The personal dynamics of first and second stage success can be pretty intoxicating. You may be the darling company that everyone wants a piece of and the talk of the town. People all over are asking you for a job, and they actually know your name. Keep your ego and aspirations in check. All this attention can get you believing that things are better than they are or that customers will now start sending you money in buckets just because you are you. It may all be true, and if so, great. If it is not true, and you believe it to be true, you and your company could be in for a rude, and sometimes catastrophic, wakeup call. It is the adrenaline rush of the first and second stage that keeps Silicon Valley startup people coming back for more.

Risk is substantially reduced when compared to the earlier stages, but the funding needs increase again since you must add manufacturing personnel, inventory, advertising, sales force, and any number of other expensive capabilities. This is when you can really make the case to the venture capital folks assuming you have an idea that shows that type of large-industry merit. This is also a time when people around you will be seeing that you have something going that is working and want to get involved. Selling shares is now easier, and less expensive, than at any other time.

Second Stage

Now you really need big money, and the requirement for effective cash flow management has never been more important. Revenues are growing in the double-digits or higher, and cash management has become almost an obsession. Sales activity is soaring, and production demand is growing like a weed. If your company has adequate operating margins and effective cash management (prompt accounts receivable collection and attractive vendor payment terms), then you might be able to internally fund this stage. More than likely, you will be short on cash and need to have some cash in reserve to cover the deficiencies that arise from having to pay vendors and employees before, sometimes months before, you have received customer payments.

There are firms that specialize in providing this second round of financing. These firms not only provide investment capital but also offer expertise on managing this perilous stage. Risk is again reduced from the first stage because you have not only a history but also a future with respect to forecastable orders and expenses. Accounts receivable can be used to fund this cash shortage as can other methods covered in Chapter 20.

It is not uncommon for a company at this stage to sell additional shares as a way of obtaining equity funding, which does not increase the cash drain on the company yet provides an important infusion of cash. This cash is really a safety net that protects the company from serious cash shortfalls, decreasing stress on management and improving the likelihood of making it to the third stage. Equity funding is not as expensive for the company to obtain since the level of overall perceived risk to the investor is much lower than at prior stages.

Third Stage (Mezzanine)

Your company is now a well-oiled machine. Your employees know their jobs, your operational systems are in place, you have an established name in the marketplace, and you are developing the next generation of products and services that will take you into the future. You are hiring managers specifically oriented toward management of a larger company, standardizing offerings, and maybe even broadening to international markets.

This level is often called mezzanine financing in that it is a growth and financing stage "between" (or bridging) two other levels: second and harvest. Management is now actively working on ways to foster the right environment within which they can harvest their prior work. This stage involves refining the company operation so that it appears as financially viable and profitable as possible, and laying the groundwork for having the share selling price seen at harvest be as high as possible. Financing obtained at this stage is usually for a relatively short period of time, and everyone involved knows that the next step is the harvest.

Harvest Stage—Exit Strategy

This is the stage when employees, founders, and early shareholders reap the benefits of their earlier investment. This stage can be the sale of the company to another group of investors or to another company, or the offering of stock in an initial public offering (IPO). The prior shareholders offer their shares for sale and take the money, often making very large sums of money in the process. If a company does a public offering, it will likely sell shares over and above those already outstanding as a way of filling the company's cash coffers while providing a way for the prior shareholders to cash in on their investment. Now your startup is a real, live, mature company that must carve a life for itself as an adult. It is a player in the marketplace. The shareholders who sell their shares "exit" the company and are no longer shareholders even though they may still be employees.

This is a time of management, employee, and focus change when leadership skills are incredibly important. Keeping now-wealthy shareholders focused on creating the next level of company success is not always an easy task. There is a big party on the day that the harvest transaction becomes final, but everyone still must come to work the next day to get on with it.

Know How Much Money You Will Need

Now that you have a solid idea about risk, reward, and company growth stages, you need to determine the amount of money you will need. In many ways, the business planning process is designed to help you determine a credible estimate of this cash requirement. The financials associated with your plan are discussed in Chapter 17. The following sections will help you frame the requirements that dictate much of your detailed financial planning.

Will You Make Money?

Before jumping in with both feet, wouldn't it be nice if you could get a better idea of whether your business will succeed? Yes, I've heard that fortunetellers can be helpful, but how about some basic financial analyses? Don't worry; you don't have to be an accountant to do this stuff.

Enthusiasm, skill, and guts will take you far, but combining these traits with cash will get you much closer to the brass ring. The reality is that *service-based businesses* (those that offer services such as accounting, consulting, or massage) generally cost less to start than *product-based businesses* (those that offer products, such as computers, clothes, or widgets). You could start a dog-walking company on little money as long as you keep your expenses on a short leash. (Sorry; the pun was too good to resist.) Seriously, though, leashes, collars, a phone line, and business cards are all you need to get into your own dog-walking business.

On the other hand, starting a product business often requires major machinery and equipment, office space, employees, and more. Maybe a lot more. Each of these items translates into more dollars and more delay before sales start rolling in.

Due to this fact of life, many companies start as service businesses and move on to include products as their cash and sales situation improves. For example, a computer programmer can start by offering software consulting (a service) and eventually develop and sell his or her own software programs (a product). Starting on a small budget doesn't mean you necessarily have to stay small, but it does help to keep expenses down when sales are lower.

def•i•ni•tion

A **product-based business** is a company that makes money by selling products that are either developed and manufactured by the company or purchased by the company for resale. Wal-Mart is an example of a product-based business. **Service-based businesses** are companies that make money by selling services, rather than products, provided by employees or contractors. Examples include doctors, consultants, and house cleaners.

How Much Can You Afford?

You don't have to have millions of dollars to start a business—far from it. Many people start small, often on a part-time basis, spreading their money between living expenses and business startup costs. Other business owners get loans for thousands and thousands of dollars. For example, some fast-food franchises cost more than $100,000 just to open.

You have to decide for yourself how much money you are willing and able to set aside to start your business. It may be less than a thousand dollars, or it may be much more. Everyone's situation is different. Just be aware that the type or size of business you start may be somewhat limited by the amount of money you have available or can reasonably obtain from others. Don't expect to start a restaurant with just a couple thousand dollars, for example; it's highly unlikely that you could afford to pay for everything you need. Even if you were able to squeak by the first month, you may be jeopardizing your future by not having enough money to fall back on.

The Plan Estimates Your Money Needs

Only by estimating how much money you can make and how much it will cost to run your business will you know whether you should continue to pursue your dream. If there is no money to be made by starting the business, then you should drop the idea. Although there are probably several reasons why you want to start your own business, the first and foremost must be that you expect to make money at it. Otherwise it is a hobby, not a business. A well-thought-out business plan is the best method for realistically estimating your startup money needs as well as your business's future prospects. Skimping on your planning sets you up for future problems and is just not a good idea.

What's Your Potential?

Let's compare the long-term earning potential of product versus service businesses. Although a service business is less expensive to start, it is also harder to grow into a larger company. Why? Simple. Every night when your employees go home, your company stops earning money. The time your employees spend on customer work is how you make money. When they're sleeping, they're not billing your customers. Your company's growth is limited by the number of hours you and your employees can bill in a day.

> **Watch Out!**
>
> When calculating how much money you need to start your business, you must include the cost of your personal living expenses during the startup phase. You will start to resent the business if you find yourself lacking a decent meal several nights in a row. This can cloud your judgment and significantly dampen your enthusiasm. It happens.

A product business, on the other hand, can make money as long as it has products on hand. You can sell 20 products on Monday and 500 on Tuesday and work your equipment extra hard Tuesday night to manufacture more products to sell on Wednesday. While you sleep, your equipment is still churning out more products.

Also, services are usually sold and provided by a set group of people (your employees). Products, on the other hand, can be sold through several different channels, such as retail stores, mail-order catalogs, and telemarketing.

Starting small, such as with a service orientation, can help to reduce your startup expenses. Later you can add products to your company's mix, when you have the money available to support it. But when you're first starting out, you need to be sure you have enough money to start up and sustain your company for at least a year.

To estimate the total startup costs of your company, determine how much money you need to start the business (*cumulative cash flow*) and how much money you need to pay yourself during that time to cover your basic living expenses. For example, if the business requires $50,000 in cumulative cash flow to start and you need $48,000 to cover your personal living expenses until the company is on its feet, then the initial investment required is not $50,000 but $98,000.

Don't scale your living expenses to the bone when you estimate these costs because, if for some reason sales are slower to appear than anticipated, you don't want to be out of business just as things start to pick up. If no additional money is available, then the initial $98,000 could be lost just as the company is getting off the ground. Once you've already received one loan to get the company started, it is even tougher to go back to your investors and ask for just a little more to keep you going. Make sure you can cover your living expenses for several months more than you expect from your plan, and give yourself some leeway.

It is either your money or your investors' money that funds the business. It will definitely be your time, and time is also worth money. Professional investors require a formal business plan before they will invest. Even if you don't need outside financing because you have the cash to invest yourself, be as serious about evaluating the opportunity as any investor would be. That's the reason you're reading this book and should work your way through all of the later chapters that deal with writing a credible business plan. Make sure that this is an investment you believe is going to pay off for you.

What else could you be doing with your money? How could it be spent if not used to start your business? All those other ways that you could have spent your money is what the financial pros call the *opportunity cost* of starting your business. Investors frequently look at

def•i•ni•tion

Cumulative cash flow is the total amount of cash needed to handle the sum of all month-to-month negative cash flow (loss) experienced until the company starts to make a monthly profit. **Opportunity cost** is the profit that you could have gained by pursuing another investment instead of the one you currently have.

situations in terms of opportunity cost: what other investment options are they giving up by investing their money with you? If the return from your business idea is lower than their next-best option, then they will not give you the money.

Basic Types of Funding

Without funding, your business idea will go nowhere. You must find a way to support the business and you while it grows into a profitable, self-sustaining entity. Here is an overview of the various funding methods and how they may apply to your particular situation. Think of this as an à la carte menu from which you can select as needed to create the funding meal that is right for your situation.

Typical Funding Action Sequence

Here are a few steps that will likely happen independent of your selected method of funding:

- Determine what you want to do and how much it will cost to do it by writing a solid business plan.

- Prepare a presentation that provides a prospective investor (even if it is you) with a justification for making the investment.

- Put the word out to the appropriate people that you are looking for funding.

- Meet with prospective investors and professionally present your case and funding need request.

- Give them some time, along with a desired decision deadline, to verify what you have told them.

- Get your money or find out why this investment is not right for them at this time. Say "thank you" either way because it is a learning experience for you when dealing with the next potential investor.

- Report to investors on a periodic basis (quarterly and annually are usually minimum) about the performance of the company and the state of their investment.

- Always be on the lookout for people who can provide your next required level of funding as your business becomes more successful.

As the top manager of your company, one primary responsibility is to ensure that the company has the money it needs to not only survive but also to capitalize on its next level of opportunity. This is a never-ending process, so just accept the fact that it is now part of your management landscape.

Funding Out of Your Own Pocket

Depending on the size of your new venture, you may be able to fund the early stages out of your own savings. If nothing else, you should plan to pay for your own living expenses for at least the first six months of business operation. If you can afford it, then you might consider funding the cumulative cash requirement as well since that way you don't have to go through a committee to make changes to the plan. You are the committee.

It all depends on how much you can afford to put into the venture and your living expenses before hitting your pain threshold or, even worse, your destruction threshold. Here are a few words of advice I hope you take to heart before using your own money:

- Don't cut your estimated need too close, or a cost overrun of some type or a slower sales ramp up could put you in a painful cash crunch.

- Make sure that your significant other(s) all buy into your using the money for this purpose, or you could really feel pressure later when it will be the least appreciated.

- If you are younger, you might be able to use a larger percentage of your nest egg, but those closer to retirement (50+) should be a little more conservative. After all, you don't have 35 years to make it back before retiring, do you?

- Ideally try to only use money that you can afford to lose. If the amount required will use all of your nest egg, then you might consider bringing in investors even if on the surface it doesn't look like you will need them. Sleepless nights over losing everything because a major client defaults on a receivable is a terrible way to live. Trust me on this one or check it out with someone who has already been through it.

Some people use the equity in their home to fund their business. This might also be a solid approach, as equity lines of credit are offered at lower interest rates than unsecured loans and you can always sell your house to pay off the debt if the worst happens to your business. You don't get back the equity or money put into the business, but you at least aren't in debt if you end up closing your doors.

Finally, there are people who start their companies using credit card financing. This is pretty expensive. Plus, once you run up your credit cards, where do you go to charge those daily items that will definitely be required? I have done this before and got myself in trouble in that I was making minimum payments instead of paying off the whole thing. I strongly recommend that you not take the credit card route unless the amount you need to start with is low enough that you could pay it off in a few months if things don't go well. Otherwise, I fear that you might dig yourself into a credit charge hole that is difficult for some, and impossible for others, to dig out of.

Brother, Can You Spare a Dime? Family Funding

Family and friend funding is a double-edged sword: (1) family may feel more inclined to help with your business idea because of a personal need to help you out, (2) they may have faith in you because they know you (or the opposite could be true for the same reason), and (3) they may hold it against you for years to come if the business fails, taking their investment with it. Can business be done with family members? Absolutely. It happens all the time. Should you be overly cautious when dealing with friends and family as potential investors? Absolutely, again. It is one thing to lose an investor. It is something altogether different to create a rift with a good friend or family member.

I have a tendency to go overboard on disclosure when dealing with friends and family. My belief is that I can always find another investor, but it will be difficult to replace this personal relationship. If they still want to be involved after all the disclosure then so be it. At least everyone's eyes were open. Also, make sure that you execute the same documents (such as loan agreements) with friends as you would with a third party. This is still a business arrangement and should be treated as such. Even (especially?) with family and friends.

Venture Capital—May Not Be for Everybody

Venture capital (VC) is a term that was bantered around a lot in the late 1990s as one Silicon Valley startup after another got funded, grew, almost became profitable (sometimes), and then went public. Who are these venture capital people, and how do you get some of their money?

First, the venture capital market today is much different from what it was in the booming 1990s. The tech-wreck of the past few years shook many of these firms to their core, and they are now far more selective on where they put their money. Plus, your venture has to meet certain requirements before a VC firm will typically even look at it.

♦ Your initial investment amount should be at least $500,000 or it is not worth their time and money to investigate.

♦ You and your management team must be top-notch since the VC invests in you first and the idea second. These people know that large amounts of money behind a great team with a hot product in a growing market will strain the seams of the company and its management personnel. They want seasoned people at the helm who know how to responsibly manage this type of growth.

♦ The idea must support large sales growth over a short period of time.

♦ The business plan must show that the VC can make at least 25–30 times their initial investment within a 5-year period or less, or they will not likely fund the company.

> **Street Smarts**
>
> Run the numbers and see what has to happen to a company's value to meet the VC valuation increase requirement. Assume the $500k in VC funding buys 25 percent of the company. This puts the initial company value at $2 million (4 × $500k). Thirty times that value is $60 million in market valuation within 5 years. Possible? Sure. Easy to do? Not usually.

◆ Venture capital funds like to work with companies that have an existing market-place, workable (or proven) product, and are credible so that the provided money enables rapid expansion. VC-funded companies are always racing the clock, so time is scarce and rapid sales growth essential.

Just on these points alone, particularly the required company valuation growth, most smaller businesses will not qualify for venture capital funding. If you feel that your idea could qualify for venture funding, you should get solid professionals involved as a reality check and in refining your plan before going out for funding.

Agency Guaranteed Bank Funding

In today's tougher business climate, state and federal agencies have put together special guaranteed loan programs. The general theme is that the public agency guarantees the loan to the lender who evaluates and processes the loan for you, the entrepreneur and borrower. If you default, the agency pays the lender for the lost loan. The intent of these programs is some type of greater economic good to the community, such as promoting small business growth as a way of stimulating the economy and increasing employment. Don't be afraid to talk to your banker about possible programs that would apply to your situation not only today but also as you grow and become more stable. Perhaps you can personally fund the company until it is large enough to qualify for one of these types of loans.

SBA and Governmental Program Realities

Without question, you should get to know the programs provided by the Small Business Administration (SBA). This is particularly true if you plan to purchase property as part of your business operation. SBA programs change, so I will not go into detail on any particular program here. Historically, SBA funding of nonproperty has been fairly restrictive, but there are rumors of the new and improved SBA being more accommodating to the realistic needs of the newer small business. The website is your best bet for initial information (www.sba.gov), but also look around your area for financial institutions that are SBA-approved to see if they can help you find and qualify for a loan that is right for your particular business.

Finally, don't overlook any leverage that you may have in qualifying for a special governmental program. This leverage may come from your being a woman, a member of a minority race, your geographic location, industry, age, education, income bracket, military background, or any number of other criteria. It never ceases to amaze me at the number of programs that the various governmental agencies offer. Someplace, somewhere, with patience and tons of paperwork, you might be able to find some funding for yourself.

Stock Sales (Not an IPO ... Sorry)

One reason to incorporate is to be able to sell stock for funding purposes. Notice that a stock sale makes the shareholders owners of the corporation, and you do not need to repay their stock investment. They are taking a risk with their investment and often get a say in the company operation in exchange. This is called equity financing or equity funding.

Equity funding is obtained through three basic means: selling shares of stock to private investors, selling shares of stock to professional investors such as venture capitalists, and "going public," which involves selling shares to the general public on one of the stock exchanges. You will initially deal with the first two financing options and, if you are successful and lucky, eventually have the opportunity to go public, which is beyond the scope of this book.

Selling shares of stock looks pretty good on the surface: you sell a portion of the company in exchange for some cash. All you give up is a little ownership in the company to get the cash you need. What is the down side? As usual, it comes down to whom you choose as your investors.

The more sophisticated the investor, the better an ally he or she will make down the road. A professional investor knows the pitfalls associated with running a business and can guide you through potential minefields. However, professional investors also tend to be demanding and relatively heartless when you do not perform as expected. From their perspective, not living up to your plan indicates a lack of business control. A professional investor will take you to task if needed because he or she has a vested interest in your success.

Street Smarts

Needing advice on how to take your successful company public with an IPO is what my brother would term a "high class problem." If you eventually get to that stage, make sure that you carefully pick your partners on that important journey and be thankful you have that opportunity.

Your Uncle Billy, on the other hand, might not need monthly reports from you on your progress and might purchase your company's stock on his faith in your ability alone. This makes getting your initial funding easier but might hurt you down the road. Suppose that the company has a rough quarter, for reasons that are out of your control, such as a flood or war. Billy might not understand why that dividend check you promised didn't arrive. He might not understand why you need more money due to unforeseen circumstances. Billy might not even have deep enough pockets to fund the next round of investing.

In fact, the optimal investor might be another company with services or products that complement your offering. This other company might buy a certain percentage of your company's shares to provide a legal link between that organization and yours. This not only provides you with cash but also allows you to partner with them on a tighter basis when approaching the marketplace. (See my book, *The Complete Idiot's Guide to Buying and Selling a Business*, for additional detailed information on this important topic.)

Never knowingly involve someone in your business that you do not trust. You will be busy enough worrying about expanding your business; you do not need someone questioning your every move and undermining what you do. Stall, work harder, cut expenses, and play with cash flow before getting involved with an investor who might be a potential integrity headache.

Ultimately, it is your job to increase the value of the shareholders' investments. You can do this by improving the company's sales while decreasing the cost of making those sales. In short, your job is to make the company more profitable from one year to the next. If the profit that the investors see is not substantially greater than what they could get from other investments such as the stock market or bonds, then why should they invest in you? Your job is to give them a better return on their investment than they could receive with traditional methods.

Seller Financing

If you plan to purchase an existing company, you may find that the seller is willing to finance a portion of the purchase price. This is sort of like a house seller taking a second note on the purchase with the bank being in first position. In this case, the seller might be the primary lender and you make monthly payments to him instead of to the bank. There is something to be said for this approach since it keeps the seller interested in the business's success and gives him an incentive to work with you to make it successful. A successful business after purchase is a win for everyone.

Ethics and Funding

It is hard to overemphasize the importance of keeping your ethics intact when looking for investors. People might take a chance on an idea that they feel is risky but has merit. Few people will give money to someone they don't trust. If you find yourself wanting to shade the truth, take a deep breath and ponder the ramifications of what you are about to do. If you are found out, the impact on your business could be devastating, not to mention the impact on your relationship with this investor. Plus, it really is a small world out there. The word will get out that you cannot be trusted, and it will take you forever to regain your good name.

In summary, fabricating information is not a very sound sales strategy when looking for funding. Plus, if you need to lie to get the money, perhaps you are trying to fund the wrong idea. The facts in your business plan should speak for themselves if presented professionally—the way you are taught in this book. Do your work up front and watch the investors convince themselves that your idea is one worth funding.

For Your Plan

Here are a few points that must be included in your business plan related to your need and request for funding:

♦ First, outline how you came up with the amounts that you are trying to get. This will involve financial analysis and some explanation about the underlying assumptions associated with the analysis.

♦ Explain why you are structuring your funding requirements as you are with respect to the use of debt and equity funding.

♦ If you already have investors, provide that information in your plan to include their relative percentage ownership.

♦ Outline what the projected harvested return would be for an investor who gets in now. Make sure that everyone knows that these numbers are *not guaranteed* but are simply estimates. Explain how that harvesting is expected to happen, such as sale of company, merger, IPO, and so on, and in what time frame.

♦ Tell how the funds will be used and how the investors will be kept informed about fund usage and progress toward the achievement of outlined business goals.

The Least You Need to Know

- ◆ Debt funding must be paid back but allows you to retain total company ownership.

- ◆ Equity funding requires that you give up company ownership but also does not require that you make payments on a loan.

- ◆ Venture capital funding is usually only right for a select group of new companies.

- ◆ Banks don't typically lend to risky ventures.

- ◆ Funding requirements, and perceived investor risk, vary with the stage of company growth.

Chapter 5

Buying Experience with a Franchise

In This Chapter

- ◆ Learn franchising basics
- ◆ Understand the benefits and drawbacks to franchises
- ◆ Determining franchiser qualifications
- ◆ Finding the right franchise for you

There was really no secret about it. Micky just loved teaching reading skills to children. It made her feel like she really was making a difference in these kids' lives, and she liked that.

Micky was a good teacher, but she was tired of having to constantly work around the whims and dictates of administrative people who signed her paycheck, but who knew nothing about literacy education.

Her brother had suggested that she start her own school, but Micky was really uncomfortable with the business side of things. Although she was a teacher, she was also willing to learn business practices if that meant that she could finally do things the way she wanted them done.

Mickey had heard good things about a new franchiser named "Words for Kids" but knew very little about their business operation. She had a little money saved up, and also knew a few other teachers who felt the same way she did and who might be interested in joining her in a new school venture. These thoughts had brought her to the franchising expo. Only by learning more about what was offered could she determine if she could teach, have control over her destiny, and make a decent living. For Micky, that would be a dream come true.

Franchises: Paying for Their Experience

Buying or starting a new *franchise* is a way to start a business using the experience and training provided by an existing company. You are familiar with franchises if you have ever eaten at a McDonald's or had coffee at a Starbucks.

The franchise process works in the following manner:

1. You decide you want to be in business.

2. You look around for business ideas that interest you.

3. You find a *franchiser* who has developed a good business concept with a successful track record helping people start similar operations.

4. You purchase the franchise rights to their procedures and name recognition in exchange for an up-front fee and a recurring annual percentage of your income.

5. After a few years, you start to resent paying the fee to the franchiser and begin looking for ways to sever the link.

(Step 5 might not always happen, but I have heard about it from enough successful *franchisees* that you may as well expect that reaction eventually.)

def•i•ni•tion

A **franchise** is a company that has created a successful business operation and concept and offers to sell the rights to the operation and idea on a limited geographic or market basis. The buyer of the franchise rights is called the **franchisee**. The seller of the franchise rights is the **franchiser**.

You benefit from the franchise relationship because it removes a lot of the risky trial and error associated with starting a new business. A successful franchiser, such as McDonald's, knows precisely how to run your business so that you have the best chance for success. That expertise does not come free, but it might save you from going under while you work your way up the learning curve. They have helped enough people set up a business as one of their franchisees that they have learned what works and what does not. That knowledge is a big part of what you pay for when you become a franchisee.

The three basic franchise flavors are distributor, chain-style, and manufacturing.

The *distributor franchise* is typically used with automobile dealerships where the franchisee (the dealer) is licensed to sell the franchiser's products. The franchisee is given some type of exclusive marketing arrangement for a specific geographic or market segment. The franchisee's main role is to sell the company's products, rather than become involved in manufacturing or other functions. An example of a distributor franchise is Ford Motor Company.

The *chain-style franchise* is used with fast-food establishments. The franchisee (the local owner) is licensed and required to prepare the food in accordance with the franchiser's standards. The local store is often required to purchase all supplies from the franchiser, maintain quality standards, and (often) hit specific sales volume targets. McDonald's is a famous example of a chain-style franchise.

In a *manufacturing franchise*, the franchisee is licensed to create a product in accordance with the franchiser's specifications. The franchise then resells the product at a wholesale price to the distribution channel. Coca-Cola is an example of a product sold through a manufacturing franchise.

A franchise arrangement allows you to start your own business with strong, experienced expertise behind you. This improves your likelihood of success and might decrease the amount of up-front cash required because many franchisers assist with the initial funding. However, it might increase the up-front total investment required (cash and loans) because you are buying a share of a proven business franchise concept. Unless you are dead set on "doing it your own way," you should consider the purchase of a franchised operation as a business option.

When you purchase a franchise, you need to set up a company just the same as if you start it from scratch. You still need to evaluate which form of doing business is best for

def•i•ni•tion

In a **distributor franchise**, the franchisee (the dealer) is licensed to sell the franchiser's products. In a **chain-style franchise**, the franchisee (the local owner) is licensed and required to prepare the product in accordance with the franchiser's standards. In a **manufacturing franchise**, the franchisee is licensed to create a product in accordance with the franchiser's specifications.

Street Smarts

Every January, *Entrepreneur* magazine (www.entrepreneur. com) does an issue on top franchises. Check it out! Their website typically shows the top franchises for the current year and for the two prior and has a special section related to franchising.

your situation: sole proprietorship, partnership, or corporation. Look to your franchiser for guidance regarding these fundamental decisions. If your franchiser does not offer assistance in these areas, you might reconsider whether this franchiser is the right horse to which you should attach your cart. These are simple questions. Where will the franchiser be when difficult questions arise?

Franchising in a Nutshell

Franchising took the country by storm in the 1980s, led by the example of immensely successful franchises such as McDonald's, Dunkin' Donuts, and Burger King among countless others. Franchising is a great idea for the right set of circumstances, which explains their popularity. According to AZFranchises.com (www.azfranchises.com) the U.S. franchising industry employs over 8 million people, accounts for 40 percent of all retail sales, has sales of over $1 trillion, and is used in over 75 different industries. Franchising is big business.

Street Smarts

The Federal Trade Commission (FTC) regulates franchise operations in the fifty states and requires the disclosure of specific minimum information from any franchiser. In addition, many states require their own level of franchiser disclosure. A disclosure document is usually filed with the FTC and appropriate state regulatory body before the sale of franchises in that state can commence operation. Often these disclosure documents must comply with the Uniform Franchise Offering Circular guidelines.

Franchising can spell big trouble if the parties or businesses involved are not working out as initially planned. To get a deeper understanding of the franchise relationship, let's cover a few basic franchising concepts:

- A company develops a successful method for performing a specific function such as changing automobile oil, food preparation, or personal fitness training.

- The company then standardizes its methodology under a legally protected brand name.

- The company prepares a set of franchise agreements and performs the required legal filings with every state in which it intends to sell franchise locations. It is officially recognized as a franchiser at this point.

- Interested parties purchase a franchise to offer these specific services or products in a given geographic or market area. Once the purchase is completed, the buyer is then known as a franchisee.

- The franchiser then provides various benefits to the franchisee such as financing assistance, volume purchase pricing, national advertising, training, and business location research, among others.

- Franchisees pay a franchise fee to the franchiser, usually based on a percentage of their sales revenues. This fee relationship usually continues for as long as the franchise is in operation.

You can see from this quick overview that there are substantial benefits associated with purchasing a franchise but that you also pay for access to these benefits. A major benefit is that you need not be an expert in a particular field since the franchiser has that expertise and can train you adequately enough to apply their model to your particular business situation. In theory, you provide the money and the personal motivation and they provide the expertise and training. Oh, if only it were that simple.

Some franchisers want to expand their market exposure in a rapid fashion but cannot afford to do it on their own. Franchising is a viable solution in that franchisees are motivated to succeed and do not need to start from the beginning in getting their business up and running. New franchisees provide money, energy, and a local presence that the franchiser could typically not have accomplished on its own for time, money, and personnel reasons, among others.

def•i•ni•tion

Disclosure document—a required filing with the Federal Trade Commission and many state regulatory agencies.

Uniform Franchise Offering Circular (UFOC)—a detailed set of franchise information disclosure guidelines that have been adopted by many states.

A problem often lies with the franchiser not having adequately prepared the training and support aspects of their franchise network. After all, the franchiser's primary function is to ensure the success of the franchisees. All of them. However, if the franchise network grows quickly due to excellent franchiser sales efforts then the franchiser might find itself stretched to the point that it cannot provide the agreed upon products and/or services to the franchisees. This leaves the franchisee in a precarious position because he may not have the years of experience needed to manage on his own, or the franchiser might not be adequately prepared to deal with the myriad questions that inevitably come up.

Other problems start to appear as the franchisees become more experienced and successful. At some point, most of them start to believe that they could perform financially as well on their own and do not need the support of the franchiser, but continue with the relationship, and fee payments, simply because they have a signed agreement. Paying the franchise fees often becomes a point of resentment, causing friction between the franchiser and franchisee. And if the franchisee falls behind in its payments, there might even be pending litigation between the two.

It is also possible that the franchiser is not maintaining its part of the agreement, causing the franchisees to believe that they are not receiving adequate services from the franchiser in exchange for royalty fees paid.

> **Street Smarts**
>
> Check with the Secretary of State's office as a starting point for specific franchiser information. If they don't have any information, they will generally point you in the direction of someone who does. A simple Google or Yahoo! Internet search might turn up important background information as well.

The franchisee needs the franchiser to be successful so that the promised purchasing economies of scale, national advertising, research, and new products or services are obtained. Otherwise, the financial model upon which the franchisees made their original purchase do not apply. The franchiser needs the franchisees to succeed or the franchiser won't be able to sell additional franchisees on its business and operational concept.

This relationship is definitely a two-way street and is complicated. Treating a franchise relationship like you would any type of partnership or other business marriage is the right approach. If you get the feeling that the franchiser is looking for you to do a lot and not provide much to the franchisee in return, then you should seriously consider putting your hard-earned money and time elsewhere.

Getting to Know the Franchiser

The more you know about the franchiser, the more you understand the reality of daily life after purchasing a franchise. The franchiser is like a parent in a relationship in that it defines many of the daily working rules. Single moves by the franchiser can have dramatic impact on the franchisees.

If possible, talk with other member franchise organizations to get their perspective on the franchiser. After all, these other locations are already part of the franchise family and can tell where the skeletons are hidden, if there are any.

Check out the franchise prospectus provided by the franchiser to new prospective franchisees. What is it offering in the new agreements that may not be included in the one you inherit with the purchase of an existing location that was started years earlier?

Ed's Lessons Learned

A few years ago a large franchiser that offered its particular brand (flavor) of fried chicken purchased one of its competing franchisers. It may have sounded good on paper, but the details of consolidating the two businesses created a lot of heartburn. Often times these two competitors were just across the street from each other. In a post-purchase environment, the consolidated franchiser had two of its own locations competing for the same customers. Many existing franchisers saw this as a violation of their franchisee agreement and took the franchiser to court. The importance of knowing your franchiser and their future business plans cannot be overstated.

You might find that the earlier agreement has more favorable terms than those contained in the later agreements. Why? Risk and reward. The earlier adopters took a higher risk and rightfully should have expected a higher reward for taking that risk. The later franchisees are purchasing a proven business model along with a lower risk, and their terms and conditions might well be less attractive.

Here are a few references that may get you started in your franchise research. Franchise Buyer (www.franchisebuyer.com) is a matching service between potential franchisees and franchisers. The American Association of Franchisees and Dealers (AAFD) is located at www.aafd.org and is dedicated to creating high quality franchising relationships. Franchise Direct (www.franchisedirect.com) provides a listing of professionals dealing specifically with the franchise side of business. International Franchise Association (IFA) (www.franchise.org) provides information pertaining to international franchising. Women in Franchising (WIF) (www.womeninfranchising.com) is located in Chicago and is specifically oriented to franchising opportunities for women.

This is only a partial listing of organizations that provide guidance, matching, and consulting services specifically for those involved in the franchise business area. Remember that no organization is a substitute for you doing your own homework, learning as much as you can, and then taking responsibility for your decisions. The next few sections provide a few basic guidelines to get you started in evaluating potential franchisers.

How Long Has the Franchiser Been in Business?

This is a pretty basic question, but one with tremendous repercussions. If the franchiser is new to franchising and you are new to both franchising and your industry of choice, then you can expect to be in double jeopardy: one from your own limited experience and the second from the franchiser not knowing what to expect from a new franchisee. Factoring an unknown risk factor, which means assuming longer times until you start to make money and more business development expense than initially estimated, is the right thing to do under these circumstances.

Determine how many franchise locations have been sold. If there are only a few and they have been operating for a few years, then this typically indicates limited acceptance of the idea. If this is the case, you want to take a close look at the franchiser's financial condition. The last thing you want to be is the last franchisee on a sinking franchiser's ship. This could be a very long, sobering, and disheartening experience.

Watch Out!

Listen with a careful ear when talking to new franchisees. They are still on their honeymoon period and might, because of their zeal and motivation, cover up an existing franchiser's flaw. On the other hand, if the new franchisee is treated the way you would want to be treated, this is also good news.

Just because a franchiser has been in business for a long time does not immediately spell success, but it surely helps in the credibility department. This is another time where talking with the existing franchisees is invaluable. It is a really good idea to talk with some who are happy with the relationship and some who are disgruntled. After all, they all have valid opinions that might affect your opinion.

Here are a few questions to ask the franchiser as a starting point. If you are not happy with the answers to these questions, then you will likely find other flaws as well:

- How many franchisee locations have you added in the last 24 months?

- How many franchisee locations have you lost in the last 24 months? Why?

- Is there any pending franchisee litigation? For what reasons and for how long? What are the requested damages?

- What does the franchiser view as its primary obligation in the relationship? What does it expect from the franchisee?

- Have the fees changed in the last five years? How much and for what reasons?

- Has the franchiser changed management or ownership in the last three to five years? Why?

- Is the franchiser publicly or privately owned and financed? Are there any pending major financial deadlines or other covenants? How would these affect the franchisees?

- How many new products/services has the franchiser added to its franchisees in the last three to five years? How many of these are actually making money for the franchisees and why or why not?

- ◆ What does the franchiser do to continually merit receiving its franchise percentage fee?

- ◆ What types of national advertising was performed in the last 12 months, and what is planned for the next 24 months?

- ◆ What percentage of the existing franchisees are actually showing a profit and how long did it take them?

Asking these questions will be like a hydra. For every one question you get answered, two more questions will likely come up. Don't be afraid to ask. After all, most of us date for a while and try to meet the family before we get married. Purchasing a franchise is similar in a lot of ways and deserves close, methodical scrutiny. Should things not work out, like any divorce, it will be a messy, expensive process that is best avoided.

Key Personnel, Methodology, or Arrangements

When purchasing a company (or franchise), you want to know where the specialized information that made the company successful resides. If it resides inside someone's head and is not well documented, then what protection is in place to protect the franchiser and franchisees from this person's loss? If it resides in methodology and procedures that are well documented and proven, then the risks are less but still worth investigating.

As a franchisee, you rely on the franchiser to keep the franchisee network current and on the leading business edge. Knowing where that edge has historically come from is a worthy research project.

It is also a worthwhile effort to verify the status of any national purchasing/sales agreements that the franchiser might have in effect. Understanding the stability of these relationships is critical to your performing a financial analysis that accurately reflects the financial risks and rewards of becoming a franchisee.

Should the agreements terminate or require a cost increase, your operating costs will increase and in turn drive down your gross

Street Smarts

You might find that the franchiser has purchased ideas from the franchisees and offered these ideas throughout its franchisee network. This approach provides an instant national presence for the franchisee's idea and could generate substantial revenues. The franchiser and the franchisees both win in this situation.

margins and income. All of this is through no control or fault of your own, because the franchiser had to make a change.

An objective assessment of the truly unique nature of the franchiser's offering is another good idea. It might be that the offering was unique when first started, such as offering hamburgers at a low price that are easily purchased from the car. Any good idea will be copied if not legally protected, eventually turning what was once a unique idea into just another similar offering.

Does the franchiser have legal protection on its products and/or methodology? If so, how much longer will that legal protection be in force? What protection is really provided and have competitors already figured out ways to work around it?

How much of the franchiser's value is associated with its name and has it diligently protected its legal trademark rights?

Has the company had recent successes or failures with introducing new products or services?

All of these things contribute to either enhancing or diminishing the franchisee value. Many are not under the direct control of the franchisee and must be maintained by the franchiser. If it has historically performed its responsibilities in an effective manner, then there is every reason to expect that it will continue doing the same in the future unless something has recently changed. The same assessment applies if it has not performed its functions properly.

Only you can make the determination as to whether or not the franchisee purchase is the right decision for you. And you can only make this determination when you have adequate, accurate information.

What About the Competition?

Nothing attracts success like success. The more successful a market and the approach to that market, the more likely it is that other companies will want their piece of the business pie.

The good news about being the first into a market is that you get to define the standards against which other entrants are compared. The bad news is that the new entrants build on the success of the trailblazers in creating their ideas and companies. If the early leaders are not careful, they might find themselves trailing instead of leading simply because they did not upgrade and improve their offering.

Franchise business is highly competitive and it is transacted at a pretty rapid pace. If you are not sure about this, take a look at the various printing and copying services that are currently available. As technology moved forward, some of the early franchisers chose to stay with their traditional printing methods. At some point, the technological advances associated with the Internet and the rapidly decreasing cost of computers made traditional printing for smaller printers less desirable from a customer's perspective. Many dedicated copying and printing businesses are no longer in business because they did not see or failed to act on market and technology changes.

Keeping ahead of the competition is critical, even if you are the early leader. Always check out the competition on both a local and national level. If the franchiser is in the lead and had a head start to begin with, then you are in great shape. If the franchiser is ahead, but the local franchisee is lagging, then you might have an excellent opportunity for a turnaround of the local location. If both are lagging, with more contemporary competitors entering the market on a regular basis, then you should seriously consider looking elsewhere for your investment.

The exception to this last point would be if the total franchise network provided a sound marketing base that needed a sound, yet well directed, kick to turn amazing returns. In this way, a few well placed investments and decisions could turn an older franchiser that is suffering from stagnation, into a well run, hungry competitor. Not only could this situation be fun to manage, but the investment returns could be enormous.

Street Smarts

Nothing will humble a business faster than resting on its past successes and not setting new goals and challenges for itself. At some point, someone will make an attempt to take some of the previously earned success away, and customers will leave if the new company provides a better value. This is particularly true with franchise operations because that newcomer can develop a national presence very quickly.

For Your Plan

- ◆ Explain the reasons for choosing the industry that you have and why this industry is still healthy.

- ◆ Discuss the reasons why franchising is a better business ownership route than starting your own from scratch.

- ◆ Present your reasons for choosing the particular franchiser you have over others that you considered.

◆ Talk about whether you plan to start a new franchise or purchase one that is already in existence, and why.

◆ Evaluate this particular franchiser's and its franchisees' historical performance and how it will apply to you in the future.

◆ Prepare information about how your particular franchise operation can be expanded should your first venture turn out profitable enough to warrant expansion.

◆ Fill in the other pertinent sections of your business plan such as management, industry, competition, and marketing as they pertain to your franchise selection.

The Least You Need to Know

◆ It is usually less risky to start a franchised business than an independent one as long as you choose the right franchiser. This is especially true if you are not an expert in the chosen field.

◆ Franchisees are heavily dependent on the franchiser for new products, services, and technologies. There will be some type of legal obligation and relationship here as well.

◆ A franchisee/franchiser agreement is like a marriage. It is better entered into slowly and with an eye for the long term.

◆ A franchisee can be seriously hurt if the franchiser does not manage its financials responsibly.

◆ The FTC and state agencies require specific disclosure filings from any franchiser before franchise sales can begin.

◆ Never ignore, or underestimate, the competition.

Chapter 6

Buying an Existing Business

In This Chapter

- ◆ Understanding the buyer and seller perspective
- ◆ The stages of the buying process
- ◆ Bringing in the right professionals when needed
- ◆ Finding the right seller

Ben was convinced that owning his own business was definitely right for him. However, he was also concerned about his ability to start a business from scratch. He knew a lot about repairing cars and had stayed current on the latest trends in car technology. He had worked for a dealership for 10 years and knew a lot about dealing with customers. In fact, one of the things that customers continually said about Ben was that he was customer oriented and that they really trusted him to work on their car.

What he did not know much about was how to find customers and how to price what he planned to sell. At the dealership, the customers came to him. He would have to find those customers for himself if he started his own business.

His dilemma was driving him, and his wife and family, nuts because he really wanted to go off on his own but he also had a healthy respect for how important customers were to his potential business success.

Then something happened on Ben's way home from work. The mechanic's shop where he origi-nally had started out, just a few miles from his house, was for sale. It had been there forever and had a solid reputation in the neighborhood. Ben had heard through the grapevine that Frank, the guy who started the place, had passed away and the other family members did not want to keep the place going. So they decided to sell it.

Ben knew that Frank had a lot of repeat business and, in fact, Ben knew a lot of Frank's cus-tomers from when he worked there before. Perhaps he could get into his own business by buying one that was solidly established instead of needing to create one from the ground up? Perhaps he should offer to buy Frank's business.

Not everyone is designed to create a business from just an idea. But this doesn't mean that these people have to give up on their dream of owning their own business. It might be right to buy an existing business with existing customers, employees, ven-dors, processes, and reputation. In this way, a lot of the risk associated with starting a business is reduced because whoever owned the business before had somehow made it work, which indicates that you can, too.

This chapter is for those of you who are convinced you want to own your own busi-ness and have the money and inclination to purchase one that is already up and run-ning. Read and consider whether paying more money up front to get started, by buying a business, is a more attractive and quicker way for you to move into small business ownership.

The Benefits and Drawbacks of Buying an Existing Business

There are a number of very real benefits associated with buying an existing business:

- An existing company has a track record that you can use to determine if future sales will provide the income you need.

- There is an existing customer base that you can tap into for future selling activi-ties which relieves some of the startup selling pressure.

- The company is already legally formed; it has a name, banking relationship, and other important business foundation aspects that you would have to create for a new business.

- The company has a reputation (good, we hope) that you can use to find new cus-tomers and business.

◆ You can get up and running in your new business possibly within weeks (instead of many months) depending on how long it takes you and the seller to complete the required acquisition steps.

But all of these benefits do not come without some potential risks.

◆ If the company has a bad reputation, it could take a long time and a lot of effort to turn it around, even if everyone knows that it is under new ownership.

◆ The company may have some legal or other obligations that would transfer to you as the new owner. You are basically inheriting the prior owner's legal and financial problems once you buy the company, so extreme care is warranted in this area.

◆ It may be possible that the prior owner is the primary reason for the business's success; and if the prior owner leaves, so does what made it successful in the past.

◆ The employees may be fiercely dedicated to the prior owner and either leave when the company is sold or, even worse, work to undermine your future success simply because you are not the prior owner.

◆ Competition may already be lining up to knock the company off of its successful block and the new owners can find themselves the target of a very aggressive business onslaught. A new company is "new" and few people even know about it, much less target it for obsolescence.

As you can see, just like any business situation, there are pros and cons. I suggest that you have a heart-to-heart with yourself about whether you are a startup person who likes to create things that are new or someone who is stellar at improving on an existing idea. Once you have an idea about where you personally fit, then you can decide if starting or buying a company is right for you.

Buying and Selling are Similar ... but Different

This might seem obvious, but it takes both a buyer and a seller to complete a business transaction. What is not so obvious is that the interests of the buyer and seller are related but very different. And these differing interests often cause miscommunication points that, if not resolved early in the process, can cause an otherwise excellent transaction to fall apart.

For example, both the buyer and the seller want the company sold, but for different reasons. The buyer is looking to the future when determining the value of the company, and filters all discussions through a "future" filter. The seller, on the other hand, is usually looking at the company from a historical perspective, and filters all buyer comments through that "historical" filter.

Although both parties show up for each of the meetings, it is very possible that each party also attended a different meeting in his own mind. Getting the buyer and the seller to agree on important points is often more of an art form than a science, but must be done to ensure a solid transaction that works for both parties.

Each party is trying to sell the other on being the right candidate. The seller is trying to convince the buyer that his particular company is the best value available. The buyer is trying to convince the seller that she can perform financially as agreed to on the contracts and that the various personal covenants included in the agreement will be adhered to. For some sellers, the personal covenants such as retaining certain employees or managing the company resources in specific ways might be more important than the actual purchase price. If the buyer is talking price and the seller is thinking employee and customer protection, there is fertile ground for misunderstanding.

Preparing to Buy

Purchasing a company is a lot like taking on a roommate and should not be pursued lightly. The right roommate can enhance the quality of your life, making your life more than it was previously. The wrong roommate can turn a good situation sour quickly and even put your emotional, physical, and financial health in jeopardy. The same can happen with a poorly managed company purchase.

def•i•ni•tion

A **strategic plan** is a business plan that sets the overall direction of a company over a future three to five year period.

An **acquisition target** is a company that you decide to investigate in earnest for potential purchase.

So where do you start your purchasing process? You first start by knowing what you personally want from the purchase. You then have to look at how much money you are willing to invest (or are capable of investing) when buying a business. You then need to determine which industries look like they are growing and present a solid opportunity for future success. This means some type of strategic planning function. From your *strategic plan*, you can determine the types of companies you should look at and the potentially attractive areas of company operation that you plan to keep or even improve once purchased. Once you know this information, you can effectively, and efficiently, start looking for potential *acquisition targets*.

At a minimum, you start by first asking yourself a few questions:

♦ What type of personal commitments are you willing to take on when buying a business?

♦ What type of geographic, financial, and industrial characteristics should the ideal company have?

♦ Do you want a company that is already doing great, or do you want one that is struggling which you can improve?

♦ How much are you willing to spend on the purchase, and how do you plan to find the money?

♦ Are you willing to work with the prior owners after the sale, or do you intend to go it alone? Beware making this decision before you know more about the company and industry you plan to enter.

♦ What assets, experience, expertise, or other capabilities do you bring to the purchase that could improve on what the company already has? These present areas where major improvements and gains can occur.

Treat this list as a starting point for generating more questions. The more questions you ask before starting your purchasing search, the more efficiently the process will proceed and the more likely you are to wind up with a satisfactory purchase. You are always better off identifying your problems earlier in the process than later so that you save time, money, and reputation.

Purchasing a business is a business decision and must make business sense, or it makes little sense at all. There are all kinds of reasons for buying a company, but unless these reasons eventually lead to improved shareholder value in the form of greater dividends, larger net worth, and/or increased price-per-share, the purchase should be re-evaluated. No business stays in business for very long if it fails to minimally maintain and, optimally, improve its financial health.

Finding the Candidate

Whether you are buying or selling, you must find your candidate. For the buyer, the candidate is the company that is a potential fit with your purchase goals.

Finding that candidate can be tricky business, which is why many companies turn to a business broker. Just as a real estate broker is familiar with the properties and buyers currently on the market, a good business broker will also be familiar with the current set of buyers and sellers.

If you choose to go without a business broker, then you must do this legwork totally on your own.

Finding a Company to Buy

As the buyer, you must first determine the general criteria for your target company. Here are some questions to consider when taking the first look at potential candidates:

- Is the company in a geographic location that meets your needs?

- Is the market segment growing or shrinking?

- Is this company's reputation one that you want associated with your organization?

- Is the company culture compatible with your own organization, or will there be a clash?

- Is the target company a leader or follower in its market segment?

- How long has the company been in business and under how many different ownership structures?

- Is the company publicly or privately owned?

- What special attributes make this particular company an attractive purchase candidate?

- Are there members of the executive management team that you would particularly like to work with after the purchase?

- Does the target company's general direction appear compatible with your preferred professional direction?

Hundreds of other items can be, and will be, added to this list as you get farther into the purchase evaluation process. At this stage, you are simply trying to make a first-cut determination about which companies are worth further evaluation. Should a company fail this first set of evaluation criteria, then you are best served dropping it from the list unless other attributes are such a strong fit that they warrant further investigation.

Once you narrow the list down to 5 companies or less, then you should perform an in-depth newspaper/media analysis. A tremendous amount of information is provided by industry publications, and most of them are in your public library. A few days in the library can round out your initial assessment and may even let you know if the company is currently for sale, whether deals have recently fallen through, or if the company has extenuating circumstances that make it an even better acquisition target. Local newspaper articles are important for learning about smaller, privately held businesses as is the local Chamber of Commerce or Rotary Club.

By the way, notice that at this stage you do not even know if any particular company is for sale or not. You are simply determining who you should talk to.

It is very possible, and probable, that your list of five companies will now be down to three or fewer. But notice that your information on these companies is now as current as possible with publicly available information. You can talk intelligently to the company management and represent yourself as a credible buyer. This may not close the deal for you, but it will certainly give you a better chance of initially getting their attention. Remember that at this stage you are simply trying to determine which companies to investigate further.

Street Smarts

If you are purchasing a smaller company, you should pay special attention to the top management team in general and the owners in particular. Quite often, these people will become your employees for a period of time after the sale as a way of ensuring a smooth transition. If the top management team has a reputation for being difficult to work with, you might just want to look elsewhere from the start.

Plan to Buy in Stages

Buying a business takes time. It also takes planning if you expect to make as much off of the purchase as possible.

It may help you to divide the pre-buying process into a few steps.

1. Prepurchase stage—Here you solidify your personal goals, direction, and finances. In this stage you are doing some soul searching while at the same time cleaning up any credit or other financial problems. You want to have as much cash on hand as possible, have as little debt as possible, and have as clean a credit record as possible. These actions will all pay off later when you try to get funding for the purchase.

2. Initial Search Stage—During this stage you put out feelers with various people to see who might be interested in selling their company. The challenge here is to approach enough companies to find a few interested sellers. During this stage

you might contact people by mail or telephone and will probably have a meeting or two before moving to stage 3. A business broker can be helpful at this stage.

3. Due Diligence Stage—This is a critically important stage for buyers and frightening for sellers because this stage requires sellers to reveal detailed information about their overall company operation. You want to make sure that whoever gets to this stage as a prospective seller is truly interested, because this stage takes a lot of work that could be for nothing if the seller backs out. It is always best to be selective about who gets to this stage, which may last a few weeks to a few months, depending on the size of the company involved and overall business complexity.

4. Proposal, Negotiations, and Close Stage—This is where purchase price numbers are discussed along with terms and conditions. The lawyers are usually pretty actively involved at this point, and many contractual terms and conditions may actually be worked out between the attorneys who come to you for final approval. This stage ends when the purchase agreements are signed, money has changed hands, and you get the key to the business's front door.

5. Post Sale Stage—Many forget about this stage, which in some ways may be the most important. Everything done in the first few stages leads to this stage. As the new owner, you get to meet with employees, customers, and vendors while taking over the reins of your company. It is in your best personal and business interest to ensure that this stage goes smoothly, because your future reputation and income will depend on it. This stage is particularly important if the purchase agreement involves stock, loans, or other financial vehicles that are tied to the company's future financial performance.

As you can see, this is not a one-step process, and you should be willing to sign up for the whole trip once you start on stage three. This doesn't mean that you can't back out at any time before the actual purchase, but don't expect to do so without suffering some type of professional, financial, personal, or legal repercussions.

The Sales Meetings

If you are the buyer, you cannot expect the seller to intuitively understand the future value that you bring to the sellers and their company. It is your job to present yourself and your plans in such a way that the seller understands and believes in the various benefits associated with selling his/her company to you.

Every contact that you have with a prospective seller should lead through the various stages of the sales process.

It seems right to present a few major points regarding effective selling techniques, which are adapted from my *StreetWise Guide to Professional Selling* training course:

◆ Sellers sell based on their belief in the benefits that they perceive will come their way from the selling in general.

◆ Sellers of small businesses may think of their employees or customers as "family" and as such might go to what you would consider extremes to protect their respective interests.

◆ Remember that all benefits come in the future, not from the past, and you are dealing more with perceived benefits as opposed to actual benefits.

◆ You can try to take emotion out of the purchase of a small business, but it will be difficult to do if the sellers are also the founders. The business has likely become a member of their family, with all of the joys and trials that come with that family membership.

Talking to sellers who do not see any benefit to themselves in selling is basically a waste of your time. If they don't want to sell, they won't.

Getting the Right Professional Help

As you get deeper into buying a business, you will find that each question generates a few more. And the more complicated the transaction, such as one involving a publicly held company, the more you will appreciate having professionals on your team that you trust and who have walked these paths before.

Let's start with your accountant. This person is important in that she can evaluate the company financial information as a sort of objective observer. Depending upon her level of involvement with the target company's accounting, she may be able to verify the bookkeeping and accounting accuracy of the information presented in the financial statements. If she is an employee or Chief Financial Officer of the target company, then her level of detailed knowledge about the information presented in the financial statements will be substantial. Make sure that you ask a lot of questions and get the detailed answers you need to understand what you are purchasing. It is not the accountant or lawyer who has to pay the debts associated with the new company, it's you! Know that this level of financial exposure makes the major decisions your decisions, not theirs, but make them with as much seasoned, professional guidance as possible.

The difference between someone with an accounting background and a Certified Professional Accountant (CPA) is that the CPA is licensed by the state in which she operates. This licensing procedure is rigorous and defines specific ethical and legal codes of conduct. CPAs typically know accounting and taxes, but they may not understand business. It is important for you to understand the limitations of your accountant. In particular, accountants are detail-oriented people who deal primarily with historical information. This information is well defined, since it has already happened. Accountants often have a hard time risking the future based on a hunch, which is where most entrepreneurial business types thrive.

Watch Out!

Just because someone such as a CPA understands accounting doesn't make him a good financial/business manager. Just because an attorney understands business law doesn't mean that she understands merger and acquisition law. Get the right professionals with the right expertise for your team and don't rush into a selection. Time spent here will save time, money, and aggravation later in the process.

So get a clear understanding about your particular accountant's personal orientation toward speculative ventures and risk. Remember, you are the business manager. She is the accountant. Her primary job is to make sure that the financial numbers shown on the statements accurately reflect the current and historical status of a company. Your job is to use that information to make business decisions. If you're lucky, you will get both financial manager and accountant in the same person, but don't expect it.

The same general advice applies to attorneys. Attorneys are excellent at making sure that contracts and other documents are "legal," but they are not really trained to determine whether something makes business sense.

For example, a "legal" agreement could be one that allows your vendors to instantly change, without prior notification or your consent, the terms on your accounts payable debt so that it is due within 48 hours instead of the initially agreed-to 30 days. If you signed an agreement containing these conditions, you would be legally bound by that agreement even if it made no business sense. Expecting your attorney to make business decisions for you is usually unrealistic, unless you are lucky enough to have an attorney who is also a solid businessperson.

You will also find that attorneys have little accounting background, which puts you and your accountant in the role of interpreting financial numbers involved with your agreements.

Company buying and selling law is a specialized animal that involves specialized areas of the law. It is likely that your standard corporate attorney will *not* have the specialized expertise needed to assist with the creation or review of business purchase documents. For this reason, it's best to look for an experienced attorney from the beginning of the process. If the transaction involves a franchise, you might even need another lawyer since franchise law is another one of those specialized legal areas.

There are special benefits derived from having a tax attorney on your team in addition to a business attorney. The tax attorney will understand both the accounting and legal aspects of your particular company. The business attorney will understand the legal aspects of the agreements you will sign as part of the transaction. The skill sets involved are unique and usually require the involvement of different people. Having an attorney who is also a CPA is an ideal combination. If this person also has business purchase experience, you should lock him in a room and not let him out.

For Your Plan

If you plan to purchase an existing company, make sure that your plan covers the following points:

- ◆ Your rationale for buying a company instead of starting one.

- ◆ Your financial justification for buying a company instead of starting one from scratch. It might turn out that the costs are similar, but buying a company gets you into business faster and with fewer uncertainties.

- ◆ Why you've chosen this type of company to buy.

- ◆ What your plans are for handling not only the purchase but also the ownership transition and future operation.

- ◆ What it is about the company you plan to purchase that makes it the right purchase for you not only today but a few years into the future as well.

- ◆ Why buying a company in general is right for you, and why buying this particular company makes sound business sense.

The Least You Need to Know

- ◆ Both buyers and sellers participate at each stage of the sale process, but sellers typically have a historical perspective whereas buyers are evaluating the future.

- ◆ General business attorneys will probably not have the specialized skills needed to evaluate the purchase agreements that you will encounter. Finding a competent and experienced business attorney that you feel you can trust is an important process that should not be rushed.

◆ Even as the buyer, you will likely have to "sell" the sellers on the fit between you and their business. Honing your sales skills will pay off as you move into the various stages of the process.

◆ Buying without a business broker means that you must find potential sellers on your own. Extensive research in trade publications, reports, and at the library are invaluable in determining likely prospects.

◆ Expect the buying process to take many months and perhaps years depending on market conditions, your readiness, and the overall complexity of the transaction.

Should You Start a Corporation?

In This Chapter

- ◆ The difference between sole proprietorships, partnerships, and corporations
- ◆ The legal implications of each type of business structure
- ◆ How taxes affect each kind of business
- ◆ The type of business structure that is right for you

Bill shouted, "What do you mean I could lose everything I own? I didn't even know Ted bought that equipment for the company."

"The problem is that you never incorporated as you planned, and the law treats the two of you as a partnership," replied the attorney. "Under the law, you are responsible for the company obligations whether you agreed to them or not."

"No way," shouted Bill. "I'm not going to pay. Let them go after Ted first."

"The equipment company will first go after the business and then you and Ted at the same time. As far as the law is concerned, you and Ted are both equally liable for paying off the debt. Sorry, but you have no choice. Next time, pick your partners more carefully and consider incorporating to avoid this situation again."

Bill didn't like it, but he accepted what he heard as the truth. How could his life savings and a thriving company take a dive so quickly based on the irresponsible actions of one person? What could he have done differently? How could he have known?

Just as one house style does not meet the living requirements of all families, no single business structure meets everyone's business needs. Depending on your current situation and future business aspirations, one business structure might meet those needs better than another. Take the time to determine where you want the company to go not only in the next few months but over the next few years, at least. A long-term perspective helps you decide on the best structure for your specific situation. In this chapter, I review the different legal business structures and discuss the pros and cons of each.

You should use this chapter as a general starting point. Understand the information presented and then apply it to your situation. This is your homework portion of the process. You should then run your assessment by the proper legal and accounting professionals to ensure that you are on the right track and to help set you up properly for your particular situation. Try to avoid the temptation to "go it alone" at this stage, because an error regarding your company's structure can have serious business, personal, and tax consequences later on.

An Overview of the Various Business Structures

The three basic business organizational structures are sole proprietorships, partnerships, and corporations. Under each category are subclasses that apply to specific situations.

A sole proprietorship is the most common and easiest type of business to create. Anyone who performs services of any kind, such as a gardener, caterer, or even babysitter, is by default a sole proprietor unless he or she takes specific action to set it up otherwise. A small company with only one employee is often kept as a sole proprietorship, but there are no restrictions on how big a sole proprietorship can become. It depends exclusively on the desires of the owner, or proprietor. The majority of small businesses in the United States are sole proprietorships.

A general partnership is formed whenever two or more people decide to enter a for-profit business venture. Typically, each partner owns a portion of the company's profits and debts, which can be set up in a written agreement among the partners. You do not need to file any special paperwork to form a partnership, but you should make sure you and your partners sign an agreement to minimize misunderstandings regarding each person's rights and liabilities. If you do not have an agreement signed by all parties, then any partnership-related disputes are handled under statutes based on the Uniform Partnership Act (UPA) used in most states. Most larger bookstores carry books that cover creating partnerships for your particular state. These books are inexpensive and helpful in making sure that you and your partners dot the right i's and cross the right t's. Once you have done the grunt work using both the book and the forms included on the companion CD, I suggest that you present it to an attorney to make sure all of the proper legal lingo is included and that everyone's interests are protected.

Corporations are often treated as an indicator of how serious you are about being in business since it is more involved and more expensive to set up and manage a corporation than to set up and manage a sole proprietorship or partnership.

When you form a corporation, you actually establish a separate organization—separate and distinct from you personally. You may ask why that's such a big deal; what's the advantage? A primary advantage is that if the corporation is sued, you are not personally responsible for any damages that might be awarded (unless, of course, you are also named in the suit, which can always happen—corporation or not). This aspect of corporations provides you with limited liability. Paperwork and record-keeping are also more involved with a corporation, which is why some people decide it's not worth the hassles. You may also find it more advanta-

def•i•ni•tion

A **corporation** is a separate legal entity created through the state where the business is incorporated. A corporation has owners who purchase shares in the corporation. A properly organized corporation bears all legal and fiscal liability, typically shielding shareholders (owners) from personal risk (unless they are also sued personally or they guarantee corporate obligations).

geous from a tax perspective to be incorporated, which can completely separate your personal and business income. If you are not careful with how you handle the administrative aspects of your corporation, you can lose your limited liability protection. So do it right to avoid unwelcome surprises later.

Corporations are legal entities created through the states where the business is incorporated. A corporation is created by owners who purchase shares in the corporation. The percentage of ownership of each shareholder is based on the number of shares owned by that shareholder compared to the total number of shares issued or outstanding.

Many corporations are formed in the state of Delaware because of its less restrictive incorporation laws. Delaware was one of the early states to allow you to incorporate while conducting business and keeping headquarters in another state. Most other states now allow the same procedure. Realize, however, that if you incorporate in Delaware and then operate in Illinois, for example, you will have to register your corporation with the state of Illinois. Now you have two states to deal with instead of one, which takes away from the Delaware incorporation benefits. Naturally, if you live in Delaware, that is where you would most likely incorporate.

Watch Out!

Don't make your business organization decision based solely on tax implications. The tax laws change on a regular basis, and the impact of the laws varies depending upon your personal income and your company's income levels. But you are right to investigate the tax benefits or drawbacks associated with each business type.

It is important to understand that the various business structures have their own sets of tax-related problems and benefits, which are outlined throughout this chapter and in the Special CD bonus chapter titled "Special Corporation Realities" that deals in detail with corporation considerations.

Just remember that the best business structure is the one that provides the required level of legal and tax protection along with enough flexibility to address future financial needs. This is a tricky balancing act that requires attention on your part.

Select the business structure that is right for you based on where you are today and where you want to wind up down the road. Consider the advantages and disadvantages of each business structure before making a decision.

Sole Proprietorship: Going It Alone

Judy makes wooden dolls and gives them as presents every Christmas. Today she sold her first one. She just became the head of a sole proprietorship.

Watch Out!

Guard against the dangers of the sole proprietorship and partnership business types. They can leave the owners personally open to any type of litigation filed against or debt incurred by the company. Years of work and personal wealth acquisition can be lost in a short period of time using these forms of business structures.

Once you begin providing and receiving money for products or services, you become a sole proprietor. Your business expenses are deductible, all income is taxable, and you assume the liabilities of the business. (More on the tax implications later.)

Notice that Judy did not have to create a separate name to start her business. She simply started her business and began selling her product, using her own name. This is why the sole proprietorship is such a popular business structure.

However, if Judy wants to call her business "Dolls and Such," she must file a Doing Business As (d/b/a) form with the local authorities, usually the county clerk's office in the area where she plans to do business. The d/b/a filing is sometimes called a *tradename*, a *fictitious name statement*, or an *also known as* (*a.k.a.*). If no one else is using the name she chooses, after filing her d/b/a form, Judy can transact business as "Dolls and Such." Filing the d/b/a gives her legal rights to the name within the jurisdiction of the governing body, which is typically the county. If someone else later uses the name within the county, Judy can ask the courts to order that person to cease operations under the name she legally owns. The other business is then forced to rename itself. Notice that this name registration is only for the county and not for the state, which could hurt Judy if she branches out to do business in other parts of the state. A corporation's name applies statewide.

A sole proprietorship is easy and inexpensive to create, and all profits go directly to the owner. The major disadvantage is that all legal and financial obligations incurred by the company are also passed directly to the owner. That means that if the company is sued for any reason, such as if a child eats one of Judy's dolls and is hospitalized, Judy is personally responsible for answering that lawsuit. Judy could lose everything she personally owns if the business-related lawsuit is lost and the damages are high. For this liability reason alone, many people choose to change their structure from a sole proprietorship to a corporation.

Liability insurance is strongly recommended for those transacting business in general, but particularly for those running sole proprietorships. Make sure that your insurance agent knows the type of business you are in and how you expect to be protected.

On the CD

A sample Assumed Business Name Certificate is included on the companion CD as document 07–01 in the Bonus Forms Section.

def•i•ni•tion

A **fictitious name statement**, also known as a **tradename**, doing business as, or d/b/a form, allows you to run a business using a name other than your own. The official name for the filing form itself may vary from one locality to another. You might also use **a.k.a.** (also known as) when referring to a fictitious name.

Being a sole proprietorship does not limit whether you have employees, although many sole proprietorships are one-person businesses. You can hire employees as a sole proprietorship, but you, as the owner, become the target for any claims made against the business as a result of any of the actions of your employees. You must apply for an employer identification number (EIN) just as a corporation does since this is the IRS's tracking mechanism for employers. (See Chapter 13 for details on obtaining an EIN.) Oddly enough, you as the owner are not an employee of the company even though you draw a salary. Who said that IRS regulations had to make sense! You file your sole proprietorship business taxes on Schedule C of your personal Form 1040 tax return.

The flexibility associated with being the only owner is often attractive enough to keep people in business as a sole proprietorship, even after the company grows large in revenues.

Partnership: A Business Marriage

Partnership is a wonderful term that evokes warm, comforting feelings. Who wouldn't want a partner to share the good and bad times in a business? Well, if you have ever been in a bad relationship, you know the damage it can do to your psychological and financial well-being. You should treat business partnerships with the same amount of respect. Your personal partner may move the ketchup from the pantry to the refrigerator, but your business partner can bankrupt you, which is a way bigger problem than cold ketchup.

On the CD

A sample Partnership Agreement (document 07-02) and sample Partnership Minutes (document 07-03) are included on the companion CD.

A sample Limited Partnership Organizing Checklist (document 07-04), Limited Partnership Agreement (document 07-05), Limited Partnership Certificate (document 07-06), Limited Partnership Consent Resolution in Lieu of First Meeting of Partners (document 07-07), and Limited Partnership Minutes (document 07-08) are included on the companion CD.

When two or more people form a partnership, they are essentially married, from a business standpoint. Either party can obligate the other via the business, and everything the business and the partners own individually is on the line. In essence, a partnership is like a sole proprietorship owned by several people. All liability is passed to the partners.

A special partnership type, called a *limited partnership*, provides certain partners with a maximum financial liability equal to their investment. To maintain this limited financial liability status, these partners, called *limited partners*, cannot participate in the daily operation of the business. The *general partner* is responsible for the day-to-day management of the business. Limited partners invest in the company and rely on the general partner to run the business.

def•i•ni•tion

In a limited partnership, some partners (called **limited partners**) invest money but do not participate in the daily operation of the business. They are liable only for the amount of money that they each have invested. A **general partner** is responsible for the daily operations of the business.

A **limited liability partnership (LLP)** is a special type of partnership that is created by a special filing with the state where the partners operate. Partners who are part of an LLP protect their personal assets from being taken if the partnership gets into financial trouble. There is really no reason not to become an LLP.

Special laws govern the operation of a limited partnership, and if they are not precisely followed, the courts might hold that the partnership was general, not limited. The formerly limited partner might find himself as liable as a general partner for business-related debts. Be aware that you must complete and file special paperwork with the state to form a limited partnership.

On the CD

A sample Limited Liability Partnership Organizing Checklist (document 07-09), Limited Liability Partnership Agreement (document 07-10), Limited Liability Partnership Registration (document 07-11), and Limited Liability Partnership Consent Resolution in Lieu of First Meeting of Partners (document 07-12) are included on the companion CD.

Corporations: Share the Wealth

Creating a corporation is like creating a new business life. A corporation is a separate and distinct business entity that is responsible for itself. Upon formation, the corporation issues shares of stock to *shareholders*, the owners. The shareholders exchange money, goods, or services to receive their shares of stock. Shareholders are, in essence, transacting business with this fictitious legal entity called a corporation and not with "real" people, per se. If you plan to start a corporation, it is absolutely imperative that you keep the difference between you and the corporation straight. Beware, however, that stock obtained from contributing an item or cash is tax free but the IRS considers stock obtained from providing a service to the corporation as income and is subject to income taxes. You see, the IRS never sleeps.

For larger corporations, a *board of directors*, elected by the shareholders, manages the corporation. This board then appoints *officers* of the corporation to handle the day-to-day affairs of the company. In essence, the board members represent the interests of the shareholders in the company operations. Depending on the state in which the business is incorporated, the business owner in many small corporations may be the primary, or only, shareholder and only board member. This same person is listed as the president, secretary, and treasurer of the corporation. A small company rarely has a board of directors except in an informal advisory capacity that does not usually involve any legal obligation on the owner and shareholder. Some states, such as Indiana, do not require a board of directors at all.

The corporation pays taxes on its annual profits and passes the profits to the shareholders in the form of *dividends*. The board of directors, or shareholders, determine the amount of the dividends.

def•i•ni•tion

In a corporation, **shareholders,** or stockholders, own a percentage of the business, expressed in terms of the number of shares of stock they own in relation to the total number of shares issued. The corporation is managed by employees who take their overall direction from a corporation's **board of directors.** A small company with few shareholders will likely not have a board of directors. Annual profits are passed on to shareholders in the form of **dividends,** although annual dividend payments are not mandatory. The amount of the dividends is determined by the board of directors. Corporation **officers** have the ability to legally commit the corporation, whereas standard employees have limited commitment ability, if any.

The major benefit associated with a corporate business form is that the corporation is liable for its own financial and civil liabilities. The shareholders risk only the amount of money they have invested in their respective shares of stock. This is referred to as limited liability.

Street Smarts

Liability issues can also be addressed through insurance, so while limited liability is one reason to choose a corporate form of organization, check with knowledgeable advisors before making a final decision.

Using the earlier "Dolls and Such" example, assume that the business is a corporation with $500,000 in its bank account. If someone were to win a judgment against "Dolls and Such" for $1 million, the company would probably go out of business, and only $500,000 would change hands. The person who won the legal judgment against the corporation would have no immediate legal basis for getting the rest of the money from the shareholders personally.

However, this is not the case with a partnership or sole proprietorship. As a partner or sole proprietor, your personal finances are put squarely at risk in this scenario, and you could lose a lifetime of work. You might end up owing an additional $500,000 to the judgment holder if that situation ever came to pass.

Another major corporate benefit involves raising money for the business by selling shares in the corporation. Once the buyer and seller agree to a price per share of stock, the buyer simply purchases the number of shares needed to equal the amount of money to be exchanged. For instance, assume you need to raise $100,000. If you find a buyer who is willing to pay you $4 per share, then you sell that person 25,000 shares of stock to receive the $100,000. Life is rarely this simple, but this example outlines the basic benefit associated with corporation finances.

To further illustrate the point, assume you still need $100,000 but don't know anyone with that kind of money on hand. Instead of selling 25,000 shares at $4 each to one person, you could sell 2,500 shares to 10 different investors for $4 each and still get the money you need. You now have 10 share-holders instead of 1, but you got the money you needed. This approach is often more attractive to investors in that they can share in your success but do not have to risk more money than they can afford to lose. Forming a corporation is the route to take if you eventually plan to raise a large sum of money by selling stock to a number of different people. Make sure that you check the stock sale registration regulations for your particular state and the Security and Exchange Commission (SEC) when doing any type of stock sale offering.

On the CD

A sample Corporation Checklist for Offering Memorandum for Investors (document 07-13), Corporation Subscription Questionnaire (document 07-14), Corporation Investor Letter (document 07-15), and Promissory Note (document 07-16) are included on the companion CD.

Standard corporations are separate entities from their shareholders and, as such, the corporation files its own tax return. It shows revenue, expenses, and net profit before tax on which state and federal taxes are paid. Net income is what is left over after all taxes are paid. Notice that the corporation may have money left over in the form of net income, but none of it has been paid to the shareholders. If the corporation wants to reward the shareholders for owning its stock, then the board of directors (or shareholders) can issue a dividend to the shareholders who then must pay tax on the dividends they receive, just as if they had received a dividend from owning General Electric or Microsoft stock.

So the corporation pays tax on its net profit before tax and the individual shareholder pays tax on the dividends it received from the corporation. This is called "double taxation." It is considered a major drawback to corporation ownership and was the motivation for creating the S-Corporation that is discussed later in this chapter.

Public or Private?

There is a difference between a publicly held and privately held corporation. Publicly held corporations are traded on the various public stock exchanges, such as the New York Stock Exchange, American Stock Exchange, and NASDAQ. The shareholders are typically large numbers of people who never come in direct contact with each other. They trust the board of directors to manage their investments for them.

Privately held, or *close*, corporations are more common. The shares are held by a few people, often family members, who also sit on the board and participate as officers of the corporation. The shares are also not offered to the general public.

def•i•ni•tion

A **close corporation,** or privately held corporation, is owned by a small number of shareholders, often only one. In this case, the corporation may be viewed as an extension of the individual. You must still act as a corporation with separate checking accounts, loans, finances, and various corporate legal notifications and documents in proper order. I know it seems silly to do all this if you are the only shareholder, but if you want to maintain the corporate benefits, then this is a necessary burden you have to do.

Unless you are planning to create a very large business, you will probably create and continue to be a privately held corporation. It is generally easier to form a small or close corporation in the state where the principal shareholders reside and work. Because state tax laws vary, be sure to check with an accountant before making this decision.

def•i•ni•tion

The **Securities and Exchange Commission (SEC)** regulates public offerings of company securities. The SEC mandates strict guidelines for the dissemination and content of company financial information to help assure investors that the information they receive on public companies is reliable and reasonably comprehensive.

If the number of shareholders exceeds 35, you must comply with the *Securities and Exchange Commission* (*SEC*) regulations for publicly offered companies. You will definitely need legal and accounting services if you plan to sell shares of stock to more than 35 people as part of your investment fundraising activities.

When a company "goes public," it offers to sell shares in the company to the general public. This is a common way for the founding members of a company to make oodles of money from the large numbers of stock shares they received during the startup stages. The founders often buy or receive this stock at the outset for a nominal price, sometimes pennies per share. When the company goes public, the shares might sell for dollars per share. You don't need to be a CPA to figure out that several hundred thousand shares sold at a public offering can add up to a lot of money. This opportunity alone keeps many people actively working for startup companies, in spite of higher risks, instead of working for larger, more stable companies.

Subchapter S-Corporations: Protection with a Smaller Tax Bite

Suppose you want the legal protection provided by a corporation but want the income to pass directly to you so that you can declare it on your personal income tax statement and avoid double taxation. For once, you can thank the IRS and Congress because they created the *subchapter S-corporation* for just this purpose.

def•i•ni•tion

A **subchapter S** or **S-corporation** is a type of corporation with no more than 100 shareholders and a single class of stock. All profits are passed directly to the owners and taxed as income, which avoids double taxation. For this reason, the S-corporation is often called a "pass-through entity." **Double taxation,** being taxed on income at both the corporate and personal levels, is avoided with the S-corporation.

In a subchapter S or S-corporation, instead of the corporation paying taxes on its income, the business income is passed to the shareholders, who then declare the income on their personal income tax statements. Subchapter S-corporations retain all the legal protection provided by a standard C-corporation (any corporation that is not converted into an S-corporation).

Why opt for the S instead of C-corporation? If you are personally in a lower tax bracket than the corporation, then passing the business income to you decreases the overall taxes paid. In addition, if the corporation loses money, you can use part of that loss to offset personal income earned from other investments you may have, up to certain limits. You can also avoid *double taxation* if you use an S-corporation, which can have a welcome tax-reduction effect around April 15 of each year. However, if you don't plan properly or if the company does better than you expected, you can find yourself with a huge personal tax bill at the end of the year because of the great performance of your S-corporation.

There are some creative cash flow issues that must be addressed every year for an S-corporation because all of the corporation's net income is passed to shareholders who pay tax on it. In essence, most of the cash available to the S-corporation is used to pay shareholders what they have coming from the fiscal year. To keep the company from

On the CD

A sample Cover Letter to the IRS for S-Corporation Election (form 2553) is included on the companion CD as document 07-17.

running out of cash, shareholders (who are also usually owners) take only as much cash as they need to pay their personal taxes resulting from S-corporation ownership and leave the rest in the corporation as an operating cash loan. As the new fiscal year starts and the corporation starts to make money, it pays back the shareholders for the loan and usually by March or April the shareholders are paid back and the corporation is again running business as usual.

If you think the S-corporation is right for you, check with an accountant and an attorney before taking the plunge. A little prevention goes a long way to avoid unforeseen problems down the road. Notice that the decision is heavily based on how much revenue and net income you anticipate the company will generate. This is why the strategic planning aspects of business are so critically important.

To form an S-corporation, you first incorporate as you would any corporation, and then file IRS Form 2553 to establish your S-corporation tax status.

Limited Liability Company (LLC)

How would you like the advantages of a corporation or partnership without some of the restrictions regarding shareholders? That's what a *limited liability company* (*LLC*) can provide.

Limited liability companies are now authorized in all 50 states. The reason for their new popularity is that LLCs provide business owners, called *members*, with personal liability protection, just as corporations do, and still provide tax profits at the individual level only, as subchapter S-corporations do. The LLC is also a pass-through entity.

What sets LLCs apart from the popular S-corporations is that LLCs do not have the traditional restrictions regarding the number of shareholders. S-corporations limit the number of shareholders to 100 and require that they be U.S. citizens; foreigners, domestic corporations, and coowners of partnerships may not participate. LLCs, on the other hand, have no limits on the number of members and do not place restrictions on the makeup or citizenship of members. In addition, LLCs can have more than one *class* (kind) *of stock* and can own stock in another corporation. An LLC allows you to avoid the double taxation of a C-corporation but provides most of the legal options regarding liability protection and stock sales that a C-corporation has. For most small business owners, setting up an LLC may be overkill. Think of it conceptually as an S-corporation with much more flexibility with respect to shareholder types and numbers.

def•i•ni•tion

A **limited liability company (LLC)** is a type of business structure available in almost every state that has many of the tax advantages of a partnership or subchapter S-corporation but fewer of the disadvantages. LLC shareholders are called **members** of the LLC.

Corporations can sell different **classes of stock,** such as preferred stock or common stock, at different prices. The various classes differ in when and under what circumstances dividends are paid. Most small companies have only one class of stock but more than one is possible.

Because of these advantages, some people expect that LLCs will exceed subchapter S-corporations, regular C-corporations, partnerships, and limited partnerships as the preferred organizational structure. Others feel that the added complexity associated with setting up an LLC will diminish its popularity. Only history will know the outcome. Increasing the S-corporation shareholder limit to 100 reduced the need for LLC formation, which now tips the argument in favor of the S-corporation for many new businesses who plan to have only a few shareholders.

On the CD

A sample Limited Liability Company Organizing Checklist (document 07-18), Limited Liability Company Articles of Organization (without manager) (document 07-19), Limited Liability Company Articles of Organization (with manager) (document 07-20), Limited Liability Company Operating Agreement (without manager) (document 07-21), Limited Liability Company Operating Agreement (with manager) (document 07-22), Limited Liability Company Member Certificate (document 07-23), Limited Liability Company Consent Resolution in lieu of First Meeting of Members (document 07-24) and Limited Liability Company Minutes (document 07-25) are included on the companion CD.

Because conversion to an LLC from another type of business structure can be costly, LLCs are generally recommended more for startups than for established businesses.

One concern about LLCs, however, is that there is no unified set of tax laws; individual states created their own laws regarding LLCs, which were then copied by other states. Check with your secretary of state and the IRS to find out more about the laws governing LLCs. In general, the LLC income passes through to the owners, who then pay tax at their personal rate on their percentage of the LLC income.

def•i•ni•tion

A **professional corporation** is a special corporation sometimes used by lawyers, doctors, and accountants. It is often subject to restrictions related to malpractice matters.

Professional Corporations

A special corporation structure addresses the needs of professionals who share a practice, such as lawyers, doctors, and accountants. The *professional corporation*, as it was initially called, provided special tax-related benefits to the participants. Many of the benefits have been reduced since 1981, however, and the growth in the number of professional corporations has declined. If you are a licensed professional who falls into this special category, check with your accountant to determine whether a professional corporation provides you any special benefits. Professional corporations use the letters P.C. after the company name.

State to State

As if life wasn't complicated enough, assume that you now want to operate your business with offices in several states. The good news is that this is possible. If the majority of your business comes from your home base in one state, you can avoid the multistate headache. The bad news is that, if this is not the case, you need to perform some filings and registrations to qualify in each state where you do business. You will have to file tax returns in each of these states as well.

Some firms specialize in setting up companies that need to operate in several states at once. Contact a law firm and get a referral to one of these firms or simply contract the law firm to perform the needed paperwork for you.

You can do all the multistate setup legwork yourself; however, this approach might become a black hole for time and effort. You are probably better off farming it out to those who do it for a living. This is particularly important when considering a name for your organization because the name must be available in all states of interest. (Read the CD bonus chapter "Special Corporation Realities" for more information about names.) If you insist on doing it yourself, contact the secretary of state in each state of interest for filing guidelines and fees.

Street Smarts

Naturally, you should make maximum use of the forms included on the companion CD to this book. They should save you tons of money in that your attorney will likely only have to confirm the content instead of writing it from scratch. If you find that these forms don't solve all of your needs, then take heart in the knowledge that there are numerous computer software packages out there that can automatically generate a wide variety of legal documents for you, from a bill of sale to articles of incorporation. Most packages even modify the documents to suit the state in which you do business. They usually cost under $100 and pay for themselves with one use. Check out *PC World*, *MacWorld*, NOLO Press, or *PC* magazine for an assessment of the software.

Don't forget that once you set up offices in separate states, you should begin tracking sales tax for these states along with the percent of corporate revenue derived from operations in these states. The tax collectors in each state want their "fair" piece of your profit pie. If you don't track it carefully from the beginning, you might spend December through March of each year unraveling your finances so that you can accurately pay your business and sales taxes in each state.

Dealing With the Tax Man

Taxes never go away, but the good news is that you only pay taxes when you are making money, which means you are making money! All you can do is try to minimize their negative impact on your profits. The impact of taxes on your choice of organizational structure is worth a brief discussion. I present only general concepts here about income taxes; talk to your accountant about your specific situation. Remember, there are many other taxes your business will have to pay. You need to learn about all of them in your area—city, county, state, sales, franchise, and so on.

The company net income will pass directly to you as owner or major stockholder (of any type of business structure except for the C-corporation). You then declare it on your personal tax return and pay tax at your personal tax rate. In corporations, all salary expenses (including the owner's salary) are deducted from the company's revenues prior to determining how much tax must be paid, but the corporation pays payroll taxes on it as well. You then pay personal income tax only on your salary, just as you do for any company.

Self-employed individuals really feel the bite of FICA (Social Security) and Medicare taxes because they pay both the employee's share and the employer's share of these taxes in the form of self-employment taxes. This is a little misleading, though, in that the overall payroll tax rate is the same whether as a sole proprietorship or corporation. It is simply paid in a different way and out of different funds.

In a corporation, however, remember that dividends paid to shareholders are subject to double taxation. At the time of this writing, there is some talk about eliminating personal taxes on dividends, so make sure that you verify whether double taxation is still in effect.

Sometimes, corporations come up with creative ways to avoid or minimize the financial bite taken out of their shareholders' dividends as a result of double taxation. Some people get so focused on avoiding paying taxes that they lose track of their primary concern: running a successful and profitable business that fulfills their personal and financial goals. We all hate giving Uncle Sam a nickel, but avoid the temptation to fiddle with your tax planning to the point that you lose focus on your business.

Individuals and corporations do not pay taxes at the same rate. You will find that the break points between tax levels differ. Depending on your situation and the company's income levels, you might be better off leaving the money in the company and paying corporate taxes instead of paying yourself a large salary and paying personal income tax. Check out the following table for the relative rates for personal and corporate taxes.

Typical Personal and Corporate Taxable Income Rates

Single		Married, Filing Jointly		Corporate	
Income	**Tax Rate**	**Income**	**Tax Rate**	**Income**	**Tax Rate**
$0 to $7,300	10%	$0 to $14,600	10%	Not a business category	
$7,300 to 29,700	15%	$14,600 to 59,400	15%	$0 to 50,000	15%
$29,700 to 71,950	25%	$59,400 to 119,950	25%	$50,000 to 75,000	25%
$71,950 to 150,150	28%	$119,150 to 182,800	28%	$75,000 to 100,000	34%
$150,150 to 326,450	33%	$182,800 to 326,450	33%	$100,000 to 335,000	39%
$326,450+	35%	$326,450+	35%	$335,000 to 10M	34%

There are additional rates for companies over $10 million in annual taxable income, and I hope that you someday need that information, which was left out of this table.

Here is an example of how all of this tax stuff can work out. Assume that you are a single person who needs $70k in salary to live off of comfortably but has a corporation earning $120k in net income before paying your salary. Your personal tax rate is 25 percent on the $70k in salary and the corporation's tax rate is 15 percent on the remaining $50k if left in the corporation and not taken as salary. Notice that if that additional $50k had been taken as salary, it would have been taxed at the 28% marginal personal rate plus applicable payroll taxes which we won't talk about here for simplicity's sake. (See Chapter 14 for more information on payroll taxes.) The 13 percent tax savings (the potential 28 percent personal rate minus the paid 15 percent corporate rate) can be left in the corporation for business use and is a lower overall tax rate than what a sole proprietor or S-corporation shareholder must pay.

Notice that a C-corporation allows you the option of leaving the money in the corporation or paying yourself in the form of a bonus or dividend. An S-corporation or LLC takes this decision out of your hands and makes you treat the leftover corporate profits as personal income, without having to apply the payroll taxes. In this case, an S-corporation shareholder would pay at least 25 percent tax on the S-corporation net income unless that income pushed the shareholder into a higher tax bracket, which might require a 33 percent or higher personal tax rate payment.

Street Smarts

Your company must pay FICA (Social Security), unemployment, and Medicare taxes for each employee over and above the standard salary. This currently amounts to around 7.65 percent. The employee also pays these taxes. See Chapter 14 for more information on taxes.

Here is how I suggest that you think about the tax aspect of the business structure decision:

- Determine what you expect your salary will need to be and assume that payroll taxes will be paid on that either as self-employment tax or payroll tax.

- Determine the amount of net income that the corporation will see if it meets your business plan projections.

- Look at the tax tables and determine whether the taxes are lower if taxed at the corporate rate or as personal income.

- If the personal tax rate is lower, then set your company up as anything other than a C-corporation. If the C-corporate tax rate is lower, then leave your company as a C-corporation so that more of the net income in the early years stays in the company for you to use in growing your young business. You will need that money the most in the early years.

- If you expect your company to show a loss for the first few years, which is not uncommon, then you might consider being a sole proprietorship or S-corporation so that the loss can be used to decrease your personal tax liability. Note that the S-corporation has some relatively restrictive loss limits, whereas the sole proprietorship loss limits are limited only by your total income.

For Your Plan

As part of your business plan, you want to address your reasons for choosing your business's legal structure. Make sure you address …

- The type of business legal structure you plan to use.

- Your primary reason for selecting that structure.

- Where you plan to incorporate, if a corporation, and the names of key officers and board members (if applicable).

- Legal protection of the company name (including whether it is available). Even better, reserve it as a website address as well. This is particularly important for those starting an Internet business. Make sure that there are no trademark conflicts with the name as well.

- Intentions related to opening offices in other states or countries and within specific time frames, if applicable.

- How the legal documents were created, signed, and recorded to provide confidence that the company creation documents are legally binding.

- The tax implications of the business type choice and thresholds at which various other changes, such as from an S- to a C-corporation, will be performed.

- Where the legal formation documents are stored and how they will be maintained and updated.

Your goal with this section is to provide the reader with a solid understanding of the company's legal structure, why that structure was selected, and how that selection benefits the company and its shareholders in the future.

On the CD

The companion CD contains a ton of additional information related to selecting the right business for you. Women and those who qualify for minority status should definitely check out the section titled, "Special Opportunities for Women and Minorities." And all should read "When to Use a Lawyer" to make sure that you legally protect yourself when setting up your business. Each state and business requirement is different, so make sure that you are set up right for your particular situation. Both of these can be found under Bonus Sections.

The Least You Need to Know

- Editable legal forms that you can adapt to your business are included on the companion CD (run them by an attorney for final okay).

- Select the business structure based on your expected business goals. Each form has its own benefits; you want to choose the one best suited to your needs.

- Sole proprietorships, partnerships, and corporations are not the same. Choose your business structure based on operational, legal, and tax considerations.

- Corporations provide the highest level of legal protection, but remember that dividend income can be subject to double taxation if a standard C corporation.

- Taxes are a part of life for any business. Recognize that you have to learn about them or find competent help to pick the right business type that fits your business and tax needs.

- Don't spend money just to create expenses as a way of decreasing your taxes. It doesn't make sense to spend $1 on an expense you don't need just to save 28 cents in taxes. Think about it. See Chapter 16 for more details on this important topic.

Part 2

Writing Your Successful Plan

In this section, you'll learn how to use marketing to get customers and keep them. You'll also discover the basics of selling, along with information about—believe it or not—how your competitors can actually help you succeed.

You will learn about employees, payroll taxes, manufacturing, operations, and your company's financials. All of these topics are presented so you can write your plan, but also as a reference in managing your business to success once you are up and running.

Read each chapter, in order, and write down the items listed in the "For Your Plan" section at the end of each chapter. By the time you get to Chapter 19, you will have completed the first draft of your plan.

Chapter 8

Determining Your Market Opportunity

In This Chapter

◆ Determine your available marketplace

◆ Find applicable research data

◆ Extract and correlate facts to determine market truths

◆ Market characteristics greatly affect your chances of success

John stood up from his chair and walked to the window before speaking. "Of course there is a market for my product. It just makes sense that people will want it."

Jason, a potential investor, shook his head and then looked directly at John.

"All right. Let's play it this way. You say in your plan that you will sell 10,000 units next year. And, coincidentally, that gets us just over the breakeven point. What percentage of your available market must buy your product before you meet that 10,000?"

"Not that high of a number. I'm not sure, but I know I can sell 10,000."

"I don't doubt that you believe that you can sell 10,000 units. What I don't believe ... scratch that ... don't have a sense of is whether that 10,000 represents a small fraction of everyone who can use this product or is more than really need it.

It can't be just Painting! Find out whats in demand in Home Remodeling/Constructi Educate yourself about it & offer it.

Example: Attic remodeling

Do you see my point?"

John just stood there and looked at Jason.

"John, just because you believe it to be true doesn't make it true. I have faith in you and your ideas, but the market will determine if we make money or not. We have to know more about the market."

Your customers make purchase decisions based on their needs, how your offering fills those needs, and their ability to buy. The more customers you have looking for products or services like yours, the better your chances of selling. The fewer potential customers you have, the worse your chances of selling. This makes sense, doesn't it? Here's the rub: how do you predict their likelihood of buying at all in general and then project their likelihood of buying from you in particular? That is the art and frustration with market and industry forecasting.

This chapter takes a detailed look at some basic forecasting and research procedures that you can use to gauge the larger market forces that shape your likelihood of success.

Understanding and Assessing the Market's Influence

It is hard to overestimate the importance of marketplace trends. Just as it is really difficult to find a winning stock when the market is in a tumble, it is difficult to find customers to purchase your offering if the marketplace is in decline (nobody is buying what you plan to sell). On the other hand, if you are lucky (smart?) enough to be offering a desirable product to a hungry market, you might continually struggle to meet customer demands. This is a good-news problem.

Let's take a closer look at an optimal buying situation before we get into the details of forecasting market trends. Optimal buying conditions would look something like this:

- The overall marketplace demand for your offering continues to grow at more than 20 percent per year when measured by dollar sales levels, and when inflation is low (under 3 percent).

- The number of units that your existing customers are expected to buy from you next year will increase, and they already have your product purchases in the next year's budget.

- The number of vendors providing products to your marketplace is few, which means that customer demand can only be fulfilled by you and a few other vendors. Less competition is a good thing under these circumstances.

- There is no pending legislation or major social change that will undermine the great market conditions that you currently enjoy.

- Your customers have enough money to purchase what you offer.

- Your customers are convinced that they need what you offer and are ready to make use of it as soon as possible.

What I just described is a market situation that any vendor would think ideal: lots of customers with lots of money, who all have a recognized need and few vendors that they can purchase from. If you can't make money in this type of marketplace, you might as well stay at home and watch TV reruns. And if you are lucky enough to have a marketplace like this come your way, take maximum advantage of it as quickly as possible because it won't last long in a global free enterprise system. Huge mar- *Google* ket opportunities create high interest on the part of other vendors who want a piece of your marketplace pie. Somebody, somewhere, will create an offering that at least matches, if not exceeds, the value of yours, putting increased pressure on you to perform. This pressure usually means that your profit margins will start to shrink even if your sales continue to increase; the opportunity starts to look less attractive than it once did. Take a look at what has happened recently with the iPod, and iPod look-alikes, as an example of what I am talking about.

Street Smarts

The forecasting process is one of trial and error. You try to find how close you are to ideal and then, when you find that ideal isn't feasible, you look to see how close you are to bleak. You are always looking for ideal but constantly watching for if and when the analysis turns substantially toward bleak. This may indicate a poor market within which even the best of ideas can't succeed. Constant vigilance to market trends is required.

Carrying this scenario to its extreme shows many vendors competing for the business of a fixed (or declining) number of customers. Now the customers are in the driver's seat regarding when, how many, and how much to pay for your offering. If you don't make it attractive enough, they will go elsewhere. As new products come onto the market that meet the customer's need, you will eventually find that demand for your product starts to diminish.

You are now in an opposite situation to that of the ideal mentioned earlier in this section:

♦ The number of new customers is stagnant or even decreasing from year to year.

♦ Industry-wide sales have flattened or even decreased from year to year.

♦ Along with this decreasing marketplace sales number comes a decrease in profit margin, so you are now shipping more product (on a unit sales basis) than ever before and making less net income than ever before.

♦ Customers invite you to provide a bid for their business but they are not sure when they will move forward and will make no commitments to any specific vendor.

♦ There are oodles of vendors selling something that looks almost exactly like your offering, making differentiation difficult, to put it mildly.

You are now in a tough situation, and the future prospects for your company and offering look grim, bordering on bleak.

Here is the question that you are trying to answer with all of this market research and forecasting work: where does your company sit in the continuum between "ideal" and "bleak"? And on what facts do you base this assessment other than your gut feeling? Anything you can do to determine objectively where you stand will not only add credibility to your business plan but also help to decrease the uncertainty and risk associated with investing time and money in your idea.

Don't Create a Market Need

I'm going to make this section short and to the point: you can't afford to create a customer need. If you want to survive the startup stages of business, make sure that people are already ready and willing to purchase your offering if it meets their needs. You don't have the resources to convince potential buyers that they really need this new idea when they aren't sure themselves. Leave the market creation to the IBM, General Motors, and Allstate Insurance companies of the world. Make your money addressing the secondary and tertiary needs that these big company market creation efforts spawn since they rarely satisfy all of their potential customers. Even a little piece of their existing pie is better than all of a pie that is still a figment of your imagination. See? Simple. Done.

Determine Overall Market Characteristics

This section presents some techniques for estimating (or *guesstimating*) you...
and projected market conditions. There is a lot more art to this process than s...
and it is heavily dependent on how lucky you are in finding the information you...
Not only are you looking for a needle in a haystack, but you also have to mentally
correlate the relationship between all of the various haystacks in the hope of gleaning
some type of meaningful trend that helps you predict the future.

You must make a number of assumptions when completing your market analysis. For
example, the percentage of available customers that you expect will pay for your product or service, called potential *market penetration*, is a key estimate in determining the
amount of money you will make if every potential customer, *your total market*, bought
from you (your *projected sales revenue*).

def•i•ni•tion

Total market is a measure, either by unit quantity or sales dollars, of what could happen
if *every* possible customer for your product or service actually bought from you.

Market penetration is a measure of the percentage of total customers who you expect
to buy from you. This is usually projected monthly in the first year and annually after
that. If there are 1 million people in your potential customer market and you expect
500,000 to buy your product, you will have captured 50 percent of the market.

Your **projected sales revenue** is the dollar value of sales you would collect if you
achieve your market penetration estimates. It is calculated by multiplying the projected
total number of unit sales by the average money received per sale.

Guesstimates are your best guess of something based on factual estimates and a little
bit of educated hunch.

You can come up with some decent projections of potential market penetration
through information from other companies
who did what you plan to do or from guesstimates from people experienced in the field.
No one expects you to know exactly how
many sales you will make during the first
year, or even the first two years. But you can
provide fairly accurate estimates by making
some educated assumptions. It is important,
however, to make it clear when you are working from verifiable industry facts and when

Street Smarts

If you become careless or,
even worse, deceptive in how
you present the facts in this
section, you might create questions about your integrity in the
investor's mind. This will almost
surely eliminate the possibility
of obtaining the funding you
require.

current
ience,
eed.

...onal or professional opinion. In this way, the reader can dif-
..."think" is true and what is indeed an industry reality.

...ng?

...wo basic flavors: dollar sales and unit sales. Dollar sales
...l amount of money spent purchasing offerings like the one
...ales deal with the estimated number of units (widgets,
...t were actually sold.

Here an imaginary set of market circumstances is used to demonstrate the procedure you might follow for uncovering overall market potential and characteristics.

Street Smarts

Notice that if you take the total number of industry dollar sales and divide it by the total number of industry unit sales, you get a marketplace average of the sale dollars/units sold. In itself, this is a valuable number to know since it lets you know if your intended offering is priced above, even with, or below the industry average.

Assume that you're interested in selling a special type of cooking dish that is used inside a microwave oven. You have looked around and found nothing else like it on the market and are convinced that this product is your ticket to national stardom and an early retirement. Let's see if this is true.

First, what do we know? The product is used in microwave ovens, which means that the only people who will use it are those who currently own, or are planning to purchase, a microwave. Let's start here.

Go to the library or cruise the Internet for retail sales information pertaining to the number of households with microwave ovens. You might even find this data in the Census or through the Department of Commerce, so it never hurts to check.

By the way, a quick Google search (www.google.com) using "Microwave oven market-place statistics" as the search terms showed 4,160 matches and led me right to the International Microwave Power Institute (www.impi.org), where all kinds of microwave-related reports are available (for a fee, of course). To really show you what is available with a simple Internet search, check out www.appliancedesign.com to see some useful data pertaining to home appliance shipments.

Assume that we find that 12.62 million microwave ovens were sold in 2006, and that this represents an increase of 6.2 percent over 2005. That tells us a lot already if you expect your product to be sold primarily at the time of a new microwave purchase. We know that your total available market is 12.62 million units and that the market grew over the past 12-month period, but not everyone will buy one of your units (sorry)—this is a different story that we address in a few minutes. Read on.

What if your product is only useful in microwaves above a certain cubic footage? Then finding the breakdown of units sold by cubic footage would further help you define your available market since this 12.62 million number deals with *all* microwaves sold. Search until you find this breakdown by cubic footage, likely on a percentage basis, and then apply that percentage breakdown to the total sales numbers you found at that last site. I went to the Wal-Mart site (www.walmart.com) to see the various microwave size breakdowns, and they appear to come in the following cubic foot sizes: 0.5, 0.7, 0.8, 0.9, 1.0, 1.1, 1.2, 1.3, 1.4, 1.5, 1.6, 1.8, and 2.0. We now have a general idea about the sizes involved.

Next assume that we want to know what the breakdown is by geography because we feel that only people in warm climates would be interested in our product. This means that we are interested in the states in the West, Southwest, South, and Southeast as prospects. This will narrow the market even more. From The Weather Channel website (www.weather.com), I found a map that showed the average temperature by state for the year, which now enables me to pick the states of most interest.

Perhaps only people above a specific income bracket or under a certain age are expected to buy our product; that would narrow the scope even more. Starting to get the picture? Assume that from all of this additional refining of the total marketplace, we now determine that of the 12.62 million new microwave units sold in 2006, only 5 million represented viable prospects for our product. We still know a lot.

> **Street Smarts**
>
> It is tremendously important to know as much as you can about the overall characteristics of your "best" potential buyer. Using these characteristics, you narrow down the overwhelming amount of information available to just that applicable to our specific scope of analysis. Typical criteria include income, location, education, or pertinent social interests such as environmental protection. I call this your "Ideal Customer" profile.

We know that 5 million microwave units are sold annually with which our product could be bundled. It is a reasonable "guess" that this 5 million units figure will increase by 6 percent or so (the national average) next year as well. We could refine this by knowing more about the percentage increases by unit types and geography and whether that 6 percent is a one-year fluke or an ongoing steady average. Five million × 1.06 (a 6 percent increase over last year) equals 5.3 million.

You're trying to determine the total number of units you could possibly sell if everyone bought your product with their microwave, and then you can scale it back to something that is a reasonable percentage of that total market. Sorry. You are not going to sell 100 percent of the new purchasers on your great product. It just doesn't happen.

The total possible units that the market could purchase next year is 5.3 million, as shown previously. Now, assume that your company can reasonably sell just 10 percent of those new purchasers on buying your product along with their new microwave. By the way, 10 percent is usually a high number for first year introduction, but it is used here to keep the math simple. You will more likely see around a 1 to 3 percent acceptance rate in the first year.

That means you could expect to sell 10 percent of 5.3 million, or 530,000 units which, if sold for $30 each, would translate into sales of $15.9 million. Not bad for a new company. You can adjust the percentage sold up or down from this starting point, but notice that you now have a benchmark for determining the quantity of units you expect to sell and the amount of sales revenue you expect to earn from those sales. Much of the rest of your plan will be determined by these two numbers, so you want to make them as accurate as possible.

Is the market forecasting process starting to tie together for you a little more? It is a process of curiosity, discovery, learning, and assimilation. The more you learn, the more you know about how to find that specific piece of data that will tie your entire analysis together. Remember that you are always trying to estimate just a few values that will eventually end up in your financial analysis spreadsheet:

◆ How many of your units can reasonably be sold?

◆ What will be the average price per sold unit?

◆ How long will it take you to get up to a certain sales level, and what percentage of the total prospective purchasing population will have to buy to make those numbers?

◆ How does the total marketplace subdivide and reduce as you apply the specific demographic traits of your most likely buyer?

◆ What is the best way to get to your prospective buyers based on their easily tracked demographic characteristics? You have to be able to find them to sell to them.

Keep your analytical eye on finding the answers to these questions, and the information will come your way. It always does once you are focused on knowing what you want. Take heart in knowing that if trustworthy numbers don't come your way, this analysis process will educate you to the point that you can make your own educated guess, which will likely be as good as anyone's.

You now have some credible market estimates. Next take a look in Chapter 12 for additional information on setting your price and estimating the number of people who will actually buy your product once they know about it. Combining the information from these two chapters will provide you with the sales revenue and unit forecast numbers that you will use to predict production, marketing, sales, cash flow, and other critical operational requirements.

It is always hard for me to believe that all of this research, analysis, and investigation come together as just a few numbers on a spreadsheet. But, oh, how important those numbers are. You just can't be too careful when estimating your sales numbers because major over- or underestimating can put you right out of business.

Who Are the Major Players in Your Market?

As mentioned earlier, your offering and company don't exist in a vacuum. You most likely already have competition for the type of product you intend to offer. Assume, continuing the example above, that we found out that Competitor A offered your target customer a product similar to yours and sold 4 million units per year. This information tells us that your maximum available market—before having to steal sales (and customers) from A—is 1 million units. Why? Because they are already buying from A, who must already be heavily entrenched in that market to have an 80 percent market share ([4 million/5 million] = 80 percent). You not only have to overcome the fact that you are the new kid on the block but also that buying from A is the customer-accepted norm.

If, on the other hand, A offers a similar but inferior product to yours and only sells 500,000 per year, then you might have a great situation on your hands. Competitor A might have created a market need for your type of offering, but it has done a pitiful job of filling that demand with one of sufficient quality. You might be able to step directly into that market need "void" with your higher-quality offering and sell a ton of product right under A's nose. If this happens, make sure to send A's president a box of chocolates and a thank you note after you make your second million dollars. See Chapter 11 for additional details related to assessing and dealing with competition.

How Long Will This Opportunity Last?

The saying "Nothing lasts forever" is particularly true of a hot marketplace. At some point, it will cool down, and you don't want to be caught off guard when it does because this can undo, in a few short months, all of the success you created over the prior few years. Take a look at Chapter 12 for information related to predicting the maturity level of your particular industry based on a life cycle analysis. Knowing your industry's maturity level helps you determine the requirements for and time frame of the level that follows. In this way, you can be prepared for that level before it actually happens, making money right up until the last minute.

Some markets, such as the novelty gift market, are highly volatile, meaning that they explode and fizzle in only a few months. Think about the Pet Rock. Others, such as steel manufacturing equipment, last for years or even decades. Your marketing window of opportunity will vary with your industry, and you should have a somewhat intuitive sense about your particular industry's market window and its unique signs of change. International pressures have the ability to quickly change U.S. markets from favorable to challenged. A healthy respect for competition blended with mild paranoia is probably a good recipe for staying competitive.

Research Data Sources Are Everywhere

One of the best ways to learn about your industry's trends is to turn to the media. Trade newspapers, magazines, reports, websites, and radio and television stations carry so much information that you can become overloaded if you aren't careful. By knowing what you're looking for, you will recognize a research data point gift when it comes across your desk. Where others would read it and move on, you will read it and add it to your analysis.

Street Smarts

Stop by your local library and ask the reference librarian about sources for marketplace and demographic information. No doubt, you will be overwhelmed with the various sources for this commonly used information. Even better, know the specific data you are seeking and let them find it for you. That is their job, and they all seem to like a good investigation challenge.

The best way to undertake market assessment research is to immerse yourself in the following:

- Industry and trade business magazines and newspapers

- Local newspapers (and local news programs)

- Publications about subjects pertinent to your offering

- National news and business publications

- Related Internet materials and websites

- Industry association trade journals

Since you already know what you want to sell but don't know how much people will pay you for it, you could narrow the focus of your research to similar businesses in your area. Study them, read all the recent articles about them in your local library's clipping files, and talk to the owners about how their businesses are going. From their experience, you will be able to gauge a reasonable price point and acceptance level for your offering.

There is really no better indicator of acceptance of an offering than to see how similar products have been purchased before. From this baseline, you can assess whether your proposed offering is more or less valuable to the customer and guesstimate this value assessment's impact on what your customers will pay.

Street Smarts

If local company owners are unwilling to share their secrets, call similar business owners in another town or state. Since you are not a competitor, they may be willing to talk with you about what they've done that has worked—and not worked. Check out online sources such as forums and discussion groups with people who can provide advice based on their experiences.

Researching Your Plan

The deeper you get into this research process, the more you will start to appreciate your local public library and the reference librarians who work there. Virtually all the information you'll ever need to research your business idea is out there. You just have to know where to look for it. These reference librarians are masters of finding that obscure fact that you simply cannot find. And if they can't find it, it just may not be out there. Get to know these reference gurus well, and use their important talent to its fullest extent.

The whole point of this chapter is to get you started on understanding your marketplace and industry so that you can make some credible predictions about your expected sales levels. Although you might have years of experience in the type of business you want to start (perhaps you've been working in your family's printing shop for decades), investors want to feel confident that your market instincts as well as your operational abilities are correct.

To show them that your ideas are on target, you have to give them proof in the form of reliable published articles, reports, and other statistics. Saying that you know the market for printing is growing exponentially each year is nice, but being able to back up that statement with a report from the Department of Commerce that says essentially the same thing gives you a lot more credibility—and that's what you need at this point. To accomplish this, all you need to

Street Smarts

Remember that increased credibility translates into decreased perceived risk in the mind of your potential investor. The lower the risk, the more likely this investor is to take a chance on your venture. Credibility is a good thing, and it comes from objectively obtained, realistically analyzed data.

do is turn to reliable experts, such as publications, reports, and market gurus. All are available by phone, fax, Internet, or at the library.

As I showed you earlier in this chapter, the growth of the Internet makes it likely that you can find much of the information you need in cyberspace. Once you become gifted at Internet searches, you might be able to avoid constant trips to the library. However, I still find that trained librarians are often able to point me in just the right direction, particularly for those difficult-to-find yet important, obscure data points. Don't be afraid to contact your local university library as well. The state universities have an incredible network of libraries that may provide the information you need, and your tax dollars have already paid for it.

Some of the most useful databases available to help you in learning more about an industry, a company, or a group of target customers include the following:

- Lexis/Nexis
- ProQuest
- Dow Jones
- InfoTrac

The following are some helpful websites you can turn to for assistance:

- **www.fuld.com** A competitive intelligence resource
- **www.thomasregister.com** The Thomas Register
- **www.dnb.com** Dun and Bradstreet
- **www.google.com** General Internet search engine

If you're lucky, you might find that more information exists than you could ever use in your business plan. Chances are good that somebody, somewhere, has compiled exactly the information you want. (I know a guy who studies the sex life of fire ants. Go figure!) The challenge becomes finding it. Once you find it, you also might need help getting it in the form you want.

Street Smarts _____

Subscribe to industry-specific publications and trade groups. They offer support and research that might not be available to the general public. Find a Federal Repository, frequently located at a local university, which contains all the latest government document information. You already paid for the research with your tax dollars, so you might as well use it. A listing of documents is also available from the Government Printing Office (www.gpo.gov). Call 202-512-1800.

For Your Plan

When writing the Market and Industry Analysis of your plan, make sure that you include the following points:

- Show that your new business idea applies to a marketplace that is healthy and growing.

- Make sure to clearly spell out your data sources and where you have made assumptions based on personal experience.

- Help your reader understand how you correlated the various pieces of information to come to some type of assessment of your intended marketplace.

- Use as many objective and credible sources as you can. Don't believe all that you find on the Internet—some of it is just someone expressing opinion not backed up with fact.

- Show yourself to not only be an expert on your product and company idea, but also in the industry into which you will sell.

The Least You Need to Know

- Credible marketplace and industry information are out there, but you may have to add scraps together to get the overall picture.

- Use Internet search engines such as Google to help you search.

- Play devil's advocate with your data and look for the holes in your analysis and assessments. If there is a hole, a professional investor will find it, and it might cost you your funding.

- Know that market forecasting is an art but one that is based on the predictable rules of business. You need buyers and buyers need products and services. Using objective numbers as a basis for educated forecasting and guessing will give you a solid sense of the market viability of your idea.

Learning on Your Competitors' Nickel

In This Chapter

- How to evaluate your offering against your competition
- Determining whether you want to lead or follow the competition
- Methods for researching your competition
- Defending yourself against competitive pressure

My boss sat back in his chair and reflected for a moment. His eyes brightened, and he smiled as he moved forward in his chair.

"I was on a plane going to Minneapolis," he said, "and two guys behind me were talking about a large sale they were working on. When one guy said the name of the company and the contact's name, I realized that it was one of my customers. He then outlined the entire sale situation, including the dollars involved, the basic technical requirements, the time frame within which a decision would be made, and who would make the decision. In short, he told me everything I needed to know to steal the sale."

"What did you do?" I asked, knowing that my boss liked inquisitive people, and also because it really was a good sales story.

"I called the customer immediately after arriving at the airport and told him that I had heard he was looking for some equipment and that I had what he needed at a price that just happened to be 5 percent cheaper than the bid provided by the guy on the plane," he replied. "I closed the deal that afternoon before the other guy even had a chance to claim his luggage."

This is a paraphrasing of a true story (except the luggage part). There is always some competitor out there who will take your lunch away, and you might not even know how it happened! This chapter shows you how to meet—and beat—the competition.

Is the Competition Real?

It's easy to overreact when dealing with the competition. You might treat your competitors as insignificant (watch your ego on this one) or as a major threat (watch your paranoia on this one). Both of these approaches are inappropriate unless you know something about the competitor. You need an honest understanding of your competition's strengths and weaknesses before deciding how you should respond.

It is very important that you spend time in your plan discussing your competition. Any investor will know that a good idea either already has competition or it will appear soon after the new idea is proven viable. A plan that does not include a detailed discussion about competitive risks is a plan that has been created in a vacuum. That is a scary prospect for any investor since it indicates a naïve approach on the part of the entrepreneurs.

In general, *direct competitors* (companies who sell the same product or services to the same customers as you) pose either strategic or tactical threats to your business. A strategic threat can affect you negatively down the road but might only make itself a minor nuisance at the present time. A tactical threat takes money out of your pocket today when your customers go to your competitor instead of you to spend their money. A large company that might enter your marketplace a few years down the road would be a strategic threat. A large company that currently offers competition to your offering is a tactical threat.

def•i•ni•tion

A **direct competitor** is a company who regularly sells a comparable product or service to the same customers that you do.

A strategic threat can easily become a tactical pain in the butt if you don't pay attention to it and take the proper actions to protect yourself. A tactical threat, if large enough, can cause major problems for you. This is especially true when you have a small customer base that provides most of your sales. If your competition takes one customer, which they will definitely try to do, they can hurt you both today and down the road when other potential customers wonder what's so special about the competitor that they were able to take a major account away from you.

When you start your business, you are in the enviable position of having no major competitor who takes you seriously. This provides you with a tremendous amount of freedom because nobody will be aiming to eliminate you in sales situations. You know that you are doing okay when competitors start to know your name and change their marketing strategy to go after you. That's both good news and bad news at once.

Because you are just starting out, you should be collecting as much information as possible about the companies in your particular market segment. People might not yet view you as a competitor and thus might be more open with their information. Sit down with that information and imagine the picture that your prospective customers have in their minds about each of your competitors. Your competitors' marketing message and positioning generally creates this image. (See Chapter 12 for more on this topic.)

How does your offering compare to your competitors'? If you were a customer looking at the two companies, would you see them as direct competitors or as two companies in separate market segments? Does this perception come from the fact that they offer different products or services or that their marketing message presents it differently?

From this approach, you can get a first cut on who to treat as a competitor. Remember that you continually want to be training yourself to see things through the eyes of your customer. Those are the most important eyes, after all.

Accumulating Competitive Information

Current and accurate information is the key to making savvy and effective competitive decisions.

Information is everywhere; keep looking for it, find it, collate it, and, finally, put it into some semblance of organization and order. It is amazing how fragments of information can give you an excellent overall picture of a competitor.

Where do you start looking for competitive information? How about the Yellow Pages? Who is listed in the category you would choose for yourself? Are they also listed in another category? If so, why? How many companies are listed there? How do they position themselves in the ad? Is it a display ad or simply a small-column ad? Grab last year's Yellow Pages and compare it to this year's. Has the number of competitors increased or decreased? Did some of the advertisers advance to a display ad?

Did their positioning change from last year to this year? Look at how much insight you can obtain about your market by simply looking at the Yellow Pages.

Other useful sources for competitive information include newspapers and magazines, your customers and your competitors' customers, annual reports, social gatherings and networking functions, sales brochures, and websites, to name a few.

Scour newspapers and trade publications for advertisements, articles, and quotes from any of your potential competitors. Ask your friends to do the same. They might find something that you missed. Start a folder for each of the competitors. (They really each deserve at least a manila folder, don't they?) Your library might also keep files on local companies that you can scan for free. Every time you find a piece of information, write it down if you heard it, or photocopy it if you found it in print. Date and place the information in that folder. I promise that you won't exactly remember it later, and the mind has a convenient way of changing its perception of reality over time.

> **Watch Out!**
>
> Beware of the tendency to spend a lot of money for market research reports prepared by professional companies that you can generally perform on your own. Having someone else perform general research hurts you on two fronts. First, you have to spend much-needed cash early in the process; second, you give up the opportunity to become familiar with the marketing information yourself. Spend the money on marketing research if you must, but try to find out some of this information on your own first. Having great research but no money to spend taking advantage of that research is poor planning.

Ask your customers what they know about your competitors. How do they like dealing with them? What do your customers like? Dislike? What is their satisfaction level? Why don't they use you for the same products and services in which they are using your competition? Notice that this discussion opens another level of communication with your customers, which is always a good idea.

Ask customers for pricing information when you have either lost or won a bid; they just might give it to you. Note that if they give you this information, they will probably share it with your competition in the same way. I have actually had clients give me a complete competitor's bid with all references to the company deleted. In this way, the information appears generic in nature and does not reveal the source, yet provides valuable insight into the competitor's overall offering. Guard this customer confidence like a diamond! It is a tribute to your client-vendor relationship when a customer opens up in this way, and you should treat it with the high degree of respect it deserves.

Review the company's own sales literature such as brochures and catalogs. Check out its website. If you don't know the website's URL, then try something like www. companyname.com or go to a search engine like www.google.com or www.yahoo.com and do a search on the company.

Their website may tell you more about the people, sites, plans, products, services, policies, warranties, and pricing than you can get anywhere else. Be aware that they will also check out your website, so don't put information there unless you want it found.

Some companies specialize in accumulating information about companies for a fee. These *clipping services* review a set number of publications for information regarding certain companies. You tell them which companies you want them to watch for and which newspapers or magazines you want them to read. They generally photocopy any articles that appear and send them to you on a regular (usually weekly) basis. This service is not free, but it might pay for itself in the valuable information about your competitors that you may have overlooked.

Finally, you can call your competitors and ask for information. A lot of times, they will send it to you. Don't use a fake personal or company name. If you misrepresent yourself, you are toying with *industrial espionage*, which is really scary. Penalties for fraud and misrepresentation can be severe and can seriously damage your business and your credibility. Just give them your name, number, and address and hope that you're talking to someone who doesn't know who you are. Don't volunteer information, and only give what you're asked. This approach is probably a safe bet when you first start out and will become more difficult as your success builds along with your reputation.

Street Smarts

If the competitor you are researching is a publicly traded company, you can get a lot of information from their annual report. Call Investor Relations for the company and ask for it. If the company won't send you one upon request, simply buy a share of stock, which entitles you, as a shareholder, to the same information that any other shareholder would receive. Try www.bigcharts.com to see if it has information you can use.

The secrets to accumulating competitor information are open ears, focused attention, closed mouths, and organized details. It's a job that requires constant diligence but doesn't take much time once you begin. As time goes on and you become more familiar with your competitors, you will get to the point that you know them almost as well as you know your own company, sometimes understanding their next move before it is even announced. If you get this good at predicting your competition, don't tell them. This is the type of skill that is best kept secret.

def•i•ni•tion

Clipping services are companies such as BurellesLuce (www.burellesluce.com) that read thousands of newspapers and magazines on the lookout for articles about or references to specific companies. Many businesses hire clipping services to watch for articles about their company and the competition. Unless you have the time to read virtually every major business magazine and newspaper, you might want to hire some professionals to do it for you. **Industrial espionage** is the practice of collecting information about competitors through devious methods. Using public information sources that everyone has access to isn't considered espionage, but rummaging through corporate waste paper baskets after hours would be.

Comparing Yourself to Them

Okay, so you've played super-sleuth and acquired a wealth of information about your competition. Put down your pipe, Sherlock; it's time to get into the trenches and start analyzing the information you've collected. How do you compare to the competition from your customer's perspective? When you find the answer to this question, you are on your way to determining your own position in the marketplace.

Here's an exercise that will help you find some answers. Take out a pad of paper or create a spreadsheet to automate the easy calculations that follow:

- ◆ Divide your sheet of paper or spreadsheet into six columns: A, B, C, D, E, and F.

- ◆ In Column A, write down the top 10 criteria your customers probably use in deciding who to buy from. Characteristics can include technical competency, service, phone support, convenience, credit terms, years in business, depth of offering, price, and so on. You can add to this listing later if you want, but only use 10 for now.

- ◆ In Column B, place a number that corresponds to the amount of importance you believe a customer places on this particular item, based on your experience. Make 1 stand for least important and 10 stand for a must-have. Although these are your opinions, they are still worthwhile to note. Your chart should look something like the following figure.

- ◆ Create individual column sets for Your Company and each of your competitors (i.e., Competitor #1, #2, etc.).

- ◆ The left column of the set is where you enter a number between 1 and 10 that gives your subjective assessment of how well each company meets customers' needs. (See Effect Columns C and E in the example.)

◆ The right column value of the set (Columns D and F) is calculated by multiplying the Importance value (column B) by the Effect value for the respective column set. For example, your company Result value is calculated by multiplying Column B by Column C. For Competitor #1, multiply Column B by Column E to get its respective Result value.

◆ At the bottom of each Results column, total all the numbers in the column for your company and each competitor. This final number provides a relative weighting assessment of how each competitor compares against the others and your company.

Ⓐ Characteristics	Ⓑ Importance (1-10)	Your Company		Competitor #1	
		Ⓒ Effect (1-10)	Ⓓ Result (B x C)	Ⓔ Effect (1-10)	Ⓕ Result (B x E)
Years in Business	4	3	12	6	24
Credit Terms	7	8	56	8	56
Hours of Operation	7	8	56	8	56
Depth of Offering	6	6	36	8	48
Prior Experience with Company	8	5	40	6	48
Certification	5	8	40	6	30
Totals			240		262
Sale Price			$75		$95

In this example, Competitor #1 has a superior market position compared to your company, as indicated by the higher total (262). This higher total helps to justify the higher product price.

How does the relative weighting number for your company compare with those of your competitors? Is your number higher or lower? The same? How does your price compare with the others when compared against the summary numbers, such as in Columns D and F in the example?

In general, you want your company's number here to be high because it indicates how close you are to ideal for your customers. Ideal is calculated by totaling the importance column and multiplying by 10—the perfect score for each item. For example, the sum of the importance column in the previous table equals 37, which, multiplied by 10, equals 370 points for the ideal.

Divide your rating (such as 240) by the ideal (such as 370) to see how close you are from a percentage standpoint (240/370 = 65 percent). What is the proper percentage level? It's a relative setting and one that is highly dependent upon your business and customer type. In general, you should strive to have a percentage rating of 75 percent or higher, which would give you a C or better in high school. It should surely be a continuing improvement goal to get closer to the ideal score.

Numbers are okay but I think in pictures, so I plot price and total relative weighting importance factor against each other for my company and my competitors. Just follow the horizontal line until you get to the proper weighting factor, and then follow your result until you intersect with the proper price horizontal line. Put a dot there and label it. Repeat this process for your company and all others. You can now see graphically where you are compared to the competition. If you really want to be thorough, you can also plot the ideal weighting against a realistic ideal price to see how you compare to it.

Notice from the example that the competitor charges a higher price and also provides a higher weighting factor, which probably justifies their charging a higher price. If you keep your products and services the same and then offer a discount price, you will continue to move down along a vertical line because you are decreasing pricing and keeping the weighting the same. Keep this up, and you will be initially busy and eventually out of business because of decreased profit margins.

On the other hand, decreasing services and keeping the price the same also eventually rings the death knell for your business because people will eventually stop buying from you. Your offering will be too expensive compared to what customers perceive they are getting. Graphically, you move to the left along a horizontal line when you keep price the same and decrease services, which decreases your weighting.

Where do you need to beef up services? Where do you get the best weighting-factor return for the dollars spent? In the preceding example, offering longer hours of operation or better credit terms increases your weighting factors on two items of high importance, whereas spending money on certification provides a lower weighting-factor return.

Okay, enough of all this graphing and other technical stuff. Will you make decisions strictly by this weighting analysis and chart? Probably not. Will the results from this analysis provide you with a structured way of analyzing your competition so that you can make informed decisions? Absolutely yes. This is a good reality check and one worth performing on a regular basis.

You should now have a pretty good idea of how you stack up against your competition. You might be less expensive than they are, for instance, but now you realize that you don't offer the extra services that they do. You can deal with the lack of services either by adding services (and potentially raising your prices) or by strongly emphasizing in your marketing program that customers will get a bargain when dealing with your company.

On the other hand, if your price is too low and you have a higher total value, you might want to consider raising the price on your offering. Why leave money on the table if you don't have to?

Price Wars Hurt Everyone

Here is the worst of all business worlds: your competition decides to gain customers by dropping their price. This often starts a *price war* where all companies try to keep their customers by matching or lowering their prices even more. This is a dangerous cycle that usually winds up with suppliers being hurt, the customer confused and dissatisfied, and substantially lower profit margins all around. The airline and computer industries go through this cycle on a regular basis. It tears the entire industry apart and takes years (if ever) to recover lost finances, and there's really no reason for it. Look at United Airlines being hurt by the pre-bankruptcy price wars but now gaining market share, after its bankruptcy, by dropping its own prices and putting pressure on American Airlines to match. It looks like other airlines will be taking turns in the bankruptcy seat.

There is a way to beat this cycle if it happens to your industry, but it takes amazing courage and fast reflexes. Instead of lowering your price, keep the price where it is. Beef up your extra services and sell the increased quality that you can provide for the higher price. Any experienced corporate business person knows you have to make a reasonable profit margin to stay in business. Instead of automatically dropping price as a reflex reaction, try this approach first, but continue to monitor your sales carefully. If you can't keep sales up, then you might just have to join the fray and hope that you survive. Look at Southwest Airlines, who maintained profit margins while the others lost billions.

> **Street Smarts**
>
> When all competitors compete based on price and keep undercutting their competitors to get sales, they are engaged in a **price war**. As each company lowers its price, others drop their prices to compete, causing profit margins across the industry to fall to critically low levels. If sales volume keeps increasing for all competitors, you may be okay, but when the market simply cannot buy any more, no matter how low the price goes, vendors will start going out of business. If your company has better profit margins than the others by having a lower cost of operation, then the price war may work out to your benefit. The most efficient and cash-flush companies generally are the ones who win price wars.

Your company is almost never hurt by continually looking for ways to keep fixed expenses low while also cutting operating expenses. If the price wars don't come, you simply make a higher profit margin than the others, which is good. If a price war does come, you have more margin to give up through price cutting before you get into serious financial jeopardy. This is also good. Keeping costs low while maintaining high levels of customer service is just plain old good business.

Are You a Specialty Store or a Superstore?

Are the other folks in your industry large companies such as Wal-Mart that have deep pockets and a wide selection of offerings? Are they smaller companies that provide a specialized, niche offering that a few people use (specialty stores such as Candles Are Us)? It's important that you understand where you want to fit in the continuum between the two types of businesses. Note that these terms apply equally well to service or product businesses. You could be a full-service health club or a specialty massage practitioner.

If you're trying to be a superstore but don't have the money to provide the required variety and volume of products needed, you will probably go out of business. The financial demands of making a business of this size work will affect your ability to maintain appropriate inventory or personnel expertise levels. Once your "shelves" appear naked or you don't provide a proper service level, customers take their business elsewhere.

If you're a smaller business that tries to cater to everyone's needs, you will probably fail—not because you lack skills or ability, but because your customers will expect more than you can offer. In addition, your smaller quantity of purchases will keep your costs and prices higher. The superstore firms will clobber you on price alone. Think about it—if your customer can purchase the same product at 20 percent less price from one of your competitors, you must offer some other very real benefit for them to purchase from you. All things being equal, customers tend to buy the lowest price. If you plan to charge a premium, you must make sure that things are not equal and that the quality/value perception is higher on your side.

It is interesting that the superstores are wary of the specialty stores eroding their business in key areas. A specialty store can provide a much higher level of personalized service to customers than a superstore can ever hope to provide. The specialty store can also charge a little more for the service because the customer perceives it as having more value. In this way, the specialty store keeps margins high and expenses low, which is always a good way to run a business. However, you need to know your customers and offer the specialty items they need.

Bookstores present an interesting example of the smaller store holding its own against the mega stores such as Barnes and Noble or Borders. These niche/local bookstores tend to know their local clientele and offer books that are specifically related to their interests. They make the bookstore not only a place to purchase specialized books, such as offering the best selection of local area gardening books around, but also a community meeting place where residents congregate as a social activity. The local bookstore becomes part of the community and is supported as such. They may not provide the wide variety of a larger store, but the shopping experience is ideally tailored for a smaller, more select clientele.

In technical areas, a specialty store may be one that not only sells hardware and software but also customizes computer equipment or software for the customer's particular needs. The company makes money on both the products and the services. The customer wins because she knows that her purchase will be handled in a low-risk, professional manner. Customers will pay for the service, especially if the cheaper or larger department store route has burned them. If the customer is looking to buy a computer and a dishwasher, the smaller store generally cannot compete.

In retail, for example, a specialty store might be one that deals only in candles and related items. The customer might be able to find a cheaper candle in a superstore, but could he find "just the right one" based on color, size, scent, etc.? Probably not, and that is the benefit of a specialty store. People expect to pay more for the added selection and service. Value is what sells; don't shortchange yourself on that count, but don't gouge your customers either. Find that right balance, and you can create a dedicated clientele and highly valued referrals.

Trying to be a superstore when you should be a specialty store is surefire trouble, as is the reverse. If you don't have the broad range of products or services to qualify as a superstore in your industry, stick with serving a small niche as a specialty store. You'll probably make more money by establishing a reputation as a specialist in a particular area, rather than a generalist who tries to do everything. And you'll probably have more fun and do a better job of it along the way. Check your ego. Make more money.

Using Market Segmentation to Your Advantage

Within every market and industry are smaller pockets of opportunity called market niches. These are a more specialized segment of a bigger market. For example, attorneys who specialize in construction industry accidents are pursuing a niche within the larger legal profession. Vegetarian restaurants are another type of business targeting that segment of the population that doesn't eat meat. Each uses a niche strategy.

Larger companies don't waste their time trying to meet the needs of a small portion of the market, but you might want to. Often the larger companies create the niches from what they don't provide that you can. Niches can be very profitable if you have the right offering.

These market niches are often like a vacuum in that once you make your product available, everything you produce will get sucked into the niche, too. You can also easily establish a strong reputation that will make it difficult for larger competitors to compete with. Even though niches might have fewer potential customers, they are often easier to sell to.

By the way, a hot unique product in a hungry niche market means you can charge more for your offering and increase profit margins. Get a good mental picture of what this means and watch the smile grow on your face.

A friend who grew up in South Africa says that they have a saying that "Many small animals live off of the crumbs from the elephant's mouth." Those elephant crumbs are looking more appetizing all the time, aren't they?

Cooperation Versus Competition

The Chinese have a saying that goes something like this: "Who knows you better than your enemies?" This also applies to business competitors.

It is not uncommon to find that you and your competitors, or even your noncompetitors, have more in common than it initially appears. They might address a particular market niche much more effectively than you do and vice versa. Combined, you might offer something that is truly more powerful than each of your individual strengths. You can cooperatively market your offerings. You can share mailing and administrative costs and aid each other in new product development activities.

For example, suppose that you are a corporate bookkeeping service that doesn't prepare taxes. It makes sense for you to align yourself or in some way partner with a tax preparation service. The benefit is that your customers perceive you as providing a higher level of service: bookkeeping and tax preparations. You send your partner tax leads and they send you bookkeeping leads. Each is happy as long as both parties play by the agreed-upon rules and don't start moving into the other alliance member's sandbox.

Ed's Lessons Learned

As a professional speaker, I am continually on the lookout for places where I can present my keynote and seminar talks on entrepreneurship, management, and communications topics. Like any business person, I am always looking for leads. Oddly enough, a lead source has come up from other professional speakers who talk on the same or similar topics. We share leads with each other for this simple reason—our customers don't want to use the same speaker year after year. They may want a talk on the same topic but will not use the same speaker they used within the past few years. I pass my colleagues' names to my contact when I finish my engagement, and they do the same with my name when their engagements end. In this way, by sharing leads, we are helping each other out as well as our customers. Who would have thought that true?

There is a potential down side to all of this cooperation. You may have to share sensitive company information (such as your customer list) with them to a much larger degree than you otherwise do with a competitor. You need to weigh the pros and cons of doing this, but if the benefits of the alliance outweigh the risks, you should go for it. Be smart about it and all can win.

For Your Plan

When writing the Competition portion of your plan, make sure that, at a minimum, you include the following information. Know that your plan readers will be keenly interested in both the competition and your reaction to their potential threat.

- A table that presents important competitor facts such as name, geographic location, public/private, nationally known or local guru, sales revenue, net income, number of employees, competitive products, years in business, and any other significant information.

- A comparison of your offering with that of your competitors. It should outline product features and where they are better than you and where you are better than them. Pricing, warranty, terms, and other significant purchase-related information should be included.

- Clearly outline your own competitive advantages so that the reader knows that you not only understand the scope of the competitive threat but also are ready to deal with it in a credible way.

- Your strategy for marketing and selling against these competitors, including the specific tactics you plan to use to win business. See Chapter 10 for more details on effective marketing.

- If your offering is substantially different from anything else out there, how do you plan to convince customers to go with you instead of staying with the established way they have previously done things? How do you plan to deal with the almost guaranteed reality that your competition will come out with a product that competes once your idea is proven worthy?

On the CD

Most of us would like to get a free ride at some point in our lives, and your business might be able to enjoy the same benefit. But you must be clear on whether your company is in the position to actually create a new market (making you a market maker) or, more likely, you are in the position of taking advantage of markets created by other larger companies, making you a market follower. Check out the special bonus section "Market Makers and Followers" for additional information on this important differentiation and topic.

The Least You Need to Know

- Competition will always exist, but that's not necessarily bad. Comparing your products and services to those of your competitors helps you stay on top of what customers want.

- Watching your competitors provides insight into what's going on in your market and what they believe customers want. This information can help you better plan for the future.

- Customers purchase value, not price. Just because your competitors drop their prices doesn't mean that you have to. A price war is usually bad news for the industry as a whole but you may be able to outlast your competition depending on your particular market segment, your profit margins, and product offering.

- You might find that working with your less-direct competitors against other common foes is a better strategy than trying to "go it alone" against everyone.

- Provide competitors with information about your company only on a "need to know" basis. If they don't need to know it, then don't give it to them. It's that simple.

- Perform the detailed competitive comparison analysis matrix once a year to objectively see how you stack up against your competition. Just collecting the data for the analysis will make you learn more about the competition and what is important to your customers.

Focused Marketing That Makes Money

In This Chapter

◆ Supporting sales success with marketing

◆ The value of target marketing and demographics

◆ Pricing strategies

◆ Promotional methods

◆ Distribution considerations

The company was spending more money on marketing and sales activities, yet it had seen a drop in its sales. The president felt that they were doing something fundamentally wrong. She had always believed that the harder you pushed something, the more it moved. For the first time in her company's history, the harder she pushed by spending more money and energy, the less she got back.

Jamie, the marketing consultant, reported her findings to a room full of company executives. "Let's start at the beginning," she said. "It appears that you have a loyal customer base and that they all come from four general industry groups. Would you agree with that?" The president nodded.

"Then why are you spending all of this time and money selling into new market areas when you still have room for growth in your target areas?"

"We can't depend on the same old customers for our livelihood. What if something happens to one of them? Then where are we?" the president inquired defiantly.

"Good point," said Jamie. "That would be true if your current customers and their respective market segments had minimal sales growth opportunity, but it appears that you are in the enviable position of having a firm market presence in a growing industry. You should first concentrate on taking care of business in your strong areas before moving into areas where you are unknown. Let me show you how a target marketing campaign to companies in your strong market segments can improve sales, decrease personnel requirements, and decrease costs. Interested?"

"What do you think?" said the smiling, yet doubtful, president.

How do you make sure your product or service is targeted to the people who can use it most? This chapter introduces you to the basic concepts of marketing and helps to round out the information presented in the other sales, marketing, and finance chapters.

Marketing and Sales: Linked but Different

Despite the fact that most people use the words *sales* and *marketing* interchangeably, the two activities really are different.

def•i•ni•tion

Marketing involves selecting or defining the right product, pricing strategy, promotional programs, and distribution outlets for your particular audience, or market. **Sales** is the part of your business that involves the steps you take to get the customer to actually buy your product or service.

Marketing consists of strategies that help to identify your customers, figure out what they need, determine what to charge them, tell them that you have what they need, and then sell it to them efficiently. In MBA programs, those are also called the "4 Ps" of marketing: product, pricing, promotion, and place of sale, which is also called distribution. If you want to get technical, they should really be called the "3 Ps and 1 D" of marketing, but let's not get nit-picky.

It is marketing's responsibility to identify the most likely customers, design the best product or service offering, set the product or service's price range, and choose the overall advertising message and presentation content most likely to get customers to buy. Specific marketing activities include market research, product or service definition development, analysis of pricing levels, creation of marketing materials and sales aids, advertising, public relations, and sales support.

It is the role of marketing to make it easier for the salesperson to sell. It is the role of the salesperson to contact customers, assess their needs, get their orders, and ensure that they remain repeat customers. Sales and marketing depend on each other but they are not the same.

Street Smarts

The essence of highly effective sales and marketing is as follows: sales efforts work best when the salesperson addresses the customers most likely to buy, with a product they are most likely to use, for a price that is within their budget, with a presentation that delivers the right message in an easily understood format. It's simple to state but difficult to do and a process that is continually being refined and updated.

Sales activities include contacting customers, making presentations, and getting the orders, among other things. The most effective marketing tells your salesperson the company type (industry or size) and contact person title most likely to buy from your company, which products they'll probably use, what pricing strategy to follow, and why the customer would use your company's products or services over a competitor's.

Effective marketing and sales campaigns require that you get close to your customers and thoroughly understand their buying motivations and habits. You might not get it right the first time, but careful planning makes sure that your darts hit the board, and experience leads you to the bull's-eye.

Know Who Is Most Likely to Buy Your Offering

We human beings like to believe that we are all unique, and on some basic level, we are. However, in other areas, we fall into certain groups that think, act, buy, and react alike. We're not all lemmings who jump off a cliff at once, but we do have certain characteristics that bind us as a group. These characteristics are often called *demographics* and include such things as age, income level, educational level, and marital status.

Breaking down your target customers by demographic characteristics is called *market segmentation*. When marketing people discuss the *demographic profile* of their ideal customer, they are looking for the common characteristics associated with their most likely customer.

A bank, for example, might segment its customers by age because people's banking needs change during different phases of their lives. People over the age of 50 are more likely than 18-year-olds to be interested in retirement-related products, and

18-year-olds are more likely to be interested in college loan details than 30-something couples who want to buy a home using a bank mortgage. Market segmentation helps the bank to group similar customers together and develop products that they will be interested in.

def•i•ni•tion

Demographics are a set of objective characteristics (including age, number of children, marital status, education level, job title, and others) that describes a group of people.

A **demographic profile** refers to a specific set of demographic characteristics that sales and marketing people use to target likely sales prospects. An ideal customer profile is a demographic description of the type of customer most likely to see the benefit from your product or service and actually buy it.

Market segmentation refers to dividing the total available market (everyone who may ever buy the product) into smaller groups, or segments, by specific attributes such as age, sex, location, interests, industry, or other pertinent criteria.

Compiling information about potential customers is the challenge for market research companies. They gather information through mail and phone surveys and personal interviews to determine people's buying habits. As a business owner, you can then buy and use this information to develop effective marketing programs to sell to these potential buyers. Remember to use your own customer database as a starting point for the types of customers who use your products. There is almost surely some commonality among your existing customers. You just need to find it and then use it to find new customers.

Anyone can buy marketing surveys (unless a specific company paid for the survey for its use only). Check with your local library first to see if it subscribes to any of these reports. Typically, the library purchases a wide variety of these reports and makes them available to the public. Look for a federal repository, which is a library that carries a lot of federal reports and documents. These reports were created with your tax dollars and are freely available to anyone who wants to read them.

This type of information may be available for free from other sources, too. The federal government compiles information about the age, household size, and financial status of all Americans in the form of a national census every 10 years (the last Census was completed in 2000) and makes it available at most libraries. The Census contains substantial information about the American public and breaks the country into areas called Standard Metropolitan Statistical Areas (SMSAs).

Target Marketing: Finding Your *Best* Customers

If you sell beef products, it wouldn't make sense to invest time and money displaying your products at a vegetarian convention. Promoting your meat products at a barbecue owners convention would make a lot more sense.

Identifying your customer is an important part of the marketing process. If you don't know who will buy your product and why, you have no idea who to contact and how to present your wares. When you don't know who your likely customers are, the result is a *scattergun marketing* approach, in which you blanket the market with a general message and hope that someone sees it and calls. This is not a very effective approach because it is costly and time consuming and results in few sales.

> **Street Smarts**
>
> There are a huge number of government and commercial websites containing useful marketing data. Check out some of these for help in researching your market: *American Demographics* magazine (www. demographics.com), Census data (www.census.gov), social statistics (www.whitehouse.gov), and business articles (www. reuters.com).

def•i•ni•tion

A scattergun sends buckshot in a wide pattern in the hope that it will hit something. Similarly, **scattergun marketing** sends marketing information everywhere hoping that someone will hear it (the opposite of target marketing). **Target marketing** involves focusing your marketing and sales efforts on those groups of potential customers most likely to need and buy your products or services. Customers buy what they need, not what you think they need. There is a difference.

Target marketing, on the other hand, focuses your financial and personnel resources on the people most likely to purchase what you offer. Suppose a particular geographic area has 100,000 potential customers for your products or services. A direct mail piece sent to this group at $1 each would cost $100,000. From this mailer, you might get a 2 percent response (which is a typical response rate). That number translates into 2,000 people wanting more information from you. Of those people, assume 10 percent, or 200 of the 2,000, actually buy your product or service. For a $100,000 investment, then, you've sold your company's goods to 200 people. A little statistics and customer characteristics analysis will probably show that these 200 people have demographic similarities that propel them into a specific market segment (which I discussed earlier).

Although promotional methods such as direct mail are discussed later, I should point out that you just spent $500 per customer ($100,000/200) to get each sale. Now, if you're selling a $10,000 item, you've done well, but if you're selling a $20 item, you've lost big bucks.

To develop a target marketing approach, you first need to define which markets contain your best potential customers. This means that you need to know something about what you're selling and who needs it most.

For example, you might find that your market segment is mostly women between 25 and 45 years of age, or that they are mostly college educated or work in specific industries. You can also use certain circumstances as market segmentation criteria; for example, businesses moving to a new location usually need new telephone equipment. To contact businesses most likely to purchase a telephone system, your first step might be identifying those who are moving or planning to move soon.

Target marketing does not waste time, money, and effort approaching people who are not good prospects. As a result, you get much better results from your sales time and money investment. The types of results you get vary widely from situation to situation, but you will always find target marketing a more manageable and efficient marketing effort than the scattergun approach.

Make sure that you keep this next point in mind when looking at your market opportunities: as a smaller company, you are most likely serving a niche of some type, which means that you do not provide something that serves a lot of people's needs. Know and accept your niche and then serve it better than anyone else to improve your chances of marketing success for the least expense.

Finding Your Right Price

Price is an interesting phenomenon in our capitalist society. It often represents more than just the amount of money that is paid for a product. Price is often viewed as a status symbol or a measure of worth over and above the amount that changes hands; the most expensive suit wins for some people. Pricing a product too low can make it appear inferior and can make people avoid it, even though it's of comparable quality to more expensive models.

Ultimately, the customer pays a price that is consistent with his *perceived value* of the offering. If the customer perceives the name on the product as having high value (such as designer clothing), then he or she might be willing to pay a high price to wear those designer duds.

def•i•ni•tion

Perceived value is the overall value that the customer places on a particular product or service. This includes much more than price; it considers features such as delivery lead time, quality of salesmanship, service, style, and other less tangible items. With a perceived-value pricing strategy, you set a price for your product or service by determining what people are willing to pay, yet making sure that you can still cover all your costs. Don't let your ego dictate your product's price. Several companies with a substantial jump on the market have fallen flat because of the faulty belief that people would pay more for their product simply because it was new, different, or had a particular company name on it! People buy benefits that are derived from their perceived value of your offering.

Pricing strategies fall into two basic categories: cost based and market based. You can calculate cost-based prices by determining the costs of producing a product or delivering a service and then adding a profit margin. This means that you'd better know your exact costs or this can really "cost" you the farm. You might think that you're doing great, only to find out that your costs were wrong and you are selling for less than your overall costs. And likely selling for less than your competition. You might be super busy but losing money on each transaction.

You determine market-based prices by studying pricing for similar products or services and then basing your prices on that competitive information. (See Chapter 11 for more details about competition.)

You need a lot of information about your product costs, your competitors' pricing, and how customers decide what and when to buy to accurately and comfortably determine pricing for your offerings. Here are some basic rules that will help you determine the best price for your services or products:

- Never price the product below your cost. You need to make a profit on every sale to stay in business unless you are clearing out inventory for the next year. Some people think that if they sell huge amounts, they'll come out okay in the end. Wrong! You can't lose a nickel on each unit and expect to make up the profit in volume.

- If you have a new company or a new product, you generally cannot match price with an established company with a similar offering. This is because the other company is already known and trusted and is a less risky choice for the customer. For the same price, its offering is considered a better purchase value. See the next point for additional comments on this important issue.

◆ You generally have to price lower than the established competition until you get a foothold in the market; unless your offering is perceived by the customer as unique and more valuable because it cannot be found anywhere else. Then you might be able to match, or exceed, competition pricing, but you better have a great sales pitch that explains the added customer benefit. Don't expect the customer to just "get it," spell it out for them.

◆ You can generally sell intangibles such as better service, deliverability, and location for up to 20 percent over a competitor's price. Over that price point, the customer will probably treat your offering as too expensive for his or her perceived value.

◆ Don't always price your offering on a cost-plus-profit-margin basis, called cost-plus-profit pricing. Although this approach is easy to compute, it usually leaves money on the customer's table that you could have otherwise put in your company bank account. *Market-based pricing* (based on competitive options) is generally more complicated but best ensures the most possible profit on each sale. In other words, if you do a better job producing the product and lowering your costs, market-based pricing gives higher dollar profits, whereas cost-based pricing cuts your sales price with each cost improvement, cutting your profit as well. (By the way, if you understood this last sentence, you are getting this important topic under your belt. If not, read Chapter 11 and this chapter until you do. It is really important.)

◆ Quantity discounts are an effective way to encourage your customers to purchase more of your product at a given time. However, watch the discount amounts, or you might find yourself selling a lot for a minimal profit.

Obviously, you can set your prices wherever you want, but your ideal price means more sales (and profits) for you because you will have figured out what your customers believe is a fair price for your goods. In return, they buy more. Knowing your competitors' profit margin can help you adjust your pricing strategy.

You must answer several key questions when determining a pricing strategy:

1. What are your competitors offering your potential customers in terms of their basic product or service price and the price of any add-on services?

2. How much does it cost you to supply the product or service desired by the customer (including those additional intangibles just discussed)? Make sure that you include variable costs, fixed costs, expected quantities, and total revenue into this portion of your pricing analysis. (See Chapter 17 for more details about costs.)

def•i•ni•tion

When your price is calculated using the cost to the company plus whatever profit margin is reasonable for your industry, you are using **cost-plus-profit pricing**. A widget that costs $1 to produce with a desired 50 percent mark-up would sell for $1 + ($1 × 0.5) = $1.50. You're simply adding on your desired profit percentage to your actual costs.

When you price offerings at a level set by what everyone else is charging, rather than by costs, you are using **market-based pricing**. With this strategy, you can generally make more money assuming your competition is charging reasonable rates and you can keep your costs down.

3. What additional features do you offer your customers that your competitors do not, and are these features worth more money? (See Chapter 13 for more information about sales and customer perceptions.)

The costs associated with a product vary, depending upon where it is in the product life cycle. The next section provides a brief overview of a new product's typical life cycle. You can use this model as a guide in determining your pricing, distribution, and marketing message strategies.

Ed's Lessons Learned

I have a friend who prides himself on his hourly consulting rate of $300, but he only bills three hours ($900) a month. Another colleague, on the other hand, charges $110 per hour and bills 30 to 50 hours ($3,300 to $5,000) per month. If the intent is to make money, then the lower billing rate is the way to go.

Street Smarts

Profit margins for a company are available, sorted by Standard Industrial Code (SIC), from the Dun & Bradstreet Reports, Robert Morris Associates' Annual Statement Studies, or the annual report of publicly traded, established companies. Most publicly traded companies will send you a copy of their annual report if you call their investor relations department. If not, buy a single share of stock, and they legally have to provide it. This provides you with a benchmark for what your profits should be.

The All-Important Life Cycle

Every product or service goes through a *life cycle* from its introduction until the time it is discontinued or taken off the market (see the figure that follows). The life cycle usually refers to products, but services go through a similar evolution.

Product/service life cycle.

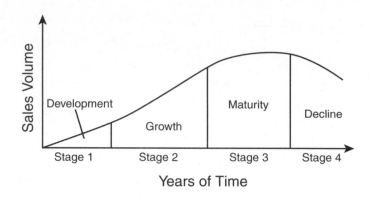

The life cycle is divided into four basic stages:

Stage 1: Market development (a.k.a. embryonic). The product or service is new to the market, having recently been introduced. Sales are slow at this stage, and customers take longer to make a purchase decision due to their lack of familiarity with the product. Only potential customers who have shown a willingness to experiment with new products or services are good prospects at this stage. That group of experimenters is often referred to as "early adopters" because they are the first to try something new. There are few, perhaps no, competitors and you determine pricing.

def·i·ni·tion

The **life cycle** is a set of four distinct phases every product or service goes through from the time it is introduced to the market to the time it is discontinued. When so many competitors enter the market that everyone has to keep dropping their prices to win sales, price erosion lowers the market price and profit margins. This is typical of a commodity product.

Stage 2: Market growth. Sales are increasing steadily, perhaps rapidly, and there is a general awareness of the product or service. Competition usually starts to show up at this point as lead times extend and you simply cannot build enough product to meet customer demands. This is a fun but also perilous time when companies often feel stretched to the breaking point and cash flow becomes incredibly important. This is that stage where you typically want to introduce your new product or service unless you are specifically financially set up to weather the slower development stage.

Stage 3: Maturity. Overall demand starts to level off as customers purchase the offering as a routine part of doing business. Customers have a high degree of familiarity with the offering and may already own one. *Price erosion* can happen at this point due to intense competition from what is now an established market for the product or service. This is sometimes called the commodity stage since it is at this stage that products are treated as basically all looking alike. Customers buy often to replace what they already have, vendors compete for customer business based on price and features. Production volume and efficiency determine which vendors make a profit and stay in business.

Stage 4: Market decline. Customer demand for the product or service starts to decline due to improved variations of the product by other companies, new technology, or other market forces that make the product inferior or obsolete. If companies do not come out with another product before they enter the decline stage, they may never recover and could be put out of business.

Although most products or services go through a life cycle in a matter of years or a decade, fad products such as novelty gifts (the mood ring or pet rock) might experience an entire life cycle in a very short period of time (such as a single Christmas buying season). Durable goods, such as microwaves, might have an extended life cycle caused by the level of technological sophistication and a high level of consumer acceptance.

Notice that the perceived value of your offering changes over the life cycle. In the early days, when customers are just learning about what you are selling, only a small segment takes a chance by making a purchase.

In the growth stage, with demand for your offering increasing, you might be in the driver's seat. This means you can charge a premium price because you have something everyone wants and few places where they can get it. The growth stage can be highly profitable, but it can also seriously strap your company for cash even though you are showing large sales revenue increases using the accrual basis of accounting.

By the time you enter the maturity stage, you probably encounter competitors who have developed similar products, which forces you to compete on price and service. For example, the personal computer industry is in the maturity stage of its development. Notice the rapid price erosion combined with improved performance that this industry has experienced. This is typical of an industry in the maturity stage of the life cycle.

The product life-cycle concept affects your pricing strategy. Once you determine where your product or service offerings fall in the product life cycle, you can make a better choice about your long-term strategy. The price you set for your rates as a new consultant, for example, is different from that of an experienced, nationally known consultant.

Use the three different strategies—cost-plus, market-driven, and perceived-value pricing—to choose the price level that will generate the most sales. Then make sure that your price is consistent with your life-cycle position.

Your Marketing Message and Positioning

I used to regularly play racquetball with two guys in their 60s, and they whipped me every time. As if getting beaten wasn't bad enough, at the end of the game, I was totally exhausted, and they were only slightly winded! One time, I finally put aside my pride and asked about the secret to their racquetball success. They replied, "It isn't the speed with which you hit the ball as much as your position when you hit it."

Market positioning is everything in sports and in business. I don't mean the geographic location of your company, necessarily, but rather the way your customers perceive (position) your company in their thinking.

def•i•ni•tion

Creating a positive image in the minds of potential and existing customers is called **market positioning**. The purpose of market positioning is to have potential customers perceive your product or service in a particular way that not only differentiates it from the competition but also makes them more likely to want to buy from you.

Take a moment and think about the hundreds of marketing-related messages that bombard you on a daily basis. How do you sift through the irrelevant ones and focus on the ones of importance to you? It depends on the way the product is presented and whether it communicates a message of interest to you. The marketing message, the essence of your positioning goal, is the key to customer perception.

The message should be simple, easy to remember, and easy to understand. The only way you can effectively position your company or your product in your customer's mind is to understand his or her thinking and lifestyle. You must know your competition's marketing approach and …

1. Make sure that your new company is seen as different from the others.

2. Make customers more comfortable with your totally new company or product by making it look a lot like your competition, which reduces perceived risk and adds validity to your company by association.

Here are some examples of typical positioning statements:

- Lower price with superior quality.
- More convenient, cleaner, and better-stocked store shelves.
- More fun at a lower price.
- Earn your college tuition in exchange for several years of training.

The range of positioning statements is infinite and limited only by your creativity. Your marketing message clearly and simply conveys the positioning benefit perception you want your customers to understand. Spend a lot of time thinking about this and try several variations on colleagues. The marketing message will appear in almost everything you produce and will create the perception your salespeople work with during the sales process. If your message is off, you are in trouble because your customers won't even think of you when they need exactly the products or services you provide!

Street Smarts

Change may be a natural part of life, but it generally causes confusion when dealing with marketing messages and positioning. It takes months (or years) to create a solid market positioning in a customer's mind, and you should not tamper with it in a careless way. Confusion is a dangerous thing when dealing with customers. Decide on the positioning and stay with it unless you are absolutely sure it doesn't work. You can tamper somewhat with the message as long as all the adjustments convey the same positioning benefits to your customers.

If you know someone who changes careers on a regular basis, you know how hard it is to discuss this person's professional capabilities. She may be brilliant, but if she cannot explain her qualifications in a simple way that means something to the listener, she remains an enigma. Enigmas are interesting at cocktail parties but rarely get hired for important projects.

The same is true of your offerings. Keep the positioning consistent, and make sure your marketing message accurately conveys the customer benefits associated with the positioning. You will get tired of using the same message well before your customers will. In fact, just as you get bored with it and want to change it is when the customers start taking notice. It may be the first time that your customer has heard it even if it is the millionth time for you.

Advertising: Balancing Push and Pull

Advertising is good for increasing awareness of your company and its offerings. Unless you're in retail, don't expect to close many sales directly from your advertising. The point of advertising is to firmly plant your marketing message into consumers' minds so that they think about you when they look for what you offer. Advertising also gets the company in front of a wide variety of people in a timely manner.

Marketers (or marketeers) call this *mind share*. This is the part of a person's thought process occupied by perceptions associated with your specific company. The greater the mind share, the more likely people are to contact you when they are looking for what you offer. If you have no mind share, then they won't even know to call. You develop mind share by using advertising, publicity, promotion, and personal experience with your company.

Advertising is useful for creating a *pull marketing strategy*, which means that the customers "pull" your product through the distribution channel by asking for it. A pull strategy is expensive because it requires massive marketing to your potential customers to alert them to your product's availability. Beware creating a national identity and customer need and not having a way for people to buy or you could lose a great opportunity. Having people order from your Internet site can help in this area today where it could not have only 10 years ago. (See CD Bonus Chapter 21 for more information.)

At the other extreme is the *push marketing strategy*, which requires you to convince distributors to carry and promote your product, hoping that customers purchase it. A push strategy might show faster initial results but depends on the activities of the specific distributor. Some companies begin with a pull strategy; then they are lucky enough to build visibility through customer demand. This often raises distributors' interest level, and it transforms into a push strategy.

def•i•ni•tion

Mind share is the portion of a person's thought processes that includes perceptions of your company's offerings. One hundred percent mind share means that any time a person needs your type of offering, he or she thinks of your company. A **pull marketing strategy** convinces your potential customers to request your offering through their suppliers. In essence, the end user pulls your offering through the distribution channel by putting pressure on suppliers to carry it in their inventory. A **push marketing strategy** sells your product to distributors, who then promote it to their customers. A pull strategy is driven by customers. A push strategy is driven by you and distributors.

Keep the following points in mind when you consider advertising:

◆ Many companies provide money to distributors for cooperative advertising. If you mention their products in specific ways in your ads, they pay for a portion of the ad. Include enough suppliers, and the suppliers can pay for the entire ad. Contact each of your suppliers for their specific restrictions.

- Yellow Page advertising is a must for any business trying to reach the general retail public, such as a restaurant. The phone book comes out only once a year, so you should plan in advance to be included. Check with colleagues about their success with the various ad types and sizes; take the plunge and hope for the best. Know that this contract will require payment for at least a year independent of what happens to your business. Try to not personally guarantee the payments if possible and look to see if you can get into a local book that goes out to those most likely to use your product or services.

- Placing an ad just one time in a paper or on TV or radio is generally useless. You need to repeat your ad on a regular basis to get the best results, so plan for 6 to 10 insertions, or don't waste your money. A smaller ad with more insertions will likely be more successful than a larger ad that only appears once.

- Advertising firms specialize in making companies like yours succeed with advertising. They also have an art department that can design an ad for you.

- Contact each publication, radio, and TV station you are interested in advertising with and ask them to send you a *media kit*. The kit includes demographic information about the people who read each publication, listen to specific radio programs, and watch individual TV shows. Typical information includes age, sex, education, household income, and marital status. This information lets you determine whether the people who will see or hear the ad are the ones most likely to buy from you.

- Ask each media supplier if they have ever run ads like yours before and what type of responses they received. This might help you determine whether it makes sense to invest in advertising there.

Infomercials are currently popular as a means of marketing products and services and must be effective, based on the rapid increase in the number of infomercials currently on television. There's a lot of money riding on the success of some of these infomercials; some cost hundreds of thousands of dollars to produce, and they are generally beyond the financial reach of the conventional entrepreneur. This doesn't mean that this avenue should not be pursued, only that the startup costs should not be ignored. Producing a half-hour or hour-long commercial is extremely expensive, and on top of that, add the cost of buying the TV time. I am not necessarily recommending or refuting the use of the infomercial as a marketing tool. I just want you to know that this avenue is available and may be right for your business, but that it requires much more investigation before taking the plunge.

There are a number of new advertising tools now available via the Internet, including banner ads, site ads, and search engine listings. For people using the Internet regularly, this can be a great way to get their attention. To explore how to use the Internet as one of your marketing tools, check out CD Bonus Chapter 21.

Advertising can be a useful tool when used properly, but it can also drain massive amounts of cash from your company with minimal financial return. Make sure that wherever your ads appear, they are seen or heard by serious potential customers for your company's product or service offerings. It is also wise to pay for professional help when producing ads. There's no sense paying big money for ad time or space only to run an ineffective, poorly designed advertisement. Spend your money where it will count the most.

def•i•ni•tion

Media kits are prepared by the advertising departments of newspapers, magazines, and television and radio stations as a means of encouraging companies to buy ads. These kits typically contain demographic information about their audience, a rate card, and an editorial calendar for publications, which tells readers what to expect in upcoming issues.

Mail Order and Direct Mail

Do you want to take on the opportunities and headaches associated with mail order? With a mail-order system, you get the order along with its payment and then you are responsible for getting the product into the hands of the customer. You have 30 days from the time you receive the order to the time you have to ship it, which gives you plenty of time in many cases to produce or acquire needed products, instead of stockpiling a huge inventory.

Street Smarts

eBay, Amazon, and other similar Internet-based companies now provide a sales outlet that was not possible even a few years ago. Many people provide their products over these services, using the service itself as its sales force. The people using these services properly and to their full extent are often making large amounts of money. Things are changing in this arena, so you are cautioned, once again, to verify the nuances of their use for yourself, but you are also well served by looking into them as a viable and potentially highly profitable sales channel. (See CD Bonus Chapter 21 for more information about making money from the Internet.)

A big down side with mail order is that customers can cancel the orders after you ship them. Credit card fraud is also a real problem with mail-order sales, which means that you might never get paid for the order. Accepting credit cards is crucial for mail-order sales because you risk having even worse collection problems if you rely solely on checks for payment. Many companies wait until a check clears before shipping the product to the customer as one way to combat bad checks.

Because there are huge up-front costs required to create and mail a catalog, companies have to be confident they will receive enough orders to at least pay for production and mailing of the catalog. With response rates in the 0.5 to 3 percent range, you must have a high profit margin on the products sold to cover the initial investment.

By law, you have to ship a prepaid order in 30 days or offer a refund to a customer who doesn't want to wait any longer. Although it might improve your cash situation to produce according to how many orders you receive, make sure you can deliver in 30 days or less. Also beware that properly collecting sales tax is an important competency to master for in-state and interstate shipments. In addition, there are now restrictions on certain products being shipped to certain countries, so check this out with the Federal Customs and Border Patrol (www.cbp.gov).

For Your Plan

The marketing section of your plan is absolutely critical, and you must spend time making it just as credible and clear as possible. Make sure that it, at a minimum, includes …

- A detailed description of your ideal target customer, including demographic profile. Make sure that you explain where you came by this profile.

 - The buying characteristics of your target customer and his or her industry.

- The synergy between your marketing approach and that preferred by your target customers.

- Your rationale for choosing the sales approach.

- Your intended positioning statement and why it was written in just that way. How does it differentiate your company and offering from others, and if it does not, why not?

- How you plan to advertise and promote your company and offering. What are the projected costs of this promotion? What are the projected sales returns for promotion dollars spent?

- Your pricing rationale and how it stacks up with the competition. Include discussion and analysis on the profit margins required for each step in your particular marketing/sales approach and how it ties in with the lifecycle analysis.

◆ A connection between this pricing discussion and your offering's cost information to verify that you can maintain adequate profit margins as defined by the norms for your intended industry.

◆ Your plans for expansion beyond your initial market introduction. What are the time frames for this expansion?

On the CD

Make sure that you look on the CD for additional information related to marketing your new company. First check out "Working with the Media" to learn ways for using the media to get free advertising. There is a proven way to work with the media so they want to work with you, and it is included in this CD bonus section. Next, take a few minutes to read "Balancing Profit Margins with Your Selling Approach." This CD bonus section helps you make sure that your distribution channel is right for your customers and also ensures that you keep your sales costs where they have to be to make money.

The Least You Need to Know

◆ Marketing lays the groundwork by communicating why customers should buy your service or your product. Sales closes the deal and brings in the money.

◆ Price is not the only buying criterion; customers look at the total value and benefits of your offering. You must remain clear on the difference.

◆ Create a simple, yet clear, marketing message that describes your company's market positioning, and stick with it.

◆ Advertising and promotion are important to positioning your company in the marketplace. A company's or product's position affects how people perceive it.

◆ Make sure that you spend your marketing dollars on the target market that is most likely to buy what you offer.

Getting Sales: The Lifeblood of Your Business

In This Chapter

- ◆ Understanding the value of effective selling
- ◆ Matching sales procedures to your company's offering
- ◆ Evaluating direct and distribution sales
- ◆ Selling services

"So what happened?" asked the board member who provided the initial funding for the company.

"The sales just didn't come in as expected," said the president, a professional engineer and former operations manager. "We've been through three sets of salespeople and can't seem to find a good group. They all seem to just want more money and don't bring in the bacon."

"Have you ever been with them on a sales call?" asked the board member.

"Not really," replied the president. "I have been working with our technical people to make sure the product can do what we promised. Selling is what I have sales managers for. Why pay them if I have to do everything myself?" He knew he was on shaky ground.

"Let's make sure I understand. We have a product and a production facility that works perfectly due to your involvement, but we have nobody who wants to buy what we build. Is that correct?" Heads nodded around the room. "What is wrong with this picture, and what are your plans to correct it?"

Picture a salesperson. What do you see? A fast-talking nonlistener who is always looking at your pocketbook? A slick dresser who continually promises to do things in "your own best interest" but who is obviously only interested in selling you something—anything—whether you need it or not?

When you go into a retail store to find a particular item, do you ask the salesperson for help or tell him or her that you are "just browsing" when she offers to assist? If you are like most people who do not use the help, it may be because you have had bad experiences with salespeople before and prefer not to have something you don't need forced on you.

Understanding the sales process and what it takes to succeed at selling is important in running a successful business. As the founder and owner of your company, the sales "buck" stops with you. You are in sales when you start your own company. The only question is whether you will fully realize that fact and set up your sales operation to support your particular sales capabilities and style.

I call sales the money funnel because no cash comes into the company unless someone has sold your product or service to a customer and you have the customer's money. Selling is your lifeline to staying in business. To succeed, you must give it the attention and respect it deserves. You can stay in business if your accounting is inaccurate or if you aren't the best of managers, but you will definitely be out of business if you cannot create sales. This doesn't mean that you must do the selling yourself, however. If you lack the interest or the ability to sell successfully, find someone who can.

You need to know enough about sales to manage those actually performing the sales function and to determine when a sales slowdown represents a problem with your sales force or a problem with your company's offering or intended market.

Remember, no matter how you feel about sales, there is one undeniable fact: without sales, you are without a business. Period.

This chapter is based on my years of experience not only as a salesperson, but also in consulting with my clients to make their sales more successful. This is my own personally developed sales philosophy and tracking method, and I encourage you to give it a try. It really works.

Manipulating and Selling: Not the Same Thing

Most of us have had someone convince us to buy something we later realized was not in our best interest. We felt manipulated by the whole process and by the salesperson involved.

Manipulation has nothing to do with sales! If you manipulate people to buy your offering and they don't want it, they will resent you, your company, and its offerings for a long time. That single sale could cost you a fortune in future revenues, not only from that one customer who will never buy from you again but also from everyone he tells about his negative buying experience with you.

Sales is the process of matching your products or services with a customer who truly needs them. You are helping the customer solve a problem by providing a service or a product that will make his or her life easier. It could be as simple as selling a pair of shoes for a special party or as complicated as setting up an experiment on the International Space Station. If the customer has a need for your offering and you provide a credible product or service that meets those needs, within the budget, then the customer will buy! It's that simple. If the customer doesn't buy, there is something wrong with your offering or your presentation, or you are not presenting to a viable potential buyer.

Manipulative selling might earn you a fast buck, but it also eliminates the chance for a future sale to that customer. Professional selling is the act of solving a customer's problems through your company's offerings. It is service-based instead of manipulation-based and has a much better chance of creating long-term customers who keep buying year after year.

Many new salespeople have shifted from average performers who just do their jobs to outstanding performers who like what they do by simply making this conceptual shift. The difference between these two approaches is the difference between not caring whether a customer needs something (manipulation-based selling) versus determining that the customer has a need that your product or service can meet (service-based selling).

Street Smarts

More satisfied customers result from professional selling than from manipulative types of selling. You don't need to be a business guru to understand that satisfied people buy more and tell their friends to buy from you. This is good.

True business and selling success usually comes from a lot of smaller successful clients instead of a single "killing." The huge deals make good press and media headlines but really don't reflect the reality of day-to-day business success.

Getting Close to Closing the Sale

The sales process takes place in a number of stages. Look at the way you buy anything. You go through your own set of questions and investigation stages before actually forking over your money. You might evaluate the available information, read about the product in magazine or newspaper articles, ask knowledgeable friends for their opinions, flip a coin, call your mom for her advice, and eventually decide on a purchase.

def•i•ni•tion

A **close** (pronounced *cloze*) is a request by a salesperson for a specific action on the customer's part. Asking for the order is the ultimate close, but smaller closes occur at each stage of the selling process to gradually move the customer toward committing to the purchase.

Professional selling involves a sequence of small events that eventually lead to the sale. At each step along the way, the salesperson makes little requests for customer action or *closes*, which eventually lead to a sale. For example, asking to meet with someone face-to-face is a small close in that you are asking the customer to take an action that leads in the direction of the sale. If the customer agrees, you are one step nearer to getting him or her to make a purchase. Once the customer is satisfied that buying your product or service is the right decision, he or she commits naturally and on his or her own to a purchase.

People expect to be asked reasonable questions that help them solve their problem, and they also expect you to ask them to buy. If you don't ask for the order, you can't blame them if they don't give it to you.

Everyone Has to Sell, but Not Everyone Closes

Nothing is more irritating to customers than to be continually asked to buy something before they're ready. Eventually the salesperson's lack of sensitivity bothers the customers to the point that they leave simply to stop the salesperson's harassment.

Everyone in your organization should support the sales process by providing information, support, service, and guidance when requested by the customer. When it is time for the final order to be placed, the salesperson takes care of writing up the sale.

Aggressive selling is closing when it is inappropriate. Professional selling is closing as needed to move the customer forward to the next sales stage while still keeping the customer comfortable with the sales process. The moral of the story: don't rush customers into making a decision, or you might lose them forever.

Ed's Lessons Learned

I have seen small business owners hire salespeople and then basically wash their hands of the sales and marketing activities of the company. Wrong move! It must be an organizational mandate that all employees, including the owners, think of themselves as salespeople with respect to serving the customer. If the phone rings six or more times before being answered and there are employees there who could have answered it, then that customer is not being served, and a sale might be lost. That employee who answers the phone must know enough about the company and its offerings to either help the customer directly or connect that customer with another employee who can. Taking care of customers is the responsibility of all employees, and when a few drop the customer service ball, especially the owners, the entire company suffers. It is the responsibility of top management and owners to make sure that there is no question in the minds of employees that the customer must be taken care of, and not taking care of the customer will not be tolerated.

Is Your Offering a Special or Commodity Item?

Your company's approach to selling is largely determined by your market positioning and message. Offerings with plenty of competition, where the products and services are pretty much the same, require that features and benefits such as price, delivery, warranty, and stability be emphasized to set your company apart. Specialty products and services, such as high-tech electronics or tailored clothing, require a higher level of personalized service and credibility as part of the sales process because each product is so different from the others on the market.

Where does your product fit? Commodities rely more on the distribution channel to effectively get products into the hands of new customers, as well as established customers who use your product on a regular basis. There is little or no difference between commodity products (milk, white envelopes, and lead pencils), and price is a major factor in the customer decision-making process.

Specialty products require a higher level of technical and sales sophistication because the product's competitive advantage must be explained well. The salesperson has to know about the benefits of the competitors' products and services and how they compare to his own company's offerings in order to sell the customer on why one is better. It is often possible to sustain higher profit margins selling specialty products because the customer is more sophisticated regarding your particular product. This is why fine wine shops, antique dealers, and high-end stereo stores charge so much more for their products. Their products are not generally available, and the salesperson provides a higher level of knowledge and service as part of the sale process.

Is Your Customer a Likely Buyer?

All the sweet-talking, wining, dining, and fancy brochures in the world will not close a sale from an unqualified prospect (someone who is not able to buy). I have seen a lot of new, and even experienced, salespeople invest valuable time on prospective customers who were really never qualified to purchase in the first place. Here is a list of five criteria you can use to determine whether you are dealing with a qualified customer.

Again, a qualified customer is someone who is interested in buying from you and has the means and capability to do so. If you can't answer a definite "yes" to these five key questions, you don't have a qualified potential customer. Get the answers, or you might waste a tremendous amount of time and energy on a prospect who cannot buy from you.

1. **Does your customer need what you have to offer?** If your customers don't need what you offer, then you can't blame them for not buying it. Would you buy something you didn't need just to make the salesperson happy? No way, and they won't either!

   Make sure you really understand your customers' needs and that they understand what you have to offer. Your challenge is to accurately identify your potential customers' needs and make sure your marketing message addresses them. If you determine that you cannot meet their needs, get out of their way.

   You might even want to help the customers find an alternate source if your offerings are not what they need. Doing this makes the potential customers feel good about your company because you are truly doing something that has no immediate reward for you (because you know they aren't going to buy from you right now). In the long run, your willingness to help find a better source might pay off with the customers coming back to buy from you later because you've already demonstrated that you really have their needs at heart. Trust is a very important aspect of an ongoing sales and business relationship.

2. **Are you working with the decision maker?** Ultimately, a single person will authorize the purchase of your offering. If you are not dealing with the person in charge of the budget, who can say "yes" and sign on the dotted line, then you are only dealing with someone who has the authority to say "no" to the sale or at best can only influence the outcome.

   Instead of wasting time and energy convincing someone who is not authorized to make a decision to buy from you, first determine who the decision maker is. This might require that you meet with nondecision makers until you find the right person. You then work to meet with that person. Meeting with anyone else but the decision maker doesn't get you any closer to making the sale and can be very expensive from a time and money perspective.

3. **Is there money budgeted for this purchase?** If there is no money available to pay for a purchase, there is no potential for a sale. It is perfectly okay to ask whether money is already in the budget for this purchase. You might find that the money is coming out of next year's budget and that the sale is on hold until the next fiscal year starts. You might also find that there is no money currently budgeted for this project, which should set off warning bells in your head. You might discover that your customer needs to spend the budgeted money by the end of this fiscal year, which provides an added incentive on his part to move the sale forward. Handling budget issues could be as simple as whether the sale is credit card or cash, as in a retail environment.

4. **Is there a pending event?** This is a critically important point that in my experience is most often overlooked by people having sales trouble. A pending event is something expected to happen in the future that affects when a decision is made. The pending event drives the time frame within which a decision is required. Typical pending events include fiscal year end (when budgeted money needs to be spent or is lost), management orders, moving offices, and mergers. If there is no pending event, the customer can, and might, take forever to make a decision. Why should they force the decision when a decision is not necessary? If there is no critical deadline, you might spend a lot of time trying to convince an unmotivated customer to buy.

5. **Is your customer politically open to using your offering?** Sometimes you can have everything in place, the deal looks like it can't help but close, and then it falls apart. It is almost as though an unknown power stepped in and killed the deal. That is probably just what happened. Many companies have divisions and subsidiaries they are supposed to buy from, and if it is discovered that they are planning to buy from another company, someone might try to kill the deal. Why would a company buy from you if it has a subsidiary that offers the same product at a comparable price? It won't! Not because the product isn't right. Not because you did a poor job of selling. Simply because there's a company policy that says all purchases must first be made from an internal business partner. Period.

Try to find out about these barriers to your sales early and save yourself a lot of frustration and anguish later. You can do this by researching all the divisions of a large company to determine whether there are groups providing the same service or the same product that you are. It might also be useful to know who the company is currently buying from to determine whether you'll be able to win business away from them. Use the competitive research procedures outlined in Chapter 9 as a starting point. Or even simpler, ask someone who works for the prospect company if there is a political conflict. That person might just tell you.

Ed's Lessons Learned

As a new salesperson, I was working on selling some test equipment systems to a major automaker. The contact people were always happy to meet with me and arranged the meetings for around 11:30 in the morning. Several other people would show up for lunch on my nickel. After several such fruitless meetings, I asked my boss what I could do to move the sale forward. He congratulated me on seeing that something was wrong and explained, "These guys only buy test equipment from Vendor A (a competitor). They have a game going to see how many times they can get a free lunch out of a salesperson before he or she realizes that there is no possibility of a sale."

The Nine Stages of Selling

Baking bread can be a frustrating and exhilarating experience at the same time. It is an art form, and anyone who has failed in the bread-baking process can verify this. You must follow specific steps in precisely the right order and at precisely the right time. Reordering the sequence or trying to rush the process invariably leads to a poor-tasting loaf.

The sales process is similar; a sale will go through specific stages before the deal is either lost or won. Performing these steps out of sequence usually leads to poor results, and skipping a step usually leads to disappointment. Plan your sales strategy to include moving the customer from one stage to another, with small closes along the way, rather than rushing the customer forward to the final close. I will now walk you through these stages and explain what occurs and what you should accomplish.

The Suspect Stage—Stage 1

At this stage, you have heard from a friend of a friend that perhaps Company A needs your products or services. This is the first stage in the process, and it usually occurs as a result of your marketing efforts, such as a direct-mail letter, advertisement, or phone calls.

When you don't know much about Company A but you think it might need your services, it is considered a suspect or a lead. There really is no close at this stage other than to make contact with a person on the staff at Company A to verify that he has a need for your services.

The Prospect Stage—Stage 2

If you make contact with a representative of Company A and learn that the company does indeed need the services you provide, you have just received confirmation and can move Company A to the prospect stage. In the first stage, you just suspected that Company A had a need, and now after receiving confirmation, you know for a fact that it has a need. Company A is now a prospective customer.

Confirmation from a prospect can come in the form of a response to your direct-mail campaign, a request for additional information, or a phone call made by your salesperson. The close for this stage is to have Company A agree to an in-depth discussion about its business needs. Not your needs, but the company's needs! This discussion can occur in person, over the phone, or by e-mail, depending on geography and industry.

The Entrée Stage—Stage 3

In the entrée stage, you have your first major interaction with the prospect. This contact is often made in person. For technical sales in particular, personal contact is usually required to understand the customer's needs and to explain your company's complex products and features.

This stage enables you to learn more about the prospect's need for your services and lay the groundwork for the next stage. Here you qualify Company A regarding money, time frame, and the decision-making process. Your close for this stage is to have the prospect detail for you exactly what it intends to buy: how many, for what purpose, when, at what price, and so on. The more you know about Company A's plans and needs, the better you can convince the company that you are the best choice for this project. It is not uncommon to leave this stage with more questions than answers, which leads to the next stage, discovery.

Watch Out!

You do lose control when you use distributors or reps to perform the sales function for your company. Major problems can erupt when distributors make commitments or promises on your behalf that you cannot or will not fulfill. Be sure that you define up front each party's responsibilities to avoid such politically and financially costly situations.

The Discovery Stage—Stage 4

In some cases, there is no need for a discovery stage because the prospect has already indicated his needs to you and has requested a specific proposal or quote. When this happens, you can proceed to Stage 5, the proposal. There is often a bidders conference date included with the request for proposal so that vendors can get additional information.

When you are dealing with larger companies, you might find that you have to speak and meet with several people before being ready to send a proposal. Often, this is because many layers of management need to give their "okay" to whatever business you might be trying to win. This might mean many presentations, meetings, or visits just to be sure you've spoken with everyone involved in deciding which vendor company the prospect should use. When you're meeting with numerous people, you have to repeat the process of learning and addressing each person's needs and concerns.

If you haven't already collected this kind of information in Stage 3, determine the prospect's situation, what might be the best way to improve the situation, the budget, how quickly the work must be done, and the most important factors in picking a supplier. Armed with this information, you can write a proposal that shows you truly understand the company's situation and that you can provide a solution that's also within the budget.

The Proposal Stage—Stage 5

Once the prospect's needs are defined and the overall sales criteria are established, it's time for you to present your best solution: your proposal. This can be in the form of a formal written document or bid, or you can simply tell the prospect that the shoes cost $75. In either case, you now explain to the prospect that you recommend a specific solution to improving his situation, and the cost is such-and-such.

On the CD

A sample Consignment Agreement is included on the CD as document 13-01.

For a large-dollar sale, this stage might involve a formal presentation to a committee of people. Make sure that you don't have food stains on your shirt or blouse and ensure that you present the benefits that the customer receives from buying from you and don't concentrate as much on your particular offering's features.

Trial Close Stage—Stage 6

In the trial close stage, you ask the prospect for his reaction to your proposal, and whether he plans to buy from you. Don't take "no" as final at this stage. "No" might only suggest that you missed something or that the prospect needs time to consider your proposal. Ask for some feedback on your proposal and just listen to what the prospect tells you. You might be surprised by what you hear. Adjust your proposal accordingly and promptly resubmit it. Feedback at this stage is your friend if the prospect doesn't accept your proposal as you presented it. Thoroughly doing your homework in the discovery stage will keep you from having nasty and unwelcome surprises when you trial close.

Some sellers who work with retailers will get over the customer's commitment resistance by offering their product on a *consignment* basis. In this way, the retailer does not pay for the seller's product until it actually sells. If the product does not sell, then the seller simply takes back the product. The only risk to the retailer with this arrangement is the energy the retailer puts behind selling the product and the floor space used up in offering the product. The seller runs the risk of the retailer selling the product and then not paying the seller for the sold products, but this is more of a credit issue than a sales one.

def•i•ni•tion _____

A **consignment** sale is one where the retailer does not pay the vendor for products displayed until it actually sells.

The Budget Stage—Stage 7

Many large purchases must go through an approval process at the prospect's company, which can take anywhere from a few hours to a few months, depending on the company and the offerings involved. This stage is often nerve-wracking for both the vendor and your primary contact who wants your offering. It requires patience. Unfortunately, all you can do is maintain regular contact with the prospect to ensure that nothing stops the positive momentum toward the sale.

For a small purchase, this stage can be as simple as running a credit card through the machine and getting an approval code.

Street Smarts _____

Start tracking and forecasting your sales as soon as you receive an inquiry from a potential customer. Monitor the prospect's progression through each of the sales stages so that you can better gauge when the actual sales transaction may occur. This gives you a consistent way of forecasting sales and predicting cash inflow.

The Close Stage—Stage 8

The close stage is when you ask for the order and either get it, find out what is missing, or simply lose the deal to another company. All prior closing stages lead to this point. If you read the situation properly and had valid information and a qualified customer, you stand an excellent chance of winning the sale. This is an exciting and scary time for both you and your customer, particularly when the sale involves a large amount of money.

On the CD

The CD contains a sample Sales Contact (document 13-02), a sample Purchase Order (document 13-03), and a sample Bill of Sale (document 13-04).

If you get a "no" or a "maybe," return to the discovery stage to find out if you missed some crucial bit of information or if the prospect's needs have changed. Then go through the rest of the stages again. If the customer meets the five qualification criteria, you should either get or lose the deal (or at least know what has to happen to obtain the order).

The Post-Sale Stage—Stage 9

You've made the sale and the deal is closed. Everyone should be happy, right? Nope. You are still not finished. Check back with the decision maker to make sure things are going okay. Make sure the customer is still happy with his or her choice and isn't having doubts or misgivings. This is an often overlooked and critically important stage to building long-term customer satisfaction. This is also a great time to ask your new customer for referrals to others who might be able to use your offering. A solid referral from a happy customer is golden and cannot be overvalued. Don't be afraid to ask for the referral, as many new customers want to share their success with others and will happily give you the referral.

On the CD

A sample Limited Warranty is enclosed on the CD as document 13-05.

It is much less expensive to keep an existing customer than to find a new one. Your most valuable assets are your repeat customers. Guard them jealously. To ensure that they continue to be repeat customers, check back with them after each sale to confirm that they are pleased with their purchase. Show your customers that you have their best interests at heart and weren't just after the sale.

A Commodity Sale Versus a Complex Sale

The sales process varies somewhat, depending on whether you're selling a CD player at a department store, a fancy house on a lake, or a $500,000 computer system. Although the timing of each stage might differ, the sequence must be followed or the sales process gets disrupted.

For example, the department store sale stages are something like this: the customer walks up and asks for assistance. This handles Stages 1 through 3. You ask what the customer is looking for and how much he or she wants to spend. There are Stages 4 and 5. You find a unit that you think matches the customer's needs and ask whether he or she wants to buy; end Stage 6. The credit card is processed, and the customer signs the receipt and walks out the door with the CD player (Stages 7 and 8). Asking the customer how the CD player is working out the next time he or she comes into the store covers Stage 9.

The sales process becomes more complex when working with high-dollar items or services, but the stages of the sale are the same. For example, trying to charge a consumer's credit card for a CD player before he or she has agreed on a unit would definitely not work in this scenario. In the same way, placing Stages 7 and 8 before the other stages would not work when selling a $500,000 computer system.

Map out your sales cycle and expected stages to set realistic expectations about what is needed at each stage of the sales process and the time frames involved in moving a prospect from Stage 1 to Stage 8.

Ed's Lessons Learned

Adding up the total time for all stages gives you an idea as to how long it will be from the time you make your first viable prospect contacts to the time when you can expect to cash your first customer payment checks. Make sure that you include normal payment terms in determining the time frame. This is an important time frame to know since it has a direct bearing on the amount of cash you must have on hand to fund operations until customer payments start coming in to help to defray expenses.

Your Sales Channels

Salespeople are important people in your organization. Just as important, in many cases, are the people who support the sales team, such as the customer service personnel. You might want to have a few salespeople responsible for finding new customers but also have a number of support people who are solely responsible for servicing and selling to existing customers.

These two tasks, finding new customers and supporting existing customers, require different skills. The support person has a relatively routine job that revolves around meeting delivery deadlines and keeping account information up to date, but the new business salesperson must create opportunities on a daily basis.

Running an efficient and productive sales team requires focused attention, enthusiasm, and commitment. But you don't have to do it all by yourself. Hire the help you need to keep sales coming in.

There are a couple of different ways that your sales staff can reach new customers. You can use independent distributors or representatives to give your company rapid exposure, or you can build a direct sales force that deals directly with customers. Both approaches have pluses and minuses.

Distributors as Sales Agents

Using *distributors* or *independent representatives* removes you and your sales force from direct customer contact. The advantage is that you now have an in-place sales force of hundreds or thousands selling your product or service. A disadvantage is that it is more difficult to get customer feedback because you have a barrier between your company and the customer. Plus, remember that the representative will deal with the customer on your behalf, and if the representative does a poor job it will definitely reflect poorly on you.

It is critical to get customer feedback so you can accurately determine whether you should be developing new products or services. It is also important for you to know how happy your customers are with the distributor, rep, and your company. Can you trust the distributor or rep to make that assessment for you? In most cases, the answer is no, so you have to decide whether the additional sales from using this independent organization are worth giving up direct contact with customers. You might have to add personnel to your staff to acquire the information you would otherwise have obtained from your sales force.

Using distributors usually means you need to hire fewer salespeople to cover a comparable geographic area or market, allowing you to keep your personnel costs down. However, you need to interview and qualify distributors as carefully as you would a full-time salesperson because that distributor is going to represent your company. Make sure you are comfortable with that. Plus, you will be giving up a percentage of each sales dollar to pay for the sales rep or distributor fees. That percentage will vary between industries and product lines. In essence, you are trading a fixed cost (your own employees) for a variable cost (the commissions), the total amount of which varies with sales.

def•i•ni•tion

A **distributor** is a company that purchases products from you at a reduced rate, keeps them in inventory, and then sells those products to its own customers. Distributors are commonly used in commodity industries. Distributors make money on the difference between the sale price to the customer and the cost of the materials as purchased from your company.

A **independent representative** is a person or company who sells your products on your behalf. Reps do not purchase or inventory the products; they only sell them to their existing customer base. They make their money on the agreed-upon commissions earned from successful sales. You are responsible for credit collections.

Should You Use Your Own Sales Force?

When is it time to set up your own direct sales force instead of selling through distributors? That is a good question, and one each company must make based on its own set of circumstances.

Here are a few things to consider when making the choice:

1. The overhead associated with an internal sales force is substantially higher than with distributors. Those overhead costs eat into your profits every month, whether the sales are there to support that overhead or not.

2. You gain more control over your customer relations when you sell direct. This provides you with better management information for decision making.

3. Selling direct does not take advantage of established customer relationships your distributors may already have in place. Your direct sales force must generate its own contacts and relationships, and that can take a longer time to develop, delaying sales in the process.

Street Smarts

Perhaps a blending of in-house and distribution selling is the right approach for your company. You might sell directly in your local geography but choose to use distribution in more remote locations such as other states or in foreign countries.

4. An internal sales force you can fully train is often better able to handle sales

of highly technical products and services and will be less likely to make promises your company can't keep.

5. Some companies start out selling direct on a smaller scale until they determine the proper sales strategy for their offering. They then approach larger distributors about introducing their products or services through the distributor's sales channels.

You have more control and flexibility with an internal sales force, but you also have higher expenses. You need to examine your marketing strategy to decide which approach makes more sense for you right now.

Selling Services Instead of Products

Services provide an interesting sales situation. The customer is buying something of value, but when the project is completed, he or she might not have anything tangible to show for it. For example, the result of your service contract with a customer might appear in the form of a new organization structure, better-trained staff, a new logo design, or a piece of software. These items clearly contribute to the company's success, but they are less obvious to the customer.

def•i•ni•tion

The agreement on exactly what services will be provided to a customer is the **scope of work**. For instance, the scope of a project might be writing a press release. Mailing out all the press releases is beyond the scope of work, meaning that those activities were not included as part of the agreement and would have to be paid for separately.

You have to keep in mind that services solve people's problems through your expertise and experience. Because the customer doesn't receive a tangible product, he or she must walk away with the belief that he or she benefited from using your service. Benefit-oriented selling is an important part of any sale, but it is critical when selling services such as consulting or training. I sometimes provide a paper summary of work performed so that customer has something tangible in her hand to refer to later when looking at how much she paid me for services rendered.

Clearly defining the *scope of work* from the beginning is critical to success when selling services instead of products. Because the customer might not have something tangible at the end of a project, it is important to clearly define at what point the project is complete. More than one company has been left holding the bag when they submit an invoice that the customer feels is too high or should not be paid at all because the customer doesn't feel he got his money's worth. The company providing the service may have done everything it was asked to do, but if the customer thought he or she was getting something else, it becomes difficult to get paid.

To avoid such situations, the best policy is to get adequate detail, in writing, about what is to be done. In your proposal to your potential customer, state clearly what you are offering to do and at what price. Make the desired outcome as specific as possible, preferably including the delivery of a final report.

On the CD

A sample Project Agreement is enclosed on the CD as document 13-06.

If there is nothing tangible you can provide to signify the completion of a contract, such as with service contracts and warranties, set a specific time period during which your services are offered. After that period is up, your services stop.

Always avoid vague, ambiguous statements such as "We will edit the new corporate brochure until the customer is happy with it," which is a time bomb just waiting to explode. What happens after you've done 25 versions of the customer's brochure and he just can't make up his mind? Is your work done, or do you have to continue to edit and reedit until the customer is satisfied? If you state exactly how many rewrites you provide as part of the agreement, the answer is probably no—you don't have to keep working forever—but with vague statements, you will probably never get paid.

def•i•ni•tion

Milestones are important target dates or goals that help you track how well you're performing against your long-term business goals. Milestones can indicate that a specific percentage of a project has been completed, once a certain step has been taken, or they can provide evidence that the project is completed. These smaller percentage completion divisions enable you to bill for portions of the project as they are completed instead of having to wait until the entire project is finished.

Instead, use carefully chosen and specific wording, such as the wording I used for a sales brochure design proposal: "We will provide an initial concept design followed by a professionally created first draft and then a second final version of the brochure that includes any requested customer changes from the first draft." Establish _milestones_—that is, measurable targets or events that demonstrate that you have provided the service and reached your objective.

On the CD

The CD contains a sample Software Licensing Agreement (document 13-07) and a sample Contract Drafting Checklist (document 13-09).

Advance payments (retainers) or down payments are always good, but they are particularly valuable with contracts for service. People have convenient memories, and a little cash on the line always seems to keep the memory of both parties active and on track. It's also an excellent sales qualifier. Any prospect who is unwilling to pay a percentage of the total project cost is not someone you want to do business with. A charge of 25 percent is the suggested minimum, and 35 to 50 percent is not out of the question. Submit invoices regularly (determined in agreement with your customer) if you are billing on an hourly basis so you receive regular payments for your work.

For Your Plan

When writing the section of your plan dealing with sales, make sure that at a minimum you cover the following points:

◆ Explain whether your offering's sales process will be routine (commodity-like) or more complex (such as a technical sale).

◆ Define the required skill set and preferred personality type of your sales force (whether direct or through distribution) and why the direct/distribution decision was made. How will these people be trained not only in your sales process but also on your offering?

◆ Describe how customer service issues will be handled once the deal is closed and the next stage of business relationship begins.

◆ Explain the timeline for a typical sale and the various actions that will be taken at each stage of the sales cycle.

◆ Explain the compensation and commission structure that you plan to use for paying your sales force. Include as much information as you can about travel and other sales-related expenses.

◆ Outline the sales tracking and management procedures you intend to follow and how that procedure will be used for sales reporting to upper management, boards of directors, and investors.

◆ Explain how leads will be generated, how they will be followed up, and how lead tracking will be coordinated. Will your company use telemarketing, and if so, how?

- Lay out a contingency plan to cover the possibility that the initial sales plan does not work and how the determination will be made to move to your contingency "Plan B."

- Outline how your sales force will implement the marketing plan's strategy for winning sales from competitors. Deals will have to be won on more than your smiles, nice as they may be.

The Least You Need to Know

- Sales are necessary for a company to survive. If you are not highly sales motivated, then you should hire someone who is.

- Selling is a process, not an end in itself, and all company personnel must be sales oriented even if they are not officially in sales.

- Every sale must go through nine specific and sequential stages before the customer is willing to make a commitment.

- Closing and selling are not the same thing.

- Don't waste time on a prospect who doesn't meet the specified qualification criteria.

- Selling direct or through external sales representatives fills different needs and requires different approaches.

Production Plans That Produce Results

In This Chapter

◆ The importance of your production plan

◆ Production considerations for product and service companies

◆ Production personnel issues

◆ The importance of automation

◆ Setting expectations

The activity level on the manufacturing floor properly impressed Vickie. Tony, her friend and the business owner, had taken his company from the idea stage and turned it into a full-blown production house.

"Wow," she said. "You really have something going on here. Stuff is stacked every-where, and you literally have people climbing the walls to get at your products. This sure looks good!"

"Well, looks can be deceiving," replied Tony with a somber look in his eye. "The reason those people are climbing the walls is because I didn't allocate enough space for inventory storage of finished products. We had to put a shelving system in place so we could stack our finished inventory along walls instead of in an inventory stor-age area as I initially wanted."

"Why are the wall storage areas color coded?"

"The red areas are for products that have not passed in-process inspection. The blue areas are for finished products that did not initially pass final inspection, have been reworked, and are now awaiting reinspection. The green areas are for finished products that are ready for sale and shipment."

Tony paused for a moment and then continued. "Not properly planning and realistically esti-mating the required square footage forced me to hire three people who do nothing but shuttle things from the walls to the production floor and back again."

"It is pretty crowded in here," was Vickie's comment, reality now sinking in. "And the activity level is pretty intense. Why not just move to another facility?"

"I got a great lease rate by signing up for a three-year minimum. I have 12 more months on the lease that I would have to pay even if we moved to another facility. The money analysis just doesn't justify the move. So here we are: one busy, big, bustling, occasionally irate family wait-ing for our lease to expire. This is a mistake I will never make again."

No matter what you plan to do, whether it is produce products or provide services, there is some type of process that will be involved. The more efficiently you plan and manage this process, the more easily you will be able to grow as your sales grow and the lower your costs of production will be.

If you plan to sell gizmos, then whoever funds your project must be convinced that you can build the gizmo you plan to sell and to the prescribed specifications. As a result, it is important to understand the production aspects of your business because if you can't produce, you won't get paid.

Production in Product and Service Environments

Think of production as the process of fulfilling the commitments that your company makes to its customers. This may entail combining raw materials, labor, and manu-facturing equipment into a finished good that can be sold. Or it could mean having nurses, a waiting room, and staging areas for a doctor's office so that customers are seen on time and with professionalism.

For example, if you are building music CDs, you have a few components that add up to your finished product: the CD itself, the jewel case in which the CD is shipped, the paper inserts, and a plastic wrapper. You must combine all these pieces so that the final product can be sold in a music store. The process does not vary from one CD to the next. As a result, you can look for ways to streamline the assembly process and develop processes that make this repeatable assembly as efficient as possible.

This type of production involves routine tasks that do not vary much from one CD to the next, except for perhaps the specific insert and CD. The more CDs that are produced, the better the assembly people become with the process and the more efficient the production process becomes. This increased efficiency translates into decreased manufacturing costs, which provide higher profits if you can keep your prices constant.

This process seems pretty straightforward for a product-based business, but what happens when you provide services, which is what most small business owners start out doing? The equation shifts: materials become a very small portion of the process and the expertise and labor portion becomes dominant.

Product businesses are based on a process that is relatively independent of the people performing the tasks; service businesses often get their work because the client wants a specific person performing the task. The process and ingredients are different, but some similarities make the analysis of the production process easier to handle.

Service businesses rely heavily on the expertise of the personnel. The jobs typically performed by service personnel are nonroutine in nature, meaning that each time the job is done it is potentially different from the next. This doesn't mean that there aren't similarities, but to use the CD-packaging analogy presented earlier, the jewel case might be a different color, the CD a slightly different shape or more than one in a case, the cover literature might need to be edited for each CD, and special handling instructions may be required. The overall process of putting it together is the same, but the specific steps required in making it all fit will likely involve tweaking for each CD.

The similarity in developing product and service processes is that you always want to find the common tasks involved in each process. This commonality presents an opportunity for applying automated, money-saving strategies to this stage of the process. Of one thing you can be sure: you will never reach high production volumes if everything you produce is a custom act of creation—you must take this into account when establishing your offering prices.

Here are some key points to remember when defining your production process:

◆ The more times you do something, the more efficient you become at doing it.

◆ Increased efficiency usually translates into reduced costs and increased profits.

Ed's Lessons Learned

If you look at a doctor's office, you see a blending of routine and nonroutine tasks and how they are delegated to the proper personnel. For example, taking temperature, blood pressure, and weight and performing other routine tasks are handled by a nurse, whereas the nonroutine tasks—the examination and evaluation of each patient—are performed by the doctor. The patient might be in the office for an hour, but the doctor might only be with the patient for 15 minutes. In this way, the doctor can see four patients in an hour instead of only one, which would be the case if she performed all the routine tasks on her own.

- The more routine (repetitive) the task, the less skilled the personnel must be to perform it and the easier it is to ensure consistent quality.

- The more tasks vary each time they're performed, the less routine the task and the higher the personnel skill level required to get it done correctly.

- Production in product-based businesses tends to be more routine, making mass volume efficiencies the goal.

- Service-based businesses tend to be more time dependent because the overall project variations can fluctuate from one time a task is performed to the next. It is difficult to estimate the amount of time something will take if you have never done it before.

- Service-based businesses should look for a methodology that makes the nonroutine tasks more routine, allowing less skilled personnel to perform the tasks without compromising quality. More skilled people can then focus on the nonroutine aspects that more fully utilize their higher skill level.

- Personal customer contact and relationships are critical to a service business (would you go to a doctor you don't like?), whereas product performance and quality are critical in a product business. (Have you ever met the designer of your MP3 player?)

Are You a Mass Producer or a Job Shop?

It's time to add another level to the analysis process. Hang in there with me because this evaluation procedure becomes second nature after a short while. The more you understand your operation, the more likely you are to make it as reliable, efficient, and profitable as possible without sacrificing the overall quality of your offering.

This section compares *mass producer* to *job shop* environments. If you are continually producing the same thing, you are a mass producer. For example, a company that produces candles is a mass producer in that once set up to make candles, the process might make thousands, or even millions, in a single run. Can you imagine how good you get at something after you have done it a few million times?

Job shop environments require more customization to complete each job. This doesn't mean that the same underlying technologies are not used. It only means that they are used in a different way for each job. For example, creating a custom software package is a job shop environment in that the software is developed once for a specific customer. You are not going to take the same software and resell it to others since few other people will need *exactly* what you developed for earlier customers. You might still perform the software programming operations using a specific programming language, but the software application itself is customized for each customer. Now, if you create the software and then package it for sale on retail shelves, the software creation process is nonroutine, but the process of packaging the software and shipping it to a retail outlet is routine for each software box shipped.

def•i•ni•tion

Mass producers continually produce the same products (routine). **Job shop** operations require more customization to produce each product (nonroutine).

Ed's Lessons Learned

I have some friends who run a small business that specializes in custom injection plastic molding of very large parts. Once the process is set up, they might produce only one, two, or three parts for a customer. This is clearly not a mass production environment, but they have a unique process methodology that allows them to create the required parts in a reliable and efficient fashion. If they based their pricing model on mass production economies, they would be out of business. They realize that their offering is unique and charge the premiums needed to cover the costs associated with a job-shop environment, yet they also ensure that the customer does not get gouged.

Linking Purchasing, Production, and Marketing Forecasts

Get ready; here comes an automation speech. If you have ever worked in a product manufacturing environment that did everything by hand, you understand the importance of automating your purchasing and inventory processes.

This can get pretty complicated, but it is really important, so bear with me. You need to order parts from your vendors before you can build your product. This means that you must have quantity projections about the products to be built. In addition, each of the components that you include in your product has some delivery lead time requirement from your vendors. This lead time can be as short as overnight for a standard part, such as a screw, or as long as several months for a custom casting part, such as the frame of a bicycle. This means that before the components can be purchased, you must know how many you plan to build, which means that you must know how many your sales and marketing people plan to sell. And more specialized parts are generally more difficult to find and more expensive to purchase.

The service equivalent of a specialized part is finding a person with the unique skill set needed to address your customer needs. You must either hire a person with the required skills, hire a less capable person and train her to have the required skills, or train one of your internal personnel to have the proper skills. In any case, lead time involved with getting the right person with the right skills must be considered. You even have a lead time involved if you already employ someone who has the proper skills. Why? Because if you are operating profitably, that person is already busy on another project and might have to finish it before he or she can start on the new one.

Oh, by the way, you also need to ensure that you have the financial means to purchase the components (or hire the personnel) because there will be some manufacturing lead time on your side before the product gets out the door and into customer hands and you receive the payment. Before you flip out, take a look at Chapters 20 and 21 and reaffirm to yourself that cash is king, credit is queen, and luck is the joker.

How can you manage the critical gap between your sales forecast and your production and purchasing requirements? You either need to handle this gap in a rigorous, yet manual, manner at first, pay someone to develop custom software, or scour the industry for a software package that addresses your specific company needs. These packages are out there, but you might pay thousands of dollars finding the package that is right for you. They are generally referred to as manufacturing requirement packages (MRP).

Is an MRP software package worth the initial investment? It depends on how large you plan to grow and how substantial your initial funding is. Paying a lot for the right production control software package could deplete your cash reserves to the point that you jeopardize the company. Clearly not a good idea. But those with aspirations of growing a large manufacturing company want to take a hard look at automating with an MRP system from early on in your company's life. At the least, start today setting up a paper tracking system that is easily adapted to an automated MRP system. If you don't, and you are successful, you will likely lose sales, customers, profits, and sleep as you deal with the intense demands that arise from rapid manufacturing growth. Make sure that you hitch your MRP wagon to a solid software product provider who will be around in the future to keep your software purchase reliable and contemporary.

In keeping with my "automate from the beginning" philosophy, I suggest that you either buy a package (if possible) or train yourself to think of your company as a process. It starts with the sales lead to the order and continues through purchasing, production, shipping, receipt of the product by the customer, receipt of the payment check from the customer, to the final cashing of the check. Ultimately, it also includes generating the operational and financial reports on a periodic basis.

Ask another manufacturer in your area for a facility tour just to see how it deals with its particular production environment. If you are building the same type of products, such as electronics, you might be able to learn from each other. Ask the manufacturer about the software it uses for MRP. It might save you headaches down the road.

> **Ed's Lessons Learned**
>
> Make sure that you spot-check your MRP reports to ensure that the numbers flowing from sales to production to purchasing make business sense based on your experience. The longer you are in business, the more accurately you will be able to estimate your sales forecasts, which better ensures proper production goal setting. But periodically spot-check the accuracy of your operational systems.

Create a Production Flow Chart

You don't have to become a process engineer to build many products, but you should have an idea of how the process flow works and what sections need special attention. This involves a big sheet of paper, or the use of a software package such as Microsoft Excel, Microsoft Project, or other software packages with flow chart drawing capabilities.

Map out the entire process on a piece of paper, and note which steps are routine or nonroutine. Also map out the weak links, or *gating items*, in the process. These are the items that restrict your ability to produce in higher volumes (mass production) or produce in less time (job shop). Making these gating items more efficient always pays huge dividends later, and you need to watch them like a hawk, for these are the items that can also put you out of business or keep you from growing.

> **def•i•ni•tion**
>
> A **gating item** is an item that limits the overall efficiency of the process. If this item's efficiency is increased, the overall process generally becomes more efficient. Track these carefully.

For example, a few years ago a large airplane manufacturer went through a huge sales growth spurt where its sales and marketing people sold many new planes to several foreign governments. Good news? Not for this company. They couldn't get many of their critical parts from their vendors in time to meet the production schedules. They had to shut down their plant for a few weeks while they waited for the gating item parts to arrive. Here is a company with a stellar sales record and a black eye simply because it outsold its production capability due to gating item parts.

> **On the CD**
>
> A sample Notice of Rejection of Delivered Goods is enclosed on the CD as document 14-01.

Finally, look at your process map, and determine the amount of space needed for each stage of production. Don't forget that the raw inventory parts you receive from your vendors need storage space along with the finished products. In addition, products that go through many stages of production need interim storage space along with those products rejected during the production process. If you don't take a detailed look at the space requirements early, you might end up like our friend in the opening story who had employees literally climbing the walls.

Successful Project Management

I am not going to go into the details of project management in this chapter, other than to point you in the direction of understanding basic project charts and tools. Check out another book in this series called *The Complete Idiot's Guide to Project Management*, an excellent introduction to the subject. I suggest using it to add meat to the skeleton outline provided in this section.

A *Gantt chart* shows you the relationship between the various project components and their required completion sequence (see the following figure). I create my Gantt charts using a spreadsheet package such as Microsoft Excel with the tracked items listed in the left column and the column headings labeled as the weeks, or days, on which each stage of the project is to be completed. I then note the dates for completion with special symbols such as "M" for milestones or "S" for start and "F" for finish for tasks that take a period of time to complete. You can use more complicated packages like Microsoft Project, but learning the package can take more time than is needed at this stage.

The *critical path analysis* allows you to determine the process bottlenecks so that you can keep an eye on them. Project management software packages perform this critical path analysis for you. You don't have to go overboard on all this stuff in the beginning, but if you don't get a realistic picture of your space and time requirements, you can be seriously hit later when you get into actual production. Plus, it is a waste to plan your production around a higher level of *throughput* and then not ensure that you have enough capability to handle the required critical path items. It is hard to say too much about the importance of knowing and managing properly your critical path items.

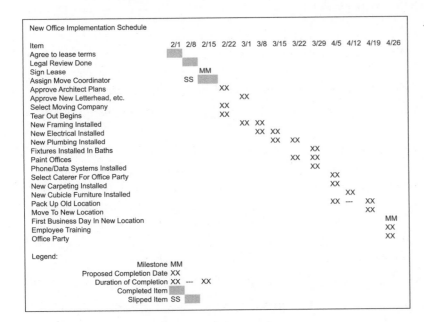

A sample Gantt chart.

By the way, the more detail you have in your planning, the more likely you are to get money from your investors. The details show them that you have thought through the steps and understand what you are doing. Without the details, you are winging it with their money. Think about it. Would you rather give money to someone who has spent the time thinking about the details or to someone who says, "Trust me; it will be okay"?

Maintaining Quality

Nothing will put you out of business faster than being a new company that gets a reputation for bad quality. Happy customer referrals are critical to the success of your business, and if you let the quality suffer, your referrals will become negative instead of positive. Ouch—then bye-bye!

I recently gave a speech to a group of quality professionals on the importance of instilling quality in small business environments. It forced me to formalize some of my thoughts on the topic. The talk was well received and they encouraged me to pass my thoughts on to my readers. So here is a synopsis of the high points from my talk for your consideration and specific application to your company environment and plan writing:

◆ Know what you sell and what your customers buy. Make sure that you or someone you trust inspects the critical qualities that your customers expect from your product or service before your customers see your offering. This applies to both product and service companies. If your company offers massage services, get a massage by each of your massage personnel every now and then to ensure that they meet your standards. If you offer tax preparation services, have one of your senior people randomly spot check the returns to ensure that they are accurate.

◆ Never let your customers become your final product inspection team. Make sure your product or service meets your expectations before you let them see it. Customers never forget that you sold them deficient goods.

Ed's Lessons Learned

Cisco Systems, the communications products manufacturer, has set up annual surveys of both customers and employees as a way of gauging satisfaction. Employees are paid a bonus or raise based on the results of their respective quality surveys. In typical Cisco fashion, they automated the survey process to make it simple and fast. Perhaps there are a few lessons here for your company as well.

◆ *Underpromise* and *overdeliver*. This is where I see many small businesses suffer. Because you are small, you might feel that you have to overpromise to compete with a larger company. You know that you are overpromising when your evenings and weekends are tied up doing extra stuff for a customer, and you are cursing yourself for having promised things that are not part of what you normally offer or you simply cannot provide. If what you promised must be there as part of the standard offering, then make the proper production changes and set up to include it as part of your normal operation. If not, do not overpromise unless you have a lot of free time. Just be careful to not "underpromise" so much that you lose deals that you credibly should have won. Keep looking for the balance, and you will find it.

◆ Never *overpromise* and *underdeliver*. You can deliver exactly what all of your brochures promote and still have an unhappy customer if the customer was promised additional items that were not delivered. This is an easy problem to fix. Promise only what you can deliver or realize that you and your company will continually be jumping through hoops complying with "loose lips" promises.

◆ Personally spot-check the products or services before they leave your business, and let everyone know that you do it. This tends to keep employees on their toes and ensures that your toes don't get stepped on. Perhaps you should set up some type of financial incentive system that is tied to acceptable quality levels.

◆ Work with customers up front to establish their expectations. This is particularly true for service agreements, or you can find yourself working for a client forever, with the best of intentions, not getting paid for it, and still having an unsatisfied customer even though you delivered what you thought the customer wanted. For example: "My company agrees to supply your company with a draft of the document, circulate the draft to the client for comments, and then incorporate those comments into the final draft." Notice how only one level of revision is included in this agreement; this means you do not waste time and resources endlessly revising your work.

◆ Define specific, concrete expectations, and do not leave them general. General (not recommended): "To deliver a product or service to the customer's satisfaction." Concrete (recommended): "To deliver a product that meets the specifications as outlined on product specification sheet 01-A, dated 09/27/2007."

def•i•ni•tion

When you **overpromise**, you make a commitment to a customer that exceeds what your company is set up to deliver. When you **underdeliver**, you deliver less than that which was promised. This behavior is almost guaranteed to generate a nasty phone call and possibly a poor recommendation from your customer.

Savvy business owners may **underpromise**—that is, promise to deliver less to the customer than they actually intend to deliver. People don't get mad when they receive more than they expected for the same price.

For Your Plan

When preparing the production portion of your plan, make sure that you consider the following points:

◆ Make sure that you understand the routine/nonroutine aspects of your offering and adjust your operation and personnel accordingly. This approach helps to ensure higher quality and avoids wasteful personnel spending.

◆ Spell out how and where you intend to perform your manufacturing and production activities.

◆ Estimate the product and labor costs associated with your offerings, taking into account the cost decreases that typically come from higher volume and more experience. This information is critically important to setting your prices and maintaining healthy profit margins.

◆ Present any labor- or skill-related issues that directly affect the production process.

◆ Explain how you intend to define and maintain an appropriate level of quality for your intended customer audience.

◆ Present a flow chart of the operational process from order receipt until the offering is received by the customer. Specify the gating components, skills, or operational steps associated with your production environment and how you plan to address these critically important concerns.

◆ It is common for the production plan to present the details associated with lead generation, order receipt, processing, invoicing, and collections. They are all part of the production process associated with a healthy business. Including this in your production section instead of in the marketing sales section is not uncommon and is recommended by some.

◆ Include an explanation of how you intend to finance and create new offerings, whether service or product oriented. At some point, a new offering must come along to take the place of the ones you initially offer, and it is good to present some thought in this regard.

The Least You Need to Know

- You must understand how your company creates and delivers its offerings and then ensure that the quality that makes you successful is an integral part of the process.

- Understand the routine and nonroutine aspects of your business, and assign appropriately skilled personnel accordingly.

- Automate as much as possible from the beginning if not cost prohibitive.

- Map out your production process and specify the personnel, raw materials, space, time, and equipment needed at each step of the process.

- Underpromise and overdeliver.

- Know the relationship between the time needed to produce your offering and when and how your customers buy.

- Spot-check quality yourself and never let your customers do your final quality inspection.

13

The Good and Bad News About Employees

In This Chapter

- ◆ Why adding people to your organization can be a good thing
- ◆ The value and risk of a personnel manual
- ◆ Effective and legal interviewing procedures
- ◆ When a contractor is really an employee
- ◆ Test-driving employees before hiring

"Tell me this again," said Julie. "Didn't you smell it when you went by her desk?"

"Sure I did," said Bill, the company lawyer. "But so what? There's nothing in your company procedures manual that covers drinking on the job."

"Because of that, I can't fire her?" asked Julie. "She carries a bottle in her purse. She takes a nip in the bathroom on a regular basis. I have even accidentally picked up one of her coffee cups to find that she was drinking Irish coffee. She's drunk on the job, and I want her gone!"

"That is understandable but not legal. Has her drinking affected her job performance in any way? Can you definitely point to business lost because of her drinking? Has it disrupted the normal flow of business in such a way that it has cost the company money?"

"I know that it must have happened, but I can't point to a specific instance," said Julie. "So you're telling me that I'm stuck with her because firing her would open us up to a wrongful termination suit based on our not having a no-drinking policy in our manual."

"Pretty much. You need to watch her closely and look for signs of poor performance that can then be documented. Then you can let her go for poor performance. In the interim, you should never mention the drinking problem to her and act as though nothing is wrong. Otherwise, you play right into her attorney's hands when you finally let her go. Sorry."

Adding employees represents a great leap for your business; there is so much demand for your product or service that you need to expand your staff. Yet managing other people brings with it a number of issues that you don't have to deal with when you work alone. In this chapter, I'll show you how to manage and lead your employees—successfully.

When You're Successful, You'll Need Help

If you follow all the great guidance throughout this book and add your own special flair, you will probably become so successful that you just won't be able to do it alone. At that point, you need to add employees to your organization. It might be only a clerical person who handles billing and answers the telephone or a complete staff of people who handle all those new projects you just brought in as a result of your incredible marketing skills.

In either case, you need to address the new challenges associated with running an organization that now has staff members. There are lots of ways to find employees, but before I jump into how to find the right employees, how to manage them, and all that detailed stuff, let me present a few bigger issues for you to consider:

1. You have been on your own, and possibly working alone, since you started your company. Make sure that you actually need an employee for functional reasons, not simply because you want someone around the office for business companionship. Have you gotten to the point that you are losing business because you don't have enough help? That is a cost, not just personal justification for hiring a new employee.

2. Employees cost money and must pay for themselves either today or in the near future. Once you hire an employee, you assume the responsibility for paying him

regularly, no matter what the business's financial condition is. Even if you have a really poor month, you still have to sign those paychecks to your employees. Are you ready to absorb that expense, or would it be smarter to push yourself a little more for a short while and build up a nest egg? Is the lack of that employee costing you money yet?

3. When you add people to your organization, you inherit a responsibility for their financial support. If you aren't making enough money to support yourself, you probably can't afford to support someone else.

4. You become the last employee to be paid if the company has cash flow problems. Are you ready to accept not getting a paycheck for a week or two (or three or four or ten) without resenting the other employees who have gotten paychecks?

5. Employees take up space, use telephones, and make decisions; you must expand your business operations to include them. They need to take responsibilities from you to help the company grow. Are you ready to let go enough to use them effectively?

6. Have you ever managed people before? Are you familiar with the challenges of encouraging and leading employees? Do you need to take some classes in effective supervision before taking the plunge? Even if you have managed workers before, a refresher is probably a good idea.

7. Know that a small business is different from a large corporation in that one employee out of a total of two makes up 50 percent of the personnel. If that person has troubles, 50 percent of the company operations are in trouble. Be aware of the large effect one person can have on your business, your customers, and your earnings.

8. If you are in a service business, make sure that your employees reflect the proper attitude and image you have worked hard to establish. A few weeks of poor telephone attitude toward your customers can unravel years of consistent service on your part. If you are really lucky, one of your established clients will tell you about the problem first, but few customers ever complain; they just leave! Teach your employees early about the level of service they are expected to provide and reinforce it with your own actions.

9. Your customers will need to adapt to working with someone on your staff. Make sure that the new employee maintains the same level of concern and dedication to customer satisfaction. The best thing that could happen to your business is for your customers to like working with your employee as much or more than they liked working with you. Now you can focus on other business issues besides

customer satisfaction. It is a good sign when customers want to work with your employees instead of you, assuming that you and the customer are still on good terms. This means that you are successfully transferring your unique style throughout the organization.

10. Don't forget that employees can always (and probably eventually will) find another job. This is your business, and you will be around long after they are gone, unless you are very lucky and find the right long-term fit with an employee. If an employee leaves, you inherit her decisions. This means that commitments made by an employee can obligate you long after that employee is gone. You, on the other hand, can't just leave and find another job because this *is* your job. Period. Find that balance between delegation and monitoring that provides the employee with effective freedom to make decisions while ensuring that the decisions made will work for you as well.

11. There are legal issues related to having employees that you could ignore when it was only you working at the company. Some form of a personnel policies manual would help you avoid situations such as the one Julie had in the introductory scenario. On the other hand, personnel policies that are too elaborate can get you into unnecessary trouble.

Watch Out!

You might be tempted to hire a friend or relative so you'll have someone on your staff whom you can trust. Be sure he or she is qualified for the job. Don't let trust be the primary reason you hire him or her or your company will suffer. Go over the details of what you really know about him or her, compared to what you have simply assumed or heard since you first met. The last thing you want is a surprise that causes you to fire a friend or relative, which disrupts the business, ends a friendship, and makes holidays even more stressful than they already are.

I have had both excellent employees and poor employees work with me over the years and have found that poor performers have a much bigger impact in smaller companies than they do in huge corporations. Larger companies can afford the luxury of one or two poor performers; smaller companies cannot. If you find employees with performance problems, such as employees who can't seem to do the work right or at a reasonable pace, let them go quickly before they do serious damage to your business.

Unfortunately, the tendency in small businesses is to take care of employees as if they were members of your family. I say unfortunately because small business owners tend to keep trouble employees on for a much longer time than do larger corporations.

One of the biggest mistakes I have seen in small business is when owners are "fast to hire and slow to fire." You should do just the opposite, be "slow to hire and fast to fire." You simply cannot afford to have the wrong people working for your small business for any substantial length of time.

Never forget that you started this business. It is yours, not your employees'. Try to let go of the daily decisions so that they can carve a place for themselves in the operation of the business, or you will wind up with morale problems down the road. Remember, however: you sign the checks, co-sign all company debts, and ultimately make the big decisions. They might also need to be reminded of this as you give them increasing responsibilities and they naturally take more initiative. How you do this is a matter of style; don't be too heavy-handed—an overbearing boss can easily drive away a good employee. (Besides, they obviously know that you own the company.) It is an interesting balancing act to promote employee initiative while also making sure that the employee doesn't get you into financial trouble.

Watch Out!

If your services company only makes money when you are there, then a vacation becomes much more costly than the trip itself. You're really paying for the actual vacation expenses, lost company revenues as a result of not being at work, and the time needed to get caught up once you return to the office. The solution? Set up your pricing so that the times you work cover the times that you are off. You could also define your operation so that the business makes money even when you are not there. This solution could involve outsourcing of routine operational components, hiring employees, or possibly more effective use of the Internet.

Once employees take on more responsibility for the company's activities, you might wonder how you ever did everything yourself. There isn't a more satisfying business experience than to find a series of orders, invoices, projects, and bank deposits that your employees created without your involvement. To call in from a well-deserved vacation and find thousands of dollars worth of revenues and profits coming into the company while you are gone is the essence of small business success.

Your business needs to be able to create revenue without your involvement, or it will never grow beyond your own abilities. That can only happen when employees get involved and have the freedom to act on their own, within certain guidelines you set.

If you want to keep your company small, then you might never need another employee, other than an occasional relative or temporary helper to handle clerical stuff. If you want to grow so the company works on a relatively independent basis, then you need employees. Accept that as a reality and plan for it in advance. That way, you can be on the lookout for the right person and get him or her onboard when the timing is right.

Ed's Lessons Learned

I tend to set dollar thresholds under which employees can make decisions within their business area before they have to contact me. For example, I might let an office manager make any decision under $250 on his or her own, up to a total of $1,000 in a month. I then review the purchases with the employee at the end of the month. In this way, I let the employee know what I expect and teach him or her how to make decisions that I would have made on my own.

This is beneficial to the employees in that they get to work with some autonomy, and it is better for me because I don't get bothered about each expense. If money is tight, I drop the thresholds. Or I start the employees at $100 per purchase and $400 per month, and increase the limits as I become more comfortable with their decision-making ability.

Good Help Isn't Hard to Find

Depending on your personnel needs, there are a few avenues you can take when you begin seriously looking for employees. First, you can try out potential employees through a part-time employment arrangement before making a full-time hiring commitment. You can also hire candidates for a specific project, as *independent contractors*, and see how they work out. Finally, temporary help agencies can serve as excellent sources of candidates who have already been screened for your particular job opening.

Other sources include college and university co-op programs where students learn on the job through structured programs that help them apply what they've learned in their course work, as well as high school programs that match interested students with part-time employers. Many colleges and high schools also encourage students to apply for internships during summer and winter vacations, where they work for an employer full-time during those breaks from school. Although internships are generally shorter term than co-op programs, you can have a student

def•i•ni•tion

An **independent contractor** is a temporary worker hired on a per-project basis. Often the contractor will sign a contract specifying the length of the project, the work that needs to be done, and the payment for that work. They may cost more in the short term, but they are not on payroll when their short project ends, which saves you money. If you keep hiring them back, then it might be time to consider them for a full-time position.

help on some important projects during a summer vacation. All these options are excellent ways to give students a chance to gain real-world experience while benefiting from their efforts at your company. You will typically use them for more routine tasks.

As your operation becomes more stable, you will want full-time employees on your staff so that you are not constantly having to train new hires that may only be around for a few months. Take your time finding the right people.

Start out the hiring process by getting a clear picture of what you want this person to do. Write out a detailed job description. Then picture the personality type you want in that job. Ask other business owners about personnel that they have worked with that might be right for your job opening. Place ads in the paper and prepare yourself for hours, or days, of reading resumés and interviewing applicants.

Independent Contractors

Independent contractors come in all shapes and sizes (literally). As with temporary agencies, you hire a contractor for a particular job, and you let him or her go when the job's done. Contractors expect to be let go at some point, so the parting is rarely accompanied by hard feelings. Typically, the length of a project is specified in a contract when a contractor is brought in, so there are no surprises about what happens when the work is done. (She leaves unless you want to hire her to work on a different project.)

Generally, these folks have an area of expertise such as accounting, computer graphics training, or specific business skills you know your company needs. You must qualify a contractor on your own and decide whether that person is the best for your specific project. The working relationship is between your company and the contractor directly, but she works as a consultant to your firm, not as an employee. You have no ongoing obligations to the contractor.

On the CD

A sample Independent Contractor Agreement is included on the CD as document 13-01. Also see the bonus "Employee vs. Independent Contractor Checklist" form.

One of the major differences between working with a contract employee and a temporary employee is that your company directly hires the contractor to do a specific task. A temporary employee is actually an employee of the temporary agency, and this agency "rents" her to you for a fee. With independent contractors, you spell out up front exactly how long you want them to work, on what project, to do what specific types of activities, and at what cost. It is also a good idea to spell out the risks that you expect the contractor to assume, such as liability insurance and all associated payroll taxes.

Temporary employees, on the other hand, really don't have any part in setting the terms of their work with you; their employer discusses those with you and then provides the individual best suited to help you out. In many cases, temporary employment contracts are open ended, so you can end them whenever you want. With an independent contractor, you work out the specific end date of the project up front.

Expect to pay more for the contractor than a temp. One reason is that the contractor is operating as a business owner, too, and must cover all his business costs with each project. Typical price ranges for writing services start at $15 to $45 per hour, document layout and design contractor fees range between $20 to $75 per hour, and professional services such as attorneys range from $65 to $250 per hour. The beauty of working with a contractor is that the person comes in with well-developed skills that are immediately applied to your situation with little or no training needed. You get the desired results quickly and efficiently. They may also have extensive expertise in a given area that you can use long after the contractor is gone.

I generally learn a lot from working with a professional independent contractor. The good ones know their stuff and put it to work quickly. Finding a good one is a lot like finding a prince: you have to kiss a number of toads before you find the right one. When you find the right one, he or she appreciates working for you on a regular basis, and you are relieved to have someone you trust and professionally respect. If you provide them with regular business, you might talk to them about a discounted rate—sort of like a quantity discount. They don't have to spend time on marketing and sales, which saves them money as well.

Fellow business owners are a tremendous referral source for specific contractors who do their jobs well. Start asking for referrals even before you have a need to use their services so that when the need arises, you have a list of qualified contractors from which to choose. You will probably need these people when some type of emergency arises, so it helps to have the relationships already established before the crisis.

When hiring an independent contractor, remember that the IRS has specific criteria that determine whether a person is a contractor or an employee. If you hire someone as an independent contractor but the IRS decides later that she was really an employee of your company, you might be liable for past payroll taxes, Social Security payments, and penalties. Be clear up front about how the IRS would characterize your relationship before taking chances with an independent contractor. See the "When a Contractor Is Really an Employee" section later in this chapter for a detailed list of criteria.

Putting Retired Folk to Work

Here is an idea for you: tap into the huge reservoir of people who have professional experience but who no longer work outside the home. This includes housewives and househusbands who now take care of their children during the day. It also includes retired men and women who might want to earn some extra money. Frequently, these workers bring substantial expertise to their work and present few personnel headaches.

In exchange for these talents, these employees require that you be pretty flexible on their work hours. People taking care of their kids need to work around school schedules, and the retired don't want work to cut too deeply into their free time, but they still want to feel like their work makes a difference. I have found these groups easy to work with and a great personnel financial investment as part-time workers. Check with the local PTA for people who are active with the schools and ask around. You might just be surprised who you find.

Take Your Employee for a Test Drive

Just as you can date for a while before deciding to get married, you can test potential job candidates before making a long-term commitment. There are several intermediate steps you can try before taking the plunge.

Because everyone is always on his best behavior during job interviews, it is very difficult to determine whether a person is a good fit for your company in that setting. You need to observe the job candidate in other situations before deciding whether to hire him.

Part-time employment is a great "try-and-buy" approach where you get to test the water with the prospective employee. Use the employee 20 to 30 hours per week, and see how you work together. If it works, you have someone who comes on full-time with a lot of background and who would otherwise need training at full-time rates. If it doesn't work, you can count your blessings and let him or her go.

 On the CD

A sample At-Will Employment Application is included on the CD as document 13-02.

def•i•ni•tion

A **probationary period** is a length of time (usually 90 days) during which both you and a new employee have a chance to see whether the employee is right for the position and vice versa. Before the 90 days are up, the employee is either let go or hired on an official basis.

Checking out college and high school students through co-op programs where the student works for you a set number of hours per week for a semester or during a summer vacation is another option for testing potential full-time employees. After working with a student for several months, you can decide whether to offer him or her a full-time job after graduation.

At a minimum, you should establish a 90-day *probationary period* that every new employee must endure. A probationary period is a time for both you and your new employee to decide whether this is the best job for him or her. Before the 90 days are up, you must let this person go, or he or she automatically becomes a full-fledged employee, which means entitlement to any of the benefits you give your other employees. In other words, on day 91, this person automatically becomes an employee.

There's no reason to rush right into hiring full-time employees if you feel more comfortable taking it slowly. Try some of these approaches to checking your potential employees before making a big commitment to them.

When a Contractor Is Really an Employee

It is incredible how complicated it becomes to determine whether a person is an independent contractor or an employee. The same person performing the same work under slightly different circumstances can be considered an employee, costing you much more financially than an independent contractor.

The IRS tends to lean on the side of finding workers as employees, not independent contractors, because it means they get more in employment taxes from you, the employer. Be sure you're clear on whether you have an employee or independent contractor working for you.

Street Smarts

Get your hands on IRS Publication 937 on independent contractors to determine whether you have employees or contractors (www.irs.gov).

The basic test to determine whether someone is an employee is whether you control the person's daily activities or whether she makes those decisions herself. A person is an independent contractor if she is held responsible only for results, and if her methods, hours of work, location at which the work is performed, and tools are under her control and not dictated by you.

Does the person perform services for more than one company? Is she responsible for her own profit and loss and is she used for specific expertise applied to specific projects instead of just showing up during regular time frames? The more restrictions that you apply to a contractor relationship, the more likely that contractor is considered an employee.

The IRS has a set of criteria that they consider when defining an employee's status. Use these criteria to substantiate your claim that a person is a contractor instead of an employee.

Make sure you have a written subcontractor agreement with the person that clearly spells out the separate liability relationship. A sample contractor agreement is included on the companion CD. Make sure that the contractor provides his own liability insurance and worker compensation insurance, or you might find yourself the recipient of a nasty legal suit if the contractor gets hurt on the job.

More Employees, More Restrictions

All companies are not created equal. Depending on the state where you are doing business and how many employees you have, you will be affected by different rules and regulations. One way to deal with these various state and federal government regulations is to develop a *company policy manual*, or employee manual, for everyone's reference.

A company policy manual spells out what the company expects of its employees and what they can expect in terms of benefits and other topics related to employment. New employees receive a copy of the policy manual and are responsible for adhering to these policies. A well-defined policy manual clears up employee confusion because everyone is given the same information. It also helps specify who should be contacted with follow-up questions. For smaller companies, the policy manual becomes the personnel policy manual. Know the laws of your individual state, and create the proper policy manual to address those state laws.

A few personnel issues apply to all companies, regardless of the number of employees. You should clearly spell out the number of company holidays provided to employees each year and the amount of vacation and sick time a person is eligible to take during the year. If you have other company policies that employees need to know, state them in the policy manual.

def•i•ni•tion

A **company policy manual** spells out what the company expects of its employees and what they can expect in terms of benefits and other topics related to employment. New employees are given a copy of the policy manual and are made aware that they will be held responsible for adhering to these policies.

Drafting your own handbook is cheaper than having an attorney write it, but a legal review is essential to make sure you haven't made significant errors.

State and federal laws kick in at different company size levels:

◆ If you have fewer than four employees (depending upon the state), you are the master of your domain and can hire, fire, and reward pretty much as you see fit.

◆ As an employer, you have to worry about a wide array of federal laws that address discrimination and other important personnel-related issues.

◆ If you have 50 or more employees, you need the same level of policy manual as IBM or General Motors. It must include policies on family and medical leave, harassment, drug-related issues, discrimination, and virtually any other workplace-related issue, such as smoking.

On the CD

See the Employee Handbook Checklist (document 13-03) and Receipt of Handbook (document 13-04) documents on the CD. Also see the "Employee Handbook" included in the bonus forms.

My recommendation regarding your personnel policy is this: until you need a comprehensive manual as outlined in the previous paragraphs, simply include those items that you absolutely want and intend to absolutely enforce. A few of these might be no drinking on the job, no smoking in the workplace, excessive tardiness or absenteeism as grounds for dismissal, no sexual harassment, no discrimination in the workplace, no stealing, and other rules that you fully intend to enforce

Watch Out!

If you write a policy manual, make sure that you comply with the written policies. It is a good idea to leave out statements regarding policies that don't apply to your company yet because of its size. Whatever you state as a policy, you must be prepared to follow.

Make sure that new employees get a copy of the personnel policies manual as part of the hiring process and that you expect strict adherence to these policies. In this way, if someone is caught drinking on the job, you can let him go for being in violation of the company policy, even if his performance has not suffered. (Thus you can avoid Julie's position as outlined in the chapter opening.) Some firms make a new employee sign a statement that they have received the policy manual so that there is no possibility of later confusion on either side of the desk.

Beware the "policies in a can" approach, which uses a standard software package or standard forms to define your personnel manual. They are probably overkill for your small organization and could open you to unnecessary exposure to legal action.

Medical Insurance

As the business owner, you probably should have your medical insurance paid by the company. Now you have an employee. Does this person get company-paid insurance just like you? What is the law? (See Chapter 16 for details on arranging your company benefits.)

To start with, the law covering medical and life insurance benefits is the Employee Retirement Income Security Act (ERISA) that was passed by Congress in 1974. This act does not require employers to provide medical, retirement, or any other benefits of any kind, but there is talk about changing these laws at the time of this writing. At the current time, ERISA only regulates how these benefits must be handled if they are provided. Employers typically offer benefits as a way to attract employees to their company and as a way of improving everyone's quality of life.

The snag comes in when you offer benefits to certain employees (such as you and members of your family) and don't offer the same benefits to other employees. In general, it is better for business and morale to offer the same benefits to everyone. The safest way to avoid this situation is to verify benefit offerings with an attorney or a benefits specialist.

The policy manual helps keep misunderstandings regarding employment benefits to a minimum, which will help you avoid possible litigation later due to unfulfilled expectations on the part of employees.

There is another potential snag depending on the type of company you own since medical insurance premium expenses may be deductible for employees but might not be deductible for employee owners. This is an area where it pays to talk with your tax professional.

> **Street Smarts**
>
> Smaller companies are exempt from many employment laws. For example, hiring relatives or friends over others is, by definition, discriminatory. This would make most small businesses in violation of federal and state laws. Call your local department of labor or your local chamber of commerce for guidelines when you begin preparing your policy manual.

Determining the right medical insurance plan for you and your employees is a potentially confusing and time-consuming process. For starters, you generally must have at least two employees (you and one other) before you qualify for most group plans. The coverage may apply to local incidents, but not cover incidents that occur out of town or out of country. Does the plan allow you to choose your doctor, or must you use doctors who are members of the plan you choose? The world of medical insurance is interesting and complicated. I suggest that you ask a few other business owners how they worked out their medical insurance situation; you might save yourself a lot of legwork.

Do your homework and don't jump at the first plan you see, or you might find yourself changing plans on a regular basis.

Ed's Lessons Learned

At one time, I (on and off) had only one other employee in my company. This meant that I was regularly having to go on and off the group policy due to the two-person minimum. (I guess one person doesn't comprise a group.) My agent let me know that I could set up a policy for myself, and then allow my employees to join my policy and set their own coverage levels. I upped their salaries enough to cover the employee's insurance premiums and insulated myself from having to define a blanket plan that applied to everyone or changed when I was back to running a solo operation. This worked pretty well. Some plans now allow you to have only one employee, so check around, as new products are coming along all the time. Know that more ways of addressing medical insurance are being created on a regular basis, so shopping and asking around are really good ideas.

Sexual Harassment

Picture this: your company is sued for sexual harassment. You know nothing happened, but you are in front of the judge, who asks about your internal policy regarding sexual harassment. He wants to see it in writing. Oops. It has been verbally expressed to all employees but never in writing. He and the jury decide in favor of the person filing the suit on the grounds that if you really meant it, you would have put it in writing. If you did not specifically state that sexual harassment is prohibited, then the opposite must be true; you must condone sexual harassment. This actually happens! I'll bet this section now has your undivided attention.

If you do not put such important policies in writing, you are in potential trouble. But be aware that if you are a small company not currently covered by the sexual harassment laws because of your size and you decide to have a statement in writing, then that statement can be used against you if you don't enforce it. Be safe, rather than sorry, and discuss the information provided in your handbook with an attorney (who will be there later if something happens) to be sure that you are not opening an unnecessary can of worms. It's always a good idea to discuss your sexual harassment policy with your attorney as a preventive measure.

Is there a lighter side to all of this? I have looked for it and can't find it. It is unfortunate that working with employees has become so dangerous, but it appears to be the nature of the beast. The best prevention for a nasty lawsuit is to avoid it in the first place. Treat all employees as people who perform a function for you. Mentally neuter them (and yourself) when you are on the job and treat them as company assets who perform a function. Nothing more.

My wife has a great saying that I suggest you take to heart when dealing with employees on just about any subject: be direct, specific, and nonthreatening. Keep it professional. Keep it courteous but also don't be afraid to expect an honest and complete day's work for a full day's pay.

Avoid the temptation to become close friends with your employees. Keep the proper amount of professional distance between them and you (while never being unfriendly). They work for you. You sign their checks. No matter what, you are never going to be one of the guys or girls. It will become difficult to handle personnel situations with authority if you spend every evening socializing with your employees.

> **On the CD**
>
> A sample Sexual Harassment Policy is included on the CD as document 13-05.
>
> A sample Employee Covenant Not to Compete is included on the CD as document 13-06 as is the Employee Confidential and Proprietary Information Non-Disclosure Agreement as document 13-11.

I've talked to several business owners, both male and female, who think of employees as nuns and priests as a way of attaching no gender at all to their employees. In all conversations, they relate as though they were talking to a member of the clergy so that no inappropriate remarks are made. This might seem a little extreme, but it seems to work for them.

You might not have to think of your business as a monastery, but don't forget that the primary reason for having employees is for them to perform a job function that makes money for them, the company, and you. Anything more than that might be misinterpreted and should be treated with caution.

Solicitation and Competition

How could these former employees do this? You spent three years building up that account, and they stole it away within 90 days of leaving your company. Their overhead isn't as high as yours, so they undercut your price by 30 percent. What could you have done to prevent this? A *noncompete clause* might have been one way to go. A noncompete clause is an agreement that your employees sign, saying that they won't steal your business ideas or methods and go to work for a competitor or become competitors by starting their own firm.

def•i•ni•tion

A **noncompete clause** is an agreement that your employees or suppliers sign, saying that they won't steal your business ideas or methods and go to work for a competitor or become competitors by starting their own firm.

Although noncompete clauses are treated differently from state to state, you should definitely look into them as one way to protect yourself and your company from ex-employees stealing your ideas and opening a business across town. When an employee signs a noncompete agreement, he or she essentially agrees not to compete with you in a specific geographic area (such as in a particular city or region of the country) for a specified period of time (such as one to two years) by performing the same function for another company that he or she did for you.

The theory says that your director of sales couldn't quit and go work for your competitor right away in a sales-related position. The reality of an employee noncompete is that it cannot keep a person from making a living in his or her chosen field. In other words, you really cannot keep a person from taking a job as a sales manager or design engineer with a competing firm. You can, on the other hand, keep that person from using any privileged, confidential, or proprietary system information in his or her new job because this information belongs to your company. A salesman can still sell; he or she just can't use your customer list. An engineer can design; he or she just can't use design procedures that are proprietary to your company. Making employees complete a Confidential Nondisclosure and Noncompete agreement lets everyone know your expectations, and when they separate from the company, the expectations are clearly stated. After that, it is up to them to determine what they will do and up to you to decide if you want to legally go after them for enforcement of the signed agreements.

Enforcing an employee noncompete that keeps a person from being able to earn a living in their selected field is a difficult, and usually fruitless, endeavor. You are better served making sure that people know that contact lists obtained at your company stay at your company and are not to be removed when the person leaves. Company confidential documents, which you should make sure are marked as such, cannot be removed from the company premises. Diligence on your part during hiring and while protecting sensitive information is the best defense you have against an employee using your information against you.

Think of an employee noncompete as a mechanism for keeping honest people honest.

Some states treat signed employee noncompete agreements very seriously and prevent a former employee from taking a job at a competing company if you file suit to that effect. Other states take the view that noncompete agreements limit where a person can work, and don't uphold them. Check with an attorney who specializes in employment law to find out whether your state supports noncompete agreements. If it does, work with an attorney to write an agreement that protects you rather than do it on your own. You might just create more headaches for yourself down the road if you handle this stuff yourself.

You cannot keep someone from making a living in his or her home town. A noncompete clause signed as part of the employment process essentially says that a person cannot earn a living in the same town as your business because he or she agreed not to compete with your company when he or she joined on. However, few courts in the country will uphold a company's rights to keep a person from making a living.

They will, however, uphold a company's rights to retain its customers without worrying about a former employee stealing those customers away. This is called a *nonsolicitation clause*, which says that the employee agrees not to pursue your existing customers for business that is related to your company. This agreement lasts for a specific period of time, usually one to two years. Former employees are restricted from using the customer contacts acquired while working with your company to aid another company, including their own.

The best way for you to cover yourself in this situation is to have the employee sign a noncompete agreement as part of his or her employment. This is particularly true for an employee who has regular customer contact. It makes you seem a little paranoid, but it might also save thousands of dollars of business from walking out your front door. When a customer starts to wave cash in front of a former employee, his or her loyalty to you will be severely tested. Without the noncompete agreement, you might end up with a personal disappointment and a financial loss without legal recourse.

def•i•ni•tion

A **nonsolicitation clause** is an agreement that your employees sign, saying that if they leave your company, they will not pursue your existing customers for business that is related to your company.

By the way, if a newly hired employee starts sharing confidential information with you about his or her last employer, even though he or she signed a confidentiality agreement with that employer, then you should reasonably assume that he or she will do the same with your information when he or she goes to the next job.

Interviewing Techniques

There are some questions that should never be asked of anyone because they are inappropriate, illegal, or both. You would probably never ask your best friend why she married that louse of a husband, or you risk losing a friend. Similarly, you should never ask certain taboo questions when interviewing people for a job.

On the CD

Sample Pre-Employment Questions (document 13-07), Employment Letter (document 13-08), Employment Contract (document 13-09), New Employee Procedures (document 13-10), and Employee Non-Disclosure (document 13-11) documents are included on the CD.

Why? Simple. If you ask an illegal question and you don't give the interviewee the job, he or she can use the fact that you asked the question as grounds for a discrimination suit—even if the question was asked purely as a conversation starter, such as "Did your children enjoy the Christmas holidays?" or "How old are they now?" The problem is that the topic should never have come up, and now you need to show that you don't have discriminatory hiring practices.

Some people try to determine information from secondary questions. For example, asking why a person moved to your city might indicate that he or she came with a spouse who was transferred. Asking if working on Sundays is a problem might raise information about the person's religious activities.

You should avoid using secondary questions to solicit the disclosure of information that could be considered prejudicial. The purpose of an interview is to determine the employee's ability to do the job—nothing else. Don't trifle with potentially discriminatory questions; nothing the interviewee reveals is worth the cost of defending an employment discrimination lawsuit!

def•i•ni•tion

A **job description** is a detailed listing of the duties to be performed by the person filling the job, also including the required skills, education, and certification levels, and other criteria directly related to the job.

Start any job search with a clear definition of what you want in the ideal person for the job. Create a *job description* that includes areas of knowledge the person must have to perform the job. Education and former experience must be clearly defined; develop objective criteria by which candidates can be screened. The more clearly you know what job you want them to perform and the kind of expertise you need, the more likely you are to find the right person to fill the open position. Be specific in your requirements if you want to minimize the amount of training this employee will require. For example, "must know Word for Windows styles operation" is specific, whereas "computer operation required" is general. If you are willing to train the employee, then you can make the requirements more general, which broadens the candidate field. Also, make sure to check out as much of what the person says about their background as possible. More than one person has inflated his or her resumé to look better on paper than was their reality.

In reality, and in the eyes of the law, you are trying to find the right person for the job, regardless of race, sex, marital status, or other criteria. The suggested interview procedures help ensure that you find the information you need without jeopardizing your company in the process.

Never bring up the following topics while conducting the interview:

- Marital status

- Veteran status

- Race

- Religion

- Nationality

- Children

- The interviewee's age

- Sex and sexual orientation

You need to know answers to many of these questions after the person is hired because emergency and medical information might pertain to children and spouses, but do not include them as part of the interview. In addition, make sure that you provide no verbal agreements about the length of employment or reasons for future possible dismissal. The person being hired might later construe these as commitments. These verbal commitments might be used against you later if problems arise with this person's performance that cause you to let him or her go.

Here are several things that you should consider doing with new employees:

- Let the applicant know the good and bad of working for you and your company.

- Avoid questions that deal with marital status, kids, religion, politics, sexual preference, and other areas that could be construed as potential ground for discriminatory treatment.

- Never lie about the company or things that might have been in the news. If you don't want to talk about it simply say so, but don't misrepresent the facts.

◆ Avoid talking about childcare.

◆ Keep notes during the interview as they relate to this person and the job.

◆ Make sure the applicant confirms that the items on the job description are things he or she can and will do and with what type of expected skill level.

On the CD

Sample Disciplinary Notice (document 13-12), Termination Letter (13-13), Employee Severance Agreement (document 13-14), Employee Information Release (13-15), Family and Medical Leave Act Request (document 13-16), and Employee Physical Accommodation Notice (document 13-17) documents are included on the CD.

◆ Make sure the applicant gets a copy of the employee manual. Question the applicant on its contents and have him or her sign the form indicating receipt.

◆ Keep your notes on a separate piece of paper and not on the resumé just in case someone else sees it, so that your thoughts cannot be construed as having prejudiced the others who interview.

◆ Have the applicant tell you about prior work experiences.

◆ Be consistent with how you interview, telling everyone the same information and asking what are basically the same set of questions.

Present the most positive aspects of the company in the most consistent manner. Your final intent is to find the best person to fill the job opening—period. If you mislead an applicant about company-related problems, you can find an employee making a substantial career change under false pretense, which can only lead to management troubles and a possible lawsuit.

On the CD

There are three great bonus sections included on the CD specifically related to employees and personnel issues. "Hire to Complement Your Existing Talents" shows you how to make sure that the employees you hire add capabilities to your company. "Making the Most of Temporary Agencies" lets you in on the secrets related to using temporary agencies to your best advantage. "Plan to Grow Beyond Your Own Capabilities" helps you understand how employees fit into your overall business growth plans. You are missing a lot of great information if you don't check out these special bonus sections.

For Your Plan

You should make a specific and visible point of discussing your personnel goals as part of your business plan. Make sure you cover at least the following points:

◆ Present the backgrounds of the founding management team, showing why they are the right people to start this particular business at this time.

◆ Discuss the startup personnel requirements from the perspective of not only finding customers but building a solid customer base.

◆ Provide job descriptions of the major positions that will perform important functions for the near term.

◆ Present a plan for expansion and how tasks will be divided as the company gets larger. Keep an eye on the division between routine and nonroutine tasks so that you spend your payroll dollars in ways that get you the best productivity return.

◆ Discuss benefits and how you plan to handle them, not only for the founders but also for the staff.

◆ Include a copy of the personnel manual so that investors can see that you have taken the right steps to protect the company and you from employee suits.

◆ Discuss the intended management style, culture, and general operational policies that you intend to implement on a daily basis.

◆ Show that you and the other founding members recognize that employees will eventually need to be added if the company meets with the success that all hope to happen.

The Least You Need to Know

◆ No man or woman is an island when it comes to succeeding in business. You must have the assistance of others if you want the company to grow beyond your capabilities.

◆ Create an environment where employees can grow professionally and financially. Allow them to feel like a part of the process, and you will reap the rewards associated with having a successful business that operates without you. But don't give employees free rein until you are sure they will act in both the company's and your best interest.

- Give potential employees a tryout before making a permanent commitment. Use probationary periods or temporary assignments to find out how they fit with your operations.

- An ineffective employee in a large organization can be disruptive, but in a small company, he or she can be disastrous because of the effect he or she has on others and on customers.

- State and federal laws kick in at different company size levels, based on the number of employees.

- Set up your minimum personnel policies to cover you on the "must adhere to" issues and add others later as needed.

- Make sure you conduct interviews in a legal and effective manner.

Chapter 14

Properly Handling Payroll Taxes

In This Chapter

- An overview of payroll taxing procedures
- Deposits and reporting deadlines
- Understanding self-employment tax
- When to consider an outside payroll service
- Rules to live—and pay tax—by

I'm a professional engineer, thought Kevin. I should be able to understand something as basic as payroll taxes. After 15 years of working and receiving paychecks, it's hard to imagine that it could be this complicated.

Okay. Deductions are made from the employee's paycheck based on earnings and several tax types. What is this FICA thing? And then there's unemployment. This is for both the state and federal taxes. I can handle that. The deposits are made quarterly for the state and annually for the federal. Or was that the reporting procedures?

Forget about that for now. Let's get this company portion of the payroll deductions under control. Hey. Wait a minute. These numbers are the same as the employee ones. Did I make a mistake, or are they supposed to be equal? Maybe the company pays it all? No, that can't be.

Wow. Now I know what a dog feels like when it chases its tail. Time to take Jill up on her offer to explain this stuff to me. It's clear that it's really unclear, and I just don't have the time to figure it out on my own.

"Hi, Jill? This is Kevin. Have I got a deal for you. What are you doing for lunch today, and were you serious about explaining payroll tax procedures to me?"

Your business won't grow without employees, but adding employees means adding responsibilities, including the need to manage payroll tax deposits. More than one company has gone under due to improper management of payroll taxes, and figuring this maze out for yourself can be costly and legally compromising. This chapter introduces the payroll process and outlines the Internal Revenue Service (IRS) guidelines for making tax deposits. Learn this well and save yourself money and grief.

Payroll Taxes: You Can't Avoid Them, So Learn How to Deal with Them

Unless you intend to be a sole practitioner all your life, you will have employees at some point, and with employees come payroll taxes. No one I know thinks payroll taxes are fun or interesting, but as a business owner, you need to have a basic grasp of the legal requirements. Otherwise, you can get tangled up in bureaucratic red tape and headaches that make asking for a loan sound pleasant by comparison. You don't have to be a rocket scientist to calculate payroll taxes, but you do have to pay attention to the details. By the way, as a sole proprietor, you still need to pay self-employment tax on your salary, so you really don't get around it even then.

As you read through this chapter the first time, you might feel kind of overwhelmed. Don't worry. Over time, this feeling will pass as you become more familiar with all the rules. Eventually, it will make perfect sense. You will have to decide if that is a scary thought in itself at that point.

Here's one of my favorite business secrets: just because you have employees doesn't mean that you have to do the accounting for your payroll. That's

> **Ed's Lessons Learned**
>
> Delaying your understanding of payroll taxes simply delays the inevitable and puts your company in financial and legal jeopardy. Spend the time today to get this information soundly under your belt because payroll taxes and the IRS are like gravity: they always win. The penalties for delaying payroll tax deposits are substantial, so don't even think about going there.

what staff (and service bureaus and accounting software) is for! Read on for an introduction to the regimented, deadline-filled world of payroll tax accounting—so that at least you can find out what you'll be delegating to someone else.

Payroll Tax Overview

Ever talk to someone from the IRS? To picture a typical payroll tax auditor, imagine that IRS representative without a sense of humor, and you're likely to be pretty close to the mark. The first thing you need to know is that all taxing jurisdictions (federal, state, and local) have their own requirements and filing deadlines that they take very seriously indeed. If you file all the right forms on time, you most likely won't have many problems.

That leads to the next question: how do you figure out which forms to file and when to file them? The three basic types of payroll taxes are income taxes (which you withhold from wages), Social Security and Medicare (you pay half, the employee pays half), and unemployment (you pay it all).

◆ States and some cities have income taxes, as does the federal government, so you need to consult both the federal guidelines and relevant state and local guidelines to determine how much to withhold and when to pay it over to the taxing authority.

◆ Social Security and Medicare are easier to figure out because they are only federal taxes and subject only to the federal rules.

◆ Unemployment is subject to both state and federal rules, with potentially complex interactions between the rules, requiring even more detailed record keeping.

To find the federal rules, contact the IRS, which has a package of tax rules and guidelines for businesses, including Publication 15, Circular E, *Employer's Tax Guide*. It's not the most fascinating reading in the world, I'll admit, but it's something you need to know about if you have employees and handle your own payroll tax accounting. The website has a wealth of information, including the forms and instructions, and is located at www.irs.gov.

For the state rules that apply to you, contact your state Department of Revenue (for income tax withholding information), Department of Labor (for unemployment tax information), or Secretary of State (in case you can't find the right bureau to answer your question). Look in the blue pages (governmental section) of your phone book under Federal or State Government to find out where to get the information.

Watch Out!

Don't rely on your computer alone! It's a good idea to manually verify tax liabilities if you typically use a software package to calculate your tax payments. If the software package is off in its calculations, you still owe the money. Depending on whether the mistake is in your favor or not, you may find yourself with more money than expected or owing more than you can pay. Software packages make mistakes, and cumulative payroll tax payment mistakes can put your company and you in serious financial trouble. The same applies to any payroll tax service you might use. Check their work occasionally as well.

Your employees will give you information about their tax status, number of dependents, and withholding allowances on a federal Form W-4. You can use this employee-provided information to look up the right withholding dollar amount in the tax tables or apply the right percentages for your state's formula. Some states have their own version of the Form W-4, which might contain different information from the federal form. In fact, some states don't have personal state income tax at all. You must check the rules for your particular state and proceed accordingly.

However, just because you figure it out once, don't think you're done for the year. If your employee's pay rate, marital status, dependent status, or address changes, the withholding amounts may also change, and you also have to be aware of the relevant ceilings ("wage base" in IRS lingo) for Social Security taxes and unemployment taxes. Providing detailed, repetitive calculations is what payroll tax reporting is all about, along with weekly, monthly, quarterly, and annual reporting requirements. If you like this sort of stuff, you will be in heaven. I, on the other hand, use a software package to keep me out of trouble.

On the CD

A sample Cover Letter to IRS for Employer ID (form SS-4) is included on the CD in the Employer and Contractor Related bonus forms section.

You've filled out the forms and followed the instructions; now you just drop them in the mail and relax, right? Wrong! Federal taxes and some state taxes are subject to depository requirements, and you can't just mail a check with your return. In essence, you deposit the taxes at your local bank either using a payroll tax coupon with your *employer identification number* (*EIN*) on it or by paying electronically. The depository schedule might not be the same as the reporting schedule or payroll schedule, so read the regulations carefully.

def•i•ni•tion

Your **employer identification number (EIN)** is a number given to any company that has employees, whether it is a corporation or a sole proprietorship. You need to complete IRS Form SS-4 and submit it to the IRS to get an EIN. You can do it over the phone by calling 1-800-829-4933 with the information required to complete SS-4. Additional EIN information is available in IRS Publication 1635, "Understanding Your EIN." You can even get an EIN from the IRS website, www.irs.gov. If you have employees, even if it is just you, you must have an EIN to ensure that all your tax payments are credited to the correct account, which is indicated by your unique EIN. Call the IRS (800-829-4933) to get your Federal Tax Deposit Coupon book (IRS Form 8109). You need a bank through which you make these tax deposits (Federal Depository). They are not mailed in.

Summary of Payroll Tax Items

Tax Type	Employee Portion	Company Portion	Total	Threshold
Federal Income	As determined from the W-4 form	None	10%, 15%, 25%, 28%, 33%, or 35%, depending on salary level	Depends on tax filing status
State Income	As determined from the W-4 form	None	Determined on a state-by-state basis	Depends on tax filing status
Social Security	6.2%	6.2%	12.4%	$94,200
Medicare	1.45%	1.45%	2.9%	Unlimited
Federal Unemployment	0%	6.2%	6.2% less the state percent	$7,000 payment
State Unemployment	0%	Depends on the state	Depends on the state	Depends on the state

Notice from the table that adding the employee and employer portions of Medicare (2.9 percent) and Social Security (12.4 percent) gives a total of 15.3 percent, which is the amount paid as self employment tax. Self employment tax is the amount paid by those who work for themselves, usually completing a Schedule C for their business and Schedule SE (self employment) on their personal return. Some people complain about this tax being higher than if they were an employee, but you can see that the amount the government receives is the same (15.3 percent)—it just seems higher because the self employed pay both the employee and employer portion of the tax, which makes sense in that you are your own employer. The IRS says that you are self employed if you "carry on a trade or business as a sole proprietor or an independent contractor," "are a member of a partnership that carries on a trade of business," or "are otherwise in business for yourself." You can figure it out from there, just know that you are not being penalized by being self employed.

Fudge on these taxes, and you will pay big time and without mercy. It is one thing to be late on a payment to a creditor. It is another to be late on payroll deposit payments to the IRS because you are essentially playing with the employee income deductions. The employer is a trustee of these trust fund taxes and as such has fiduciary responsibility to make proper payment to the IRS. The IRS will eat you alive in late payment fees and interest if you delay, so make sure that you read the next section and file on time. Think of it this way: you are holding the employee payment portion for the IRS, so if you do not make the payment, you are essentially stealing from the employee. That puts a little different spin on it all, doesn't it?

Filing and Paying Payroll Taxes

You have performed the calculations, made the payroll deductions, and paid the employees their well-earned paychecks, but there is still more for you to do. You now need to report the deductions to the IRS and make a bank deposit or electronic deposit to ensure that the IRS gets the money you've so carefully deducted from everyone's paycheck. Once again, refer to IRS Publication 15 (Circular E), Employer's Tax Guide, for a lot more information.

Tax Deposits and IRS Form 941, Employer's Quarterly Federal Tax Return

Make your payroll tax deposit with a company check at your local bank along with the Federal Tax Deposit Coupon that tells the IRS which company is making its deposit. The coupon should have the deposit amount filled in, along with the box associated with the quarter to which the deposit is to be applied and the type of tax based on the particular IRS form number (in other words, 941, First Quarter). The bank will give you a standard deposit receipt in return.

You deposit the federal payroll taxes on either a monthly or semiweekly basis, depending on the size of your payroll. If your total tax deposits exceeded $50,000 in the period of July 1 of the prior year to June 30, then you probably have to deposit semiweekly. If not, you can deposit on a monthly basis on or before the fifteenth of the month. The IRS will let you know, but you are ultimately responsible even if the notice was not received. For your first year in business (when you do not have a prior four quarters) you file monthly except under very specific circumstances. It is a good idea to keep tabs on the amount of tax you pay. In general, you deposit taxes on a monthly basis for your first year. Your payroll tax service should be able to provide you with this historical (or projected) information, or you can simply pull it from your accounting package. This scheduling is a little confusing at first, but get it on your calendar and stick with it so it simply becomes part of doing business.

Make sure that you get your payment into the bank before the end of the banking day. There is a time difference between the end of the banking day and the time the bank closes. Be sure you know when the banking day ends. For example, the banking day might end at 2:00 P.M. even though the bank closes at 4:00 P.M. The deposit must be in the bank by 2:00 P.M. in this situation.

The IRS has moved into the twenty-first century and set up the Electronic Federal Tax Payment System (EFTPS). The plan basically dictates that employers who must make total combined deposits of employment, excise, and corporate income taxes in the prior year of $200,000 or more must make electronic deposits. Once again, the IRS will notify you if you must comply with the electronic filing requirements, but you probably shouldn't trust them on this one either. You must complete and return to the IRS an enrollment form at least 10 weeks before you plan to make your first electronic deposit. (For more EFTPS information, call 1-800-555-4477 or go to www. eftps.gov.)

If no wage payments are made in a month, no deposits are needed. If the fifteenth falls on a holiday or weekend, you can deposit on the following business day and still be on time.

Street Smarts

Depository banks don't have to accept checks from other banks for payroll tax deposits, so when you are choosing your business bank, make sure that it can accept payroll tax deposits.

Semiweekly depositors must stay on top of things. If you pay your employees on a Wednesday, Thursday, or Friday, then your tax deposit must be made by Wednesday of the following week. If payday falls on Saturday, Sunday, Monday, or Tuesday, then deposits are due at the bank on the following Friday. There is a special three-day rule that adds a day to the deposit deadline for each day that a holiday falls between the payday and deposit date.

Street Smarts

The semiweekly and monthly deposit designations have nothing to do with when you pay your employees. The IRS expects to receive payroll deposits monthly or semiweekly (depending on the size of your payroll).

You report all the deductions you've taken from the payroll to the IRS for a given calendar quarter on IRS Form 941, Employer's Quarterly Federal Tax Return. This is for payroll tax information only. The form must be in the mail and postmarked by the last day of the month following each quarter. For example, for the first quarter (January through March), you must complete and mail the 941 form by the last day of April. At this time, you should evaluate the amount of money you owe in taxes and what you actually paid throughout the quarter. If the amount you still owe is less than $2,500, which it should be if you are calculating and depositing your payroll taxes properly, simply enclose a check for that amount with your Form 941.

The following table summarizes the payroll filing procedures for you.

Payroll Deductions Made	When Payroll Checks Are Written
Federal bank deposits required	Either semiweekly or monthly, depending on deposit levels. Deposits are made with IRS coupon form 8109 or electronically.
Payroll deduction form	On a quarterly basis on the last day of the quarter for which the 941 was completed and postmarked the month following each calendar quarter.
State unemployment	Usually quarterly, but the last day of reporting and payment the month following each quarter.
Federal unemployment	Annually, using IRS form 940 and reporting payment deposit coupon form 8109. Quarterly if owed amounts exceeds $500.

Payroll tax calculations, deposits, and reporting are initially confusing but become a routine part of operation in a short period of time. Ignore them, and you will pay stiff penalties, so step up to the table and do it right from the start.

Based on how you pay your employees, you might annually have to also file Form 945, Annual Return of Withheld Federal Income Tax, which is for tax withheld for nonpayroll items. This gets pretty arcane, so check with your tax professional to see whether you have to file this form as well.

Here are a few additional forms to think about that will be obvious to you once you see them: you must furnish employees with their Form W-2, Wage and Tax Statement, by January 31 of the calendar year following the tax year in question. You then send the IRS a copy of the W-2 forms along with a Form W-3, Transmittal of Wage and Tax Statements, by the following February 28. Similarly, you must provide contractors with their Form 1099 (such as 1099-MISC, Miscellaneous Income) by January 31 of the calendar year following the tax year in question. You then send a copy of these 1099s to the IRS along with Form 1096, Annual Summary and Transmittal of U.S. Information. Notice that the W-2 and 1099 are to provide payment record information to the employee and contractor, respectively. The W-3 and 1096 are to inform the IRS about those payments. I think of them as a way for the IRS to close the loop on who received payments from your company. You are required to provide these forms, so just do it and don't let anyone talk you into not providing a 1099 to them if you paid them more than $600 in the tax year.

State and Federal Unemployment Taxes

This part gets easier. After you've been accruing unemployment payments with each payroll period, your state will make you complete a reporting form and deposit the required funds on a quarterly basis by the last day of the month following each quarter. For example, you make first quarter (ending March 31) payments by the end of April. The federal reporting is done on the IRS Form 940, which you must complete annually by the end of January of the year following the reporting period and mail along with a check for the proper amount remaining that was not paid throughout the rest of the year.

The state tells you what rate you must pay for unemployment, based on historical unemployment benefits paid to past employees. This unemployment rate indicates their assessment of the amount of risk your company poses to the unemployment fund. If a number of your employees leave your company and file for unemployment compensation, you see your unemployment tax rate increase. Tax rates reflect expected costs for your industry but are adjusted based on your specific experience. If no one leaves your company and files for unemployment, after a few years, your rates might even decrease. Sure. I believe in the tooth fairy as well. Sigh.

Rules to Live (and Save Taxes) By

Here are a few rules that I learned the hard way. I relay them here with embarrassment and with the hope that I can save you from the same mistakes:

1. Report your payroll taxes—yes, all of them on all of the nice little forms—when the reports are due. That's right—on time!

2. Make sure that your deposits are accurate and on time. Only an act of God can save you from IRS penalties and fines if they are levied against you or your company.

3. Use a payroll software package such as QuickBooks, which includes a payroll service to ease the payroll process. If you don't use a software payroll package, then investigate a service to handle payroll for you. If you only have a few paychecks, you might try manually determining and entering the data yourself using the tables supplied with IRS Publication 15.

4. Find someone who understands the payroll tax calculation and reporting process. Have them show you their completed forms and walk you through the process when you first start issuing payroll checks. If there is anything nonstandard about your payroll process, then have a professional verify your approach and your first few paychecks and deposits.

5. Stay on top of things, and always include the additional payroll tax expenses when considering an employee raise. Perhaps you should offer your employee additional benefits instead of a raise because a raise has the additional payroll taxes attached, and certain types of benefits do not incur the incremental taxes.

The payroll tax reporting and deposit procedures will eventually become second nature to you, but it is definitely confusing when you first start out. I had a tough time finding all of this information in one spot and made some serious blunders that cost me thousands of dollars. Don't make the same mistake. Get the right advice early in the process and follow it. The late fees are tough to swallow.

Street Smarts

Your unemployment tax rate fluctuates, depending on how many employees have ever filed for unemployment. If former employees file for unemployment benefits, you see your unemployment rate increase, unfortunately.

As a final note, don't fiddle with these taxes. If you look at where the money comes from, you can see that you are holding your employees' money until deposited. If you are delinquent in making these deposits for any length of time at all, it might be viewed as theft, and you can get yourself into serious legal trouble that you really don't want. Don't take chances with payroll tax liabilities. If your company goes under, you still owe these taxes, so pay these guys before you pay everyone else. Have I made myself perfectly clear on this matter? It is really important.

Using a Payroll Accounting Service

You always have the option of giving this task to someone else. Your accountant will generally do payroll tracking for you as part of a standard service offering. Outside payroll services specialize in nothing but payroll accounting. This might be too much for what you need at this time, but you might ask your fellow business owners about how they handle their own payrolls. These payroll services have also been adjusting their service offering to accommodate businesses with a small number of employees. The payroll tax process is an important concern for all business owners regardless of size and age; experience is a good guide in this area.

The Least You Need to Know

◆ Employee-paid payroll taxes include Social Security, Medicare, and federal and state withholding. The company and the employee pay equal amounts of Social Security and Medicare. The company pays all the federal and state unemployment tax.

◆ Payroll tax deposits are required semiweekly, monthly, or electronically, depending on the size of your company's payroll. The first year you will probably make monthly payments unless your payroll is large.

◆ Federal payroll taxes are reported on a quarterly basis using IRS Form 941. Similar forms are necessary for state payroll tax reporting.

◆ Federal unemployment taxes are paid quarterly if the unpaid liability exceeds $500. Otherwise, they are reported and paid annually using IRS Form 940.

◆ Don't be late on reporting or deposit deadlines—the penalty fees are huge!

Chapter 15

Accounting: How Business Keeps Score

In This Chapter

- ◆ Why you need to understand accounting procedures
- ◆ Basic accounting principles
- ◆ An overview of balance sheets and income statements
- ◆ Cash flow analyses
- ◆ Comparing cash flow to accrual income statement
- ◆ When to use an accountant or CPA

Jake, who lived in Tulsa, was in Chicago for a business seminar and was excited about seeing his friend Dan. They had worked on cars together in high school and now each owned their own auto repair businesses. It was great to talk about business; they shared the same problems and could be honest with each other because they were not competitors. Dan's business was in its fifth year of operation. Jake started his about two years ago and was clearly not making it. Things were tough, and this seminar was his last shot at turning things around before he had to "bag it" and get a "real job."

"I don't understand," said Dan. "You're a great mechanic and you love working with people. What's wrong with your business that you aren't making ends meet?"

Jake looked out the window and back at Dan. "Good question. I'm busy as all get-out and often have to turn business away, but at the end of the year, my accountant tells me I don't have enough money to pay myself what I need. Something's wrong, and if it doesn't get fixed soon, I go back to work for the dealership."

"What is your percentage profit margin?" was Dan's initial question. "And how does your pricing compare with the competition in town?"

"I have the lowest prices around," said Jake proudly. "I dropped our prices 20 percent last year, and that was when things really cut loose. We're doing more work than ever, and my sales are twice what they were last year. I even had to add space to my garage to handle the new business."

Dan smiled and then looked Jake squarely in the eye. "High sales and profits do not always go hand-in-hand. If you can't keep your profit margins where they need to be, you're in trouble. What's your percentage profit margin?"

"I don't know," replied Jake. "I let my accountant take care of all that financial stuff for me. I do cars; he does numbers. I just tell him what I want our prices to be and he takes it from there. That's what I pay him for."

"So he makes your financial decisions?" Dan asked. "What does he know about the car business? Does he care if you don't make money? You really don't review your financial statements more than once a year? I have a bad feeling that you're a great mechanic who never made the transition to being a business manager. Let's get a copy of your financial statements and compare them to mine. I bet we can get an idea of where things are going wrong. Your business means too much to you to let it go under due to bad pricing and financial decisions."

Jake nodded somberly, silently hoping that Dan would buy lunch. He started to realize that just looking at sales instead of the whole business might have hurt his dream of independence. This time, he would stay awake during the seminar's financial analysis segment.

Like Jake, most business owners treat accounting as a necessary evil. I understand that attitude completely because I did the same thing. And because I did not treat the accounting aspects of managing my company seriously, I made a few financial decisions based on bad information, much to my regret. I now strongly believe in the value of accurate accounting, and I encourage you to learn from my mistakes.

This chapter won't make an accountant or bookkeeper out of you. Relax. It will, however, introduce you to important accounting terms and methods so that you will learn enough to manage an accountant in a way that is valuable to your own business situation. Remember that your accountant works for you, not the other way around. Get him involved early so that he understands your needs, but remember that you inherit the financial impact of your decisions, not your accountant.

It is important to remember that your books have to be right for tax accounting purposes, but they also have to provide you with the information you need to make solid business management decisions.

Accounting 101

Communication is a wonderful thing—when it works. Communication takes on a new importance when it's about money. Money is a basic necessity of life, and most people treat threats to their money as threats to their person. Accounting procedures and statements provide a standardized way for people to communicate about financial and business situations.

> **Street Smarts**
>
> If you're publishing financial information for use outside of your company, you need to consider an additional set of special accounting rules (called *GAAP*, or *Generally Accepted Accounting Principles*) when you prepare your financial statements. For managing a business, however, you only need to make sure your accounting system makes sense to you and to your financial advisers. Most software packages will handle the bookkeeping part of things. Your accountant can help you set up the procedures that keep you GAAP compliant without a lot of complexity.

The purpose of the highly structured world of accounting is to provide business managers and others with the information they need to manage a business or evaluate their investments. Accounting is how business keeps score, and, just like keeping score in baseball, there are numerous rules and procedures to accurately reflect the results of the actions on the field.

You need to accumulate information that is timely, reliable, and useful, and you don't want to take valuable time away from making money. Fortunately, accounting principles and policies can make accounting for your business easier. Several software packages are now on the market that make accounting a much simpler task than ever before. I talk about them in more detail later in the chapter.

The following sections provide some basic accounting concepts so that you can understand the considerations involved in setting up and maintaining your accounting systems. Time spent up front planning and developing good accounting procedures can save you countless hours of frustration down the road.

Accounting Periods

Accounting periods are periods of time, such as months, quarters, or years. Keeping records by accounting periods allows a company's financial reports to be compared from one time frame to another. It's a good idea to review your company's performance on a regular basis so you can become aware of potential problems, such as running out of cash, higher product or fixed costs, or lower sales figures, before it's too late. Watching how your financial condition changes from one period to the next provides important *trend* information that tells you early on if you are doing better or worse than before.

Accounting periods also provide a basis for comparing company performance from one period to the next, from quarter to quarter, or from year to year. Additionally, to file your tax returns, you have to determine in what month you want your year to end so you can report your profit or loss for that year. Most small companies use a *calendar fiscal year* (January to December).

For starters, you need to determine when your company will evaluate its financial performance. Most companies, small and large, look at their basic financial statements at least quarterly (every three months) to measure their progress toward long-term goals, and most managers review their financial statements on a daily or weekly basis. It's always good to know where your sales are coming from and how your money is being spent.

The next question is, "When does my company's financial year begin and end?" A year in a company's history is a *fiscal year*. Unless there is some reason to do otherwise (as recommended by your accountant), keep your fiscal year the same as the calendar year, from January 1 to December 31. This means your quarters will end on March 31, June 30, September 30, and December 31.

Of course, you need to consider whether the IRS has any relevant rules before you can comfortably select a fiscal year end. The good news is that you can always change your fiscal year after you have been in business for a while, so you shouldn't worry too much about this selection. Start out with a standard calendar year and change it later if needed.

Sales and Costs

Assume that your client pays you today for work you intend to perform in 60 days. First off, kiss this customer and keep him happy; this type of client is rare, indeed. Second, take a look at whether you should declare that payment as earned income. (In other words, can you spend the money today knowing you won't have to give it back, or should you wait?)

def•i•ni•tion

Accounting periods are set calendar time intervals (months, quarters, or years). Keeping your records up to date by accounting period will allow you to compare one period to another. A year in a company's history is called a **fiscal year.**

When the company's financial reporting period is the same as the calendar year, which extends from January 1 to December 31, it is called a **calendar fiscal year.** Most companies use a calendar fiscal year, and you should, too, unless told otherwise by a tax professional.

Sales revenue is the first item on your income statement and represents the total amount of sales that your company earned during the accounting period. This means that you substantially completed the work *and* fully expect to be paid for it.

The **cash basis** of accounting recognizes sales and expenses when cash is actually received or spent. The **accrual** basis focuses on the earning process and matches sales revenue and expenses required to earn that sale to the period when the earning process is completed. Accrual also records transactions when commitments are made, not necessarily when cash changes hands.

Income is the general term for money received from selling a product or service to a customer. Any money paid to you before the product or service is fully given to the customer is **unearned income.** If the customer can cancel his or her contract and get the money back, you have not truly earned it.

Money you have received for work performed or for products provided is known as earned *income*. You've done everything the customer requested, according to some formal or informal agreement. You can consider the money yours since you have no situation that could create a legal obligation to return it. At this point, the transaction can be considered a sale and booked as *sales revenue*.

In the *accrual* accounting world, when you receive payment from a customer for work that hasn't been completed yet, for accounting purposes, you need to show that payment as *unearned income* until the work is done. When the earning process is complete, the accrual basis of accounting reports that transaction as sales revenue and eventually income. Accrual accounting is discussed in more detail in a few more pages.

If the customer can cancel his order, then the money really hasn't been earned yet, has it? You are essentially holding the money for him until you complete the work. In short, if you haven't finished earning the money by meeting all the terms of your contract with the customer, you shouldn't consider the revenue from those sales as truly yours. Many businesses hedge on this requirement and eventually get themselves into cash trouble. Treat it as a refundable deposit until you do the work to earn it.

If you have a noncancelable contract along with a nonrefundable advance, then the money you received is yours. At that point, you can include it as sales revenue.

If you use the *cash basis* of accounting (described in the next section), you don't need to know the difference between collections and earned income. In the cash-based accounting world, everything you receive from sales is considered income when it is collected, and you don't make any special accounting entries to show when it is earned.

Cash or Accrual: Which Accounting Method Is Right for You?

Here's a fundamental accounting question: when do you actually incur an expense? Is it when you use the product or service, or when you pay for the product or service? The answer is different depending on whether you use the cash basis or accrual basis of accounting. These are two approaches to accounting, and you need to know a little about both to effectively manage your business.

The cash basis of accounting recognizes sales and expenses when money (cash) is actually received or spent. The accrual basis of accounting focuses on the earning process and matches sales revenue to the period when the earning process is completed, not simply when the cash is received. The accrual basis also matches expenses incurred to generate those sales to the period in which the income is reported. It is often said that accrual accounting recognizes an expense or income at the point where a commitment (agreement) is made, not necessarily when cash actually changes hands.

If your business has substantial inventory, the IRS says you must use the accrual basis of accounting, so that decision is made for you. However, if you run a service business, especially if you are a small business that does not offer credit payment terms to its customers, you might find that keeping your books on the cash basis is much simpler.

Here's an example to illustrate the differences between the two methods.

Assume that you run a small consulting firm, and you're working on only one project right now. Last month, you spent $400 on supplies and office expenses, paid your staff $1,000 (both fixed expenses), and billed your client $2,500 for the project. This month, your client pays the bill (and the check clears the bank!). Under the cash basis of accounting, you show a loss of $1,400 last month because you paid for the supplies and salaries then and received no cash customer payments. You show a profit of $1,100 ($2,500 – $400 – $1,000) this month because you collected the cash payment now and still had the $400 and $1,000 fixed business expenses. Under the accrual basis, you match the expenses incurred last month with the revenue earned last month (you issued a customer invoice for $2,500 for work done) and in that month show a profit of $1,100 ($2,500 in revenue less $1,400 in expenses). Note, however, that this does not mean that last month you put that $1,100 in the bank. This is the scary part of not understanding the implications of accrual accounting statements. You may see a positive *net income* on your statements but have no money in the bank. Why? Because your customers owe you the money and have not paid you. Their earned income is accruing and continues to accrue until they pay you. If they never pay you, that accrued income never turns into cash, which ultimately is what you really care about.

If you have a fairly simple business, with expenses incurred close to the time sales revenues are collected, the cash basis of accounting might give you information that is accurate and timely enough to let you run your business. However, most larger businesses use the accrual basis of accounting, for some or all of the following reasons:

def•i•ni•tion

Net income is the amount of money left over after *all* expenses have been deducted from the sales revenue figure. **Earnings** is another term for net income.

- ◆ They have inventories, so the IRS makes them use accrual accounting.

- ◆ There can be long lags between the time expenses are incurred and the time customer payment for sales are collected, and the business managers feel that cash basis accounting gives them a distorted picture of operations.

- ◆ The business sells a small number of large items, and showing *earnings* based on collections results in dramatic swings in reported performance from month to month, even though the underlying operations might not be fluctuating nearly as much.

- ◆ The business has more than one owner, and the owners want a clear picture of the total accumulated earnings of the business, not just the cash collections. (Cash basis accounting gets particularly messy when partners split up.)

Watch Out!

Beware simultaneously tracking part of your business on cash basis and part on accrual. This can get very confusing when reading financial statements. And it is guaranteed to make your banker question the validity of the rest of the numbers. But if you use the cash basis of accounting, you must make a nearly obsessive commitment to tracking what your customers owe you along with when and how they pay. All this accounting stuff is important and interesting, but your business success starts and ends with creating sales, collecting customer debts, and keeping your company able to pay its bills. Never lose your emphasis on creating sales and collecting customer payments no matter what accounting procedures you use.

The Cash Basis Accounting Method

How do you track money owed to you when you're using the cash basis of accounting? Very simply, you complete work for customers and you bill them. In some businesses, you receive payment right away, such as if you are running a restaurant; customers pay after they eat. You keep track of who owes what by having waiters and waitresses use order slips. At the end of the night, you total the amount on all the order slips collected and match them with the amount of money in your cash register. You then deposit most of that money in your bank account and keep some in the register to use as change the next day.

If you run almost any other kind of business, however, you probably have to wait to receive payment. You might bill a customer on the first of the month and have to wait 30 days until the check arrives. To keep track of who owes what, create a file of all the invoices sent to customers. As customers pay, you deposit their checks in the bank, record their payment as a sale, and take their invoice copies out of the file. You can always check to see whose invoice is outstanding by looking in your file. Once more than 30 days have passed, you want to give the customer a call and find out if there is a problem. (See the Special CD Bonus Chapter 25, "Making Sure Your Customers Pay," for more important information on collections.)

The Accrual Accounting Method

Accrual accounting imposes an additional accounting step; now you have to use the accounting system to track when a customer is billed as well as when the collection comes in, and you might be (and probably will be) making accounting entries at times when no cash has changed hands.

Furthermore, accrual accounting might report handsome profits while you have no cash in the bank to pay suppliers—because all those sales show up as revenue and accounts receivable (an asset on the balance sheet), but your customers haven't actually paid you any cash yet. When managing any business, large or small, remember that cash is like air, and track your bank balances and expectations about cash flows using the techniques discussed later in this chapter. Many businesses have shared the sad experience of running out of cash before all the bills have been paid while showing great sales; try not to join them!

Ed's Lessons Learned

My primarily service-oriented company runs on the accrual basis for management and tracking purposes, but files taxes using the cash basis. I usually recognize the sales revenue at the time of invoice generation, track my accounts receivable, and monitor my balance sheet cash account like a hawk. I found that tracking only cash transactions while also providing credit payment terms to customers became too confusing. It impaired my credit collections and did not give an accurate assessment of my company when I ran my financial reports.

Accrual accounting might also impose tax complications. No one likes paying taxes on reported income before the cash from those sales has been collected, but that can be the way accrual accounting works. Your accountant or tax adviser can give you suggestions on techniques to minimize this source of pain. (I'll bet that last statement got your attention.)

The following table summarizes the advantages and disadvantages of cash basis and accrual basis accounting.

Cash Versus Accrual Accounting

Cash Basis	Accrual Basis
Advantages	
Relatively simple to use	Provides a conceptually more correct picture of the results of your business operations if not compared to cash
Understandable to anyone who has balanced a checkbook	Consistent with the way bigger companies report their financial results
Reports income when you have cash to pay the taxes	Required by the IRS if your business has inventory
	Simplifies accounting during change in ownership
	Makes reporting to outsiders (bankers, potential investors, and so on) more comprehensible because they are used to accrual basis statements

continues

Cash Basis	Accrual Basis

Disadvantages

Cash Basis	Accrual Basis
Can distort the results	Can be costly and time-consuming of operations, possibly leading to bad business decisions
Not acceptable to the IRS if your business has inventory	Might not match reported income and cash availability
Not comparable to the way bigger companies report their financial concepts and their reported results	Requires some thought and expertise to understand
Complicates accounting during changes in ownership	
Can make your company's financial condition appear worse than it is if you offer credit terms to your customers	

Understanding Financial Statements

Settle down in a comfortable chair and make a pot of coffee; it's time to learn the language of accounting. It's not nearly as fun as the language of love, but stick with me. Even if you intend to use an accountant to manage your records, you still need to understand basic financial terms so you can make reasonable financial decisions on your own. And if all of this understanding makes you tons of money, you *will* love it. Trust me.

Understanding financial statements isn't difficult. Yes, even you can pick it up. Using financial statements effectively along with a valid sales forecast gives you a preview of good and bad times before they hit, so you can take proactive measures if necessary.

This section introduces you to financial statements and explains their basic purpose. There are three basic financial statements: the *income statement, balance sheet*, and *statement of cash flow*. The income statement shows you the sales revenue, expense, and net income level of your company during a specific accounting period, which is usually a fiscal month, quarter, or year. The balance sheet shows you how much you own and how much you owe at a particular point in time, which is usually calculated at the end of a fiscal quarter and on the last day of the year. The statement of cash flow shows exactly how much cash you actually received and how much cash you spent on a periodic basis. You really need to watch your cash flow statement carefully, especially if you use accrual accounting. Your cash flow statement keeps you informed about how much money you actually have in your bank account to pay all your bills.

def•i•ni•tion

There are three basic financial statements. The **income statement** reflects all income and expenses for a particular period of time (usually a month, quarter, or year). The **balance sheet** shows your total assets (what you own) and liabilities (what you owe) on a given date, usually the end of the accounting period. The **statement of cash flow** (or cash flow analysis) shows exactly how much cash you received and how much you spent on a monthly basis. This statement helps you understand the cash reality of the accrual basis income statements.

The income statement and balance sheet will have different numbers for the same accounting period if you create these reports first using the cash basis and then again using accrual accounting. Modern accounting packages enable you to report using either technique. If you understood why the accrual- and cash-basis reports for the same period will have different numbers, you are starting to understand this section. If not, keep reading this section until you get it. This topic is simply that important.

A Chart of Accounts

One of the procedures accountants use to make record-keeping easier and more understandable is summarizing transactions so that similar transactions are grouped together. They do this by using a *chart of accounts*, which lists all the possible categories of transactions and organizes them to make producing financial statements easier. Accounts that summarize the assets and liabilities of the company are grouped together to form the balance sheet. Accounts that summarize the sales and expenses of the company are grouped together to form the income statement. Those statements, taken together, describe the total financial condition and results of operations for the company. The statement of cash flow uses information from both income and balance sheet statements.

It is critically important to set up these accounts so that they are not only useful for tax purposes but also so that you can get the financial management information (reports) you need to make effective financial decisions. Remember, you don't get to report any taxes on income if you do not manage your business successfully enough to have a positive net income at the end of the year.

def•i•ni•tion

A **chart of accounts** is a list of all the categories used by a business to organize its financial expenditures and sales. These accounts will be defined so that they track the way you run your business even though many of these accounts are standard between most companies.

Please take the time to understand this important example. Tax accounting only requires that you know the amount of revenue received and the total costs associated with earning that revenue. From this information, you can calculate the total net income on which income tax is owed. Management accounting may additionally track the revenues and costs associated with specific product or business areas, so that management can determine which business activities are profitable and which are losers. This has nothing directly to do with tax preparation but has a lot to do with profitably managing your business.

The specifics of setting up these management accounting categories depend on your particular business, but the importance of setting up these management accounts early in the process applies to all businesses.

Don't feel that you need to reinvent the wheel when creating these accounts. Try to get your hands on a copy of the chart of accounts for a company like yours, and you will likely find almost all of their accounts will apply to your company as well. Make life easier for yourself.

If you are using the accrual basis of accounting, you also need a financial statement that details cash flow activity, which is likely to be different from the activity shown on the income statement. Cash basis companies might not need as elaborate an analysis to generate a good understanding of their cash flows, but they should still be aware that lags between billing and collection could adversely affect their cash position.

The Income Statement

Your income statement (or profit and loss statement, or P and L) tells you whether your business is profitable. The income statement totals the amount of *revenue* and then subtracts the expenses associated with making that revenue. The result is the *pretax profit* and, after taxes are paid, net income.

Income statements show you how much you sold and how much it cost you to create those sales during a particular period of time. Most businesses prepare year-end income statements so they can see how they did during the year. You can, and most likely should, prepare income statements for shorter periods such as monthly, quarterly, or year-to-date.

Expenses fall into two categories: *cost of sales* expenses and *operating (fixed) expenses*. Cost of sales expenses (also called the cost of goods sold, or COGS) are those directly related to producing your product or providing your service. These generally include the cost of raw materials, the cost of labor to run the machine that produced the widget you sold, and other expenses required to obtain or create the product or service. COGS will vary with sales volume and are often called *variable expenses*. Sell nothing and COGS = $0. Fixed expenses do not change with sales volume. Sell nothing and rent stays the same.

def•i•ni•tion

Revenue is the total sales amount received by the company. **Pretax profit** is the amount of money left over after all expenses, except for tax payments, have been deducted. **Cost of sales,** or **variable expenses,** are the costs directly linked to the production or sale of a product or service (raw materials, labor, and other expenses). **Operating expenses,** or **fixed expenses,** are those expenses associated with running your company (salaries, rent, utilities, and so on).

Your **gross profit** (also called gross margin) is the amount of money left after you cover the cost of sales: gross profit = revenue − cost of sales (also called cost of goods sold, or COGS). Out of gross profit, you pay your operating (also called fixed) expenses. Sorry for the jargon confusion, but I wanted you to see the various terms here first.

For example, suppose you sold a coffee mug for $5.00 and it cost you $3.00 to purchase it. The cost of sales is $3.00, which is what you paid for the mug. The *gross profit* calculation associated with this single mug's sale is revenue − cost of sales = gross profit, or $5.00 − $3.00 = $2.00 gross profit. The cost to your company of providing products for sale varies with the quantity sold, or is said to "vary with sales," so it is called a variable expense. This sentence is important enough for you to review it until it makes sense.

Operating (fixed) expenses are those expenses associated with the daily stuff that keeps your business running. You still have some amount of these expenses regardless of how much you sell in a month. These include your salary, your rent payment, the cost of the electricity in your office, insurance, administrative salaries, commissions, and other similar costs of operating the company. Operating expenses are paid out of the gross profit. Notice that operating expenses include commissions that vary with the sales level, so they are not strictly "fixed" expenses but are often treated as such when performing financial analysis.

Now that I've given you an overview of what the income statement provides for you, take a look at one.

Remember the earlier coverage of accrual and cash basis accounting? Look at the income statement that follows in the next section and notice how the relationship between expenses and revenues is linked directly to profit calculations. Unless the two are synchronized, there is no way to accurately determine if you made money during the time period that you're examining.

The Balance Sheet

Whereas an income statement reflects the flow of money in and out of a company during a specific time frame (as videotape records events over a period of time), the *balance sheet* shows the amount of company assets and liabilities at a particular point in time (a snapshot of how things are at a particular moment). The balance sheet is based on a fundamental equation of accounting: assets = liabilities + owner's equity.

Assets are those items of value the company owns, such as cash in the checking account, accounts receivable, inventory, equipment, and property. The value of an asset is based on its initial purchase price minus any applicable *depreciation* (an accounting method for tracking the decrease in value that occurs as an asset ages).

Watch Out!

When you are analyzing the depreciation of an asset, don't confuse book value with market value. For example, your 10-year-old car might have $0 book value. Does that mean that the car is no longer worth anything? Not necessarily. The car probably has some market value in that someone would be willing to pay you something for it. The market might think that an asset has value even after it is fully depreciated.

For example, cash is an asset. You obtain the cash either from selling stock, obtaining a loan, or selling your services or products. Cash is money you can spend on the spot. It is called a *liquid asset*; you can use it immediately to pay off a debt or to purchase items. Other common liquid assets include accounts receivable and inventory. Liquid assets are part of current assets and represent those assets that you expect to be converted into cash within a year.

def•i•ni•tion

Assets are items of value owned by the company, including cash, property, and machinery. The value of an asset is based on its initial purchase price minus any applicable **depreciation** (the decrease in value that occurs as an asset ages). Different assets will depreciate at different rates, and this is an area where accountants can really help.

Liquid assets include cash and anything that can be quickly converted into cash in less than 12 months (such as inventory and stock and bonds). **Fixed assets** are those that are difficult to convert quickly, such as buildings or machinery.

The **book value** of an asset is its purchase price less the total amount of depreciation that has already been applied to the asset. The market value of an asset is what someone would pay for the asset, even though it may have been partially or fully depreciated.

A typical income statement.

A Simplified Income Statement
Jackson Surveying—Income Statement
For Fiscal Year Ending December 31, 20XX
Income Statement

Item	Dollar Amount	Description of Its Income Statement Function
Sales	$250,000	All revenues
Cost of Sales (variable costs)	$95,000	Variable costs associated with the revenues
Gross Profit (Gross Margin)	$155,000	Sales - Cost of Sales
Operating (Fixed) Expenses:		All nonvariable expenses:
Salaries	$65,000	Usually administrative and executive salaries
Rent	$18,000	What you pay to keep your doors open
Marketing and Sales	$55,000	What it costs you to sell your offering
Total Other		
Expenses	$138,000	Total of All Other Expenses
Pre-Tax Profit	$17,000	Gross Profit - Total Other Expenses
Federal/State Taxes	$5,950	Taxes due on the Pre-Tax Profit
Net Income	$11,050	Pre-Tax Profit - Federal and State Taxes

Fixed assets have a longer life and are more difficult to convert into cash quickly. Typical fixed assets include buildings, machinery, and land. The net *book value* of an asset is based on its initial purchase price less any depreciation. Different fixed assets have different depreciation terms, or depreciable lives. Check with an accountant to determine the proper depreciable life of a given item.

def•i•ni•tion

Liabilities are amounts that you owe, including loans, credit cards, and taxes. **Short-term liabilities** (those due within 12 months) are also called **current liabilities**. **Owner's equity** is what is left when you subtract your liabilities from your assets.

Liabilities are amounts that you owe. Typical liabilities include accounts payable, which reflects amounts you owe to suppliers, loans, credit cards, taxes, and other people or organizations. *Short-term liabilities*, which are paid back within 12 months, are also called *current liabilities*. Long-term liabilities include the portions of mortgages and equipment loans that are not due in the next 12 months.

Owner's equity is the portion of the balance sheet that displays what is left over when all liabilities are subtracted from all assets. Take what you own, subtract what you owe, and you are left with owner's equity. This is the number that you want to maximize because it can reflect the book value of your company. The initial investment of your company stock and accumulated retained earnings are added together to calculate owner's equity.

The amount of net income (see the sample income statement earlier in this chapter) determined at the end of the year is added to an equity account named retained earnings. You add the current period's net income to the prior period's retained earnings to calculate the company's retained earnings at the end of the period in question. A negative retained earnings is often a flag for a company in financial trouble. If you think about it for a second, it will make sense to you. The only way that the retained earnings can become negative is if there are negative net income values added to it, which means that the company lost money during the period that created the negative net income.

The following table is an example of how to organize your accounts in preparation for making your balance sheet.

Typical Balance Sheet Accounts

Assets	Description
Cash	Bank accounts, petty cash, investments.
Accounts Receivable	What other companies (customers) owe you on a credit basis, to be paid usually within 30 days.
Inventory	Raw materials, finished goods, products being built, retail merchandise, product manuals, and so on.
Fixed Assets	Land, buildings, machinery, office equipment, depreciation expense.

Liabilities	Description
Short-Term (Current)	Must be paid in less than 12 months. Includes accounts payable to suppliers, unpaid wages, taxes, credit card debt, short-term loans, and long-term notes with less than 12 months left on their term.
Long-Term Liabilities	Due over a period that is longer than 12 months. Includes mortgages, equipment loans, bank loans, and other long-term financial obligations.

Owner's Equity	Description
Equity Equation	Owner's equity = assets – liabilities .
Capital Stock	Owned by shareholders. Includes common stock and preferred stock.
Retained Earnings	Current and cumulative prior years' net profits or losses as accumulated from prior- and current-year income statements.

So here you are with accounts and numbers. Now look at the following figure to see how to put them together to create a balance sheet.

As your company grows, the numbers on your assets and liabilities and equity lines usually will grow larger and larger because you'll be purchasing new equipment, increasing your accounts receivable because of higher sales, or improving your cash situation. Companies just starting out will typically have a small number on their assets and liabilities and equity lines. Focus on having a positive net income, which will create a positive and growing retained earnings, thereby increasing your owner's equity.

Street Smarts

It is common for small business owners to manage their business so that they show a negative net income and, as a result, pay no taxes. Since privately owned companies do not have to face the scrutiny of the public investor marketplace, like that of a publicly traded company, there is minimal pressure to show a positive net income. You can also take this approach with your business, but be prepared to answer some pretty tough questions if you ever need to present your negative income financial statements to outside investors such as bankers, venture capitalists, or the like. Or worse, the IRS.

This typical balance sheet shows the format for organizing all your balance sheet accounts.

A Simplified Balance Statement Jackson Surveying—Balance Sheet Period Ending December 31, 20XX	
Current Assets	
Cash in Bank	$15,000
Accounts Receivable	$25,000
Inventory	$18,000
Other Current Assets	$7,000
Total Current Assets	$65,000
Fixed Assets	
Land and Building	$250,000
Machinery	$75,000
Office Equipment	$35,000
Accumulated Depreciation	($25,000)
Total Fixed Assets	$335,000
Total Assets	**$400,000**
Current Liabilities	
Credit Cards	$3,000
Wages Payable	$9,500
Taxes Payable	$3,000
Line of Credit	$5,500
Accounts Payable	$4,500
Total Current Liabilities	$25,500
Long-Term Liabilities	
Mortgage Loan	$185,000
Machinery Loan	$55,000
Equipment Loan	$30,000
Total Long-Term Liabilities	$270,000
Total Liabilities	**$295,500**
Owner's Equity	
Common Stock	$45,000
Retained Earnings	$59,500
Total Owner's Equity	$104,500
Total Liabilities and Equity	**$400,000**

Owner's equity, your company's net worth, is calculated by subtracting the liabilities from the assets. This means that as your assets (what you own) increase and your liabilities (what you owe) decrease, your equity increases. This makes logical sense, and the balance sheet puts it into a form where it can be calculated precisely. Realize, however, that your owner's equity usually does not reflect your company's market value. Setting the market value for an ongoing company is usually a complicated matter and heavily industry dependent. It depends on what someone is willing to pay you for your business.

Although your balance sheet might not change drastically from week to week, it's a good idea to regularly review whether you are taking on more debt or increasing the equity of the company. Most financial software packages can easily provide you with a balance sheet and income statement whenever you want to look at it. Always make sure to know if you are looking at an accrual or cash basis report and watch your cash and accounts receivable like a hawk.

Cash Flow Analysis

A cash flow analysis can be your most important financial statement because it tells you whether you have enough cash to pay your bills. Never forget that cash is as important as air for your business. Period. Although tracking your assets and liabilities is important over the long term, when you're just starting out, the key challenge is keeping more cash coming in than is going out.

A cash flow analysis, or statement of cash flow, looks a lot like an income statement (see the following figure). The major difference is that your income statement focuses on earnings from operations, whereas the cash flow analysis also reflects investments, borrowings, repayments of loan principle, and other balance sheet changes. Cash flow from operations might also be significantly different from reported earnings, especially if you are using the accrual basis of accounting. Remember also that your income statement might be based on accrual accounting methods, whereas your cash flow statement is based on actual cash in and out flows.

It is common to add another line to a new business cash flow statement which is underneath the net income (loss) line. This line is named "cumulative cash flow" and represents the cash totals either received by the company over the period in question (when the company is making money) or the amount of money required by the company to keep running during the months when it is operating at a loss.

Referring to the cash flow analysis, you can see that the company will lose money through July of the year listed. If you add up all of the negative net incomes (losses) from January through July, you get a grand total loss of $26,991. This figure means that you must have at least $27,000 on hand before you start your business to cover what you predict to be the total amount of loss before you begin to make some money in August. August is called your "break even" month because it is the month where you sell enough to create enough gross profit to cover your ongoing fixed expenses.

Notice also that the company starts to make money pretty quickly after August such that between August and the end of November, enough positive net income is predicted ($25,352) that it almost completely repays the initial $27,000 required to get you past July. After November, this company is really expected to generate substantial positive net income of around $16,000 per month!

Notice that a few important goals present themselves with this cumulative cash flow analysis:

◆ You know the minimum amount of money you have to have in savings or from investors to cover your company during those lean early months ($26,991).

◆ You know when you expect the company to start generating a positive net income (August).

◆ You know the sales level you have to reach to have the company generate a positive net income ($11,367).

◆ You know the approximate amount of product and services you have to sell to generate the needed break even revenue ($9,094 and $2,273, respectively).

◆ You know that your fixed expenses are $7,200 per month and if there is a way you can reduce them, at first, you will more quickly get to a positive net income.

Are you starting to see how important this simple statement is to your overall business planning and analysis procedures? I hope so, because much of the work you do preparing the rest of your plan will wind up as numbers inserted into this cash flow analysis statement. Get to know the numbers you put in here, believe in their reality, and see how the numbers fall. If you can show that your plan makes you money within the required timeframe and you have access to adequate cash to cover the initial losses, then you have come a long way toward determining if this business idea is right for you.

> **Street Smarts**
>
> You can and will spend cash in ways that will not show up as an expense on your income statement. For example, the interest that you pay on a loan is deductible as an expense, but the principle portion (the part that decreases the amount of outstanding loan balance) is not an expense. You pay cash to reduce the loan payment, but it does not become an expense. For this reason, the statement of cash flow will not match your income statement.

The reason you need both an income statement and a cash flow analysis is that you might have a really good month of sales followed by a really bad month of sales. So bad, in fact, that you have to get a loan to cover your expenses. By watching your cash flow analysis, you can see in advance when you will start to run out of cash during that month. However, because an accrual based income statement records when obligations are made, not when the cash is either spent or received, the good months and bad months often even themselves out. You wouldn't know by looking at your income statement, but August almost put you out of business due to lack of available cash.

Your monthly cash flow analysis would alert you to potential problems before they become real problems. You should now see that you must use all three financial statements to get an accurate picture of your company's financial condition.

It is also a good idea to become good friends with your receivable aging report. This is the report that tells you who still owes you money and how far past due they are with their payments. If you offer net 30-day terms, and you see most of your clients paying in 45 to 60 days, then you are providing them with additional credit for the extra 15 to 30 days. In essence, you are taking out a loan to cover for their delayed payment. If that is okay with you, then you are more generous than most small business owners I know. Get your collections in order, and you might find your need for cash decreases accordingly. See Chapter 25 for actions you can take if they don't pay.

	January	February	March	April	May	June	July	August	September	October	November	December	20XX
Revenues													
Product Sales	$1,200	$1,620	$2,187	$2,952	$3,986	$5,381	$6,995	$9,094	$11,822	$15,368	$19,979	$25,972	$106,556
Services	$300	$405	$547	$738	$996	$1,345	$1,749	$2,273	$2,955	$3,842	$4,995	$6,493	$26,639
Net Revenues	$1,500	$2,025	$2,734	$3,691	$4,982	$6,726	$8,744	$11,367	$14,777	$19,210	$24,973	$32,465	$133,195
Cost of Sales													
Product Cost	$300	$405	$547	$738	$996	$1,345	$1,749	$2,273	$2,955	$3,842	$4,995	$6,493	$26,639
Services Cost	$45	$61	$82	$111	$149	$202	$262	$341	$443	$576	$749	$974	$3,996
Total Cost of Sales	$345	$466	$629	$849	$1,146	$1,547	$2,011	$2,614	$3,399	$4,418	$5,744	$7,467	$30,635
Gross Profit Margin	$1,155	$1,559	$2,105	$2,842	$3,836	$5,179	$6,733	$8,753	$11,378	$14,792	$19,229	$24,998	$102,560
Fixed Expenses													
Salaries	$3,500	$3,500	$3,500	$3,500	$3,500	$3,500	$3,500	$3,500	$3,500	$3,500	$3,500	$3,500	$42,000
Payroll Taxes and Benefits	$700	$700	$700	$700	$700	$700	$700	$700	$700	$700	$700	$700	$8,400
Advertising and Promotion	$300	$300	$300	$300	$300	$300	$300	$300	$300	$300	$300	$300	$3,600
Depreciation	$150	$150	$150	$150	$150	$150	$150	$150	$150	$150	$150	$150	$1,800
Supplies and Postage	$100	$100	$100	$100	$100	$100	$100	$100	$100	$100	$100	$100	$1,200
Professional Fees	$175	$175	$175	$175	$175	$175	$175	$175	$175	$175	$175	$175	$2,100
Printing	$200	$200	$200	$200	$200	$200	$200	$200	$200	$200	$200	$200	$2,400
Telephone	$250	$250	$250	$250	$250	$250	$250	$250	$250	$250	$250	$250	$3,000
Equipment Rental and Repair	$50	$50	$50	$50	$50	$50	$50	$50	$50	$50	$50	$50	$600
Travel	$650	$650	$650	$650	$650	$650	$650	$650	$650	$650	$650	$650	$7,800
Miscellaneous	$225	$225	$225	$225	$225	$225	$225	$225	$225	$225	$225	$225	$2,700
Office Space	$900	$900	$900	$900	$900	$900	$900	$900	$900	$900	$900	$900	$10,800
Total Fixed Expenses	$7,200	$7,200	$7,200	$7,200	$7,200	$7,200	$7,200	$7,200	$7,200	$7,200	$7,200	$7,200	$86,400
Net Income (Loss) Before Tax	($6,045)	($5,641)	($5,095)	($4,358)	($3,364)	($2,021)	($467)	$1,553	$4,178	$7,592	$12,029	$17,798	$16,160
Provisions for Income Tax													
Federal Income Tax	$ -	$ -	$ -	$ -	$ -	$ -	$ -	$ -	$ -	$ -	$ -	$ -	$0
State Income Tax	$ -	$ -	$ -	$ -	$ -	$ -	$ -	$ -	$ -	$ -	$ -	$ -	$0
Total Tax Provisions	$ -	$ -	$ -	$ -	$ -	$ -	$ -	$ -	$ -	$ -	$ -	$ -	$0
Net Income (loss)	($6,045)	($5,641)	($5,095)	($4,358)	($3,364)	($2,021)	($467)	$1,553	$4,178	$7,592	$12,029	$17,798	$16,160

Note: Tax deductions not included to simplify analysis.

A typical cash flow analysis.

On the CD

More important information about financially managing your company is included as bonus sections on the companion CD. "Using Financial Statements" helps you more effectively use the information contained in your financial statements so that you can make more profitable decisions. "To CPA or Not to CPA" helps you understand what you really get from using a CPA for your accounting requirements. For many smaller businesses, a CPA is overkill, but for the right circumstances, a CPA is a great professional to have on your side. One tip from these sections could pay for the entire book, so make sure you check them out.

For Your Plan

- Start collecting the data you will need to create an income statement and balance sheet for your new business.

- Follow the standard format shown in this chapter for both statements. If you plan to use accrual accounting, then you will have to prepare a separate cash flow statement as well.

- Project the first year on a monthly basis and then show years two and three as totals. I suggest that you use a spreadsheet package like Microsoft Excel to prepare these statements so that you can "tweak" the numbers once the initial analysis is completed. This is usually a pretty interesting time and perhaps my favorite in the whole plan-writing process.

- Calculate the cumulative cash flow requirements for the first three years to determine the total amount of cash you will need to cover the initial startup negative net income. This will show when you plan to break even and also how much positive cash you can expect once the business is up and running as well as when you expect to recover the initial investment.

- Plan a cash safety net as part of your analysis and investor discussion. For example, if you think you need $27,000, based on cumulative cash flow analysis, then you might try to find $35–40,000 just in case you don't ramp up sales as quickly as expected. Life almost never turns out like we predict.

- Make sure that you spell out all of your assumptions and sources related to where the numbers contained in the cash flow analysis came from. Why? First, you will forget where you got them from if you don't write them down. Second, investors will want to know how you estimated future sales growth and associated expenses.

The Least You Need to Know

- Accounting is the tool used to determine the financial health of your business. It is a necessary and integral part of your business, and you should pay close attention to it from the start.

- Financial statements include an income statement, statement of cash flow, and balance sheet.

◆ Accrual and cash basis accounting provide different profit and loss information for the same accounting period. Make sure that you always track your cash and don't always believe the accrual based income statement.

◆ Bookkeeping is basically clerical in nature once the procedures are set up; financial accounting involves analyzing financial performance and comparing current results with prior accounting periods.

◆ When in doubt, get an accountant. You might not need a CPA right away.

Chapter 16

Reaping *All* Your Small Business Benefits

In This Chapter

- Understand double taxation problems
- Learn the difference between expense deductions and tax credits
- Determine your personal and business tax benefit situation and opportunities
- Review benefits that your company can offer
- Learn the various ways to get money out of your company

Douglas was a happy man. He had a great family, his weekends free, and a services corporation netting, after-tax, over $250,000 annually. And that was over and above his salary of around $110,000 per year. He was debt free and the company's prospects looked good. That knot in his stomach that had been there since he started his company was finally starting to fade. Whew!

But now he faced another dilemma, which he called a "high class problem." His company had had liquid assets of $200,000 going into the last fiscal year. It now had $450,000 in liquid assets with the addition of last year's $250,000 earnings.

The company really didn't need that much in assets to provide the needed level of financial protection, and Douglas sure wanted to have that money for his personal use.

What was the best way to get that money from the company's accounts into his own? And if the future continued in this way, he should really devise a strategy not only for the current situation but also for dealing with future gains as well. Should something happen to the corporation, he wanted to make sure that some of that gain went to paying for his children's college education and a solid play-plan for him and his wife. They had sacrificed a lot for the company over the last few years and he wanted to find a way to make it up to both of them.

He had tried to read the tax books on his own, and had felt like a visitor to a foreign country. And he knew that not handling this properly could cost him dearly in taxes, which were already too high in his opinion. He needed help and now he had the motivation to find it.

When first starting your company you look for ways to ensure its survival. In fact, you may not even be able to imagine a time when its survival will no longer be in question, but that day will come. In many cases the company starts to make so much money that the owners must decide how much to leave in the company and how much to take for their own benefit. This is a great problem and one that requires some advance planning or you might find that taking money out of the company costs you more than you expect. This chapter takes a look at some of the problems related to getting money out of your profitable company.

The Grim Truth

The sad fact is that, from a tax perspective, there are really only a few ways that you can transfer money from your company to you or your family:

◆ As salary, which means that the company and you will pay payroll taxes on the money paid, up to a threshold amount for Medicare and Social Security wages. The company does, however, get to deduct your salary as a business expense, which does decrease its tax payments.

◆ As dividends that are paid from after-tax company dollars; you then have to pay personal tax on the money you received as dividend income, but this money is not subject to payroll taxes. The company does not get to take this payment as a deduction.

◆ As an employee benefit that is paid from pretax dollars that are often deductible to the company. Various benefit programs can fall into this category. Depending on your type of business (sole proprietorship, partnership, S-corp or corporation, etc.) along with your respective percentage company ownership, these benefit payments will be treated either as an expense by the company with no tax impact on the employee/owner or as an expense to the company but taxable income to you the shareholder/owner. More on this very confusing topic later in the chapter.

♦ As allowed in various unique circumstances where the money is transferred to you but the company treats it as an expense and can deduct it. You treat it as income that is not subject to payroll taxes but subject to income tax. For example, when you lend money to the company, the interest paid by the company on that note is treated as an interest expense deduction to the company and interest income to you on which you must pay personal tax. Rent paid by the corporation to you as the landlord would also fall into this category.

♦ By selling some of the company stock that you own or selling the company outright. Selling your own company stock is treated with the same short and long-term tax rates as publicly traded stock sales.

Remember that Social Security tax is only paid on payroll amounts up to $94,200. Regular federal income tax is paid on all personal income at your personal rate. Medicare is taxed on all compensation at a rate of 1.45 percent for you plus 1.45 percent for the corporation, for a total of 2.9 percent on all money earned with no ceiling. Turn to Chapter 14, "Properly Handling Payroll Taxes," for more details on this very important topic.

As you find with any tax-related topic, the right approach to managing business expenses depends on your specific circumstances. Here is why.

Assume that you are just starting out and your annual salary from your company is $28,000, which puts you in the 15 percent federal income tax bracket if you are married filing jointly. Assume also that your C-corporation company is doing pretty well and has a net profit before tax of $100,000, which puts it in the 34 percent federal tax bracket.

> **Street Smarts**
>
> Dividends are a very expensive way to pay yourself. I suggest you use the dividend compensation method as a final resort to avoid paying corporate tax and then paying personal tax on the dividend you receive.

Now assume that you need $10,000 for a special, personal, expense item that is completely unrelated to your company and the company has over $75,000 in cash that it does not need to cover short-term expenses. You want that money and you are the owner. You should be able to take it, right? Sure, but taxes are going to be paid somewhere along the line. How can you take that money from the company for your personal use and pay the least amount of tax?

Assume that you take it as salary and that all of the $10,000 goes directly to your personal taxable salary. You now show a taxable personal income of $38,000 ($28,000 salary + $10,000 bonus) which is still in the personal 15 percent federal bracket. When you take the $10,000 as a bonus, you and your company will pay a combined 15.3 percent ($1,530) in payroll taxes before you personally ever see the bonus money. You will then personally have to pay federal income tax at a 15 percent rate on the remaining $9,235 ($10,000 − $765 payroll taxes) which equals $1,385. Adding the two taxes together we see that the total tax paid to give you that $10,000 is $2,915, or a combined 29 percent.

Now assume that you own an S-corporation and can wait until the end of the year to take the $10,000 as an S-corporation shareholder distribution. The S-corporation pays no corporate tax but you still have to pay tax at the personal 15 percent federal income tax rate on the distribution. Because the $10,000 is not treated as salary, payroll taxes are not due (saving 15.3 percent), but you pay $1,500 (15 percent) of the $10,000 in federal personal tax. This second scenario saved $1,415 in taxes simply by how you chose to pay yourself the money. Is waiting a little while worth saving $1,400? Only you can decide, but I would almost always rather keep the $1,400 in my pocket instead of giving it to Uncle Sam.

Here is the problem with trying to give a blanket statement about a tax advantage that is true for everyone. If you change the business income levels, personal income levels, marriage status, number of dependents, and any number of other variables related to the analysis, it can change the tax analysis dramatically. It really does depend.

Ed's Lessons Learned

Of one thing you must remain absolutely clear. If you own a corporation, you and your corporation are not legally and financially the same entity. Mixing your personal expenses with those of the Company, Inc. is a likely way to have any separation between you and the corporation be disallowed by the IRS, which now turns everything into a completely new tax ballgame, and likely to your detriment. You sole proprietors and partnership members are legally linked, but it is still a good idea to separately account for your personal and business activities.

Here is a rule of thumb that applies to almost any business situation. You should start today thinking of your business as a separate entity from you personally. When you are at work you make financial decisions that are best for the company. When you are at home you make financial decisions that are best for you personally. Make business expense choices that make sense for the business while always, in the background, keeping an eye out for those times when what is financially good for the company is also financially good for you personally. Don't spend company money on things that aren't needed by either you or the business.

When you find these overlaps, you should set up the agreements between you and the corporation just as you would with any other "arms-length" employee since, after all, that is what you are as far as the IRS is concerned. This is particularly true for corporations.

If you borrow money from the corporation, execute a loan agreement just as you would with anyone else. If you personally lend money to the corporation, execute a loan agreement just as you would with any other person or company that borrowed money from you. Collect on the loans just as you would expect from any other borrower. Make your payments just as you would on a normal loan. But structure the transactions to your and the company's best financial and tax advantage. Why not? You have an in with the executive management team.

A business tax deduction of $1 will only save you a maximum of 38 cents in tax payments. This is because the $1 you spend on the business expense reduces your net profit before tax by $1. The maximum corporate income tax rate is 38 percent, so reducing your net profit before tax by a dollar reduces the amount of tax you owe by 38 percent of $1, or 38 cents. Spending $1 on something that you don't need, just to keep from paying tax, is like giving someone a dollar when they promise to give you 38 cents in return. You would never so easily give up 62 cents in a business transaction—why would you do that to avoid taxes? Create great sales, be smart about how you manage your expenses, and let the taxes take care of themselves. This isn't very sexy, but my accountant told it to me long ago and I think it's still good advice.

Are You Self-Employed or an Employee?

This may sound a little strange at first, but hang in there. This is an important concept and tax-related distinction to make when you are an owner/employee.

You can only be an employee of a corporation. You cannot be an employee of your own sole proprietorship or partnership. How can you be an employee when you *are* the company? You can't, which is why these two business forms have different tax deduction rules from corporations.

Corporations have shareholders that own the company. Employees run the company to the benefit of shareholders. You may be the only employee and shareholder, but remember that the corporation is a completely separate legal entity that employs you for its financial gain. All employees of a corporation receive a W-2 form that is used when filing their personal income taxes. This distinction applies to C, S, and LLC-type of corporations.

Watch Out!

Avoid the temptation to try to treat yourself or others as contractors with the intention of avoiding payroll taxes. Taxes always get paid by someone. If you don't take them out of contractor payments and the IRS later determines that they were employees and not contractors, you will have to make up any back payroll taxes owed, plus penalties. At 15.3% of historical payroll dollars paid, that can add up to a lot of money all payable at one time. Beware if you own an S-corporation and do not take a salary but instead take all of your income as S-corporation distribution at the end of the year. The IRS knows you are working every day at your company and, as such, you should have a salary and pay payroll taxes. You better be prepared to make a solid case in the event of an IRS audit or you may find yourself owing 15.3 percent payroll tax on all of those year-end distributions.

A sole proprietorship or partnership is owned by the owner(s). They are not employees. Money paid to owners, even if it is earmarked as salary within the company payroll system, is really not payroll as far as the IRS is concerned. Owners are treated as self-employed individuals who must then pay 15.3 percent self-employment tax on all income obtained from the operation of the business. Or as my accountant put it to me one day regarding a sole proprietorship, "You have to pay self-employment tax (complete Schedule SE) whenever you have income resulting from the completion of a Schedule C." (He is always cracking great accountant jokes like that.) Owners must also make 1040-ES estimated tax payments and filings during the tax year, as needed, to keep their outstanding tax obligations to a minimum.

By the way, the income shown attributable to the general partner of a limited partnership (as shown on Form 1065 and Schedule K-1) is subject to self-employment tax. The other limited partners are not subject to self-employment tax on their portion of the partnership's income (loss) but are subject to the passive investment rules, which may limit the amount of their limited partnership losses that partners can deduct when preparing their taxes.

There are exceptions to these rules pertaining to the payment of payroll taxes for full-time traveling salespeople, full-time life insurance salespeople, certain types of home-makers, agent-drivers or commission-drivers who distribute various types of services, and some types of corporate officers. If you fall into any of these categories you should seek advice from a tax professional.

Had enough? My head is starting to hurt just explaining all of this. I just figured that you should be aware of the incredibly complicated tax miasma that exists in the United States. There is no reason why you should be an expert in all of these various areas of tax law. You have experts out there who know all of this stuff already. Pay a few hundred dollars to sit with a tax professional and/or financial planner, explain your current situation and where you plan to take your business in the future. This person will give you your best shot at determining the right business structure for your situation. Pepper this advice with some legal advice regarding liability issues and you will be on your way to starting out on the best possible legal and tax footing.

Differentiating Various Business Types and Taxes

Keeping the various income, expense, and tax relationships straight is difficult for the owner of any small business. Sometimes you emotionally feel that your fate and that of the company are intertwined to the point that they cannot be separated. But they should be separate from a personal perspective and have to be from a tax perspective.

Take a look at this table to see a summary of the various ways that company income and loss transfer to you as the owner, shareholder, and/or employee.

A Summary of Various Business Tax Situations

Business Type	Income/Loss Transfer	Tax Impact	Comment
Sole Proprietorship, Partnership	Company profit/loss passes directly to the owners with no restrictions on loss transfer.	Taxed at the owner's personal income tax bracket. Self-employment tax (15.3%) must be paid, which is basically FICA for both company and personal portions.	A successful business could quickly put the owner in a high tax bracket. Owners must make separate tax deposits to cover their own tax liability. Owners are not employees and do not receive a W-2, but other employees are and do receive W-2s.

continues

Business Type	Income/Loss Transfer	Tax Impact	Comment
C-Corporation	Corporation itself shows a profit or a loss that is carried forward.	Corporation pays tax at the corporate rate. Dividend payments to owners are taxed at the owner's personal tax rate.	Owner is likely also an employee and receives a W-2 and pays payroll taxes just like all other employees. Nearly all employee benefits are deductible by the corporation.
S-Corporation, LLC	Corporate profit or loss passes to the shareholders with some restrictions on loss transfer.	Corporate income or loss is transferred to the owners, who are then taxed at the owner's personal tax rate that may or may not be lower than the C-corporation tax rate.	Owner/employees pay personal income and payroll taxes on their salary as shown on the W-2, just like any other employee. They must also pay personal tax on their portion of the corporation profits but also absorb corporate loss from Schedule K-1. Many benefits are deductible by the S-corp, but the owners must show these payments as income upon which they pay tax at their respective rate.

You can understand, at this point, the attraction of the S-corporation when viewed from a tax perspective. Corporate net income (loss) passes to the shareholders in proportion to their respective percentage ownership. Any loss can be used to offset other personal investment-related gains of the same type (*active/passive*), but profits require the payment of taxes at the individual taxpayer rate. Importantly, the S-corp involves only one level of taxation—the personal level—and avoids double taxation. Cash payments are made to the shareholders from the S-corporation in equal amounts to the income levels reported on the Schedule K-1 so that shareholders have the cash with which to make their tax payments. This year-end cash distribution can strap the S-corp for cash at the beginning of the new year, so special loan arrangements are typically worked out between the corporation and the shareholders.

def•i•ni•tion

The IRS generally divides your business and investment activities into two categories. You are **active** if you materially participated with your business or other activity. Material participation is explained by the IRS in its Publication 925 and can generally be thought of as when you participated in an activity for more than 500 hours in a year or when your activity constituted the bulk of total participation by anyone else involved with the activity. There are other forms of material participation as well and this topic gets pretty complicated. If you do not actively participate but have something at risk in an activity, then your involvement is considered **passive**.

If you want to grow your company, then you will have to leave money in the corporation, which makes the S-corporation option less attractive. If you want to drain the company of its assets every year to put as much money as possible in your own pocket with minimal tax bite, then the S-corporation is probably your best bet. As I have said before, "It depends!" Talk with your tax professional about this very important topic and make sure that you truly understand the details of year-end tax and cash resolutions and take the proper preparatory steps. Otherwise, you may find yourself with a huge personal tax bill and no money with which to pay it.

By the way, the tax laws change all the time and often make no sense at all. So don't feel bad if you are not up to date on all of the various tax implications. You would have to dedicate most of your efforts to tracking taxes and not to making money in your business. Make the money first and then worry about the tax implications, but be as smart and prepared as possible along the way.

You Still Need a Retirement Fund

Planning for retirement is one of the reasons that most of us work. If you are like most of the people I talk to, you do not really expect to receive much benefit from Social Security when your time comes to collect. So you are planning to retire on your own resources, hoping that Social Security will provide the easy-living gravy if it is even there at all. You pay FICA and/or self-employment taxes to meet your Social Security and Medicare obligations. Your retirement funds are something else completely.

Retirement planning could fill a book in its own right. I am going to distill most of it down to information pertaining directly to those of us who run our own small business. A lot of this will be my opinion, simply in the interest of space and reading time.

Please do not treat this small section as a comprehensive guide to retirement plans. It is not. I strongly suggest that you talk with your tax advisor about the various options and their applicability to your particular situation.

Be aware that there are retirement benefits available to you as a business owner that should not be ignored.

The Standard IRA and Roth IRA

Most of you are probably familiar with the standard Individual Retirement Account (IRA) plan that has been around for years. In essence, it allows you to put up to $4,000 annually into an account and defer tax on not only the $4,000 that you initially deposit but also on any income earned by the IRA account. Deferred, that is, until you start taking money out of the account, which cannot happen, without your paying huge penalties, until you are 59 $\frac{1}{2}$ years old.

If your spouse, or you, or both are members of a qualified plan (such as a 401(k), SEP, or other pension plan), then you may find some restrictions on your ability to contribute to an IRA. If your modified adjusted gross income (MAGI) is between $75,000 and $85,000 for a married couple filing jointly, then you will find that you cannot take the full $4,000 as a deduction. These limits and reduced deduction rates change over time, so check them. Here is the interesting part about an IRA for business owners—you can have one for yourself, independent of the type of company you own, and not have to offer it to the rest of your employees. This makes it attractive but only allows you to protect $4,000 of your annual income from income taxes, which will likely not be enough for you to retire on.

The Roth IRA is designed for you folks who believe that your tax rate later in life will be higher than it is today. With a Roth IRA, you make the deposit today and pay tax today on the money you deposit. The good news is that all interest earnings associated with the account, and later withdrawals of account money, are tax-free. You can make deposits even if you are an *active participant* and can even make deposits for your spouse if your spouse has little or no income.

There are income-based phaseout rules associated with the Roth IRA which are similar to those outlined earlier pertaining to the standard IRA. The phaseout starts for married couples at $150,000 and has some special provisions for those over 50. Once again, check with your tax adviser for additional information. Withdrawals cannot begin without penalties before the money has been in the account for a specified period of time and the recipient has reached age 59 $\frac{1}{2}$.

> ## def•i•ni•tion
>
> **Active participant** refers to whether an employee is involved with an employer-maintained retirement plan at any time during the tax year. Covered plans include qualified pension, profit sharing, or stock bonus plans such as 401(k). If the "Pension plan" Box 15 of the employee's W-2 is marked, the employee is an active participant.

An SEP and SIMPLE Plan

An IRA is a basic retirement investment that almost everyone should consider if they meet the threshold requirements. But self-employed persons, or those who own closely held corporations, have other options that enable them to contribute much more than is possible with an IRA. These plans are *simplified employee pensions* (SEPs) and *savings incentive match plans for employees* (SIMPLEs).

The SEP is a retirement plan that the employer sets up with a brokerage house, bank, or insurance company. The employer sets the criteria for an eligible employee and then sets a percentage of an employee's salary that the company is willing to contribute to the SEP account on behalf of that employee. All employees over 21 years of age who earn at least $450 and worked for you at any time during three of the prior five years must be covered by the plan and using the same percentage contribution criteria.

The employee makes no contribution into the SEP and the company does not administer the SEP. The company makes arrangements with a SEP administrator, such as a brokerage, by completing an IRS Form-5305. The company then gives employees the name of the administrator so that the employees can set up their own accounts under the company umbrella. The company makes contributions to the SEP on behalf of the employee. The contributions can be for up to 25% of the employee's salary or $44,000 per employee, whichever is less. This means that you could pay yourself a salary of up to $220,000 and put (defer tax on) an additional $44,000 in a SEP. The company uses the SEP contribution as a tax deduction and the employee pays no taxes on the SEP contribution until they start to withdraw money during retirement.

The overall SEP is created by your company, but each employee account is managed by the respective employee. This means that the employee can invest in money markets, mutual funds, stocks, or other investments as fits that particular person's investment strategy; the company is not liable for any activity except for making the contributions.

You must, however, understand that whatever percentage level you set for yourself must apply to all other employees as well. You do have some limited flexibility in setting eligibility requirements for joining the SEP, but you cannot set eligibility based on income level or position in the company.

> **Street Smarts**
>
> Start out with 25 percent of your salary going to the SEP every year. At the point where you hire employees or when times get financially tight, set the SEP level to a lower percentage, or even zero, until things get back on track.

The SIMPLE plan is much like a SEP, with one very important distinction: employees make contributions to a SIMPLE (up to $10,000 annually) and the company can (and really has to) match to a maximum of 3 percent of the employee's salary. An employee making $100,000 would contribute $10,000 (which reduces his taxable income to $90,000 from a tax perspective) and the company could contribute $3,000 that it takes as a tax deduction. The combination allows the employee to add $13,000 total annually into a retirement plan. You file IRS Form 5304-SIMPLE with the SIMPLE plan administrator to get it started.

The IRS only offers the SIMPLE to "small" employers, which it defines as those having 100 or fewer employees who received at least $5,000 in compensation in the previous year.

Notice a big difference between the SEP and the SIMPLE approaches. The SEP takes money from the company and puts it into a tax-deferred account for your later use. The SIMPLE requires you to make a contribution from your paycheck to increase the retirement account. And the maximum contribution levels possible from the SEP are much higher than those of the SIMPLE.

If you have a lucrative small business and several of your family members work for the company, you might want to seriously consider an SEP as a retirement vehicle. This way you get as much money as possible out of the company and into your family's hands, and on a tax-deferred basis. Sure, they can't touch it until they are 59 ½, just like any deferred plan, but at least the money is working directly for your family.

Both plans are pretty easy to administer, with just a few forms being required to open them and minimal administration in the following years.

Various Other Deductions

Another way to get money out of your company is by having your expenses overlap with the company's in some way. Just remember that any expense deduction taken by the company is only justifiable if it is an expense that the company must incur in the normal course of its doing business. You may think that the company, which takes up a room in your basement, should pay all of your home's utilities, but that just isn't the way it works. The business uses a portion of the home's resources and only that portion is deductible in a way that stands a remote chance of passing an audit. If you are allowed the deduction, you should take it. But if you are not you might want to not push the issue to keep from raising audit flags at the IRS.

Home Office Deductions

If you use a portion of your house to perform your business activities, then that use provides you with a possible tax deduction that may help defray the cost of home ownership. You are giving up the use of that space to the company, just as you would any other tenant, and the company is obliged to pay for the use of the space.

You can rent the space to your corporation, which then deducts the payments as rent expense on the corporate return. You, on the other hand, must declare the rental income on your personal return. You just became a landlord to your corporation for that rented portion of your house. You should charge fair market value for the space, which might turn out good for you and the corporation because it can be difficult for businesses to rent small spaces.

Assume, for example, that your business uses 300 square feet of space in your 1,800 square foot home. This is ⅙ of the total space in your home, which is the percentage of expenses you can now take as a deduction. If office space rents in your area for $2.00 per foot, including utilities, then your corporation writes a rent check to you for $600 per month. You legally got $7,200 ($600 × 12) out of your corporation without payroll tax impact.

You can even depreciate that portion of the house used by the corporation, but know that it will impact your taxes at the time you sell the house. Once again, talk to a tax professional before assuming that you have everything related to a home office deduction well understood. It can be complicated and the laws change, sometimes with no apparent reason. Sole proprietors should consult IRS Publication 587 for all the details on deductions applicable to home offices.

Street Smarts

If you are a sole proprietorship, you can only claim home office deductions to that point that they equal your business income for the year. You can, however, carry forward any unused loss from one year to the next. So calculate it for sure!

If you plan to take the home office deductions, make sure that you meet these minimum criteria:

◆ You must use that portion of your home regularly to transact business.

◆ You must use that portion of your home exclusively for business activities. No personal activity can go on in that space.

◆ Finally it must either be your principal place of business, a place where you meet customers in the normal course of conducting business, or it must be a separate structure that is used in relationship to your business.

As I said earlier, you should take this deduction only if you really qualify for it. But know that keeping your personal and business lives separate is tough enough when you go elsewhere to work. When you simply walk down the hall, you really must be disciplined to not only go to work when needed, but also to not use the business space for personal activities. Otherwise you can negate the home office deduction in the event of an IRS audit. See CD Bonus Chapter 22 for more tips on handling a home office.

Medical Benefits

Given the cost of medical treatment it is imperative that you and your family have medical insurance. One trip to the hospital for just a few days can cost tens of thousands of dollars, and a major illness can bankrupt you. It is simply not worth the risk to live without medical insurance if at all possible.

Getting affordable medical insurance is far easier said than done. This section is intended to give you a few tips on how to handle medical insurance for you and your small business.

First, it is totally optional for you to provide medical insurance to your employees except in rare circumstance. Will you have to offer it to attract the best employees? It depends on that person's specific circumstances and whether he is covered by his spouse's employer's program. There is no reason for you to offer medical insurance for employees and yourself if you and all others are covered under your respective spouse's employer's programs. The major drawback to this approach is that you do not own the policy and whenever a spouse changes jobs, you are subject to the terms and preexisting condition restrictions of the new plan. Preexisting condition issues can be difficult. Owning your own plan gives you control over your medical insurance future in a way you just don't get with an employer-provided plan. You are the employer.

Just to give you an idea of where you stand with respect to the competition, the Kaiser Foundation has reported that 60 percent of small businesses with between 3 and 24 employees provided healthcare insurance. By the way, medical insurance coverage payments made by the company are tax deductible to the company, except as outlined below.

Sole proprietors, partnerships, and S-corporation shareholders who own more than 2 percent of outstanding shares have special tax rules for handling medical insurance payments. The IRS treats you folks as owners, not employees, and you are not subject to the same rules as employees. The company can pay your insurance premiums or you can own your policy and pay your own premiums. If the company pays your insurance premiums and your insurance is provided as part of a company plan for all employees and their dependents, the company must report the total annual payments to the IRS on your Schedule K-1. You must treat those payments as income to you personally. The premiums aren't treated as salary but as a fringe benefit that is subject to personal income tax but not payroll tax.

The IRS allows you to deduct the amount reported by the company on your personal tax return, whether you itemize deductions or not. You still get the deduction, but it appears on your personal return and benefits you on your personal return.

The Health Savings Account (HSA) is another option that some business owners choose to use for their medical coverage. The HSA is a way for you to contribute money to a fund, on a tax exempt basis, that you can later use to pay for medical expenses. To use the HSA you have to also set up a High Deductible Health Plan (HDHP) that will cover any major medical expenses but will typically also have a high deductible of several thousand dollars. The deductible is paid from the HSA account and can be carried over from one year to the next. The general theory behind this approach is that the HDHP will cover any major illnesses and your HSA will cover the checkups, flu shots, etc. and your overall premiums should be lower. This approach is becoming more popular with small businesses as well as those with a larger number of employees.

A Final Word About Providing Benefits

Many of my small business clients feel that they must offer all of the benefits of a large corporation to attract the high-quality talent they want. This is often not the case.

People leave large corporations for smaller companies because they are unhappy with the corporate environment. Just leaving for them is a benefit in itself. Many times these corporate refugees are retired and have their own pension, medical coverage, and life insurance. If that is the case, there is no reason for you to provide it as well.

Plus, there are all kinds of other benefits that you can offer that have nothing to do with spending money. Here is a simple starting list for your consideration:

- Offer a discount on your products or services to employees and their families.

- Offer flexible working schedules for those who have to schedule around children, school, or other personal situations such as caring for a sick relative.

- Offer to pay for employee training classes or even offer college tuition reimbursement. You improve the employee's skill level, likely increase their allegiance, and also get the tax deduction.

- Keep the working environment interesting, professional, and fun. This is a huge benefit just in itself.

- Provide employees with ways that they can grow personally and professionally while working for you and making you money.

- Offer special treats such as annual parties, internal employee competitions, or trips to great places as employee incentives. You may take these places for granted but for employees they are really special.

- Offer umbrella packages for medical insurance, life insurance, profit sharing, and other benefits so that you are not incurring the costs but enabling the company employees to participate at group rates at their own discretion. Those who need the benefit take it, pay for it, and save money doing it because they work for you.

This is a quick list to get you thinking. The items mentioned are not recurring expenses as is the case with salary increases or paid benefits. They are occasional and relatively inexpensive.

The Least You Need to Know

◆ The C-corporation pays dividends to shareholders in after-tax net income. The shareholders pay personal tax on the dividend, causing expensive double taxation.

◆ Both salary and bonus income require the payment of the corporate and personal portions of FICA taxes up to the applicable income thresholds.

◆ There is a tax difference between owners taking out money as salary, dividend, or S-corporation disbursement.

◆ A home office deduction is a valid tax reduction strategy that simultaneously enables your business to reduce its overhead expenses in the early years.

◆ An SEP and SIMPLE plans enable owner/employees to transfer money from the company to their own retirement plan.

◆ Tax deductibility of benefits expenses varies between sole proprietorships/ partnerships, S-corporations, and C-corporations. Owners and employees may or may not be treated equally from a tax deduction perspective.

Part

Running a Successful Business

Your business plan is a major step in getting your business started, but you will need additional information and skills to make and keep your business successful once it is up and running. Your business will need cash as much as you need air. And cash availability is tied directly into your credit policy— which is tied directly into your policy on collecting bad debts from people who don't pay. This part tells you what to do in these important areas.

It also helps you work with your commercial banker, explains how to take full advantage of automation, and describes ways to handle health insurance and other small business benefits. There is also a special new chapter that explains the basics related to dealing with China, a major force not only internationally but also here in the U.S.

The prior parts got you going. This part helps you continue on that road to sustained success.

Cash Is Like Air for Your Business

In This Chapter

- The value of cash in your organization
- Turning receivables into cash
- How rapid sales growth can jeopardize your business
- Using credit to your advantage
- Determining total cash requirements

Laurie stared in disbelief at her conference room table. She had heard of this happening to other companies; she couldn't believe it happened to hers.

"We're out of money," she said. "I can make payroll, but I don't have enough left over to pay our suppliers."

"That's impossible," said Philip, the VP of Sales and Marketing. "We just had three of our best months this quarter. In fact, our current revenues are triple that of last year at this time, and our income statement clearly shows a profit for this quarter. What gives?"

Jerry from accounting shifted uncomfortably and then started to speak. "The net income shown on our statements is right—we have recently closed some great deals, but our cash is way low. As you know, we haven't collected payments on those large sales. And we've had to pay our workers and suppliers even though our customers haven't yet paid us. It'll be great when all those sales are collected, but if we keep growing as we have been, we're likely to need even more cash."

"So are you trying to tell me that our sales success has put the company in jeopardy?" cried Philip.

"Not at all," said Laurie. "We simply did not plan for the rapid increase and came up short with our lines of credit and other ways of getting cash into our bank account. It was my and Jerry's responsibility to plan for this, and we blew it. We need to tell our vendors our dilemma. I think honesty is the best policy. Let's just hope they will let us stall our payments. We can't let it happen again!"

Everyone nodded his or her head at the seriousness of the situation. They had been so happy about being successful that they had forgotten that cash is like air for your business.

Keeping the cash flowing into your business is key to growth and expansion, not to mention paying your bills in a timely manner. This chapter will help you develop strategies for keeping the money flowing into your business so that you don't run into the same trouble Laurie's company did. It also shows you how to determine the amount of cash you will need to keep afloat.

When You're Out of Cash, You're Out of Business (Usually)

Love may make the world go 'round, but it's cash that keeps the lights on while you're spinning. Try to retain an employee when you can't pay him, and you will understand that cash is the business equivalent of air. Lose your employees, the good ones, and you have substantially hurt your business. Once they're gone, they're usually gone for good.

Take a look at your vendors. How long will they keep providing you with the materials you need if you can't pay your bills? About as long as a snowball would last in a west Texas desert. Once again, you can't blame them for putting a stop to your credit line. Guess who is paying employees out of his or her own pocket because he or she gave you credit and you can't pay? Your vendor! Your vendor has to cover his or her own behind just like you do.

Now, what about you? What happens if you can't pay yourself? How long will you keep the business alive and pay your employees when you are not being paid? A few months, maybe, but when it becomes a way of life, you will be seriously tempted to pull the plug and "get a real job." Not because you don't love what you do, but simply because that's what an organism does when its air supply is taken away.

A cash problem hurts your employees, your vendors, and you personally. Lack of cash might cause your usually professional employees to become disgruntled, might cause the quality of your product to decline, and might lead to your own loss of enthusiasm. The result is that your customers will be affected, and they probably won't like it. Their opinion of your company might drop as employees become snippier over the phone or in person. Unfortunately, customers don't really care why the quality has declined; they just recognize that it has, and they might decide to take their business elsewhere if it continues.

All this because you forgot that cash is king! Income is great. Equipment is wonderful. Receivables are heartwarming. Inventory gives you something to count on boring weekends and at the end of the year. But cash is the oil that makes it all work smoothly on a daily basis.

How Success Can Kill Your Business

How good can it get? Here you are with a 300 percent increase in sales over the past six months. Your people are flying high, and you just can't seem to do anything wrong. As a matter of fact, the projects coming your way are larger than you ever thought you would have, and it looks like you'll get them all! Your initial dreams have come true, and you're on the verge of becoming unbearable to everyone around you. Don't worry. Life is about to humble you, unless you have taken the proper steps to deal with the growth.

Have you ever met someone who told you that he was so successful, he went out of business? If not, you should look for such a person and buy him dinner (or a drink, depending on how he dealt with the loss). Just as you don't need to go through a windshield to learn that seatbelts are a good thing, you don't need to go out of business to learn the dangers of rapid growth.

Picture this scenario: you used to provide $10,000 per month in services, and all your customers paid cash on delivery or by credit card. When you completed the sale, you got the cash and it went straight into your business checking account and was used to pay your bills. Everyone was happy. Then customers began asking for credit terms. After all, your competitor offered them credit, and they have consistently used your company instead. It wasn't such a big deal, and they were stable. Why not offer them credit? So you did.

Take a look at what happened when you agreed to offer credit payment terms instead of cash. You delayed the cash payments you would have previously received this month (precredit) for at least a month. You, however, still need to pay your employees and vendors at the end of *this* month. Where is that money going to come from? Unless your company has a lot of cash on hand (and wouldn't we all like that situation?), it will have to come from you, the owner. When the customer pays, you will simply pay yourself back the amount you loaned the company and all will be fine. So far, so good. Sort of ….

Watch Out!

Don't put all your eggs in one basket. As dangerous as it is to grow your company quickly, it's even more risky for that growth to be the result of a relationship with just a few big customers. Keep trying to expand and diversify your customer base while managing your growth or a lack of payment by a single large customer can seriously cripple your business and cost you some sleepless nights.

Now let's be really successful and bump your monthly sales to $30,000. Wonderful! Who is going to provide the cash needed to cover the month-end bills? You? Do you have the $30,000 on hand to lend the company? Even if you do have the cash at $30,000, you might not when monthly sales hit $50,000 or $100,000. What about if customers start to take liberties with the net 30 day payment policy and start paying in 60 or 90 days instead? Can you now come up with the $60,000 to $90,000 it will take to cover the cash flow during that delayed payment period? I should now have your attention.

My point is this: someday you will no longer be able to personally provide this kind of cash advance to the company. Uh-oh! There go your employees and all those wonderful vendor relationships. When they leave, they place everything that made you successful in jeopardy. In short, the whopping success that you enjoyed has just put you precariously close to being out of business. Isn't it amazing how a few short (or very long, sleepless) weeks can turn your business on its ear? That is exactly what will happen if you don't take steps to avoid a cash crunch.

I'm not trying to talk you out of making your business as wildly successful as you can imagine. I'm just trying to open your eyes to the fact that success can destroy all that you have built if you don't also deal with its potential risks. Use the information in this chapter in conjunction with that in Chapter 18 to ensure that your credit and collection policies are rock solid, which will minimize the cash pressure on you and your business.

Factoring, Credit Terms, and Loans

Here you are, all dressed up to go to the dance with a hot date and no cash to pay for the cab. Now what do you do? You go to someone and borrow money against your next paycheck or income tax refund. Well, the same thing can be done with a business, and it's called *factoring*. With factoring, a company gives you a percentage of what customers owe you, sort of like a short-term loan using what is owed you as collateral. This is pretty expensive short-term money to get, but it is common practice and viable if you are in a cash crunch.

You can also improve your cash situation by providing your customers with a discount incentive for paying their bills early (or even on time) and delaying payments to your own vendors with whom you have credit. This improves your cash position (for the short term) by decreasing the time *float* between when you must pay your bills and when you receive money.

Finally, you can get a short-term loan that is secured by your receivables from a bank or other funding source. This technique is less expensive than factoring and provides greater stability, along with other benefits such as improving your lending relationship with your banker.

def•i•ni•tion

Factoring is the process of receiving money now for payments your customers are expected to make to you in the next few weeks. There is a cost for having that money now, however, which is paid in the form of a percentage fee to the factoring company or factor. It is expensive to do on a regular basis but can be effectively used if needed. But you must plan ahead with the factoring company to factor your receivables. **Float** in this context refers to the time frame between when you earned the money due you and when it is actually received. It can also mean the time frame between when you actually receive money and when portions of the money are due payable to others.

Factoring Receivables

If you need cash now to cover business expenses, there are companies out there who will provide you with cash for your receivables in exchange for a fee. Here's a general outline of how factoring, or discounting, of receivable notes works. (Use this as a way of understanding the process and verify the percentages with prospective factoring companies that you can find with a simple Internet or Yellow Pages search.)

1. You close the deal and the customer agrees to pay you for your product or service.

2. The company that plans to factor your receivables issues an invoice to the customer (usually on your letterhead), which the customer is to pay.

3. The factoring company immediately gives you cash worth between 80 and 95 percent of the receivable value.

4. The factoring company then gives back a portion of the fee (usually up to half of the initial 5 to 20 percent discount) if the customer repays within the specified time frame.

For example, assume that a client contracts to buy from you $10,000 worth of your product or service. Assume that you can realistically expect to receive that money within 45 to 60 days, which can put you in a bind depending on your company's cash situation. You could factor the note using the previously outlined procedure and have the numbers work out as follows:

1. You close the deal for $10,000 and perform your side of the agreement so that the revenue is now recognizable.

2. The factoring company issues an invoice to your customer for $10,000 and indicates the terms in which the payment should be made to the factoring company.

3. The factoring company immediately writes you a check for between $8,000 and $9,500, depending on your agreement with the factoring company.

4. If the customer pays within the allowed 30 days, then the factoring company writes you another check for around 10 percent (or $1,000) when payment is received. (The longer it takes for your customer to pay the factor, the less of the original invoice amount you get back.)

On the CD

A sample Receivables Purchase Agreement is included on the CD as document 17-01.

Assuming that you receive an 85 percent factoring rate with a 10 percent additional payment received within 30 days, you see $8,500 immediately and $1,000 within 30 days. You give up 5 percent, or $500, to get your money up front instead of later and for pushing the collections issue over to the factoring company. Collection becomes their problem, not yours.

If you are in a cash crunch, factoring can save your hide. However, the down side is the expense, which is not trivial. If, rather than factoring, you used a typical bank line of credit, with interest-only payments, at a 5 percent per year interest rate (which may be low depending on the money markets), then borrowing that same $10,000 for one month would cost you $10,000 \times 0.05/12 = \$41.67$ instead of the $500 that factoring would have cost you. When you receive the $10,000, you pay off the line of credit. Simple. Wow! You have saved a lot of money using the line of credit instead of factoring.

Factoring is a pretty expensive way to have your cash earlier instead of later. On the other hand, if you need it, you need it. Don't stand on principle and put your company in cash jeopardy.

Here is something that you might consider if you have the personal cash on hand. You can minimize the sour taste that factoring percentages can create by performing your own factoring services. If you have substantial personal resources and you own a corporation, you can use your own money to replace the need for factoring. You can buy the receivables from your corporation with your personal funds and provide the same terms as a factoring company. At least the interest is going into your favorite account (yours!) instead of some other company's. You will, however, need to declare the interest income on your personal tax return. After all, it is income that you earned as a private individual even if the money did come from your own corporation. Prepare a factoring agreement and perform the transaction just like you would with a third party. I have even factored receivables to friends as a way for them to make more money on their savings than they would get from a bank or CD. I made it clear to them, however, that if the customer defaulted on the receivable, it was their problem, not mine, and that was why they were receiving a higher interest rate on the factored notes.

Unfortunately, you can only factor up to the limit allowed by your personal resources. You then must look for other options.

Using Credit Terms to Enhance Your Cash Position

Timing is the secret to success, and that is particularly true when working with money. The time that money is in your hands, or in someone else's, either makes you money or costs you money. You must make every possible effort to turn your sales into cash as quickly as possible, paying as little as possible to get your money faster, such as by factoring, lines of credit, or offering fast-payment discounts.

You have an excellent opportunity to improve your cash flow by simply changing the way you pay your bills and collect receivables from your clients. If you must pay in 30 days and your clients must pay in 60 days, you have a problem. On the other hand, if your customers pay in 10 days and you pay your vendors in 45 days, you are in excellent shape. You accomplish this by simply offering your customers a discount (such as 2 percent of what they owe you) for payment within 10 days. Many companies will

On the CD

Sample Credit Application (document 17-02) and Credit Information Release Authorization (document 17-03) documents are included on the CD.

jump at the chance to save the 2 percent, and it's certainly cheaper for you to offer this discount than to pay a factoring service 5 to 15 percent for the same result! From your customer's perspective, they are saving 2 percent off of their product costs (which improves their gross margins) by simply paying early, which may not be a problem for many of them. You will hear this credit policy referred to as "2 percent in 10 days/net 30 days" credit terms.

Street Smarts

Don't tell the IRS that I told you this, but you can improve your cash position for a two-week period by holding your monthly payroll taxes until the middle of the month, assuming your payroll situation allows you to do that. Sometimes, providence will shine on you when that big check you've been expecting arrives just in time to make the payment. If not, you better be ready to come up with the cash needed to make the tax payment. Remember, this approach is not recommended and should be treated as a very last resort because delinquent payroll taxes can land you in big trouble with serious legal consequences.

Think about it. Plot out on a piece of paper the timing of payments made and received. Assume that a $10,000 sale is made today. Mark on a calendar when you expect to provide the products or services, when you plan to receive the payment made under your credit terms, and when you have to pay your vendors and employees. Notice that the arrows for money going out and money coming in have a delay between them that usually doesn't work in your favor. You must pay the suppliers before you receive payment. Now mark where payment would be received with a 2 percent discount in 10-day incentive. Isn't life easier when the cash is in your hands, instead of in your customer's account? Plus, when you have the money, you don't have to worry about it becoming uncollectable, a horrible circumstance in which I hope you never find yourself.

Buying on Credit

Your grandmother may have always told you to stay debt free because a person in debt is a person in trouble. Well, that might be true for certain people, but credit is the lifeblood of a growing company. Credit in itself is not bad. It is how you use this credit that can either save your hide or hang it out to dry.

Try this technique for increasing your cash situation. Instead of paying $25,000 in cash for that bunch of computer equipment you intend to buy, why not go to your bank and have them give you a loan secured by the equipment? The bank will probably want 20 percent ($5,000) down and the rest financed over 24 to 36 months at the going interest rate. Notice that your monthly expenses go up, but you have $20,000 cash in your bank account, that you avoided spending today because of the loan, to handle unexpected cash shortfalls. Heck, some vendors are even offering, at the time of this writing, "buy now, no interest or payments for up to two years" payment terms. This is really pretty scary from a customer perspective because you could take full advantage of this offer, run up a huge debt to this vendor, spend the customer payments on growing your business, and find yourself unable to pay the debt when due in two years. It takes a lot of self-discipline to manage this type of debt/credit opportunity properly and not put your company in jeopardy. Remember that credit is never free and at some point charged items must be paid for with real cash.

> **On the CD** _____
> Sample Security Agreement (document 17-04) and Guaranty (document 17-05) documents are included on the CD.

Even your grandmother would agree that paying your bills while keeping some cash on hand is a healthy state of financial being.

Taking Out a Loan

You can imagine that every business has the same problems in turning its receivables into cash. It should not surprise you that people, even banks, provide loans designed to cover exactly this short-term timing situation. It is essentially a line of credit secured by the receivables, and you are expected to pay it down as quickly as possible. The interest rate is some variation of prime plus a few percentage points annually, instead of the 60 percent that you get with a factoring company, and you establish a credit history with your bank. That always pays off in the long run because the bank can become an integral partner as your success requires higher and higher borrowing levels.

Applying Break-Even Analysis to Determine Startup Cash Requirements

A thriving, dynamic business always has something new happening. It might be the business itself when you are first starting up, or it might be introducing a new product line. In either case, it is important to get a solid idea of when and whether your business or new offering will make money. The financial technique used for estimating that time frame and likelihood is called *break-even analysis*. Notice that knowing the break-even point is important to determining the amount of cash you need to have on hand. The further out your break-even point, the more cash you need to keep you solvent until you get past break-even and start making money. The closer your break-even point, the less demanding your cash requirements. Without knowing your break-even point, you are simply guessing, which is scary.

def•i•ni•tion

A **break-even analysis** is a calculation of how much sale revenue and resulting gross profit you must create to cover your basic fixed costs of doing business. This dollar sales value can also be translated into a unit sales level. Above that level, you're making money. Sounds like a pretty important number (and initial target) to know. The formal definition is when your gross profit equals your fixed expenses.

In a nutshell, a break-even analysis tells you how much you have to make in dollars or products sold to cover all your costs. Obviously, your goal is to do much better than that, but start first with ensuring you can at least pay for the products or services to be produced. When you operate at break-even, it is not costing you anything to keep your doors open, and when you are above break-even, you are actually making money.

A break-even analysis takes into consideration three pieces of information:

- ◆ The average sale price of what you sell, which can be either products or services. Just estimate how much your typical sale will be and divide it by the number of units you sold (or hours you spent) to earn those sales.

- ◆ The average variable cost to you to produce what you sell, or how much it costs to produce your typical sale. Once again, add up your total estimated variable costs and divide them by the number of units (or hours) involved to create those total costs. Ideally, you want the number of units used in this step to match the number used to calculate the average sale price. This is your average variable cost.

- ◆ Your total fixed costs per year (and then per month), which are your total expenses for the year that you have to pay no matter how much you sell. This includes things such as rent, your phone bill, insurance, tax, employee salaries, and utilities.

Your break-even point in dollars is calculated by calculating

Fixed cost ÷ (1 − % average variable cost) × average sales price

Remember that when calculating your average cost of producing products, you will have to add all of your expenses associated with manufacturing, such as raw material costs, labor costs, and waste and divide it by the number of products produced. That's your average. Some individual units may have cost more than others to produce, and some less, but over time and larger quantities, the cost evens out to some average.

Similarly, the average sale price of your product can be determined by adding your anticipated sales for the next year and dividing by the total number of units you expect to sell. While you may sell some for higher or lower prices, this calculation averages them into a single number, which simplifies the analysis.

For example, if you have annual fixed costs of $30,000 and sell software programs that are sale priced at an average of $100 and cost you $20 to produce, your break-even in dollars is $37,500:

$$\$30,000 \div (1 - 20 \div 100) = \$30,000 \div .8 = \$37,500$$

This means that you must have sales of $37,500 a year just for the business to break even (pay its fixed expenses and product costs). To calculate the number of software programs you have to sell, just divide $37,500 by the price of the program, which is $100:

$$\$37,500 \div 100 = 375 \text{ units}$$

These example numbers will mean nothing to your particular business, but if you put in some estimates of your average sales price, cost, and total fixed costs, you will get an idea of what you can expect for your company. Once you figure out the break-even in dollars and units, think about whether those figures seem high, low, or reasonable for your particular business environment. (This is a marketing question, isn't it?) Notice that you now have a target for unit and dollar sales and if you believe you can hit this target, then you at least can get your business to the point that it is supporting itself. That is a huge milestone in itself.

For those of you starting a service business who think there's no way to figure out an average sale price, here are some pointers. Keep in mind that calculating your break-even point isn't supposed to be exact at the moment. You're just trying to get a rough idea of whether you can ever sell enough of your product or service to pay all your expenses and make some money.

If you're not selling a product, there are other ways of estimating your break-even point. If you are thinking of becoming a consultant, for instance, you determine your hourly rate and divide your fixed costs by your hourly rate. That tells you the minimum number of hours you need to bill each month to break even. (*Note:* it is common for consulting businesses to have very low variable costs since they provide only services and not products.) If you come up with 10 or 11 hours per week, or 40 per month, you're doing well. The average number of hours that a new consultant bills weekly is around 14; this number should get up to around 24 to 30 hours per week once the company gets up and going. If you're having trouble choosing an hourly rate, call some of your competitors and ask what their rate is; that is a guide for what local clients are willing to pay.

Street Smarts

When you perform a break-even analysis, be sure to divide the average cost by the average price first, before subtracting the number from 1. This gives the answer in dollars, not units. You then calculate the number of units needed to break even, which is also very important to understand.

Even if you are selling a product and you can't figure out the average sale price, just take the prices of all or most of your products and calculate an average. If you own a restaurant, you can estimate the average meal price by taking the average price of an appetizer and adding it to the average entrée price and drink price. This number may run anywhere from $5.00 at McDonald's to over $100 at an upscale eatery. Now estimate your average cost of providing those appetizers and entrées. Subtract that average cost from the average price to get the average gross margin (gross profit) per meal. Now divide your estimated monthly fixed costs by this average gross profit per meal number. This final quotient tells you how many people you need to feed each month just to keep your doors open and the lights on. Does it look feasible given the number of hours you'll be open and your neighborhood? Remember that if your restaurant is in an industrial district, you might not have many customers outside of breakfast and lunch. These are the types of questions you're trying to answer with this exercise.

If you come up with a number that is much higher than you think you could ever reasonably achieve, your business may have serious problems staying financially solvent. Are there ways you can reduce your fixed costs, such as by setting up a home-based office or putting off hiring employees until later? Those are the kinds of decisions you need to make to create a successful business. However, if your break-even appears well within reason in terms of sales, look again at your numbers to be sure you haven't forgotten to take something into consideration. If your calculations appear accurate, then you are in luck and are well on your way to starting a successful business.

Break-even analysis is one of the most valuable and simple to use financial analysis tools available, and you should get to know its usage. It will pay off for you well into the future.

Knowing When Enough Is Enough

There are worse fates than having a business fail miserably due to a single, catastrophic event. One of them is having it fail gradually so that it slowly bleeds your reserve funds and energy. It never really takes off, but it never really is bad enough to close the doors. Beware because the steady drip-drip-drip of cash leaving the company on a monthly basis will keep you around while draining your finances. When this happens, you find yourself digging into your personal savings each month to keep the company afloat, all the time believing that it will turn around. The problem is that both you and the company may eventually go bankrupt.

For this reason, I suggest that you set some time frame and financial guidelines for when and how you will evaluate your company's performance. These milestones should include desired, or even required, levels of personal income and time investment to keep the business running. If you exceed these goals, then you and your business are successful. If you are below those goals, then you need to make some goal adjustments or business management adjustments. At that time, you can choose to either recommit to the venture or decide that it's time to call the idea a bad one and move on by either closing, selling, or restructuring the business to meet your desired goals.

Get your family involved in this goal-setting process. It is important that they know the sacrifices on their part are only in place for a set period of time, after which things will be reevaluated. If the business does well, you'll all benefit; but if it never takes off, your family can take comfort in knowing you'll shut it down after a certain period of time and try something else. Believe me when I say that your family is afraid for you and for themselves if the business goes under.

The hardest question to answer is, "How long do I keep investing in the company before I can expect a profit?" This is a tough question, but you can expect to lose some money for at least 12 to 24 months, and you should be making a decent living between 36 and 48 months. It is certainly common for the owner to pay all of the bills during the startup period of time and not take home a salary. (These are simply rules of thumb based on discussions with other business owners and do not represent scientific findings.) If you have a smaller service-oriented company that you can operate out of your home, then you might make money much sooner because your overhead is low and you get to break-even earlier. Are you starting to appreciate this tight relationship between your sales price, your variable costs, and your fixed costs? They are inextricably linked. In summary, the more you can reasonably charge your customers, while keeping your variable and fixed costs low, the sooner you will take home the money needed to support yourself and grow your business.

Street Smarts _____

> Assume that you need to cover at least six months of personal living expenses
> before the company becomes profitable enough to pay you a salary. Expect that it
> may take 18 to 24 months, but use 6 months as an absolute minimum. If you plan
> 18 and it takes 6, you are ahead of the game. If you plan 6 and run out of money
> at month 7, you are out of business. This is a sobering thought, so don't be too aggres-
> sive in your sales and profit projections.

Projecting Startup Cash Requirements

Your income statement summarizes how much money you made and how much
money you spent for a specified period of time, which is typically one year but will
be broken out on a monthly basis for the first year of operation. It allows you to look
at the big picture of how much money you expect to make (or lose) over a period of
time.

Use a balance sheet to determine the value of what you own (your assets) and what
you owe (your liabilities) at a particular point in time, usually the last day of the year.
Bankers are interested in this statement because it gives them an idea of what your
business is worth and whether you can pay off your loan by selling all your assets.

Now for the clincher: remember that your income and balance sheet might be based
on accrual accounting and may not reflect cash received. You can look good on these
two statements and be completely out of cash, which happens to more of my clients
than you want to know. You really want to know the total amount of cash that you will
require during the startup phase to cover not only initial startup costs but also the net
cash outflow that will happen monthly until you make it past break-even—the point
where your monthly net income goes from a negative number to a positive one.

Remember that each month of cash-basis negative net income (net cash outflow)
increases your total cash requirement, and each month of cash-basis positive net
income (net cash inflow) decreases your total cash requirement. Adding the inflow/
outflow from one month to the next tells you the total you need (cumulative) over the
period of time of your analysis. (See the "Typical Cash Flow Analysis" chart included
in Chapter 15 for an example of a cumulative cash flow calculation.)

This cumulative cash flow requirement is so important that it is hard to overemphasize. This is the total estimated cash you must have available to pay all of your bills
while you are ramping up your sales to break-even and beyond. You can have this

money in the form of cash on hand, ready loans, equity partners willing to buy in, or any number of other, creative ways. But you must have it available, or you may find yourself running out of cash at the very moment when your business is poised for success.

For Your Plan

Any investor knows that cash is the air supply of your company and will want to understand the uses of your cash, how you plan to manage it, and how much you need to stay afloat. Make sure that your plan presents the following information:

- A monthly cash flow (loss) projection for the first 12 months and then annually for years two and three.

- The amount of cumulative cash you will need for your venture, including a detailed description of the sources of this cash.

- Your intended cash management strategy, including the use of factoring, bank lines of credit, or other sources.

- Your intended credit management policies and your justification for why you set them up the way you did.

- Your expected break-even point from both a sales and units perspective. These numbers will be used to set goals for the initial marketing and operations portions of your plan.

- How these break-even projections tie in with the marketing and sales plan, which must be designed to create sales sufficient to exceed the break-even within prescribed time frames.

The Least You Need to Know

- Cash is the lifeblood, or air supply, of an organization. Without cash to pay employees or vendors, you are out of business.

- Cash will become scarce at some point in your business growth; of that you can be certain. Set up credit lines today that will help you when it happens.

- Factoring is a convenient, yet expensive, way of turning receivables into cash.

◆ Banks will give you short-term lines of credit secured by receivables, but you generally need to have set this line of credit up before you actually need it.

◆ Don't be afraid of credit. Purchasing capital equipment items with credit instead of cash shifts the purchase from a large cash outlay to smaller monthly payments, which improves your cash position as long as you don't go overboard. But plan to pay it off when it becomes due.

◆ Understand the cumulative cash requirements of your company to make sure that you are not caught short on cash just when your company is ready to take off.

Properly Handling Credit Card Sales

In This Chapter

- ◆ Comparing standard terms with credit card sales
- ◆ How much do credit sales cost you?
- ◆ Protecting yourself from fraud
- ◆ Telephone sales versus in-person credit card sales
- ◆ Determining the right credit card policy for you

Jamie was pumped up! Sales were going through the roof, and things appeared to be financially on track. Why did his accountant want to talk with him? What could possibly be wrong? His trusty accountant, Raymond, was smiling but also shaking his head.

"Jamie, how would you feel about having another $500 in your pocket this month without lifting a finger?" asked Raymond. He knew Jamie well enough to already know the answer.

"Sure, and what's your cut for bringing this opportunity to me?" asked Jamie.

"Not a nickel. This one is on the house. Do you remember those two large training contracts you signed last month? The one for $17,000 and the other for $15,000? Well, guess what? The clients decided to charge the sales to their American Express card, and American Express charged you 3.5 percent for processing those charges! These clients both have great credit records and probably would have jumped on the 2 percent discount we offer for payment within 10 days. In short, you gave up at least 1.5 percent of the sale price because your salespeople wanted to get credit for the sale before the end of the quarter!"

"Hmmm," Jamie thought, punching numbers into his calculator. "3.5 minus 2 is 1.5 percent. And 1.5 percent of $32,000 is $480. The sales reps just cost me enough to pay for a great evening out on the town for me and that wife of mine I never see! What do you suggest?" asked Jamie.

"Let your salespeople know that credit card sales cost the company extra money because the credit card company charges a processing fee. Cards should be used only for sales under a certain dollar level and limited to specific situations, such as new customers without a solid credit history with our company. If they continue taking a credit card for everything, then bring the credit management procedure away from them. If you don't set some limitations on credit card sales, you give money away to credit card companies when you can have the cash in your pocket. Credit cards are an excellent way to avoid collection problems with new customers, but they get expensive with established customers who you know will pay."

"Thanks, Raymond," said Jamie as he walked out the door. "You can bother me with this kind of feedback any time you want."

Credit cards may well be the new form of legal tender. I know people who carry credit cards and an ATM card but little or no cash. You simply cannot ignore the implications of credit cards on your business no matter what type of business you run. It is important to consider whether offering your clients the opportunity to pay using a credit card, instead of cash or a check, is a good thing.

More than likely you will find that taking credit cards is a convenience that most of your clients will want, especially if you deal with consumers instead of established businesses. However, if you'll be selling consulting services to companies and billing tens of thousands of dollars, a credit card is probably not the best way to get paid. Instead, request a completed credit application and a company check to verify that they will pay, and save the credit card processing fees. This chapter helps you get set up in the right way with policies that make credit work for you.

The Way Credit Cards Work

A person (consumer) obtains a credit card from a bank, which provides a line of credit to the person whose name is on the card. The credit card is issued as a Visa, MasterCard, Discover, or some other brand name. (American Express produces its own cards, which require payment in full each month for most charges unless special arrangements are made, and provides its own credit processing operations, which I discuss in more detail later.)

You, as a business owner, set up your own merchant account so that you can process credit card sales and then have money deposited into your account. You are issued a *merchant number* by your credit card processing company that helps them identify exactly who you are, the applicable processing fees to charge, and where your money should be deposited.

> **Watch Out!**
>
> Some credit card processing companies have restrictions that prevent them from authorizing certain types of businesses. If you fall into any of these categories, be aware that you might have to do a little more shopping around to get a good deal: home-based businesses, mail-order firms, start-up businesses (those less than a year old), and businesses done primarily over the phone.

The customer's credit card is generally *unsecured*, meaning the bank has nothing that it can take and sell to repay the person's debt if the person defaults on payments. The only recourse is to cancel the card, destroy the person's credit record, and bother him until he pays. Fortunately for you, the business owner, you get paid whether your customer pays the credit card company or not. That's what you pay the credit card companies for. They, not you, absorb the risk of their credit card holder not paying his balance. If you don't know your customers, the credit card processing fee can be viewed as inexpensive payment insurance.

When a person purchases something from you and pays using a credit card, he is using his line of credit from the bank. The bank is essentially agreeing to pay the person's obligation to your company and takes the responsibility for obtaining payment from the person whose name appears on the card. In short, the bank is giving the person a loan that he uses to buy a product or service from you. In return for taking the responsibility (and risk) for collecting payment from the cardholder, the bank charges you a fee. Of course, you still get paid even if the credit card company doesn't, but you did give up a percentage of your total sale amount to them for absorbing this risk.

You can generally think of a buyer who uses a credit card as someone with a line of credit from a bank. The company whose name appears on the card, such as Citibank or Chase, handles the cardholder credit application and marketing of the card. You process a customer's purchase using the credit card and signed receipt. In return, the bank deposits the amount of the purchase (minus the fees) into your bank account. The company that processes and clears your company's credit card transactions, debiting the charged amount from the proper credit card and then crediting your bank account, is called the card processing company. Such a company can be an independent business just like yours, and thus not affiliated with the credit card issuer. On the other hand, some banks now have their own credit card processing units.

PaymenTech (1-800-619-1982) is one credit card processing company you might want to contact. Another is US Bank Merchant Services (1-800-432-9413).

def•i•ni•tion

A **merchant number** is a number given to your company that is used to identify which account should be credited when a customer makes a purchase. It also verifies that you're allowed to accept credit cards in payment. When you call your credit card processor for authorization to charge a customer's credit card, he or she asks for your merchant number, the customer's card number and expiration date, the security code shown on the back of the card, and the amount of the purchase before giving approval with its associated authorization code. An **unsecured** line of credit is a line of credit that is not backed by some form of collateral. The interest rate on this type of credit line is usually much higher than a loan secured by something of value other than your good name and promise to pay.

The Costs of Credit

Sounds pretty simple, doesn't it? Run the card through the credit card machine, punch in the purchase amount, and press Enter. You've just gotten paid. Too cool! Too easy! What's the catch?

The catch is that there's a cost to this great service. Take a look at who gets a piece of that simple transaction.

For the purposes of this discussion, I assume you are processing the transaction electronically as opposed to manually. With a manual system, you have to call and request authorization by voice, rather than let the credit card machine dial automatically by modem. The processing company also typically charges a higher fee for manual processing. Electronically is truly the way to go unless you only process a few credit transactions per month.

Terminal Fees

First is the cost of the equipment used for processing the cards. It is sometimes called a swipe machine because you can either type in the numbers on the keypad or swipe the card through the slot on the top of the unit. The machine comes from a *credit card transaction processing company*, a company that is often a bank or a bank's sales representative who acts as a liaison between your company and the credit card processing network. The machine is essentially a small computer terminal that connects you directly to your credit card processing company. This can also be computer based for those of you who intend to incorporate the credit card processing in with your billing or accounting system.

The credit *card processing company* typically charges you an application fee ($65 to $100) and a programming and installation fee ($35 to $50). For these fees, you can accept payment by Visa, MasterCard, and probably Diner's Club, but not American Express or Discover, both of which have their own special requirements.

American Express (1-800-445-2639) has its own processing network, called the Electronic Draft Capture (EDC) network. Once American Express receives and completes your application request, you must contact your terminal provider (the folks who are renting you the credit card processing machine) and make sure that they program your machine to process American Express transactions.

American Express strongly recommends that merchants set up their processing to be electronically based since it is easier for them and less expensive for the merchant. Of the organizations I worked with in setting up my accounts, American Express was by far the easiest to work with.

def•i•ni•tion

A **card processing company** processes and clears your company's credit card transactions. Card processing companies are independent businesses, not affiliated with a credit card issuer. A **credit card transaction processing company** acts as a liaison between your company and the credit card processing network.

Watch Out!

Trying to avoid hassles by not going electronic will probably cost you money. Everyone is better protected with electronic processing because you lessen the chances of mistakes and omissions. You should probably just take the electronic plunge from the start or expect to pay higher discount and transaction fees.

But wait, there's more! The Discover Card also has its own network and requires the same actions. Call Discover at 1-800-347-6673 to start the process and get the electronic terminal.

Should you simply buy your own terminal instead of renting one? Good question. The answer depends on your volume, monthly rental fee, and current cash situation. Rent for a few months and see how it goes. If after six months you start to resent the monthly charges, you should either go back to a hand processing system (in which you manually call in each charge for verification) or buy your own electronic terminal. Typical costs for such new terminals are $500 to $800.

Here you are with your credit card terminal and some customers, ready to sell your product or service using credit cards. You thought the analysis was over, but it is really just beginning. In addition to the setup charges and terminal costs, the credit card companies also want a percentage of the transaction amount and often a per-transaction fee as their compensation for guaranteeing the charge. Read on to find out how much you have to pay for this privilege.

Monthly Fees

First, you pay a monthly fee for the electronic terminal rental ($25 to $55) that is automatically deducted from your bank account by the service company. You are also going to pay a monthly service fee ($5 to $10) for the reporting of your account activity during the month. This is also automatically taken from your company checking account.

Street Smarts _____

Here are a few statistics that will fit in with your incentive to accept credit cards. Consumers already use credit cards for 25 percent of all of their spending, and these consumers typically spend more on a transaction if it is by credit card than by check (204 percent more) or cash (20 percent more) since they are not limited by the amount of cash that they have on hand. To pay a few percent in transaction fees to increase the transaction amount by 20 percent or more is a simple justification to make, don't you think?

The credit card company then charges your company a percentage of the transaction amount for each purchase. This fee varies among service providers, credit card companies, the type of transaction involved, the size and frequency of the transaction, and whether the transaction is processed electronically or manually. The bank charges you a transaction fee for each deposit made to your account. The following table shows typical discount and transaction fees for the various credit card types.

Typical Discount and Transaction Fees

Credit Card Type	Discount Rate (Percentage of Purchase Amount)	Transaction Fee (Cost to Deposit in Bank Account)
Visa	1.6 to 3.0%	20 cents
MasterCard	1.6 to 3.0%	20 cents
American Express	2.95 to 3.5%	None
Discover	(Would not disclose.)	

Keep in mind that home-based businesses may have special requirements to qualify for full merchant account status. Have your marketing literature ready to prove that you are a real business.

Here is what you get for the fee and how the process works when you have an electronic system:

1. You run the card through the credit card machine (called swiping the card). The terminal reads the card number and card type off the black magnetic strip on the back of the card.

2. The credit card terminal requests the transaction amount and expiration date of the card. You type both when requested and tell it to process the transaction.

3. The terminal dials the card processing company and sends the information to the computer, which then confirms the card isn't stolen and the cardholder has enough money available on the card to process the charge.

4. If everything is okay, the computer responds with an approval code that you write (or is printed) on the sales receipt. If your machine is connected directly to a printer, the receipt prints automatically when the transaction is approved, just as you see in most restaurants and high-volume retail stores these days.

5. The credit card processing company deducts the proper percentage from the purchase amount and deposits the rest in your business checking account. You essentially get the money right away instead of waiting for 30 days and taking the risk that the customer won't pay. Make sure that your bookkeeping system is set up to track these charges if you plan to do a lot of these. Check with your processing company to see if it has a point-of-sale system that is right for your particular situation and requirements.

6. Most banks charge businesses a transaction fee for each deposit you make, so you are also charged by your bank for credit card deposits.

Street Smarts

Find a company that provides access to Visa, MasterCard, Discover, and American Express as a single service. If the company you use doesn't want to do this, at least find out how to set up your machine so that it processes all the different credit cards you expect to accept from your customers.

7. The processing company sends you a summary statement every month that outlines all transaction dates, sale amounts, credits applied (product returns), discount rates applied, and net deposits. This statement is handy for reconciling your bank deposits, invoices, and receivables when you have customers paying by different methods. Your bookkeeper definitely needs this statement, so don't throw it away. Many modern electronic processing machines can provide you with a summary statement of transactions processed, which helps in verifying the statement provided by your processing company.

Covering Your Legal Bases

We are always happy to sell our products or services and receive payment, but what happens if the client later contests the charge and refuses to pay? What if the person using the card isn't supposed to be using it? You could be stuck with a huge bad debt that takes a large number of healthy sales to correct. The following table lists a few things you can do to minimize the chance of those situations occurring. Without question, ask your credit card processing company about their recommended (or required) procedures for verifying credit card purchaser identities. The following list gives you a general idea of what is involved, but work with your vendor for the most current specifics.

Credit Card Sales Protection Procedures

When Someone Charges Something in Person	Actions and Reasons
Check the expiration date to make sure that the card is still valid.	Look at the Valid From and Good Through dates on the card to make sure that the card is still valid. Check that the information is embossed and not just printed.
Look for a hologram or other security mark.	These emblems are difficult to duplicate. If you can't find one, you might be holding a fake card.

Disclose the terms of the sale and get a signature, if possible.	The more that's in writing and signed by the customer, the harder it is for him or her to contest the charge. Make sure terms, conditions, and return policy are easily spelled out on the receipt.
Run the card through an imprint machine or electronic terminal, fill out the sales draft completely, and get a signature.	Take the customer's card and run it through an imprint machine or electronic terminal using the proper sales receipt. Make sure that you get a signature and that it is legible and completed with all pertinent information included. Verify that the signature on the card matches that provided by the customer on the sales form. Don't accept an unsigned card.
Get an authorization number for each transaction.	Run the card, amount, and expiration date through the electronic terminal to receive a sales authorization from the service company. Write the authorization number on the sales draft.

The preceding information is taken from the December 1992 issue of the Agency Inc. Newsletter, Volume 3, Number 12 and is applicable today.

If you plan to take orders over the telephone without seeing the customer and getting his signature, you can still take a few steps to better protect yourself. Because the chances of getting burned over the phone or by mail are much higher than in person, the credit card companies will probably charge you a higher discount rate for this type of transaction. These types of transactions are often called mail order, telephone order, or Internet (MO/TO) orders.

When processing a telephone transaction, follow these steps:

1. Get all credit card information and repeat all numbers, dates, and names that appear on the card. Write "MO" or "TO" on the signature line to indicate that the customer was not present.

2. Enter the transaction immediately into your electronic terminal to verify that it is a valid card and that the card is authorized for the amount of the purchase. Get an authorization number and write it on the receipt.

3. Verify the card's CVC2/CVV2 validation code that is printed on the card if it is a Visa or MasterCard. American Express uses a Card Identification Number (CIN) as part of its validation checking procedures.

4. Verify the person's billing address using the address verification system (AVS), which is only available for cards issued within the United States. AVS will verify whether the address given by the purchaser matches that on record for that particular card.

5. If possible, get customers to come by to pick up the merchandise. Have them sign the sales form at that time. Or have them complete a signature card that indicates their willingness to have your company transact charges against their account. This will not be possible with Internet orders, so make sure you follow the previous steps.

If you are processing a credit card sale by phone, if at all possible, fax the customer a copy of the invoice including all credit card information. Request that he sign the invoice and return it to you by fax for a rough "signature on file" agreement. A signature on file agreement means the customer agrees to pay you for all future charges against that credit card by the same customer. A formal signature on a file card includes the agreement duration of effectiveness, the names and sample signatures of all persons authorized to charge against this credit card, an imprint of the credit card, credit card expiration date, termination stipulations, and change-related conditions. This may sound cumbersome, but it is still done, especially if you are working with local customers.

What to Do if a Charge Is Contested

Unfortunately, even if you have a credit card payment approved, you can still run into problems. There is a lot of credit card fraud floating around these days, and certain people take advantage of situations if given the chance. Your established customers are not usually the problem. New customers or those you will never see again can leave you with a bad bill or a contested charge that can cost you a lot of money.

This is really important, so stay awake for this paragraph: when a transaction is challenged by the customer (called a *chargeback*), the burden of proof that the transaction actually occurred falls on the merchant's (your) shoulders, not the customer's.

def•i•ni•tion

A **chargeback** happens when a customer contests a charge and you as the merchant have to prove that this person did indeed make the purchase indicated. If you do not have the right paperwork, this customer could get your product or service and you won't get paid.

Taking the steps outlined here might seem like a hassle, but you will have a fighting chance with the credit card company if the charge is ever contested or disputed by the customer. If the customer signed the sales draft, saw the terms and conditions, and clearly knew what was being purchased and the proper amount, you have an excellent case in your favor. The more of the transaction that was handled in writing, the better the chance you have of keeping the money. Caution and procedures make the solution to this possible trouble area. Define credit terms, stick with them, and fight for your money when the time comes. And make sure that you comply with the filing and contesting deadline time frames set by the credit card companies, or you could lose the sale proceeds even if the facts are on your side.

Watch Out!

Beware of how discount and transaction fees affect your profits. Accepting American Express for a $10,000 charge from a solid account customer, for example, puts $295 to $350 in American Express's pocket instead of yours. In that case, you might be better off persuading the customer to pay by other means, such as a 2 percent discount for check payment. Using American Express instead of net 30-day payment terms with solid credit customers can cost you thousands in unnecessary credit protection expenses.

Responding immediately to any inquiries from your credit card companies is essential to maintaining your merchant status. For many retailers, losing merchant status would be disastrous. Don't test the system. Answer their questions, provide any information requested, and enjoy the additional sales you're earning because you are able to accept credit cards.

Street Smarts

Credit card processing companies can help you deal with what you think might be a fraudulent or otherwise suspicious credit card purchase. They call these Code 10 Procedures. Call your processor to ask for a Code 10 authorization, and it will lead you through the process, which might involve keeping the card. Don't risk taking the card if the customer may become dangerous, but know that you have avoided a fraudulent purchase if a Code 10 authorization showed up a stolen card. Contact your processing company for more instructions on dealing with Code 10 situations.

The Least You Need to Know

- You probably have to accept credit cards in one form or another or risk losing customers, especially if you run a restaurant, retail store, or other end-user, consumer-related business.

- Electronic processing is the easiest and least expensive way to process credit card transactions. Investigate a point of sale system that might inexpensively make your credit card processing easier and more accurate.

- The various credit card companies charge between 2 and 4 percent of the transaction amount in exchange for their guarantee of payment, which can be very expensive when applied across the board to all transactions.

- Treat each sale as a legal agreement. Get signatures and transaction details to back up any claims made by the customer at a later date that he or she never made that purchase.

- Telephone and mail-order credit card sales are more expensive due to their higher likelihood of fraud. Fraud deterrent procedures are mandatory if you plan to accept credit cards over the phone or by mail order.

- Get an authorization number from the credit card company for each transaction. This, along with a signature, is your best protection for your credit card sale transactions.

Chapter 19

Banking On Your Banker

In This Chapter

- ◆ Your banker is an ally, not an enemy
- ◆ A banker's perspective on lending money
- ◆ The importance of your business plan to bankers
- ◆ Working with the Small Business Administration

"These guys have absolutely no vision," said Bill. "This is a great idea, and all I need is $25,000. That's nothing to a bank their size, but NO-O-O! They want all of this supporting documentation before they will even consider the loan. Why do I bother with banks in the first place?"

"They have money, and you need money. Isn't that right?" asked Bill's father.

"Sure, but why make it so complicated? It makes me want to pull my account and take my business to another bank that appreciates a good deal. I know this business. They have no idea what they're throwing away."

"That might be the key to your problem," his father said quietly. "If they don't understand the opportunity, can you blame them for not seeing its value? After all, whose job is it to convince them to give you money? Theirs or yours?"

This might seem obvious, but at some point in your company's life, you will have to work with a bank. The relationship might involve something as simple as a checking account or might be quite complicated. One thing is for certain: your relationship with the bank is easier if you understand how bankers think.

This chapter introduces you to the banker mentality along with an overview of the services you can reasonably expect from a bank.

I wish someone had told me this stuff when I started my business. Read, learn, understand, and move past any preconceived notions you might have about banks and learn how to keep this important and useful relationship productive instead of frustrating.

What Does a Bank Bring to the Table?

In a word: money! In a second word: services. As your company grows, its need for cash and more complex financial services also grows. Banks are storage houses for money, which is the one element most lacking in a new company. To get an idea of what it is like to be a banker, think about the last time you lent someone money and they were slow in paying you back. How does it feel to be a banker? Are you going to be more cautious the next time you lend someone money? Keep that feeling in mind when you talk to your banker, and you will have a much better understanding of that side of the desk.

Where does a bank fit into a new business's life? In the beginning, you will have a business checking account, but most likely you will have to turn to sources other than a bank for business financing—the money you put into the checking account. When you are just starting out, the bank has no experience with you, and your company has little or no financial track record. On what basis is the bank going to lend you money? Your good intentions? Your smile?

> **Street Smarts**
>
> Banks must report to federal regulators who then insure the deposits made at that bank. For this reason, banks must make certain that their lending programs meet clearly defined federal guidelines, or they could lose their insurance coverage, which is a very bad thing for a bank. Sometimes banks can't lend you money due to those guidelines.

Initially, expect the bank to provide checking services and accept wire transfers, federal tax deposits such as payroll, and credit card deposits, along with other standard banking services. Over time, the bank will see your record of frequent deposits and a growing bank account, thus documenting solid growth and financial performance. Then, the bank will be more willing to risk loaning your company money. When you want a line of credit or a loan secured by a business asset of some type, you will likely want to work with a bank.

Banks exist to serve customers, but as the old joke says, "The only way you can get a loan is to prove you don't need it." Consequently, many startup companies have difficulty getting a loan from a bank—even if they have the best idea in the world. This is where your personal credit becomes very important.

You will have to deal with a bank in some way. Period. It's a good idea to start early to develop a good relationship with your bank—and with the loan officers at your branch. Why? Well, one of these days your business will be well established, and a banker who understands your company can be a great resource in supporting your profitable growth.

Start now, long before you ask for money, to lay the groundwork that will convince your banker that you are a solid customer and a good business risk. Besides, bankers see a lot of different businesses, and you might be able to get some good business advice from your banker at the best price: free! And getting free stuff from a banker is a really good feeling.

Why don't banks lend to companies just starting out? The banks have to be convinced that they will get their money back, with interest, when it is supposed to be repaid. Startup companies are notoriously bad about paying loans back on time, if at all, and after the turmoil in the banking industry with the savings and loan crisis of the mid-1980s and the uncertainties of the past few years, loan officers tend to shy away from risky situations. Yes, they might be missing a golden opportunity to support your business in the early stages, but they also miss the opportunity to lose the money they loan you if your company doesn't work out the way you hope.

> **Street Smarts**
>
> Get to know several loan officers at your branch and the main branch so if your main contact leaves, you don't have to start from scratch getting to know someone else. It is also a good idea to get to know your loan officer's boss.

The Loan Officer Is Your Friend. Really.

To whom would you rather give money—someone who treats you with contempt and antagonism every time you meet, or someone who appears to appreciate you for what you have to offer? Would you give money for a risky venture to someone you barely know, or to someone you have known for a while and trust? The answer to these questions is simple, and my point is probably already made. Meet the loan officer responsible for your account when you first open the account—before you need money. Keep him updated on your progress and help him become more familiar with your company. You'll find that bringing him into the loop early will make him an ally when you need to ask for a loan. Don't wait until you're desperate for money to bring him up to speed on your activities.

Make sure that this first meeting goes well—no matter what! Appear to know what you're doing, even if you're feeling doubtful. The doubts will pass, but the initial impression on the loan officer will stay. Look and act like the president of your own company, like someone who deserves as much money as you want! This meeting doesn't have to be lengthy, but you must leave a positive impression so the loan officer will remember you when you need to borrow money.

Don't underestimate the value that this loan officer brings to your business. As with any bureaucracy, it is really good to know someone inside who can steer you through the maze and support your cause when needed.

Banks Will Give You Money Only When You Don't Need It

Banks make money by lending it to individuals and businesses. The loan officer's obligation to the bank, and its shareholders, is to make loans to the businesses that are most likely to pay the bank back.

The lending policies of nationally regulated banks are monitored by some combination of the Federal Reserve, the state's Office of the Comptroller of Currency (OCC), and/or the particular state's Department of Insurance and Financial Institutions. (You can recognize a national bank by the word "national" or letters "NA" in its name.) The loan officer of a national bank must walk the line between pursuing the best business opportunity for the bank and complying with their respective regulatory agencies. Larger banks handle such a large loan volume that they tend to evaluate loans on a template basis instead of individually. Private and community banks, on the other hand, are more able to get to know the specifics of an applicant's situation and, as such, better understand when a loan is still a solid investment even when it is outside of the template guidelines.

> **Street Smarts**
>
> When you request a loan for an amount greater than the loan officer's lending authority, the loan officer must get approval from her supervisor or from a loan committee that makes decisions regarding larger loans. Plan to invest some time learning your banker's lending authority to potentially make both of your lives easier.

From a bank's perspective, lending money to a small business provides risks and advantages that are different from those associated with a large company. Take a look at some of these risks and advantages.

The smaller business loans have a higher risk associated with them because the business is usually newer and might have fewer assets to be used as collateral. The newer business has a limited profit track record as well. These risk factors will increase the interest rate the small business must pay, which in turn increases the revenue banks receive. Small businesses are also attractive as loan customers because funds from a loan can usually be covered by money from company checking and savings accounts at the bank. Because small businesses are likely to keep their money in only one bank, banks are becoming more willing to lend them money.

Larger companies have large lending needs that require extra attention from the bank—401(k) plans, a lock box, and so on. These lending services generate fee income for the bank, but the loans are priced at a lower interest rate because the larger customers are in a better negotiating position. However, larger businesses rarely have all their money in one or two accounts; it's invested in several other places.

To get any lender to provide you and your company with money, you must sell them on your company, your ideas, and on you, or this money may go to other, less risky ventures. Be prepared to present a case to your banker on why you should get the loan. Is your business plan looking important again?

In addition, it is generally safer for a bank to invest money in several ventures, rather than all in one basket. Several small business loans spread the risk over several businesses so that even if one business owner starts to have trouble repaying his loan, the whole bank is not threatened.

Street Smarts

To give you an idea of how much a default costs a bank, consider a company with a $10,000 loan that defaults. The bank has lost the $10,000 plus the interest on the loan, which is generally 2 to 3 percent in profit (the difference between the interest rate it pays depositors and the interest it receives on loans). To make up that loss, the bank has to lend an additional $333,333 just to get its money back within a 12-month period. Here is why: a $333,333 loan would generate close to $10,000 in net interest income to the bank in a year assuming a net 3 percent interest rate.

The primary reason banks have conservative lending policies is that loan defaults are expensive. Consequently, banks only provide loans that are acceptable risks in the eyes of their depositors and the regulatory agencies to which they report. They are not in the business of providing high-risk, high-profit potential venture capital loans.

As a small business owner, you must create a personal and business track record in advance that will qualify your company for a loan when you need it. Here's what you can do:

◆ Keep your personal and business financial situation healthy by using standard accounting practices and watching your personal cash flow. Try to get your debts as low as possible and your cash reserves as high as possible before starting your business.

◆ Try to get a small line of credit early on to get your credit established with the bank. A business line of credit is usually increased when you pay it off on a regular basis.

Banks often use tax returns as the basis for determining a business's and individual's financial (and consequently loan) status. Keep both your company and personal returns in order to improve your loan chances with the bank.

Calling your loan officer and saying, "I need the money tomorrow" is a red flag that something is out of control with the company and its management. A panic situation raises questions about your managerial ability. Plan ahead to make sure that you can get a bank to lend you money when you really do need it.

You can also expect to personally guarantee any loans given to your company by a bank. Every bank that I have ever worked with has wanted the same thing, and the first time you sign the papers giving the bank the right to go after your personal stuff should the business loan go into default, you can feel your skin crawl a little. It just comes with the territory, and you should not take it personally. As a business banker friend of mine put it, "Why would you expect the bank to give you money for a business idea when you aren't willing to put your own assets behind it?"

Bank Loans You Can Get

Now you understand the world of finance from the bankers' perspective. How does this translate into your ability to get money when you need it? Here are some loan options for you to consider.

This is really important: banks are always coming up with new ways to make money lending to others. A tight economy and heavier dependence and respect for small business is making otherwise tight financial organizations and the governmental agencies take on more risk than they would under better times. Don't make any assumptions about what a bank can or cannot do. Get to know your banker and let him or her see if there is a program out there that is good for both your company and the bank.

An unsecured line of credit can be given on a personal basis to the company officers. This is essentially a personal loan to officers (based on the personal credit history of the individuals), who then loan it to the company. The bank does not give this loan directly to the company because the company has not proven it can pay the loan back. The officers then arrange reasonable repayment terms with the company. If you are an officer of a corporation, make sure the loan conditions, such as the interest rate and the term of the loan, are similar to those you would see in normal business transactions.

A secured line of credit is the next best option. In this scenario, the bank loans the company money to purchase an asset, such as new equipment or a new building. The asset is then used to secure the loan until the company pays it back, just like a house secures a mortgage, which is simply another kind of loan. In this case, the company typically must provide at least 20 percent of the purchase amount. (A $50,000 purchase requires $10,000 invested by the company and $40,000 by the bank.) If the loan can't be repaid, the assets are sold to recover the bank's investment. Liquid assets, such as a certificate of deposit, a receivable note, or inventory are the most desirable and easiest to loan against because they are the easiest to sell if the company defaults on the loan. Next best are fixed assets such as equipment and computers.

You might also be able to get *short-term loans* (under a year) by using receivables or inventory as your collateral. This type of loan is really a line of credit with special provisions. You provide a summary to the bank showing that your company has a certain level of liquid assets—accounts receivable from customers, inventory, or CDs—that can be used as security on the loan. The bank will only loan 70 to 80 percent of the value of the assets, which is recalculated each month. The danger is that if your assets decline from one month to the next, you might have to shell out some additional money. The nice part about this type of loan is that it generally requires interest-only payments, but the entire balance must be paid off at specified periods, usually quarterly.

That is the strict letter of the relationship. Now, here is what usually happens in reality. You talk to your banker and show a historical record of receivables, inventory, and receivables aging. (See CD Bonus Chapter 25 for more details on receivables and collection procedures.) From the amounts and aging, you and your banker agree on a reasonable amount of liquid asset value, and the bank opens a line of credit for that amount. The 70 to 80 percent rule still applies, and my experience has been that this keeping of the loan no more than the agreed-upon 80 percent value is handled on the honor system. My banker only asked for my receivables value at the one-year anniversary but reserved the right to investigate them monthly if desired. Your banker will probably only exercise this right if he or she believes that the note or the company is in jeopardy.

Street Smarts

The value of assets is usually discounted when used as security for a loan. As my banker says, "We are in the business of lending money, not selling items to recover debt."

Notes, or loans, secured by larger assets such as major equipment and property are considered long-term and can have a 36- to 60-month repayment period. When calculating the value of your inventory, bankers typically use 50 percent of the retail price as the value. They don't consider the inventory worth the full price you paid for it because the bank must sell it for much less if you go out of business. Some banks even discount *cash on hand* to cover potential collection and account closing costs in the event of a default.

For example, assume that you secured your line of credit last month with $50,000 in receivables, giving you $35,000 in credit (70 percent of $50,000). If your receivables drop to $40,000 the next month, your collateral is worth only $28,000 (70 percent of $40,000). The $7,000 difference between the $35,000 and the $28,000 value of your assets must be paid to the bank immediately to meet the terms of the original loan agreement. This can be a tough check to write if you haven't planned for it. Will you get caught if you try to stretch the situation? Probably not. Is it worth the risk? I think not, because if you are caught, you are in violation of a banking agreement, which can torpedo any prospects you have for keeping that banker on your side. Plus that would likely make the bank call the entire note altogether, which can really put you in a cash pinch.

Sell Your Banker on Your Company

People naturally avoid risk, and bankers make risk avoidance an art form. There is only one issue ever discussed with a loan officer whether it is explicitly stated or not: how will the bank get the money back if the loan defaults? Where will the money come from? A new company has no established source of cash. The entire business is assumed very risky. The only thing the loan officer has to refer to is the business plan.

Your bank wants to be sure you've thought through all aspects of your business and believe it can work. If you don't believe in it, why should they? Can you imagine giving $50,000 to people who are wishy-washy about where they plan to go, how they'll get there, when they'll arrive, and how they'll pay you back? I can't! Remember, your business plan is your opportunity to explain what you want to do and how you intend to succeed.

The bank is going to expect something from you before it gives credit. First, you must do your homework and prepare a comprehensive business plan with realistic sales and expense projections. Next, you must provide personal financial statements to give the bank an idea of your own financial situation, separate from the company. People with 20 percent or more ownership in the venture are typically required to personally guarantee the debt, meaning that they agree to repay all of it personally if the company defaults. Period. Later you will have more negotiating room, but early on, this is the norm.

Your challenge is to convince the bank that you are credit worthy. As a new business owner, your personal credit history along with a well thought-out business plan are the best cards that you can play. My banker told me that the loans I received were based on my personal credibility, personal asset value, and the strength of my business plan. So far, so good!

Banks will evaluate you based on the five Cs of lending:

- **Character.** What are you like? Confident? Ethical? Self-assured? This is treated as a very important consideration when first starting out. Make the initial meetings count!

- **Capacity or cash flow.** Can you repay the debt? Do you have the cash flow to support the monthly or periodic payments required?

- **Collateral.** What can the bank take if the loan defaults? Make it clear that you don't intend to default, but that the bank is covered should the worst happen.

- **Condition.** What is the general economic condition of the area, and what is the intended use for the money?

- **Capital.** What is the company's net worth or equity?

Remember that banks make their money by lending money, and they are always looking for solid loan prospects. If banks don't lend money, they don't make money. Interesting, no? If you have a clean financial report, both personal and business, and a company with a solid, proven financial record, you can get money from your bank. Notice that you must perform to a certain level before your bank will consider lending you money, and only for minimum risk opportunities.

Commercial Checking Accounts: A Different Animal

Balance your commercial checking account just as you do your personal checkbook—but do it more often because the dollars and complexity involved are much higher! Your company writes checks and makes deposits as you do in your personal checking account, but the rules are slightly different, as is explained a little later. You can shop around and find a better deal on fees and transaction costs on business checking accounts, but make sure the rules and requirements fit your needs. Don't overlook the important factors of convenience and security; after all, you hope to be taking a lot of money to the bank, so make sure the bank you select is accessible and safe.

Keep the following in mind when you set up a commercial checking account for your company:

◆ You are charged for your commercial account based on the number of transactions and the average account balance.

◆ You can expect to pay a fee for each check you deposit, along with a transaction fee for the deposit. (Can you believe it? Only a bank would bill you for giving it money!) At some banks, the rate billed for each check varies according to whether it is local, in state, out of state, or from your cousin Vinnie!

◆ You are also billed for each check you write.

◆ You receive a statement from the bank that outlines the charges billed to your checking account for those transactions. This statement is in addition to the basic checking statement listing all the checks and deposits that have cleared. The formal term for this is an *analysis statement*.

def•i•ni•tion

An **analysis statement** is a statement from your bank that outlines the various bank charges and credits incurred with respect to your business account. An **earning credit** is a credit offered by the bank in the place of earning interest because federal law does not allow you to earn interest on a business checking account.

◆ Banks charge transaction fees for each deposit you make and each check you write, but they also give you an *earning credit* on the money in your account, which you can use to pay those transaction fees. By keeping enough in your account to offset transaction fees, you save some money.

◆ Verify the bank's policy on handling international transactions and letters of credit. This becomes very important when dealing with foreign customers. See Chapter 20 for more on going international.

♦ Talk to the bank about the services it offers related to conventional and Internet-based processing of credit cards.

Shop around to get the best overall services package that is right for your company. It will be based on your expected number of checking transactions and the other business services that you will need. Do your homework up front to ensure that you get set up with the right bank from the start. It is really a drag to cultivate one bank only to find that it cannot serve your needs as you grow and you have to start building that relationship all over again with another bank.

Enter the Small Business Administration (SBA)

When nobody else will help, the Small Business Administration (SBA) comes to the rescue. Maybe. It used to be difficult to get an SBA loan, but the SBA has changed and might be able to help if the loan amount is under $100,000. What used to generate a one-inch folder of paperwork is now down to a two-page application as part of the LowDoc loan program. This is good news, but you should understand the process to see how the SBA can help you in the early days.

The SBA doesn't give you money. A bank actually issues the check. The SBA just guarantees the bank that the loan will be repaid and charges you a 2 percent fee for the insurance policy. A guarantee from the SBA that the loan will be repaid makes the loan very attractive to a bank.

Why would the SBA lend you money when a bank won't? Because the federal government thinks that small business must flourish for the domestic economy to grow, and its guarantee is the SBA's way of putting its money where its mouth is. The SBA lets the bank do the legwork and then either approves the guarantee or not.

Not all banks are SBA lenders, and you should check with the bank before starting the process. Some banks are in a position where the SBA will always approve a loan guarantee request from them. Call the local SBA office for information regarding these banks.

Don't assume that you need an SBA guarantee to get a loan. Fill out a loan application at the bank of your choice, which will require your personal financial information and a business plan. Should your loan not meet the bank criteria for lending (the five Cs presented earlier), the bank can then turn to

Watch Out!

The SBA requires that you keep thorough records. The bank and the borrower must account for all funds disbursed. The record-keeping load is substantial, so be ready for it.

the SBA for a loan guarantee. If the SBA approves, the loan is funded from the bank with a guarantee provided by the SBA. The bank approves the loan if the SBA provides an 80 to 90 percent repayment guarantee. Quite often, banks would rather give you the loan themselves instead of involving the SBA because it makes working with the loan more complicated for the bank.

There are several different SBA loan types, and they change on a regular basis. Contact your local SBA office (www.sba.gov) and sit through one of their introductory talks (around one hour long). The talks provide a solid basis for understanding the procedure and how to work with a bank to obtain a loan. Preferred SBA vendors do a lot of business with the SBA, so get a listing of them and work with one of the preferred banks from the beginning. The SBA website has a special page dedicated to financing your business that provides a great overview of this important topic.

Big Banks, Small Banks

Which is better—a small bank with easy access to the lending managers or a big bank with deeper pockets and higher approval levels? The answer: it depends.

All banks have lending guidelines, but the internal policies are more flexible with a small bank. The officers are more likely to take the time to work within the rules in a small bank than in a big one. With a small bank, you get to know the officers better and quicker, but the loan amount that can be approved might be smaller. This means that you should check out the bank's philosophy of operation and verify that it actually does what its marketing literature says it does. Ask for a few references of companies in your size range, and then call these references and ask them questions.

Start with the banks where you already have a relationship. If the big banks give you grief, go to a smaller one. You might look like a large fish in a small pond, so beware that the pond might not be deep enough as you grow beyond a certain level, at which time you might have to change banks.

Average small business loan amounts are in the $25,000 to $50,000 range, which is well within the reach of any bank. Be aware that because it takes just as much paperwork to process a $25,000 loan as a $250,000 loan, most banks prefer to process the larger amount, where they earn more interest.

The Least You Need to Know

- You will need the assistance of a bank as your business succeeds and your cash requirements increase, so get to know the officers of your bank now.

- Your personal credit history and business plan are your best selling points when trying to get money in the early stages.

- Banks make money by lending money, but they have to lend a great deal of money to make up for a loan that goes into default.

- The five Cs of lending determine your credit worthiness. Make sure that you have effectively addressed all of them to increase your chances of success.

- The SBA requires the same amount of preparation for a loan guarantee that a bank does. Apply for a loan at a bank first, and if you are turned down, the SBA might be able to help get it approved by guaranteeing repayment for you.

Chapter 20

International Business—Did I Mention China?

In This Chapter

- Your international business opportunities
- Conducting international business on the Internet
- Tips on taking international orders
- Using letters of credit for payment
- Incorporating China into your plans

"Hey, boss! Check this out," cried Gary as he ran into the room. "We just got an order for 15,000 units from a guy in Singapore. He found us on the Internet and obviously likes what we do."

Brenda looked up from her desk. She was busy getting ready to leave town for a well-deserved vacation and only had a few hours before she and her family caught a flight to Florida.

"How many units?" gasped Brenda. "15,000? That's more than we've seen from a single buyer all year. Let me see that," she said as she reached for the fax. She didn't even know that they spoke English in Singapore.

Sure enough, here was an order for 15,000 units from a company she had only heard about on the Discovery Channel. She certainly wanted the revenue generated by this sale, but Singapore seemed a long way away. Why now? Why at the last minute before she left town on vacation? Well, this might be business that paid the rent for next month. She sighed.

"What do you want me to do with this?" asked Gary. "Do you think it's legit?"

"Hey. What do I know about Singapore other than it has great Chinese food? All I know is that 15,000 units is a lot of product for us to commit to provide unless this is a real order. Give me a few minutes to do some homework," was her reply.

As Gary left the room, Brenda hit the speed dial button for her banker. "Hi, Jim? Brenda. Listen. I just got an order from Singapore and have no idea how to handle it. Can you and the bank help me out with this?"

"Well, hello to you, too, Brenda," said Jim. "It looks like the world has discovered your little gold mine. Let me take a few minutes and talk to you about letters of credit."

History and literature are full of stories of entrepreneurs who weathered the high seas and foreign cultures to create business empires for themselves. These stories make international business sound like the last bastion of "wild west" entrepreneurship. In fact, international business is nowhere near as perilous as the stories might have you believe. It happens every day and has a well-established set of procedures. These procedures may just be new to you.

Is doing business internationally more complicated than selling domestically? Yes. Are the risks associated with international business higher? Yes. Are there opportunities that exist on the international market that just do not exist in your country? Yes. Can you turn those opportunities into financial rewards for you, your company, and your family? Absolutely, but you need to be smart about how you take advantage of them. This chapter shows you how.

However, this chapter is not designed to teach you how to create an international business. That topic is far too complicated to cover adequately in a single chapter, and Appendix D lists several books that provide an excellent starting point. My intent is to explain the realities of international business transactions so that when you start getting marketing interest or orders from international customers, you are prepared with enough information to transact the business in a credible way.

In addition, a special section has been added to the end that relates to the massive impacts that China and India are not only having on their local areas but in the U.S. as well.

International Business and the Internet

Believe it or not, if you have an Internet presence, you could find yourself in the international sales business, whether intended or not. Remember that when dealing with the Internet, a person in Tokyo is just as close to you as a person in Chicago … until you start shipping, that is. Assuming that the Tokyo person can read your site, which is possible because English is rapidly becoming a primary international business language, then that person might want to order what you advertise on your site. How do you get the product to them? How do you make sure that you get paid? How do you collect if they default on payment? How do you plan to service your product if it has trouble? By the way, there are many English-speaking countries around the world, such as Australia, New Zealand, South Africa, England, Canada, and others that minimize the language barrier issues. But you have the same collection, delivery, and service problems with them as you would with the prospective Japanese customer.

Street Smarts

Faxing and electronic mail are great in that they transcend all time zone barriers, but beware the cost of sending faxes internationally because these costs can mount quickly. Using the Internet and e-mail for international communication is much cheaper and quicker. It is also more interactive, which is important when dealing across language and cultural barriers. If you do a lot of international calling, you might want to look around for a Voice Over Internet Protocol (VOIP) service that will send your calls over the Internet almost for free.

In short, as soon as you present a site on the Internet, you open yourself to international orders. Is this good? I believe orders in almost any language and denomination are good, as long as the customer gets what he expected when he ordered and you get paid as you expected. Read the rest of this chapter to familiarize yourself with the basics of taking an international order, shipping the product, and receiving payment. Take the fear out of doing business with that enormous international community by setting a few procedures based on these simple rules. You will learn more on your own as your success builds, but these rules can help get you started.

Taking and Processing Orders

I remember when my company got its first international order request. First we were excited, but as we walked through the many details associated with filling the request, we started to panic.

Use your international customer as a resource with respect to determining the best way to ship from your country to theirs. Ask them about the methods that have worked best for them, use their advice, and then protect your financial interests. In this way, you can save a lot of legwork, get your customers the products and delivery schedule they want, and minimize your financial exposure. Communication is always important, but it is particularly important when dealing across cultures.

I have also found that many non-English native speakers can write excellent English, making electronic mail a more effective method of communication than the telephone. This is counter-intuitive but it has been my experience, especially when you are just beginning to work together. As you get to know each other, the phone might become a better communication tool, but precision is still best maintained by e-mail.

Giving Product Information

Look for clues everywhere in the transaction to determine the best methods of communication. For starters, look at the information request. Remember that the person at the other end of the request might not speak English as a primary language, and you should make this process as simple for him or her as possible.

If you received a request for information by a posted letter, fax, or e-mail message, responding with a lot of words is generally not a sound approach. Responding with product number, prices, and pictures is better. Keep your message short, polite, and clear, and you stand a better chance of your response being well understood and received.

Finally, you may want to investigate the use of a translation service that will convert your literature from English into your selected foreign language. There are even some computer programs that claim to do a solid translation job, but I have never tried one myself. You might try one of the programs and then give the translator both the original copy and computer-generated translation for a critique. It might save time on the first translation and may save money on future ones.

Shipping and Handling

Both you and your customer should understand that shipping products internationally takes a longer period of time. When you ship internationally within shorter periods of time, the costs increase substantially. For this reason, international customers will often want to buy in larger volumes to amortize the shipping costs over more units, which decreases the shipping cost per unit.

Your customer is responsible for paying the shipping and insurance costs associated with the order. Let the customer tell you how the order should be processed so that it passes through his or her country's customs service with the least amount of headache and unnecessary expense.

If you incur the shipping charges because your customer bills them against your account, then make sure that you have a guaranteed method of payment with either a letter of credit or credit card (as discussed later in this chapter). If possible, use one of the customer's designated shipping accounts so that you can avoid as much of the risk associated with international shipping as possible.

Let's face it: boats sink. Planes crash. Countries go to war and economies falter. You don't want to be in a position where you ship $15,000 worth of products to a country that just began a civil war and find out that you cannot get paid.

Pricing and Exchange Rates

When you establish prices, you do so using your home economy denominations, such as U.S. dollars. Designate this by including "USD" after all prices or by stating on the invoice that all amounts are in U.S. dollars. In this way, your customer inherits the *exchange rate liability* because you are paid in your home country currency.

If you keep up with international *exchange rate* trends, it is possible to make money off the exchange rate variations between countries by quoting prices in the currency of your customer's country or by specifying an exchange rate that is used for the transaction. (Assume that there are no exchange fees to simplify the discussion.) There is money to be made here, but it will take diligence on your part. And I suggest that you get your international business up and running before you worry about optimizing exchange rate financial opportunities.

For example, assume that your product sells for $10 USD, and the German Mark (DM) is trading for 1.79 DM per dollar. This means that a person buying your product must pay you 17.9 DM (1.79×10) to buy the product. You then convert that 17.9 DM into $10 US ($17.9 \div 1.79 = 10$). Simple so far. Yes? This example is simple because it assumes that the exchange rate does not change between the

def•i•ni•tion

Exchange rate is the comparison of one country's currency in exchange for another's. For example, you can exchange a certain number of U.S. dollars for a certain number of French francs. **Exchange rate liability** is the negative impact of a fluctuation in the exchange rate from the time that you make a purchase agreement to the time the money actually changes hands.

time that you agree on a price and the time that you receive the payment and convert it into your home country's currency. Now, look at the same example and see what happens when the exchange rate fluctuates.

Street Smarts

Check the business section of your newspaper for the world's most common currency exchange rates. You can check out exchange rates on any number of Internet websites that deal with financial and business information, such as www.cnbc.com.

For the day in question, you quote a price of 17.9 DM. Assume that the exchange rate on the day that you convert the DM payment into USD is 1.60. When you convert your 17.9 DM into dollars, you now receive 17.9 ÷ 1.6 = 11.19, or $1.19 more than the price in USD. Why? Simply because the international exchange rate changed enough, and in your favor, to allow you to squeak an extra $1.19 out of the transaction.

Could the exchange rate have just as easily gone the other way and cost you money instead? Absolutely. Prove it to yourself by using an exchange rate of 1.85 DM per USD and show that this type of fluctuation would have cost you money.

Making Sure You Get Paid

Collecting from deadbeat customers in your home country is bad enough. Now try collecting from a deadbeat who lives in a small village 10,000 miles away where they don't speak English. Not a chance! Extending credit for international shipments is very risky business indeed and should only be considered once you have an excellent working relationship with the client and you understand the legal safeguards on both sides for the specific country in question.

When getting paid, cash is always king, but few people are going to send cash internationally—and in today's international terrorism intelligence environment, a large cash transaction could invite unwelcome governmental attention. You can start out with your terms being "Shipment upon receipt of payment in full in USD as a cashier's check for products and shipping" and see how this is received. If it works, great. If not, then try some of the other approaches.

Credit cards are another excellent way of ensuring that you get paid for internationally shipped products. The credit card transaction is basically the same throughout the world, and most people are familiar with the process of paying for something over the phone with a credit card. Talk to your credit card processing company to find out what they require for international orders above certain dollar levels.

For smaller dollar amounts and working with smaller companies, I have found this to be the best approach. You perform a standard credit card verification, just as you do with a domestic shipment. In this case, however, make absolutely sure that you get a fax of the order signed by the cardholder with his or her printed name and date next to it before shipping your products. You don't want an international order going into dispute. As the dollar amounts and companies become larger, you must use other payment methods. Discuss this with your credit card processing company.

Street Smarts

Don't assume that the laws of your customer's home country match those of yours. Even in the U.S., laws vary between states. Assuming a law to be true is setting yourself up for a disappointment at best, and a disaster at worst. Check with a specialist on your target country or make sure that you are financially covered before committing yourself.

Some clients may offer to send a set of financial statements from which you can provide credit. This is risky business in that there is no guarantee that their financial statements were created using the same GAAP guidelines used in the United States. In short, you may not really understand what you are reading, and the statements could be more fiction than fact.

The most common form of international financial transaction for sale of products or services is a *documentary letter of credit* (L/C). With this type of payment, your bank deals with your customer's bank and both banks act as intermediaries to ensure that the transaction happens as agreed. This provides protection to both of you. The following steps outline a standard *irrevocable L/C* transaction between your customer (suppose she's in India) and your company in the United States.

1. You and the customer agree upon the terms of the sale, usually by e-mail or fax. Typical items agreed upon during this stage are price, quantity, time frame, shipping dates and method, payment terms, revocability of the L/C (discussed later), the banks involved on both the buyer and seller sides, whether partial shipments are allowed, when the letter is opened and when it expires, and how the letter is to be transmitted between the parties. Notice that the banks are not involved in any of these terms; you and your customer must work them out.

2. The customer goes to her bank, in India, and establishes the L/C.

3. The customer's bank opens an irrevocable L/C naming your company as the recipient, which includes all the terms and conditions that you and your customer agreed upon.

4. The customer's bank sends the L/C to your bank, requesting confirmation of its receipt.

5. Your bank then faxes to you a copy of the L/C along with a confirmation letter.

6. You review the L/C and confirmation letter for proper terms and conditions. At this time, it is a good idea to verify with your *freight forwarder* that it can meet the delivery deadlines specified. If not, then you should contact the customer to change the L/C terms to reflect the proper dates. The banks then reissue the documentation.

7. You arrange with your freight forwarder to ship the product as indicated in the L/C.

8. When the forwarder has the products ready for shipment, it prepares all the needed documentation, including the *bill of lading*, which lists products included in this shipment.

9. The freight forwarder sends a copy of the paperwork, including the bill of lading, to your company.

10. You present the documentation to your bank, indicating that the shipment is on its way.

11. Your bank usually airmails the documentation to your customer's bank, which then reviews the paperwork and sends it to your customer.

12. Your customer uses the paperwork to claim the goods when they arrive in India.

13. Your bank then honors the L/C payment terms and deposits the proper amount in your account. The timing of this deposit is based on the terms agreed upon at the beginning of the procedure.

Notice that the documentation is critical to proper execution of an L/C transaction. If the documentation is not executed properly and consistently, it is very likely that your product shipment and payment receipt will be held up for a long time.

Here are some things to check when executing an L/C:

◆ Make sure that you have an irrevocable statement that states that the L/C is confirmed by the designated bank.

◆ Verify the spelling of the name and address of both the customer and your company. It must be consistent across the board.

def•i•ni•tion

A **bill of lading** is a document that accompanies shipments and contains information about the origin, destination, shipping means, and items included in the shipment. An **irrevocable L/C** is one in which the customer who issued the L/C cannot change the L/C terms. A confirmed L/C obligates your bank to make payment on the L/C to you upon presentation of the proper paperwork. This means that your customer's bank is extending the customer enough credit to cover the purchase. A **documentary L/C** is a financial arrangement set up between your bank and your international customer's bank. The banks act as third parties that verify receipt of product and transfer the funds. A **freight forwarder** is a company that manages the shipping of products from your country to others. Freight forwarders handle all the paperwork required to legally ship your product to the desired customer country.

♦ Make sure that the L/C amount is enough to cover not only the product involved, but also the shipping, insurance, and other fees associated with the shipment.

♦ Beware of shipping or other documentation dated outside of the date range defined on the L/C.

♦ Watch for extraneous markings on the invoice that are different from those found on other documentation.

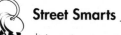

Street Smarts

It is not uncommon to request payment in advance for a percentage of a large order. This is a good-faith gesture on the customer's part, and it provides you with some protection later if the customer is slow to pay. (By the way, this rule holds equally true for domestic orders.)

♦ Make sure you allow for breakage or loss during shipment, called *shrinkage*. To accommodate this situation, include the term "approximately" or "about" before the L/C amount. Each industry will have its own accepted shrinkage norms, so check with someone already shipping internationally to determine what is right for your situation.

def•i•ni•tion

Shrinkage refers to breakage or loss of products during shipping or from theft.

♦ Watch for inconsistent pricing, quantities, product descriptions, or other terms of sale.

Is this starting to look like a lot of paperwork? It can be, but that's better than not getting paid. Notice that this bank-to-bank handshake confirmation provides protection for both the seller and the buyer. Plus, international bankers work in this world every day, so use your banker as an advisor.

Are you going to handle all of this paperwork yourself? Probably not in the early days. Instead, you want to work with a freight forwarder who can walk you through the paperwork maze. A freight forwarder is a company that manages the shipping of products from your country to others.

> **Street Smarts**
>
> Notice how important your bank is to the L/C process. Once again, you see that it is important to have a solid working relationship with your bank and banker. If you plan to do a lot of international work, then you should align yourself with a bank well versed in this type of business. Otherwise, you may be held back by your bank, which is unacceptable.

Find a forwarder who works with your target countries by looking in the Yellow Pages under Freight Forwarding. Try this procedure for selecting a freight forwarder: pick a typical shipping scenario regarding the country, products, and so on that apply to your company and have several forwarders bid on the cost of their services for handling this shipment for you. Compare the services and costs and then make the decision that is right for you.

There are various types of L/Cs; talk with your banker to determine the one that is right for your particular situation. The first few times you go through this letter of credit process, you might wonder why you ever got involved, but once you see the checks appearing in your bank account, you will wonder why you waited so long.

Going International—All the Way

Assume that you have been bitten by the international bug and want to make that a primary focus of your business. I admire your fortitude and sense of adventure, but I want to caution you on the complexity of your intended venture.

It is difficult enough to run a successful business within your own country. Those difficulties increase exponentially (that is, a lot!) when you decide to cross cultural, language, economic, and geographic boundaries. Unless you have a specific country, market niche, and maybe even product in mind for your international venture, I suggest you test it at home first.

Many people I know who go into import/export do so to feed their travel lust. In this way, their business travel becomes an expense and they can travel abroad more often. This sounds good on paper, but you have to eventually make some money or you will be out of business.

Opening up foreign markets takes time and money. Most small businesses have limited amounts of both. To address this situation, they look for established outlets in their target countries and allow these outlets to sell and distribute their products for them. You get ready market exposure, and the distributor gets products that might otherwise be unavailable. Once you find the right outlet in your target country, follow their advice on how to present the product for best acceptance.

Pick your countries carefully, or you can find yourself spread all over the globe and not making money anywhere, including at home. Most people I know choose countries where they once lived or where they have relatives. Speaking the local language is also a plus that is hard to overemphasize.

Also, don't underestimate the overall complexity of selling a product or service internationally. You must comply with legal and governmental regulations, or you can incur the wrath of your government, the target country's government, or both. Check with your country's consulate office in the target country for advice on how to break into the local market. They often employ people who are dedicated to fostering economic relationships between the two countries. These people can save you hours of struggle and introduce you to people who can provide the services you need. You should also determine if what you intend to ship is allowed based on the U.S. Government's international product shipment restrictions. For example, certain advanced technologies are not allowed for shipment to certain restricted countries. This list changes continually, so keep an eye on it.

Street Smarts _____

UPS, Federal Express, Airborne, and other major shipping companies have people who will help you complete the proper paperwork and act as your forwarder. They are happy to help so that they get your shipping business.

Street Smarts _____

When you become much more experienced, you might decide to perform the freight-forwarder function yourself.

Can it be great if it works? You bet. Can it be overwhelming as it ramps up? Yes again. I suggest that you take your international orders when they come and follow the letter of credit procedures outlined in this chapter. As your experience in other countries increases, you will find the natural migration path for taking your company and offerings international.

Working with China

Unless you live in a cave without television or radio you have heard something about the effect that China is having on the global economy. It is difficult to pick up something in the stores and not see "Made in China" on it. And the connotation associated with those three words has changed from that of something "cheap" and unreliable to quality and value. That perception shift in itself is worthy of notice, but it really gets amazing when you consider that China is an old country with a rich history that is transforming itself like a startup right before our—and the world's—eyes.

This section provides a brief overview of China and some of the specific and unique aspects of either using Chinese vendors or seeking Chinese customers.

Some Facts About China

First, let's get a few facts about China on the table:

- China's population is around 1.3 billion people (20 percent of the global population of 6.5 billion). The United States has 298 million people and the European Union has 456 million. This makes China's population almost twice that of the U.S. and European Union *combined!* (By the way, India is just behind China at around 1.1 billion.)

- China and the United States are roughly the same geographic size.

- A 2005 report by Mercer Human Resources stated that the Chinese workforce is composed of 718 million people, of which 16 percent have production jobs and 27 percent are skilled (white collar) workers. The U.S. has a total nonfarm employment of 135 million, of which 14 million (10 percent) are in manufacturing.

- The U.S. has a per-capita gross domestic product (GDP) of $42,000, where China's is $6,800. This means that the economic output of the U.S. per person is more than six times that of China. To give you a basis of comparison, Mexico is at $10,000 and Canada is at $34,000. This is all according to the CIA website at www.cia.gov.

- A U.S. product engineer will be paid around 10 times that of her Chinese equivalent, and China graduates 350,000 engineers annually where the U.S. graduates 90,000.

◆ Chinese production workers make about $1/20$ of the hourly wage rate of the average U.S. production worker, but this ratio will vary depending on where you get the data. What is consistent is that the average Chinese production worker makes a lot less than his American counterpart.

This all adds up to a country that is about the geographic size of the U.S. with four times the population, whose economy is growing like a startup weed but which still has a very low per-capita production rate compared to developed countries. So why is there all of this fuss about China, anyway? Here is where size and history really do matter.

The Importance of Relationship in Business

First, a little about China's recent history. James McGregor has written a great book titled *One Billion Customers: Lessons from the Front Lines of Doing Business In China*. In this book, McGregor spends a lot of time talking about how the history of China cannot be separated from doing business today in China. China is a communist country with centralized control, but there is a wide range of legal and operational reality based on where you are in China. Plus, there is a tradition of authority figures saying one thing but doing something else, which has created a high level of distrust among persons that is usually only overcome with time, experience, and personal contact. And money. McGregor claims that the traditional congratulations shared for the Chinese New Year translates into English as, "Congratulations on getting rich." He contends that the fluid nature of politics and corruption in China has forced people to place their faith in the one thing that they can somewhat control: money. So, money talks in China.

In addition, relationship is critically important in China. Chinese workers are known to pledge allegiance to their company, but in reality are pledging their allegiance to a specific person or leader. If the company takes care of the workers, then the workers will take care of the leaders and then the company. There is a strong family-like aspect to Chinese company environments.

Alliances and business relationships between companies work along similar lines. They tend to view relationships as longer-term commitments instead of brief opportunities. It is not that making money isn't important, it is, but the ongoing relationship is important as well. It is also important to know who you are dealing with, which also stems from the prior mentioned history. For this reason, negotiations with the Chinese can proceed at a snail's pace for westerners, who are used to meeting, quickly setting goals, defining terms and conditions, and moving forward with the business relationship. A first meeting with the Chinese may entail dinner. The contract is very important to westerners, where to the Chinese it is less important than the person with whom that agreement was made. Oh, and there has to be money made as well.

The Importance of Size

China is so large, and its population so huge, that even small sales opportunities that can be exploited can translate into large revenue opportunities.

China is experiencing a massive exodus from its rural communities to its cities. Those in the cities are making much more money than those in the country, and with that increased household income, and the sheer number of Chinese receiving more of that income, a massive purchasing engine is being created. Some estimates are that China has around 100 million middle class citizens, and this number is expected to reach 200 million by 2010! (Remember that this is around two-thirds of the total U.S. population.) Chinese total purchasing is expected to increase at 18 percent annually until 2016, where the United States is expected to grow at only 2 percent over the same period. Marketers have even created a term for these Chinese equivalents of the yuppies—"Chuppies." The late Chinese leader Deng Xiaoping stated that "to get rich is glorious," and these young Chuppies certainly appear to have adopted that part of the doctrine.

The Challenges

Labor rates are cheap compared to the U.S., professional skills are less expensive compared to the U.S., and there are hundreds of millions of new consumers with money to spend arriving on the scene. How can you take advantage of this combination so that you and your business can flourish? Here are a few things to consider:

- ◆ China is on the other side of the world. Flying parts back and forth is generally expensive enough to seriously offset the labor savings of manufacturing in China. Products are generally shipped by water.

- ◆ Shipping by water takes at least 20 days and may take as many as 30, meaning that a longer lead time is involved in getting your products from China to you so that you can sell them to customers.

- ◆ Moving things around in China is also difficult because of the rough state of the roads, trains, and other infrastructure. The situation is improving (25 percent of all worldwide steel production goes to China), but you will have to spend extra time, money, and effort ensuring that the manufactured product gets to your door from China in acceptable condition. Packaging becomes critically important under these circumstances and should be given special attention.

♦ To make headway into the Chinese markets or manufacturing areas, you must have some type of personal relationships established or you may find yourself thinking you have commitments, deadlines, and agreements only to be painfully and often expensively disappointed. You have to invest time and money in finding these contacts, establishing relationships of trust with them, and then moving forward with them.

♦ To sell products in China, 40 percent of the product must be manufactured in China. Notice how personal relationships again become important when doing business in China.

As a result, those intending to manufacture in China must forecast, plan, and manage over time horizons that can be years instead of weeks or months as is possible using U.S. vendors and customers. Project management skills start to take a much higher priority when using China as a manufacturing partner. It is hard enough to start a business when you have vendors, customers, employees, and alliance partners in your same geography, speaking the same language, and sharing the same culture. Adding Chinese partners to the startup situation may add a level of complexity not worth pursuing unless you have a high level of familiarity with the specialized issues involved.

On the other hand, if you can produce in China at a substantially lower price than entrenched competition, it might give you the pricing advantage needed to get established in the market. Just be respectful of the risks involved.

The Least You Need to Know

♦ Expect that your Internet site will generate international interest.

♦ When you transact international business, work with credit cards and letters of credit to ensure that you are paid.

♦ Use freight forwarders to handle your international sales.

♦ Don't go international until you have a revenue stream at home or deep enough pockets to fund the slower startup.

◆ Target countries that you know, and work with local channels to increase your likelihood of success.

◆ Keep your eye on the benefits of working with China as you start to get some success in your new venture.

Business Buzzword Glossary

accounting period   A period of time used to correlate revenues and expenses, usually defined as a day, week, month, quarter, or year.

accrual basis of accounting   A method of accounting that relates revenues and expenses based on when the commitments are made as opposed to when the cash is spent or received.

action plans   The steps needed to achieve specific goals.

advisory board   A group of business associates who act as advisors to your company on an informal basis. You can set regular meeting dates and times for the group to come together to discuss business issues, but you do not compensate advisors for their advice. You may want to pay for dinner, however, so they know you appreciate their time.

also known as (a.k.a.)   *See* doing business as.

analysis statement   A statement provided by your bank that details the various deposits and charges associated with your business account. It is used to detail the bank account service fee amounts.

angel investors   People, or groups of people, who invest in ventures that nobody else wants to touch.

articles of incorporation   A set of documents that are filed with the secretary of state's office that formally establish your corporation in that state.

assets   Those items of value the company owns, such as cash in the checking account, accounts receivable, equipment, and property.

authorized shares   The total number of shares of stock the corporation is permitted to issue. For instance, if 1,000 shares of stock are authorized at the start of the corporation, only a total of 1,000 shares can ever be sold to shareholders—no more than that unless the articles are amended to allow more authorized shares.

bad debt ratio   The amount of money you believe customers will never pay (also called uncollectible funds), divided by total sales and expressed as a percent.

balance sheet   One type of financial statement that you (or your accountant) create for a specific date to show all the company's assets and all the liabilities and equity owned by investors. The value of your assets must equal the value of your liabilities and equity for the statement to balance, which is where the term came from.

banking day   The days of the week that banks are open for business. You must make deposits at the bank before a certain time of day, which is usually around 2:00 P.M., for the deposit to be credited on that same day. If you make the deposit after the 2:00 P.M. cutoff, the deposit is not credited to your account until the next banking day, which may be the next day. If you make a deposit at the end of the week, the next banking day may not be until Monday of the next week.

benefit   What the customer gains by using your product or service. For example, the benefit of a drill bit is that it makes holes.

board of accountancy   The group of accountants who make decisions regarding generally accepted accounting principles.

board of directors   A group of experienced business leaders who are asked or elected to serve as formal advisors to a company. The board votes on major corporation changes, plans, and procedures. In return for assuming responsibility for the long-term growth of the company, directors generally receive either cash compensation or shares of stock. In other cases, the largest shareholders may ask for or require a seat on the board of directors as a means of protecting their large stake in the company.

bookkeeping   A system for accurately tracking where your money is coming from and where it is going. You can hire a bookkeeper to manage your record-keeping or invest in a computer program to do much the same thing. Bookkeepers are not necessarily accountants, although they do help organize all your information for use by your accountant.

break-even analysis   An analysis technique used to determine the quantity of an item that must be produced or sold to cover the fixed expenses associated with the time period in question.

break-even point   The quantity point where the gross margin equals the fixed expenses for the period in question. Above the break-even point, the company makes money, and below the break-even point, the company loses money.

browser   A software program that runs on a computer and allows Internet HTML (website) pages to be properly viewed.

business inertia   The inability of a company to change its thinking or ways of doing business. Generally, larger, more bureaucratic companies have more inertia than smaller, leaner businesses that can respond quickly to changes in the marketplace, giving small businesses a competitive advantage in many cases.

business judgment rule   A concept that protects members of corporate boards of directors from lawsuits filed by shareholders, customers, or others if the decision that caused the lawsuit was made in the best interests of the corporation.

business plan   A document that outlines your overall business objectives, their viability, and the steps you intend to take to achieve those objectives. Can be for internal use, external use, or both.

bylaws   The overall rules for operation of a corporation. Bylaws are an integral part of the corporation filing procedure.

C-corporation   The default corporation structure used primarily to protect owners from liability exposure. Most major corporations are C-corporations so that they can sell shares of stock to the public. Other forms of a corporation, such as a Sub S, have restrictions on the number of shareholders that can exist, but a C-corporation does not.

calendar fiscal year   A financial year that starts on January 1 and ends on December 31.

card identification number (CIN)   A number printed on the face of an American Express card that is used to verify validity of credit cards presented for purchases.

card processing company   A company that processes the credit card transactions for the retailers by verifying the account validity, the credit amounts available, and the transfer of funds into your company checking account.

cash basis of accounting   A method of accounting where expenses and revenues are tracked based on when cash is received or actual checks are written.

cash flow analysis   A financial statement that shows how much money the company had at the beginning of the month, how much money came in through sales and payments, how much went out in the form of payments, and what was left at the end of the month. Successful entrepreneurs carefully watch the amount of money coming in and going out of a company (cash flow) so the business doesn't run out of cash.

chain style franchise   A franchise arrangement where the franchisee pays a fee for an established chain store outlet like Midas or McDonald's.

chargeback   When a credit card processing company charges a sale back against your account, usually because the customer denies having actually made that particular purchase. It is the merchant's responsibility to show that this purchase actually happened, or the merchant could have to take the loss on the transaction.

chart of accounts   A list of all the categories a business uses to organize its financial expenditures and sales.

class of stock   Corporations can issue different types of stock that each have different legal rights with regard to dividends, voting, and other rights. Each of these different stock categories is called a class of stock.

clipping services   Companies such as Bacon's and Luce Clipping Services that read thousands of newspapers and magazines on the lookout for articles about or references to specific companies. Many businesses hire clipping services to watch for articles about their company and the competition. Unless you have the time to read virtually every major business magazine and newspaper, you might want to hire some professionals to do it for you.

close   A request by the salesperson for a specific action on the customer's part. Asking for the order is the ultimate close, but there are smaller closes that occur at each stage of the selling process to gradually move the customer closer to the sale.

close corporation   A company where owners or shareholders are active in the daily management of the corporation, which has no public investors.

commodities   Products that have no distinguishing features or benefits, such as flour, salt, and pork bellies, so that there is little or no difference in pricing between competitive products.

company policy manual   A manual that outlines the overall company policies that apply to all employees.

consideration   Something of value, such as money or a right to do something, that is usually given at the signing of a contract.

content (website)   The information included in a website that is viewed by Internet visitors.

corporation   A legal entity that is created as an umbrella under which business operation can occur. Corporations are chartered with the state and come in various forms, such as the S-corporation and the Limited Liability Company (LLC).

cost of sales   The costs directly linked to the production or sale of a product or service, also called the cost of goods sold (COGS). These generally include the cost of raw materials, the cost of labor to run the machine that produced the widget you sold, and other expenses that were required to sell the product or service.

cost-plus-profit pricing   Calculating your price using the cost to the company plus your desired profit markup. A widget that costs $1 to produce or purchase with a desired 50 percent markup would sell for $1 + ($1 × 0.5) = $1.50.

credit card transaction processing company   An organization that processes the typical credit card transaction and handles the transfer of funds from a credit card account into yours.

cumulative cash flow   The total amount of cash needed to handle the sum of all month-to-month negative cash flow (loss) experienced until the company starts to make a monthly profit when it hits break even.

current assets   Company assets that are liquid or can be converted to cash in less than one year.

CVC2   A three- or four-digit value that is used by MasterCard to verify the value of the information embossed on a credit card. If the card embossed information does not match the CVC2 value, then the card may be a forgery. Similar to CVV2 for Visa.

CVV2   A three- or four-digit value that is used by Visa to verify the value of the information embossed on a credit card. If the card embossed information does not match the CVV2 value, then the card may be a forgery. Similar to CVC2 for MasterCard.

cyberspace   A term used to designate the networked computer world that continues to permeate business.

debt financing   A means of securing funding to start or expand your business by way of a loan of some sort. The business takes on debt, instead of investors, as a way of getting the money it needs immediately while not giving up ownership.

demographic profile   Usually refers to a specific set of demographic characteristics used by sales and marketing to target likely sales prospects. Sometimes called an ideal customer profile.

demographics   A set of objective characteristics that describes a group of people. Includes characteristics such as age, home ownership, number of children, marital status, residence location, job function, and other criteria.

depreciation   A tax-related accounting procedure that deducts a certain amount of an asset's worth for each year of its operation.

direct competitor   Anyone who can, and will, eat your lunch today if you let them. Companies that sell the same product or service your company does, going after the same customers.

direct shareholder vote   A voting procedure where the shareholders personally cast their votes instead of voting by proxy.

discount rate   Refers to the amount (percent) that a credit card processing company charges a merchant for processing each transaction.

distribution channel   However your product or service gets from your facilities into the hands of customers. Different ways of distributing your product include direct sales, employees selling your offerings, retail stores, mail order, the Internet, and independent sales representatives or manufacturers' representatives.

distributor franchise   A franchise arrangement where the franchisee actually acts as a distributor for a major manufacturer's products, such as with a large auto dealership.

dividends   Money paid to shareholders out of the C-corporation's net income (after taxes are taken out). This is a form of compensation to the shareholders for having made the investment in the corporation by purchasing shares. Shareholders declare and pay tax on received dividends when filing their personal income tax return.

doing business as, or d/b/a   When you start a sole proprietorship that is named something other than your given name, you must complete some forms to officially use that name. The form you complete is a doing business as, or d/b/a, form. For instance, Jane Smith & Associates would need to file a d/b/a at the county clerk's office because the name is something other than just Jane Smith. Sometimes called a tradename or a.k.a. (also known as).

domain name   A unique name used to define an Internet location.

double taxation   Where the business pays tax on its annual profits and then passes part of that income as a dividend to you, the majority shareholder, who again gets taxed at the personal level; thus, the same sales revenue dollar is taxed twice.

earned income   Income attributed to completed business operations during a specific period of time.

electronic mail, or **e-mail**   A method of sending mail from one location to another using an electronic delivery medium such as the Internet.

employee manual   A document prepared by the company and issued to all employees, indicating the company's policies and procedures.

employer identification number (EIN)   A number issued by the IRS to any company with employees. May also be called FEIN or TIN.

entrepreneur   Someone who is willing to take personal and financial risks to create a business out of a perceived opportunity. A cool person who bought this book and wants to make more money than the rest by running the show.

equity financing   When someone gives you money in return for ownership of a portion of your company. You are giving up equity in the business in return for capital, which is equity financing. The other kind of financing is debt financing, which is when you get a loan that is paid back later. Equity financing does not get paid back. Investors get their money back by selling their shares to someone else, receiving dividends or Sub S-corporation distributions.

exchange rate   The rate at which one form of international currency is converted into another.

exchange rate liability   The uncertainty that comes from holding a purchase/sale agreement that is not in your home country's currency in an environment where exchange rates change.

factoring   The process of receiving money now for payments your customers are expected to make to you in the next few weeks. There is a cost to having that money now, which is paid in the form of a percentage fee to the factoring company or factor.

feature   The different objective characteristics of a product or service. For example, the features of a drill bit might include its size, length, and the type of material it is made of.

federal tax deposit coupon   Coupon issued by the IRS for collection of employee withholding taxes on a regular basis. Your employee identification number (EIN) and the amount due for the tax period are printed on the coupon. The coupon then accompanies your check made payable for the amount due.

fictitious name statement   See *doing business as*, or *d/b/a*.

firewall   A hardware or software device that is designed to keep those already on the Internet from entering your particular systems or network unless specifically authorized by you to do so.

fiscal year   The period of time over which you track and report your annual business accounting operations for tax and regulatory purposes.

fixed expenses   Business expenses that do not vary each month based on the amount of sales, such as rent, equipment leases, and salaries. Payments for these expenses are essentially the same each month, whether you achieve $1 million or $1 in sales.

float   The time period during which you have to cover expenses that should have been paid out of money received from customers. During this time, you are essentially lending money to your customers.

forum   A site on a computer service in which people with similar interests can post and read messages.

franchiser   A company that has created a successful business operation and concept that offers to sell the rights to the operation and idea on a limited geographic or market basis. The buyer of the franchise rights is called the franchisee.

freelancer   An individual who works for several different companies at once, helping out on specific projects. Freelancers are like consultants; they are paid a set rate for their services and receive no benefits, no sick pay, and no vacation allowance. The advantage is that freelancers can usually set their own hours, earn a higher hourly rate than they would get from full-time employment, and work with more than one company at a time.

freight forwarder   A company that specializes in shipping, duties, customs, and other administrative complexities related to international commerce.

Gantt chart   A simple yet effective method of tracking project items so that their order of completion, time frame, dependencies, and status are easily monitored.

gating item   The section of a process that limits the overall process speed. Increase the gating item's throughput, and you increase the overall process throughput.

gross profit   The amount of money left after you cover the cost of sales. Out of gross profit, you pay your operational expenses. Gross profit = revenue – cost of sales.

Hypertext Markup Language (HTML)   The programming code embedded in a website's pages that is interpreted by a browser for display on the user's computer.

imprint   When a credit card transaction is recorded by running the customer's credit card and carbon paper through a special roller machine.

income   The amount of money left over after all expenses and taxes are deducted from the sales revenue amount.

income statement   A type of financial statement that reflects all the income and expenses for a particular period of time, which is generally a year.

independent contractor   Another word that the IRS frequently uses for a freelancer. It means that the company you're doing work for is not your employer. You have the freedom to decide when, where, and how you will get the work done that your client has given you. You pay your own taxes and benefits, but you can also deduct expenses associated with getting your work done, such as a business phone line, travel, and supplies.

industrial espionage   The practice of collecting information about competitors through devious methods. Using public information sources that everyone has access to isn't considered espionage, but rummaging through corporate waste paper baskets after hours would be.

inertia   Indisposition to motion, exertion, or change; resistance to change. "This is the way we have always done things, so we will keep doing them this way even if they don't work" is an example of ineffective inertia.

initial public offering (IPO)   A stock trading event where the stock for a corporation is offered to the general public for the first time.

interests   Things that you enjoy doing, including the parts of your current job that you like the most, as well as what you do for fun in your spare time. Combining your personal interests with your business interests is a great goal.

Internet   An electronically connected network of computers that spans the globe. Once you are connected to it, the usage is typically provided at a flat fee for unlimited usage.

Internet service provider (ISP)   A company that provides access to the Internet for users who provide their own computer, modem, and the proper software.

job description   A detailed listing of the duties to be performed by the person filling the job in question; a listing of the required skills, education, certification levels, and other criteria directly related to the job.

job shop operation   A company that has a process flow that creates unique items at lower production volumes for each of its customers, as opposed to producing a standardized product in high volumes.

letter of credit (L/C)   A financial note that is set up through international banks by buyers and sellers who reside in different countries. Establishes a third-party, bank-to-bank handshake to ensure that both sides of the financial transaction are executed properly.

liabilities Amounts that you owe. Typical liabilities include loans, credit cards, taxes owed, and other people to whom you owe money. Short-term liabilities, which are paid back within 12 months, are also called accounts payable. Long-term liabilities include mortgages and equipment loans.

life cycle The four general phases that a product or service goes through between being introduced to the market and being discontinued or taken off the market.

limited liability company (LLC) A new type of business structure available in almost every state that has many of the advantages of a partnership or subchapter S-corporation but fewer of its disadvantages.

limited liability partnership (LLP) A special type of partnership wherein the partners protect their personal assets from being taken if the partnership gets into financial trouble. It blends the benefits of a general partnership with the liability protection of a limited partnership.

limited partnership A special form of partnership in which one partner acts as the general partner and is fully liable for the business and the other partners are limited partners and as such can limit their liability to what they invest in the partnership.

link A technological tool used to connect one Internet site's pages with website pages either on the home site or on another. A simple click on a link takes the viewer to the next page location attached to the link.

liquid assets Anything the company owns that can be quickly sold and turned into cash, such as accounts receivable, computer equipment, or stocks and bonds. Assets such as buildings or huge machinery would not be considered liquid because selling them would take a considerable amount of time.

local area network (LAN) A network setup inside of a company that connects computers and peripheral devices such as printers so that all network components can be shared.

logistics The set of activities that deal with making the daily routine effective. The daily grind of answering the phone, mailing letters, and dealing with customers takes time. You will probably need clerical help once you become successful to offload the daily routine paperwork so you can have time for other activities.

long-term goals Goals that typically extend beyond the next 12 months. For dynamic industries, only a few months can be considered long-term.

maintenance temperament Preference for keeping established systems running like a well-oiled machine and not creating new stuff.

managerial accountants   People who help you use your financial information to make business decisions. Generally, these accountants are on staff at a company and are responsible for record keeping and specialized reporting.

manipulation   When customers feel that they are not in control of the sales process—that they will be encouraged and persuaded to purchase something they don't really need. Underlying this activity is the sense that the salesperson really doesn't have the customer's needs and interests at heart. Can be useful when repeat sales are not desired or needed, but generally counterproductive if repeat sales are desired.

manufacturing franchise   A franchise arrangement where the franchisees are licensed to manufacture a specific product, such as Coca-Cola.

manufacturing requirement package (MRP)   A software package that integrates production forecasts with purchasing volumes to ensure that component parts needed to assemble a final product are available to meet production schedules.

market maker   A company with the clout to create an entire market opportunity simply by its involvement. IBM and Microsoft are examples of market makers in the high technology area.

market niche   A segment of the market that has an existing need for a product or service that nobody currently offers.

market penetration   The percent of prospective users of your products or services who are already existing customers.

market positioning   Creating a positive image in the minds of potential and existing customers. The purpose of market positioning is to have potential customers perceive your product or service in a particular way that makes them more likely to want to buy from you.

market segmentation   Dividing the total available market (everyone who may ever buy) into smaller groups, or segments, by specific attributes such as age, sex, location, interests, education, number of children, industry, or other pertinent criteria.

market value   The value of a product or service as determined by what the market will pay for it. Market values change with market activity and represent a type of collective marketplace survey of perceived value.

market-based pricing   Where offerings are priced at a level set by what everyone else is charging, rather than by what it costs you to make it (see cost-plus-profit pricing). With this strategy, you can generally make more money, assuming your competition is charging reasonable rates and you can keep your costs down.

marketing   Selecting the right product, pricing strategy, promotional program, and distribution outlets for your particular audience or market. Effective marketing makes it easier for salespeople to sell.

marketing theme   The overall thought that pops into people's minds when they think of your company and its offerings. For example, Pepsi's theme is "youth." Its soda is the drink for people who feel, or really are, young—the "new" generation.

markup   The amount of money over and above the cost of producing a product or service that is added to pay for overhead expenses and profit.

mass producers   Companies that produce the same product(s) in very high volume as opposed to a large number of products with very small production runs.

merchant number   A number given to your company that is used to identify which account should be credited when a customer makes a credit card purchase. It also verifies that you're allowed to accept credit cards in payment.

mind share   The portion of a person's thinking processes that includes perceptions of your company's offerings. One hundred percent mind share means that any time a person needs your type of offering, he or she always thinks of your company.

mission statement   A simple statement that clearly defines the overall goals, or mission, of the company.

momentum   Describes the direction in which things are naturally moving and implies the amount of work or energy that would be needed to change the natural course of the business as it is currently operating.

MO/TO   A credit card processing company acronym that refers to mail orders and telephone orders. Has also been extended to include Internet orders.

net income   Money left over after all company expenses and taxes have been paid out of revenues. Net income can be either positive or negative, depending on how good a year you had, but it can't stay negative for long or you'll be bankrupt.

noncompete clause   An agreement that employees or suppliers sign indicating they won't steal your ideas or business methods and go to work for a competitor or become competitors by starting their own firm. Generally, noncompete clauses are one section in a larger employment agreement.

nonsolicitation clause   A statement included in most noncompete agreements that restricts former employees from contacting prior customers with the intention of soliciting business from that customer for the employee's current employer.

nuisance   Someone who takes up a lot of your time but really poses no threat to your lunch plans.

objectives   Goals that define the overall direction of an organization, which can be divided into a number of shorter-range action items.

officers   Senior members of a management team or board of directors elected to serve as secretary, treasurer, president, and vice president of the corporation or board. Officers can usually legally commit a corporation in contract negotiations.

operational expenses   Those expenses associated with just running your business. No matter how much you sell this month, you will still have these expenses. These include your salary, your rent payment, the cost of the electricity in your office, and other similar costs of operating the company.

opportunity cost   The profit that would have been gained by pursuing another investment instead of the one currently in process. For example, if you go out on a date with one person, you lose the potentially good time you could have had with someone else. Sound familiar? That is opportunity cost.

outsourcing   Corporate-speak for hiring outside consultants, freelancers, or companies to provide services that in the past have been provided by employees.

overpromise   When you promise more to a customer than you actually deliver. It is never a good idea if you want to keep happy customers.

overdeliver   Delivering more to the customer than was agreed to, or more than the customer expected. It is usually a good idea if you can afford it.

owner's equity   What is left over when the liabilities are subtracted from the assets. Take what you have, subtract what you owe, and you are left with owner's equity. This is the number that you want to see increase from year to year because it reflects the value of your company. The initial value of your company stock and retained earnings are added together to calculate owner's equity.

partnership   When you and one or more people form a business marriage; your debts and assets are legally linked from the start. Any partner can make a commitment for the business, which also commits the other partners.

pending event   A future event with a specific date that forces business people to make decisions that they would otherwise put off until later.

perceived risk   The risk assessment as seen through the eyes of the investor or customer. You always want to be working to minimize the level of perceived risk on the part of the investor.

perceived value   The overall value the customer places on a particular product or service. This includes much more than price and considers other features such as delivery lead time, quality of salesmanship, service, style, and other less tangible items than the price. Essentially, a perceived value pricing strategy means determining what people are willing to pay and charging that amount, assuming you can still cover all your costs.

percentage markup   The amount of money a business adds into a product's price, over and above the cost of the product, expressed as a percent. A piece of candy costing $.05 to produce that has a markup of $.10 (meaning that the price to the consumer is $.15) has a percentage markup of 200 percent. This is calculated by taking the original cost, dividing it into the amount of markup, and then multiplying the result times 100.

performance to plan   A measurement tool used by investors to determine how close an organization is to performing according to the initial business plan goals.

personal attributes   Things such as being patient, working with other people, taking initiative, and other intrinsic personality-related traits.

point of sale system (POS)   This is a system set up to automatically record a customer sale transaction. Often, these systems are tied into the accounting system so that the sale transaction is automatically added to the accounting system, keeping sales automatically current.

potential sale revenue   A measurement of the total amount of money that can be made from a specific customer or event.

pretax profit   The amount of money left over after all the business expenses and costs of goods sold are subtracted from total sales, but before taxes have been subtracted and paid.

price erosion   When competitive sales present enough alternative product selections to your customers that you must drop your price to keep their business. This erodes both price and profit margins and usually occurs when market maturity is reached.

price war   When all competitors compete based on price and keep undercutting their competitors to get sales. As each company lowers its own price, others drop their prices to compete, resulting in profit margins in the industry as a whole falling to critically low levels.

probationary period   A time frame within which an employee is evaluated by the company, and vice versa. At the end of the probationary period, the employee and company can part ways with no negative implications or connotations.

processing company   A credit card-related company that acts as an intermediary between your customer's credit card sale transaction and your bank account where the sale amount, less a processing fee, is deposited.

product positioning   A conscious attempt on the part of your company to differentiate between your offering and those of your competitors. You position your product in people's minds by creating a perception of your product or service so that potential customers think of your products or services when they have a need.

professional corporation   A type of corporation, such as the subchapter S and subchapter C, used by professionals such as attorneys and accountants. Such corporations have P.C. after the company name to indicate the company is a professional corporation.

pro-forma balance sheet   A balance sheet comprised of numbers that are calculated based on historical performance and known future events. Typically used to project future financial expectations.

prospectus   A formal legal document a company prepares before being able to sell shares of stock to the public. The prospectus details all the pros and cons of investing in that company, so the potential purchaser of the company's stock is fully informed of the potential risks up front.

proxy statement   A form distributed to shareholders who will not be attending the company's annual meeting so their votes regarding the election of the board of directors, or other issues, can be counted. If a shareholder cannot attend the company's annual meeting but wants to vote, he can submit a signed proxy statement turning over the right to vote a certain way to the board.

publicity   Working with the media to have your company covered by the professional media such as magazines, newspapers, TV, and radio.

pull and push marketing strategy   A pull strategy convinces your potential customers to request your offering through their suppliers. In essence, the end user pulls your offering through the distribution channel by putting pressure on suppliers to carry it in their inventory. A push strategy sells your product to distributors, who then promote it to their customers. A pull strategy is driven by customers. A push strategy is driven by distributors.

registered agent   The official contact point for all legal matters. The registered agent is located at the registered office, which is the official address for corporate business.

retained earnings   A balance sheet item shown in owners' equity that indicates the amount of net income that is accumulated year after year. A positive net income increases retained earnings and a negative net income reduces retained earnings. When stock ownership does not change, the retained earnings provide a quick measure of year-to-year income performance.

revenue   Money you receive from customers as payment for your services or the sale of your product. Some people also call it sales, and it is the first item listed on an income statement.

reward   What an investor expects to receive for having made the investment in the first place. This is usually some form of payment to the investor within a specified time frame.

risk   The possibility that something, like an investment, will not turn out as well as expected. The higher the risk associated with an investment, the higher the expected return on investment.

routine tasks   Things you do that are pretty much the same as the last time you did them, except for minor variations. Printing out monthly invoices or counting inventory are two routine tasks that don't take much brain power but that have to be done.

S-corporation   A type of corporation, formed by making a special filing with the IRS, that has a limited number of shareholders. The profits are passed directly through to the owner, avoiding double taxation.

sales   Begins where marketing leaves off and involves all the steps you take to get the customer to buy your product or service.

sales revenue targets   The sales goals you set that affect all the other financial and production figures.

scattergun marketing   A scattergun sends buckshot in a wide pattern in the hopes of hitting something. Scattergun marketing sends marketing information everywhere in the hopes that someone will hear it and buy—the opposite of target marketing. Target marketing is usually more cost and time effective.

scope of work   A highly recommended section of a proposal that defines the overall intent of the work to be performed. This can be detailed or simple, depending on the work to be performed.

search engine   Internet technology that allows a program to categorize website information in such a way that a search can be performed on the site based on specific key words.

secured line of credit   A line of credit that has some form of asset such as accounts receivable or equipment as collateral for the loan.

Securities and Exchange Commission (SEC)   A regulatory body that monitors and defines policy for the exchange of stock on the public markets.

shareholders   Any individual or organization that owns shares of stock in a company.

short-term goals   Goals that occur within a short period of time, typically less than 12 months, and ideally lead to the completion of a long-term goal.

short-term loan   A loan that is to be paid off within one year.

shrinkage   The loss of product due to any number of means including loss in shipment or theft.

skills   Acquired skills include typing, speaking a foreign language, playing golf, and so on. Natural skills are inherent and less quantifiable, such as speaking voice quality, physical appearance, running speed, and so on.

sole proprietorship   You transact business without the legal "safety net" associated with a corporation. You are personally responsible for all the business's obligations, such as debt, and report your business activities to the IRS on your personal tax return's Schedule C.

startup temperament   Someone who thrives on (or even craves) new and exciting projects and challenges.

strategy   A careful plan or method; the art of devising or employing plans toward a goal.

suite   A term used in relation to software where a number of different application programs are sold under the same name, so that purchasing a single product actually provides a variety, or suite, of other software packages.

sunk cost   Money already spent that you cannot recover. Does not take into account opportunity cost or how else you could have spent the money.

superstore   An organization that provides a little, or a lot, of everything as opposed to specializing in a specific area.

swipe card   The action of running a credit card through a machine so that the magnetic strip on the back side is automatically read for transmission to the processing company.

tactics   Relating to small-scale actions serving a larger purpose, such as a strategy.

target marketing   A marketing approach involving focusing your marketing efforts on those groups—those potential customers—most likely to buy your products or services.

tasks   Things that need to be completed as part of working toward goals.

tax accounting   A type of accounting concerned solely with how much money you will have to pay in taxes. Tax accountants can help you take steps to minimize your tax bill.

underdeliver   Delivering less to the customer than you promised. Guaranteed to create a disappointed customer.

underpromise   Promising less to a customer than you actually plan to deliver.

underwriter   A company responsible for marketing and selling shares of stock in a company to outside investors.

unearned revenue   An accrual accounting term for payments made by a customer for work that has not yet been performed but still shows up as revenue on the financial statements. There will usually be a special account with this name.

unqualified prospect   An individual who says he or she needs your product or service, but who has not yet confirmed that he or she is able to make the purchase decision or met the other five qualification criteria (see Chapter 11).

unsecured line of credit   A line of credit such as a credit card that a company can turn to for cash and that is not backed by some form of collateral. Secured lines of credit are usually backed by some form of deposit, accounts receivable statement, or other company asset that the bank can use to pay off the debt if the company can't pay off the line of credit.

variable expenses   Those costs that vary according to how much of a product or service is produced. Just as things usually cost less when you buy them in bulk, producing a product in large quantities works the same way. The more you produce, generally the lower the cost per product. The cost of sales varies according to how much is produced.

wealth   Consistently having money left over after all your bills are paid. Real wealth is usually built by continually saving money over a longer period of time and is rarely acquired in a single "huge deal."

World Wide Web (www)   The interconnection of many Internet locations, or sites. These sites consist of HTML-coded pages that are read by a user's browser. These sites also refer to each other through links so that users can easily move from one Internet site to another.

The Kwik Chek Auto Evaluation Example Business Plan

Recommendations for Using This Business Plan

What follows is an actual business plan I wrote a while back for a used car evaluation service business called Kwik Chek. I wrote this plan to determine whether the idea would fly as an independent investment with national franchise potential or whether I should go back to the drawing board and find a new idea. I did not want to actually operate one of the Kwik Chek services myself, which is important to understanding the conclusions. The plan is included as a model to help you get a flavor for what is involved in writing a plan for your own business.

Don't get lazy and try to use this plan as is. It won't work for you or your idea, even if you have the same idea! You will clearly need to do your own research, write your own content, create your own financial analysis, and fill in the sections in a way applicable to your particular business idea.

Street Smarts _____

The flow, format, style, analysis process, and presentation are what you should be looking at when you review the plan. Don't get put off by the plan's data being from the 1980s. The analysis process is still valid.

Although I did not implement the plan, it served its purpose at the time it was written. The plan showed that the idea wasn't right for me since I did not want to be doing the work on the cars myself, and the analysis shows that owner/operator management was the way to go. Notice that the plan did what was expected of it. It told me that this idea did not fit my criteria for a business venture that I wanted to sink my time and money into.

Use this sample plan as a road map for the development of your own plan, and don't take the specific plan content literally. Think of it as a sample shell into which you will pour your own content.

Remember also that your plan should address the questions of the intended readers—this means that sections should be added or deleted as needed. Your levels of detail, section flows, and writing style will likely differ from that presented in the Kwik Chek plan. That is okay. Just make sure that you include an executive summary, the business description, competition, marketing plan, organization personnel, operations, funding requirements, and financial statements sections. The industry analysis, market analysis, and conclusion section contents will vary based on the market familiarity of the intended readers. The more familiar your reader is with the target marketplace and its unique attributes, the less detailed these sections need to be. The less familiar your reader is, the greater the need for detailed explanations in these sections.

These next few points are very important.

1. Write the executive summary after you have completed the plan. This sequence keeps you from writing something that meets your "picture" of how things should be as opposed to how they really are as supported by plan data and analysis.

2. The overall plan contents should support the conclusions outlined in the executive summary.

3. The appendix should support the overall plan contents and add details that were simply too much for the chapters themselves.

No single sample plan can do justice to the numerous business opportunities and entrepreneurial styles that exist. Read this, or any plan, as a guide, and make your business plan your own. Good luck, and start writing.

Cover Sheet

(Do not include this "Cover Sheet" text on your actual cover sheet. They will know it is the cover sheet.)

Plan Number: _____ Presented to: _____ Date: _____

Kwik Chek, Inc.

(A Texas Corporation)

(Corporate Office)
123 Balcones Drive
Austin, TX 78751

Phone: (512) 555-5555
Fax: (512) 555-5556
Web URL: www.kwikchek.com

Primary Contact: John Doe, President and Founder

The management of Kwik Chek has prepared this business plan for the expressed purpose of securing funding from the parties to whom the plan is presented. This business plan and all of its contents, methods, data, procedures and other proprietary information are company confidential information. No part of this plan may be revealed, copied, or duplicated in any way without the expressed written permission of Kwik Chek management. Copyright 1989 by Kwik Chek. All Rights Reserved.

Table of Contents

(Include page numbers on your final plan.)

Executive Summary

This plan presents Kwik Chek, a mobile used automobile inspection service, to determine whether it is a profitable business venture to pursue as either an investor or owner/operator. The report begins with a brief description of the service concept and then proceeds with an in-depth look at the services proposed, an in-depth look at the used car market for purchasing characteristics, an operational analysis of the requirements for providing the service, and a financial analysis of the cash flows expected over the first three years of operation.

The results of the study show that Kwik Chek, when treated as an absentee owner investment only, requires over $100,000 in cash to accommodate negative cash flows in the first year of operation and shows a positive return on investment in Year 3 of operation.

Further analysis shows that Kwik Chek, when treated as an owner/operator business, still requires $70,000+ in cash, but it shows a positive return on investment in less than two years instead of three and shows a substantial positive cash flow in Year 3 and beyond. The return on investment time period is reduced by one year.

There is already competition in the used automobile inspection area, but there is substantial market share to be had by each entrant. The Kwik Chek analysis assumes that only 20 percent market penetration is achieved by Kwik Chek to achieve the goals outlined—this is reasonable given the anticipated competitive environment.

It is not recommended that an absentee owner pursue Kwik Chek as strictly an investment because the return on investment period is over three years and the longer-term positive cash flows are nominal. It is, however, recommended as an investment for an owner/operator who can serve as both owner and inspection technician with another family member working as dispatcher. This scenario provides the family with an opportunity to generate in excess of $100,000 in household income by the end of Year 2.

A Description of the Proposed Kwik Chek Service

Kwik Chek is a user vehicle inspection service designed to provide prospective buyers with objective information about the mechanical condition of the vehicle that they intend to purchase. The inspection is performed at the vehicle's location, and a complete report of the mechanical and electrical condition of the car is provided. Kwik Chek inspects automobiles and light trucks.

To schedule an appointment, the customer telephones a local Kwik Chek office and schedules a time and location for the inspection. This provides a major benefit in that the customer does not have to "borrow" the car to bring it to a mechanic and the vehicle seller does not run the risk of someone unknown driving the car around town. When the inspection is completed, the customer is provided with a sheet detailing the condition of the vehicle. In total, approximately 90 points are inspected. The customer can be assured that the major vehicle components will be inspected and that any major defects will surface during the inspection.

Street Smarts

Notice that this description not only provides details about the service being provided but also presents the major customer benefits derived from using the service. The reader not only knows what Kwik Chek is about but also why someone would be interested in using the service. Notice that everyone has experience with buying or selling a car, so you can assume a certain level of familiarity with the need for this type of service. Gauge your description to your reader's experience level with respect to your industry. The detailed listing of inspected vehicle components simply adds credibility to your story by showing that you have thought out the details.

A detailed listing of the inspections performed during a Kwik Chek inspection is included in the next section.

The inspection time takes around 40 minutes once the mechanic is set up. Each Kwik Chek technician is an experienced mechanic. The equipment in the Kwik Chek van is designed to streamline the inspection process as much as possible. (See Exhibit X for a detailed listing of van equipment.)

The primary benefit being purchased by the user is the peace of mind associated with an objective, informed, third-party opinion of the used car purchase. Most people want to know what they are buying and not be surprised by major defects later when the vehicle is theirs. The Kwik Chek information can also be used by both buyer and seller as a negotiating tool to achieve a more equitable price for the vehicle.

In summary, the benefits associated with the Kwik Chek service are peace of mind and convenience. The major marketing questions are how many people are willing to pay for the service, and at what price? The Market and Industry Revenue Potential Analysis section addresses these important marketing-related issues.

Kwik Chek Tests Performed

Engine Diagnostics

Compression

Rotor

Cap

Capacitor (as required)

Points (as required)

Electronic ignition

Oil leakage

Spark plug fouling

Spark plug wires

Belts

Exhaust for age and leaks

Oil consumption/burning

Suspension and Steering

Tire wear

Shock absorbers

Alignment (from tire wear in front)

Torsion bars tightness

Cracked leaf springs

Spare tire condition

Brakes

Check pads/shoes for wear

Check one rotor/drum for wear

Check for pulling when braking

Check emergency brake

Accessories

AM/FM radio/cassette

Power windows

Power locks

Power seats

Air conditioning

Heater and fan speeds

Gauges

Speedometer/odometers

Cigarette lighter

Windshield washer

Windshield wiper operation and blade condition

Transmission

All speeds

Clutch slip and adjust (manual)

Reverse

Lights

Headlights (low/high)

Turn signals

Hazard lights

Backup lights

License plate lights

Dome lights

Instrument cluster lights

Outside lights

Fluid Levels and Condition

Oil

Transmission

Differential

Clutch

Brake

Coolant plus hoses for leaks

Battery

Washer fluid

Steering

Hydrometer test of coolant for antifreeze

Electrical

Alternator charging

Battery load test

Slow leak test

Body

Undercoating

Accident repairs

Rust

Fading/peeling paint

Proper closure of doors and windows

Mirrors (inside and out)

Trailer hitch hook-up residuals

The Market and Industry Analysis

The automobile marketplace has been in a state of transition since the beginning of the 1980s. There has been a trend in recent years away from purchasing new automobiles and toward purchasing an automobile on the used car market.

It has recently become common knowledge to the general public that a new car purchased from a dealer loses a tremendous amount of its resale value almost immediately. This amount of initial loss is generally financed and paid for by the owner over a three- to five-year period and consequently does not get amortized as quickly as the car loses its value. A used car, on the other hand, does not lose value as quickly after purchase because the bulk of the "new car" depreciation has already occurred by the time of purchase.

Street Smarts

This section presents the big-picture case for the service. It helps the reader understand the nuances related to the marketplace and its trends over the past decade or so. In this way, the reader learns that this is not a temporary opportunity but one indicative of a longer-lasting nature.

Data from the 1988 Motor Vehicle Manufacturers Association Facts and Figures, as shown in the following table, shows that the total number of registered vehicles on the road today has increased steadily from 1980 to 1988, and the mean and median ages have also increased.

Registrations and Vehicle Ages

	1980	1988
Registered vehicles	150 million	180 million
Mean age of vehicles	6.6 years	7.6 years
Median age of vehicles	6.0 years	6.8 years

There are many possible reasons for this recent trend. The increased need for fuel-efficient cars, combined with difficult financial times for the public at large, have made people more cautious about how they spend their money. They are tending to treat an automobile purchase as an investment decision, rather than an impulse buy.

The major problem with a used automobile is that the buyer generally purchases the vehicle in "as-is" condition. The buyer is typically unaware of the mechanical condition of the vehicle and consequently purchases the vehicle on faith that it does not have major mechanical or electrical problems that will substantially increase the overall cost of ownership.

The current alternative to buying on faith is to take the car to a mechanic for a complete mechanical review. This action takes time and money on the part of the buyer, and trust by the seller. In addition, the scheduling of the mechanical inspection is typically done during the day when the buyer is at work. In essence, it is a hassle at best and prohibitive for many. Consequently, even though everyone agrees that an independent inspection is a good idea, few people actually have the inspection done.

From the seller's perspective, it is valuable to have an independent inspection report of the mechanical condition of the vehicle to assure potential buyers that there are no hidden defects in the vehicle.

This procedure is similar to that done when a person buys a house and arranges an inspection of the physical condition of the house. In some states, it is a legal requirement to have a house inspection before the house can be sold. Because a house and a car are typically the two largest purchases the average person makes in a lifetime, it stands to reason that they should both be treated with the same level of care.

It makes intuitive sense that a service that offers reliable mechanical inspection of vehicles in a convenient way and for a reasonable price would be well received by the used-vehicle buying public.

Market Opportunity Estimate

It is assumed that the Kwik Chek service proposed would be most applicable to used car purchases because new car purchases come with a warranty, providing the purchaser with post-purchase security. This report concentrates on the used car market as the potential opportunity for Kwik Chek. It initially looks to verify the business concept in the Austin, Texas area (the founder's home town) and then expand it across the country if shown viable.

Street Smarts

Notice that this section so far helps the reader understand not only the total number of used cars that will be purchased in Austin over the next 12 months, but also that 67 percent of these cars will be purchased on the open market, with the remaining 33 percent being purchased from dealers. Also note that the reader is clearly made aware that 67 percent/33 percent national average ratio being applied to the Austin market is a clearly stated "assumption" on my part. They may not agree, but there is also no sleight of hand here.

The Scarborough Report on Austin Automobile Purchases for 1988 shows that 31 percent of all adults in Austin are planning to purchase an automobile, and 47 percent of those are planning a used car purchase. This implies that 14 percent (47 percent of 31 percent = 14 percent) of all adults in Austin are planning a used car purchase within the next year. (See Exhibit I.)

There are 569,000 adults in the Austin SMSA according to the most recent Census data. Fourteen percent of this number (those estimated to be looking to purchase a used vehicle) indicates that it can be estimated that 81,190 (569,000 × 0.14) used cars will be purchased each year. (See Exhibit I.)

The Scarborough report also shows that, on a national basis, 23,386,400 used cars were purchased in 1988. Of these, 7,607,172 (33 percent) were purchased from dealers according to the Wards report. It is then assumed that the remaining 15,779,228 (67 percent) were purchased on the open market. (See Exhibit I.)

For purposes of analysis, it is assumed that the 33 percent dealer/67 percent open market ratio outlined in the previous paragraph of used car purchases is indicative of the entire nation, including Austin, in determining the number of used cars purchased from dealers or on the open market.

Referring to Exhibit II, it can be seen that Austin should be purchasing more used automobiles than indicated in Exhibit I because the total purchases divided by the total registrations indicates a holding period of 4.6 years per purchased vehicle. This is more than the 3 to 4 years indicated by the *Medical Economics Journal*, February 6, 1989, page 174.

Street Smarts

These last two paragraphs provide justification to the reader that I am not being too aggressive with my estimates. In fact, I make the case that, if anything, the number of used cars that could use the Kwik Chek service is actually larger than that estimated here. This is always good news to investors who want you to have more people to sell to instead of fewer. Makes sense to me.

The estimated new car purchases are assumed accurate because they come from manufacturer data. An increase in the total number of used cars purchased would decrease the holding period for vehicles and indicate a larger turnover than estimated for this analysis. A larger turnover would decrease the holding period and make it closer to the 3 to 4 years estimated. Consequently, it is assumed that this analysis is conservative and reflects a slightly pessimistic case for analysis.

These unit market potential estimates will be tied in with the pricing and other pertinent data to present Kwik Chek's projected financial performance.

Pricing of Kwik Chek Inspections

Exhibit III reflects the price demand curve for the Kwik Chek service at different prices. The curve is derived from data obtained from a survey of prospective purchasers of the service. The curve indicates that only 70 percent of used car purchasers would use the service at any price and that none would use it if priced at more than

$110. The curve is most flat in the $40 to $60 range, with most people saying that $49 sounded "about right." It should also be noted that some mentioned a tendency to price the evaluation service at a percentage of the purchase price of the vehicle in question.

Verification of the $49 price came from the Credit Union National Association *Guide to Buying and Selling a Used Car*. The guide indicates that "If you think this is a car you want, hire a mechanic or car care center to evaluate the car. You can usually do so for $40 or less."

Based on the added convenience of performing the evaluation on site instead of having to take it to a mechanic as is assumed in the Credit Union guide, a $49.95 price seems reasonable and justifiable. A graph of Exhibit III data indicates that with a price of $49.95, the available market of potential users of the Kwik Chek service becomes 37.5 percent of the total number of used car purchasers.

In summary, Kwik Chek proposes to offer its service to the general public for $49.95 and expects that 37.5 percent of all possible used car purchasers are viable prospects for using the service at that price.

It should also be noted that national purchases are somewhat seasonal in nature, as indicated from the Scarborough report data shown in Exhibit IV. The peak buying season appears to be March (9.6 percent of purchases) through August, with the end of the year and the beginning of the year relatively slow (6.98 percent of purchases according to Exhibit IV). It is recommended that Kwik Chek be introduced to the buying public in January to allow familiarity with the concept in time for the March to August buying peak. The moderate Austin climate may reduce some of this seasonality, but it should be assumed highly pertinent in areas that experience cold winters.

Street Smarts

Notice that this pricing discussion is based on "real world" feedback in the form of personal interviews and then verified with a reality that already exists in the marketplace. This type of confirmation helps to add credibility to your estimates and assumptions. It accepts a mid-range price as a way of getting more customers and selling more inspections.

Street Smarts

Notice that the plan has now laid the foundation for a total revenue potential analysis. The assumptions related to the total number of unit sales are presented, as are the dealer and open market pricing estimates. It is now time to do the math and see where the national and Austin revenue potential winds up. These estimates are shown in the next section.

As mentioned previously, 33 percent of all used cars are purchased from dealers. Kwik Chek can provide a similar service to the dealers as it intends to provide on the open market. The dealers will probably want a discount of 20 to 25 percent off the retail price, based upon past experience of Kwik Chek management. Kwik Chek can justify this discount because of the ease of inspection of many vehicles in the same location, instead of many locations all over the city. The reduced travel time reduces time and travel expenses, which enables the lower dealer price. The dealers will use Kwik Chek so that their mechanics can be working on more expensive and complicated repairs.

It is assumed that there will be two classes of service: (1) the dealer service at $39 per inspection, and (2) the open market at $49.95 per inspection.

Market Sales Potential

Exhibit V indicates that at the $49.95 price, and with estimated 37.5 percent of the used car buyers as potential customers, the total U.S. revenue potential is $438M. This exhibit also shows that if 20 percent of national potential customers use the Kwik Chek service, $87.6M in sales will be generated. It is assumed by management that Kwik Chek cannot obtain more than 20 percent penetration due to competition. Note that this exhibit and Exhibit VI do not include a breakdown for dealer/open market inspections. This breakdown is presented in Exhibits VII and VIII.

Street Smarts

We now have total possible revenue projections for the Austin marketplace and for the nation. These projections are based on market conditions, *not* what I "think" should be true, other than the assumptions that are intrinsic to the analysis. It is now time to determine if Kwik Chek, its owners, and investors can financially survive with these revenue projections and to assess its competitive challenges.

Exhibit VI indicates that the Austin market alone has a total potential market of $1.5M at the $49.95 price, and that a 20 percent penetration of that market will generate $304,000 in annual revenues.

Exhibit VII indicates that the national potential revenues with 20 percent penetration of both the dealer and open markets is $76M, down from the previous $87M estimate but still a substantial number.

Exhibit VIII outlines the same breakdown as mentioned in the previous paragraph, but for the Austin area. It is seen that Austin can be expected to generate $282,000 in revenues and perform 6,090 inspections per year with 20 percent potential market penetration.

Competition

Kwik Chek already has two competitors in the Austin area: Auto Chek and No Lemons. In addition, a potential competitor named CheckOut may be about to launch a national franchise.

Auto Chek

Auto Chek has been in business for almost one year. The president is a successful entrepreneur who recently sold another company and started Auto Chek a short time afterward.

The president has every intention of making Auto Chek a national franchise and has already sold the franchise rights to organizations in Dallas and San Antonio.

Auto Chek wants an initial franchise fee of $25,000 and an 8 percent royalty on sales. It has advertised widely in Austin, but an informal survey of people regarding the service showed that there is awareness of the service but not the name of the company. There is a potential free rider opportunity available to Kwik Chek.

Auto Chek charges $49.50 for its services and checks 90 points on each car, making it comparable with the Kwik Chek offering.

No Lemons

No Lemons has come onto the market in the past month. It charges $59.50 for its service and claims to inspect 120 points, but it inflates the number a little (by treating each tire as an inspection point, wipers as two inspection points instead of one, and so on).

Rumor around town is that many dealers are shying away from doing business with No Lemons. We intend to find out more about what these problems may be between No Lemons and the dealerships to determine if there is an opportunity here for Kwik Chek. It is definitely in the market and already out there with a van and providing the service. No Lemons is planning to franchise nationally. Fees and royalty information were not available.

CheckOut

CheckOut is an inspection company in New Jersey that has been providing services for over five years but is confined primarily to the New Jersey/New York area. It charges $59 for its service and checks around 90 points.

CheckOut is rumored to have started a national franchise, but to date, I haven't found evidence of that being the case.

Marketing and Sales Strategy

The most powerful tool for promoting Kwik Chek's success is positive word of mouth where one satisfied user tells several friends about the value received from using the service. This applies equally well for the dealer and open market segments, with the dealer segment involving a much smaller number of people. The most difficult initial problem is increasing the public's awareness about the service availability and benefits. A special referral reward system should be established where a person can earn a free inspection for recommending 10 people for the service. Vouchers can be used to track the referrals.

A monthly marketing expense of $2,500 is assumed, and it should be spent in the following areas:

Monthly Yellow Pages advertising	½ page ad at $1,200 per month = $1,200
Direct-mail pieces to dealers	200 pieces at $1 each = $200
Direct-mail pieces to households	$400 as an insert in a bulk mailing pack
Commissions for part-time sales	$700 per month at 10 percent of partial revenues

It is also assumed that around $10,000 will be spent during the first few months on radio and newspaper advertising. In addition, special promotions should be set up with the dealers around town in conjunction with radio simulcasts where free used car inspections are provided if you bring your car in for inspection while the radio station is broadcasting and on-site.

Street Smarts

Notice that this plan not only presents details with respect to advertising and sales activities in the first few months of operation, but also provides a rationale as to why this approach is taken.

Given the more ready access to the dealer market and its decision makers, a special sales push will be applied to the dealer segment during the first few months of operation. The special emphasis to the dealer will be that using Kwik Chek to inspect the cars is less expensive than them paying their own mechanics to perform the check. This is justified by the assumption that the dealer pays around $70 per mechanic hour, including overhead and benefits, and a 40-minute inspection would cost the dealership $47 and revenue lost by that mechanic not being able to repair a dealership customer's car. At $39 per inspection, Kwik Chek should be attractive to the dealership.

Operations Plan

Exhibit IX outlines the logistical analysis used to determine the total number of vans that would be required to address Austin at the 20 percent penetration rate. Twenty percent was used to determine the state of the company when working at its peak efficiency.

It is assumed that inspections are provided 11 hours per day, 7 days per week. Dealer inspections will occur during the week, and open market inspection will occur additionally on the weekends and evenings. Initially one person may try covering this number of hours and, if successful, a second person should be added to reduce hours to a normal work week for both.

It is assumed that a dealer inspection will constitute 33 percent of inspections. Using the estimated 40-minute inspection time per vehicle, dealer inspection of each vehicle is expected to take 0.67 hours (40/60 minutes). The open market inspections cannot be scheduled in closer than 1.5-hour (90 minute) intervals due to 45 minutes of assumed travel time between appointments and other unforeseen circumstances.

Street Smarts

Notice the level of detail included with this operational assessment. There is a quantifiable justification for the analysis and its findings, which is substantially different from just projecting hunches. With these numeric estimates, the reader can make his or her own determination as to the validity of the analysis, and you have something concrete and specific to discuss in coming to agreement. Notice the comment related to adding another driver to cover part of the 77 hour work week. This is a decision usually made on the fly, but at least you start with some concrete idea of requirements.

Based on these assumptions—and the 33 percent dealer/67 percent open market split mentioned previously—a maximum of 272 inspections can be performed by one van in one month. The chart indicates that at the 20 percent penetration rate, an average of 1.9 vans will be needed to meet estimated maximum demand in Austin.

It is recommended to start out with one van with Mr. Doe performing the inspections and then add a technician along with progression to a second van when the number of inspections warrants the addition, sometime in Year 2 of operation when the total number of monthly inspections approaches the maximum per van of 272 indicated in Exhibit IX. (See Exhibit XI and XII for inspection rampup details.)

The initial plan is for the Kwik Chek office to operate out of Mr. Doe's home, which is assumed acceptable since customers will never have to visit the office. All inspections take place at the customer's location and not at the Kwik Chek office.

The van driver/mechanic will carry a cellular phone and also have a two-way radio so that scheduled appointments can be passed to the driver on a real-time basis. It is important that drivers and the dispatcher/office telephone operator be in regular communication with each other to ensure that customer schedules are kept and delays are immediately acted upon and relayed to the customer.

The Management Team

John Doe is the author of this plan and the president of the new company. He has worked as a mechanic for over 10 years and has experience repairing both domestic and imported automobiles. He has served as the shop foreman for the local Ford dealership for the past two years. His foreman duties also include profit and loss projections for the service segment of the local dealership's operation. Mr. Doe will be the initial inspection technician, with others hired as business grows.

His wife, Judy, intends to work as the secretary/dispatcher to make the initial Austin, Texas operation a success and to improve their income from the business. She has experience as both a switchboard operator for a large corporation and as an executive secretary.

Mr. Doe has a wide network of mechanic colleagues who are interested in working with Kwik Chek once the idea proves successful.

Financial Analysis

This section presents a detailed financial analysis of the Kwik Chek business idea. It first looks at the variable and fixed costs associated with the business operation. This section includes a profit analysis for each van, determines the break-even number of inspections needed to support the van and its driver, and then ties the pieces together into a complete profit and loss analysis over a three-year period.

Fixed- and Variable-Cost Analysis

Exhibit X outlines the fixed and variable costs associated with the operation of Kwik Chek.

It can be seen that the van with its equipment has a cost of $24,140. If financed over a three-year period at 10 percent interest rate, this becomes a payment of $779 per month. It is also assumed that a technician/mechanic is dedicated to the van with a salary of $1,800 per month, which is initially paid to Mr. Doe. Adding in paging, service, and maintenance, the fixed costs associated with operating a van are expected to be $2,925 per month.

The general overhead cost is outlined in Exhibit X to be $7,191 per month. This number assumes that most equipment such as computers, copiers, and so on will be financed over a three-year period at 10 percent for a monthly payment of $336. It also assumes a secretary who doubles as an appointment scheduler and earns $1,500 per month and $2,500 in monthly marketing expenses. The general overhead number also includes a $417 monthly amortization of a franchise fee of $15,000 that is equally divided over 36 months. All appointments for inspection are scheduled through the main office operator/dispatcher. This $7,191 figure includes 20 percent margin for error to allow for things that were not initially anticipated, so it should reflect a maximum amount.

Exhibit X also shows that the variable costs associated with dealer inspection is $10, and it is $11 for the open market inspection because gas mileage is involved. Included in this cost is a $5 incentive to the mechanic for each inspection performed and paid for by the customer. This is to keep the drivers motivated to complete as many inspections as possible while assuring quality work.

It can be seen from Exhibit X that total contribution to overhead for operations when at 20 percent (and working with 2 vans) is $16,475 per month. The total overhead (fixed cost) is expected to be $13,040 (2 × $6,520), which leaves the net profit before taxes at $3,435. Up to this point, there has not been any allowance for owner income other than the income earned by Mr. Doe as the test technician. At this point, it appears that the maximum before-tax income to the owner of the Austin Kwik Chek franchise would be $3,435 per month

Street Smarts

Notice also the level of detail included in this analysis.

There is a lot of information here, and a case can be made for it being a reasonable projection of the future. The breakeven numbers provide initial operational goals to shoot for so that, at a minimum, the business is paying for itself with Mr. Doe at least taking home some salary.

or $41,220 per year. If the franchise were owned as a subchapter S-corporation, the owner would still need to pay taxes on this amount.

It is also seen from Exhibit X that the inspection break-even for the entire operation with 2 vans is 402 inspections and that the incremental costs associated with another van are covered with 90 inspections.

Overall Financial Analysis

Exhibit XI shows the financial results expected from Kwik Chek operation when the owner is not involved with the inspections. Exhibit XII shows the expected financial results when the owner actually performs inspections from one of the vans. The owner/operator actually makes the $20,000 allocated to the van operator and retains whatever profits are left over at the end of the year.

Street Smarts

Look at how important that cumulative cash flow number is to the total attractiveness assessment of this business venture. Notice also that the company hits its break-even point somewhere between Month 12 and the end of Year 2. If the break-even quantity is reached earlier than in Month 12, then the amount of cash required to open the business is reduced and the return on investment improves accordingly.

It is assumed that Kwik Chek acquires one percent additional market share for each month it is in operation. At the end of the second year, Kwik Chek is assumed to be at the 20 percent penetration target.

The chart also indicates that there is a substantial negative cumulative cash flow during the first year. The peak negative value is $102,026 for absentee owners and $72,000 for the owner/operator. The profits derived by the second year of operation begin to erode the negative cumulative cash situation. Kwik Chek is still in a negative cumulative cash flow situation by the end of Year 3 for the absentee investors but shows a positive turn for owner/operators. Absentee owner/investors begin to show a return on their investment beginning in Year 4.

The chart shows that the company operates with a negative net operating income over the first year of existence for absentee investors and turns slightly positive for the owner/operator and turns positive for both scenarios in Year 2. The owner/operator stands to make substantial money after the first year should business plan projections be accurate.

An additional van is required during the second year to meet market demands. When included in the expenses of the second and ongoing years, Kwik Chek can be expected to yield a net profit before tax of $41,208 for absentee owners and $89,808 for owner/operators.

Anyone who invests in a Kwik Chek franchise must be willing to risk between $70,000 and $100,000 in cash and wait between 2 and 4 years for a positive return on that investment.

Summary and Conclusion

It can be seen from the previous discussion that the investment potential of a Kwik Chek franchise is not a viable option for a person who treats it exclusively as an investment.

Exhibit XII shows what happens to the financials of the project if the owner is also the mechanic for the first van. This creates a saving on two counts: (1) The $5 incentive per inspection is not needed to motivate the mechanic because the mechanic is the owner, and (2) there is an $18,000 savings per year in the salary paid to the mechanic.

It can be seen from Exhibit XII that there is still a substantial negative cumulative cash flow for the first year, but, for the investor scenario, the cash flow drain reverses direction in Month 11 as opposed to some time in Year 2. We see that the project becomes a positive cumulative cash flow project by the end of Year 2 and becomes a generator of substantial cumulative cash, $107,841, in Year 3.

It still requires $75,000 (plus living expenses) to ensure minimum cash reserves for the business. If the marketing penetration rampup is greater than expected, then the business will generate cash faster.

It is thus concluded that Kwik Chek is not a viable investment for someone who does not intend to operate the business himself, performing inspections in one of the vans. It does not generate a positive return on investment until Year 3 and requires over $100,000 in cash reserves to start. This time frame is simply too long for most investors.

If a person wants to invest his own time in the project and operate one of the vans, then there is substantial future revenue-earning potential from Year 3 onward. There is still over $75,000 in cash required to fund the business, but the long-term prospects for return are much improved over treating the project as only an investment.

Kwik Chek should be started in Austin by a mechanic who wants to start his or her own business. If it begins to show the returns expected, then the project should be set up for national franchising to mechanic/investor groups who want to provide the service. At that time, additional funding can be obtained based upon the company's successful track record.

Exhibits

Exhibit I: Scarborough Report on Automobile Purchases

From the Scarborough Report on Austin automobile purchases (1988)

Percent of adults planning to purchase a car:	31%
(This fact implies that people change cars every 3.2 years)	
Percent of adults planning a used car purchase:	14%
Total number of Austin SMSA adults:	569,355
Percent of women adults buying used cars:	69%
Total number of planned used car purchases:	81,190
Women planning to buy a used car:	56,021
Men planning to buy a used car:	25,169

Notes:
1) The median price range for women's purchases is $6,900
2) The median price range for men's purchases is $10,300
3) The bulk of those buying used cars have median incomes of $27,000

4) The total number of licensed drivers in the U.S.=	164,000,000
There are Number of male drivers=	85,000,000
Number of female drivers=	79,000,000

Assuming the Austin ratios for adults purchasing used cars is valid for the
the entire U.S., then we can assume that the total number of used car purchases
in a year are:

Total number of drivers:	164,000,000
Percent buying used cars:	14%
Percent buying new cars:	16%
Total used car purchases:	23,386,400
Cars purchased by women:	16,136,616
Cars purchased by men:	7,249,784
Cars purchased from dealers:	7,607,172 [from Wards, p. 166]
Cars purchased on open market:	15,779,228

Exhibit II: Validation of Conservative Estimates

To determine whether Austin is representative of the U.S. in general, we
can compare the new car purchases nationally to those expected in Austin.
Austin is expecting new car percentage purchases of 15.5%.

New car information:

1988 new vehicle purchases:	15,245,843
Percent of licensed drivers:	9%

This information indicates that the national average of used car
purchases may actually be higher than that seen in Austin.

Total new car purchases:	15,245,843
Used car purchases:	23,386,400

Total annual purchases:	38,632,243
Total registered vehicles:	179,000,000
Percent purchases to registration:	22%
Average holding period:	5

The national average for holding a car is 3-4 years. These numbers
indicate that the numbers used for analysis are conservative and that
more used cars are probably sold annually than predicted.

Sources:
Motor Vehicles Manufacturers Association Facts and Figures (1988)
Wards Automotive Yearbook, 1989

Exhibit III: Price Demand Curve

Price ($)	Demand	Tot Rev ($)
0	100	0
20	70	1,400
40	50	2,000
50	38	1,875
60	25	1,500
110	0	0

Exhibit IV: Seasonality of Buyer Purchasing Habits (1987-1988)

Month	1987	% of total	Cumulative %	1988	% of total	Cumulative %
1	1,001,879	5.99%	5.99%	1,211,704	6.98%	6.98%
2	1,249,911	7.48%	13.47%	1,412,058	8.14%	15.12%
3	1,527,827	9.14%	22.62%	1,667,601	9.61%	24.73%
4	1,554,248	9.30%	31.92%	1,493,641	8.61%	33.34%
5	1,464,754	8.76%	40.68%	1,629,931	9.39%	42.74%
6	1,584,114	9.48%	50.16%	1,634,603	9.42%	52.16%
7	1,478,519	8.85%	59.01%	1,426,720	8.22%	60.38%
8	1,522,813	9.11%	68.12%	1,446,218	8.34%	68.72%
9	1,413,512	8.46%	76.58%	1,339,803	7.72%	76.44%
10	1,330,895	7.96%	84.54%	1,381,685	7.96%	84.40%
11	1,231,478	7.37%	91.91%	1,313,526	7.57%	91.97%
12	1,352,231	8.09%	100.00%	1,392,945	8.03%	100.00%
	16,712,181			17,350,435		

Exhibit V: National Potential Sales in Units and Dollars at 5, 10,& 20% Penetration

Month	1988 Percent	Used Car Sales (Units)	Total Kwik Chek Market @ $49.95 (Units)	Total Kwik Chek Revenues @ $49.95 (Dollars)	At a 5% Penetration of Total Market (Units)	At a 5% Penetration of Total Market (Dollars)	At a 10% Penetration of Total Market (Units)	At a 10% Penetration of Total Market (Dollars)	At a 20% Penetration of Total Market (Units)	At a 20% Penetration of Total Market (Dollars)
January	6.98%	1,633,238	612,464	$30,592,594	30,623	$1,529,630	61,246	$3,059,259	122,493	$6,118,519
February	8.14%	1,903,293	713,735	$35,651,048	35,687	$1,782,552	71,373	$3,565,105	142,747	$7,130,210
March	9.61%	2,247,735	842,901	$42,102,891	42,145	$2,105,145	84,290	$4,210,289	168,580	$8,420,578
April	8.61%	2,013,257	754,971	$37,710,821	37,749	$1,885,541	75,497	$3,771,082	150,994	$7,542,164
May	9.39%	2,196,960	823,860	$41,151,814	41,193	$2,057,591	82,386	$4,115,181	164,772	$8,230,363
June	9.42%	2,203,258	826,222	$41,269,771	41,311	$2,063,489	82,622	$4,126,977	165,244	$8,253,954
July	8.22%	1,923,055	721,146	$36,021,228	36,057	$1,801,061	72,115	$3,602,123	144,229	$7,204,246
August	8.34%	1,949,336	731,001	$36,513,505	36,550	$1,825,675	73,100	$3,651,351	146,200	$7,302,701
September	7.72%	1,805,901	677,213	$33,826,784	33,861	$1,691,339	67,721	$3,382,678	135,443	$6,765,357
October	7.96%	1,862,353	698,382	$34,884,203	34,919	$1,744,210	69,838	$3,488,420	139,676	$6,976,841
November	7.57%	1,770,483	663,931	$33,163,353	33,197	$1,658,168	66,393	$3,316,335	132,786	$6,632,671
December	8.03%	1,877,530	704,074	$35,168,491	35,204	$1,758,425	70,407	$3,516,849	140,815	$7,033,698
		23,386,400	8,769,900	$438,056,505	438,495	$21,902,825	876,990	$43,805,651	1,753,980	$87,611,301

Notes:
1) 1988 percentages taken from Exhibit IV: Seasonality of Buyer Purchasing Habits
2) Used car sales derived from data in Exhibit II for total national used car purchases
3) Total Kwik Chek market derived from Exhibit III. 37.5% demand expected at $50 pricing
4) 20% penetration is the maximum expected due to future entrants and other competition

Exhibit VI: Austin Potential Sales in Units and Dollars at 5, 10 & 20% Penetration

Month	1988 Percent	Used Car Sales (Units)	Total Kwik Chek Market @ $49.95 (Units)	Total Kwik Chek Revenues @ $49.95 (Dollars)	At a 5% Penetration of Total Market (Units)	At a 5% Penetration of Total Market (Dollars)	At a 10% Penetration of Total Market (Units)	At a 10% Penetration of Total Market (Dollars)	At a 20% Penetration of Total Market (Units)	At a 20% Penetration of Total Market (Dollars)
January	6.98%	5,670	2,126	$106,208	106	$5,310	213	$10,621	425	$21,242
February	8.14%	6,608	2,478	$123,769	124	$6,188	248	$12,377	496	$24,754
March	9.61%	7,803	2,926	$146,168	146	$7,308	293	$14,617	585	$29,234
April	8.61%	6,989	2,621	$130,920	131	$6,546	262	$13,092	524	$26,184
May	9.39%	7,627	2,860	$142,866	143	$7,143	286	$14,287	572	$28,573
June	9.42%	7,649	2,868	$143,275	143	$7,164	287	$14,328	574	$28,655
July	8.22%	6,676	2,504	$125,054	125	$6,253	250	$12,505	501	$25,011
August	8.34%	6,767	2,538	$126,763	127	$6,338	254	$12,676	508	$25,353
September	7.72%	6,270	2,351	$117,436	118	$5,872	235	$11,744	470	$23,487
October	7.96%	6,465	2,425	$121,107	121	$6,055	242	$12,111	485	$24,221
November	7.57%	6,147	2,305	$115,132	115	$5,757	230	$11,513	461	$23,026
December	8.03%	6,518	2,444	$122,094	122	$6,105	244	$12,209	489	$24,419
		81,190	30,446	$1,520,790	1,522	$76,040	3,045	$152,079	6,089	$304,158

Notes:
1) 1988 percentages taken from Exhibit IV: Seasonality of Buyer Purchasing Habits
2) Used car sales derived from data in Exhibit I for total Austin used car purchases
3) Total Kwik Chek market derived from Exhibit III. 37.5% demand expected at $50 pricing
4) 20% penetration is the maximum expected due to future entrants and other competition

Exhibit VII: National Dealer/Open Market Potential Sales in Units and Dollars at 10 & 20% Penetration

Dealer Percentage: 33%
Open Market Percentage: 67%

Month	1988 Percent	Used Car Sales (Units)	Total Kwik Chek Market @ 37.5% (Units)	Potential Dealer Sales @ 33% (Units)	Dealer Revenues @ 10% Penetrat. of Dealer Potential & $39 Price (Dollars)	Dealer Revenues @ 20% Penetrat. of Dealer Potential & $39 Price (Dollars)	Potential Open Market Sales @ 67% (Units)	Open Market Revenues @ 10% Penetrat. of Open Mrkt. Potential & $49 Price (Dollars)	Open Market Revenues @ 20% Penetrat. of Open Mrkt. Potential & $49 Price (Dollars)
January	8.14%	1,903,293	713,735	232,165	$905,443	$1,810,887	481,570	$2,405,441	$4,810,882
February	9.61%	2,247,735	842,901	274,180	$1,069,303	$2,138,607	568,720	$2,840,758	$5,681,517
March	8.61%	2,013,257	754,971	245,579	$957,756	$1,915,512	509,393	$2,544,417	$5,088,835
April	9.39%	2,196,960	823,860	267,987	$1,045,148	$2,090,297	555,873	$2,776,587	$5,553,175
May	9.42%	2,203,258	826,222	268,755	$1,048,144	$2,096,288	557,467	$2,784,546	$5,569,093
June	8.22%	1,923,055	721,146	234,576	$914,845	$1,829,690	486,570	$2,430,418	$4,860,835
July	8.34%	1,949,336	731,001	237,781	$927,348	$1,854,695	493,220	$2,463,632	$4,927,265
August	7.72%	1,805,901	677,213	220,285	$859,112	$1,718,224	456,928	$2,282,354	$4,564,709
September	7.96%	1,862,353	698,382	227,171	$885,967	$1,771,935	471,211	$2,353,700	$4,707,401
October	7.57%	1,770,483	663,931	215,965	$842,262	$1,684,525	447,966	$2,237,592	$4,475,183
November	8.03%	1,877,530	704,074	229,022	$893,188	$1,786,375	475,051	$2,372,882	$4,745,764
December		0	0	0	$0	$0	0	$0	$0
		23,386,400	8,157,436	2,653,466	$10,348,517	$20,697,034	5,503,970	$27,492,329	$54,984,657

Notes:
1) 1988 percentages taken from Exhibit IV: Seasonality of Buyer Purchasing Habits
2) Used car sales derived from data in Exhibit II for total national used car purchases
3) Total Kwik Chek market derived from Exhibit III. 37.5% demand expected at $50 pricing
4) 20% penetration is the maximum expected due to future entrants and other competition
5) It is assumed that dealers will want a 20% discount off of retail to use the service
6) The breakdown of dealer to open market sales percentages is taken from Exhibit I

Exhibit VIII: Austin Dealer/Open Market Potential Sales in Units and Dollars at 10 & 20% Penetration

Dealer Percentage:	33%												
Open Market Percentage:	67%											Open Market Revenues @	

Month	1988 Percent	Used Car Sales (Units)	Total Kwik Chek Market @ 37.5% (Units)	Potential Dealer Sales @ 33% (Units)	Dealer Revenues @ 10% Penetrat. of Dealer Potential & $39 Price (Dollars)	(Units)	Dealer Revenues @ 20% Penetrat. of Dealer Potential & $39 Price (Dollars)	(Units)	Potential Open Market Sales @ 67% (Units)	10% Penetrat. of Open Mrkt. Potential & $49 Price (Dollars)	(Units)	Open Market Revenues @ 20% Penetrat. of Open Mrkt. Potential & $49 Price (Dollars)	(Units)
January	6.98%	5,670	2,126	692	$2,697	69	$5,395	138	1,435	$7,166	143	$14,332	287
February	8.14%	6,608	2,478	806	$3,143	81	$6,287	161	1,672	$8,351	167	$16,702	334
March	9.61%	7,803	2,926	952	$3,712	95	$7,425	190	1,974	$9,862	197	$19,724	395
April	8.61%	6,989	2,621	853	$3,325	85	$6,650	171	1,768	$8,833	177	$17,667	354
May	9.39%	7,627	2,860	930	$3,628	93	$7,257	186	1,930	$9,639	193	$19,279	386
June	9.42%	7,649	2,868	933	$3,639	93	$7,278	187	1,935	$9,667	194	$19,334	387
July	8.22%	6,676	2,504	814	$3,176	81	$6,352	163	1,689	$8,438	169	$16,875	338
August	8.34%	6,767	2,538	825	$3,219	83	$6,439	165	1,712	$8,553	171	$17,106	342
September	7.72%	6,270	2,351	765	$2,983	76	$5,965	153	1,586	$7,924	159	$15,847	317
October	7.96%	6,465	2,425	789	$3,076	79	$6,152	158	1,636	$8,171	164	$16,343	327
November	7.57%	6,147	2,305	750	$2,924	75	$5,848	150	1,555	$7,768	156	$15,536	311
December	8.03%	6,518	2,444	795	$3,101	80	$6,202	159	1,649	$8,238	165	$16,476	330
		81,190	30,446	9,904	$38,624	990	$77,248	1,981	20,543	$102,610	2,054	$205,221	4,109

Notes:
1) 1988 percentages taken from Exhibit IV: Seasonality of Buyer Purchasing Habits
2) Used car sales derived from data in Exhibit II for total national used car purchases
3) Total Kwik Chek market derived from Exhibit III. 37.5% demand expected at $50 pricing
4) 20% penetration is the maximum expected due to future entrants and other competition
5) It is assumed that dealers will want a 20% discount off of retail to use the service
6) The breakdown of dealer to open market sales percentages is taken from Exhibit I

Exhibit IX: Operations Breakdown for Austin to Determine the Number of Vans Required

Dealer Price:	$39.00
Open Market Price:	$49.95

Number of inspection hours per day:	11
Number of days per week:	7

Inspection hours per week:	77
Inspection hours per year:	4,004
Average inspection hours per month:	334
Maximum inspections per van/month:	272
(Assuming 33%-67% dealer-open market split)	

Inspect time (Hrs.):	1.50	(Open market inspection time including 30 minutes travel)
Inspect time (Hrs.):	0.67	(Dealer inspection time of 40 minutes)

Month	20% Penetrat. of Dealer Potential & $39 Price (Dollars)	(Units)	Inspection Hours Required	20% Penetrat. of Open Mrkt. Potential & $49 Price (Dollars)	(Units)	Inspection Hours Required	Total Num. Inspt.	Total Van Hours Needed	Total Vans Needed
January	$5,395	138	92	$14,332	287	430	425	523	1.6
February	$6,287	161	107	$16,702	334	502	496	609	1.8
March	$7,425	190	127	$19,724	395	592	585	719	2.2
April	$6,650	171	114	$17,667	354	531	524	644	1.9
May	$7,257	186	124	$19,279	386	579	572	703	2.1
June	$7,278	187	124	$19,334	387	581	574	705	2.1
July	$6,352	163	109	$16,875	338	507	501	615	1.8
August	$6,439	165	110	$17,106	342	514	508	624	1.9
September	$5,965	153	102	$15,847	317	476	470	578	1.7
October	$6,152	158	105	$16,343	327	491	485	596	1.8
November	$5,848	150	100	$15,536	311	467	461	567	1.7
December	$6,202	159	106	$16,476	330	495	489	601	1.8
	$77,248	1,981	1,320	$205,221	4,109	6,163	6,089	7,483	1.9

Exhibit X: Fixed and Variable Cost Breakdown per Van and Inspection

Van Equipment	Cost
The van	$15,000
Test equipment:	$290
Compression	$50
Calipers	$50
Depth gauge	$50
VOM	$125
Hydrometer	$15
Scope and analyzers	$3,500
Portable personal computer	$3,000
Other equipment:	$1,350
Generator	$200
Hydraulic jack	$200
Jack stands	$150
Scooter	$50
Misc hand tools	$750
Van Customization	$1,000
Total Van Cost:	$24,140

Van Fixed Costs:	$2,925	
Monthly payment	$779	(Finance over 3 years at 10%)
Technician wages	$1,800	($20k per year + benefits)
Paging service	$25	
Insurance	$220	
Maintenance (@ 5%)	$101	

General Overhead Costs:		$7,191	(Including 20% buffer for error)
Office rent		$450	
Postage		$150	
Marketing		$2,500	
Insurance/benefits		$500	
Franchise fee ($15K)		$417	(Divided over 36 months)
Telephone		$140	
Secretary/appointment		$1,500	(Includes appointment scheduling)
Office equipment:		$336	(Finance over 3 years at 10%)
Computer	$5,000		
FAX	$900		
Copier	$1,500		
Furniture	$1,500		
Telephone	$500		
Misc	$1,000		
Total	$10,400		

Fixed Cost per Van Assuming Two Vans Are in Operation: $6,520

Van fixed cost	$2,925
Office overhead (pro-rated)	$3,595

Fixed Cost per Van-Hour of Operation (The Scarce Item): $20

Pro-rated cost per dealer inspection	$13
Pro-rated cost per open market inspection	$29

Variable costs per Inspection: $11

Gasoline	$1 (Assume 10 miles/call @ 10mpg & $1/gal.)
Misc consumables	$5
Incentive to tech	$5

Profit Margin Analysis for Dealer and Open Market Inspections

	Open Market	Dealer
Revenue	$49.95	$39.00
7% franchise fee	($3.50)	($2.73)
Variable cost	($11.00)	($10.00) (No gas for dealer insp.)
Contribution	$35.45	$26.27
Inspections per month:	342	165
Segment contribution:	$12,138	$4,336

Monthly expected total contribution:	$16,475
Less: total fixed cost	($13,040)
Net total profit before tax:	$3,435

Assuming a 33% Dealer/67% Open Market Breakdown in Inspections:

Break-even monthly inspections quantity:		402
Total 2-van fixed cost:	$13,040	
Dealer inspections:	133	
Open market inspections:	269	

Break-even Quantity for Justifying Another Van Purchase:

Van break-even for 33%/67% split:		90
Van incremental fixed cost:	$2,925	

Exhibit XI: Summary Financial Analysis for Kwik Chek in Austin

	Start	Mo. 1	Mo. 2	Mo. 3	Mo. 4	Mo. 5
Market share	0%	1%	2%	2%	3%	3%
Dealer inspections	0	8	17	17	25	25
Open market inspections	0	17	34	34	51	51
Total inspections	0	25	51	51	76	76
Number of vans needed	1	1	1	1	1	1
INCOME FROM PRODUCTION ACTIVITIES						
Dealer sales ($)	0	322	644	644	966	966
Open mkt sales ($)	0	855	1,710	1,710	2,565	2,565
Less: cost of good sold						
Variable costs	0	(271)	(542)	(542)	(813)	(813)
Franchise royalty	0	(82)	(165)	(165)	(247)	(247)
Gross margin	0	824	1,647	1,647	2,471	2,471
OPERATING EXPENSES						
General fixed costs	(7,191)	(7,191)	(7,191)	(7,191)	(7,191)	(7,191)
Van fixed costs	(2,925)	(2,925)	(2,925)	(2,925)	(2,925)	(2,925)
Net operating income	(10,116)	(9,292)	(8,469)	(8,469)	(7,645)	(7,645)
ADDITIONAL EXPENSES						
Promotion cost	(10,000) [Initial advertising, public relations, etc.]					
Misc. startup cost	(5,000)					
Net profit before tax	(25,116)	(9,292)	(8,469)	(8,469)	(7,645)	(7,645)
CUMULATIVE CASH FLOW	(25,116)	(34,408)	(42,877)	(51,345)	(58,990)	(66,635)

Assumptions:
1) There is a 33%/67% quantity split between dealers and open market inspections
2) Dealer inspections cost $39.00 and open market inspections cost $49.95
3) The maximum number of inspections per van is 272 per month
4) Office fixed expenses can handle up to 4 vans without expansion
5) Demand will never exceed 37.5% of all used car purchases
6) Kwik Chek can achieve a 20% share of the demand within 2 years
7) More than 20% share may not be possible due to competition
8) Available market for dealers and open market inspections in units is:

            Dealers: 9,904   (From Exhibit VIII)
            Open Mkt: 20,543   (From Exhibit VIII)

Mo. 6	Mo. 7	Mo. 8	Mo. 9	Mo. 10	Mo. 11	Mo. 12	Year 2	Year 3
4%	4%	5%	6%	7%	8%	9%	20%	20%
33	33	41	50	58	66	74	1,981	1,981
68	68	86	103	120	137	154	4,109	4,109
101	101	127	152	178	203	228	6,089	6,089
1	1	1	1	1	1	1	2	2
1,288	1,288	1,609	1,931	2,253	2,575	2,897	77,251	77,251
3,420	3,420	4,276	5,131	5,986	6,841	7,696	205,225	205,225
(1,083)	(1,083)	(1,354)	(1,625)	(1,896)	(2,167)	(2,438)	(65,003)	(65,003)
(330)	(330)	(412)	(494)	(577)	(659)	(741)	(19,773)	(19,773)
3,295	3,295	4,119	4,942	5,766	6,590	7,414	197,700	197,700
(7,191)	(7,191)	(7,191)	(7,191)	(7,191)	(7,191)	(7,191)	(86,292)	(86,292)
(2,925)	(2,925)	(2,925)	(2,925)	(2,925)	(2,925)	(2,925)	(70,200)	(70,200)
(6,821)	(6,821)	(5,997)	(5,174)	(4,350)	(3,526)	(2,702)	41,208	41,208
(6,821)	(6,821)	(5,997)	(5,174)	(4,350)	(3,526)	(2,702)	41,208	41,208
(73,456)	(80,277)	(86,274)	(91,448)	(95,797)	(99,323)	(102,026)	(60,818)	(19,610)

Exhibit XII: Owner/Mechanic Summary Financial Analysis for Kwik Chek in Austin

	Start	Mo. 1	Mo. 2	Mo. 3	Mo. 4	Mo. 5
Market share	0%	1%	2%	2%	3%	3%
Dealer inspections	0	8	17	17	25	25
Open market inspections	0	17	34	34	51	51
Total inspections	0	25	51	51	76	76
Number of vans needed	1	1	1	1	1	1
INCOME FROM PRODUCTION ACTIVITIES						
Dealer sales ($)	0	322	644	644	966	966
Open mkt sales ($)	0	855	1,710	1,710	2,565	2,565
Less: cost of good sold						
Variable costs	0	(144)	(288)	(288)	(432)	(432)
Franchise royalty	0	(82)	(165)	(165)	(247)	(247)
Gross margin	0	951	1,901	1,901	2,852	2,852
OPERATING EXPENSES						
General fixed costs	(7,191)	(7,191)	(7,191)	(7,191)	(7,191)	(7,191)
Van fixed costs	(1,125)	(1,125)	(1,125)	(1,125)	(1,125)	(1,125)
Net operating income	(8,316)	(7,365)	(6,415)	(6,415)	(5,464)	(5,464)
ADDITIONAL EXPENSES						
Promotion cost	(10,000)	[Initial advertising, public relations, etc.]				
Misc. startup cost	(5,000)					
Net profit before tax	(23,316)	(7,365)	(6,415)	(6,415)	(5,464)	(5,464)
CUMULATIVE CASH FLOW	(23,316)	(30,681)	(37,096)	(43,511)	(48,975)	(54,439)

Assumptions:
1) There is a 33%/67% quantity split between dealers and open market inspections
2) Dealer inspections cost $39.00 and open market inspections cost $49.95
3) The maximum number of inspections per van is 272 per month
4) Office fixed expenses can handle up to 4 vans without expansion
5) Demand will never exceed 37.5% of all used car purchases
6) Kwik Chek can achieve a 20% share of the demand within 2 years
7) More than 20% share may not be possible due to competition
8) Available market for dealers and open market inspections in units is:

                Dealers: 9,904 (From Exhibit VIII)
                Open Mkt: 20,543 (From Exhibit VIII)

Mo. 6	Mo. 7	Mo. 8	Mo. 9	Mo. 10	Mo. 11	Mo. 12	Year 2	Year 3
4%	4%	5%	6%	7%	8%	9%	20%	20%
33	33	41	50	58	66	74	1,981	1,981
68	68	86	103	120	137	154	4,109	4,109
101	101	127	152	178	203	228	6,089	6,089
1	1	1	1	1	1	1	2	2
1,288	1,288	1,609	1,931	2,253	2,575	2,897	77,251	77,251
3,420	3,420	4,276	5,131	5,986	6,841	7,696	205,225	205,225
(576)	(576)	(720)	(864)	(1,008)	(1,152)	(1,296)	(65,003)	(65,003)
(330)	(330)	(412)	(494)	(577)	(659)	(741)	(19,773)	(19,773)
3,802	3,802	4,753	5,704	6,654	7,605	8,556	197,700	197,700
(7,191)	(7,191)	(7,191)	(7,191)	(7,191)	(7,191)	(7,191)	(86,292)	(86,292)
(1,125)	(1,125)	(1,125)	(1,125)	(1,125)	(1,125)	(1,125)	(21,600)	(21,600)
(4,514)	(4,514)	(3,563)	(2,612)	(1,662)	(711)	240	89,808	89,808
(4,514)	(4,514)	(3,563)	(2,612)	(1,662)	(711)	240	89,808	89,808
(58,953)	(63,466)	(67,029)	(69,642)	(71,303)	(72,014)	(71,775)	18,033	107,841

Legal Considerations

The primary legal issues that should be considered in establishing Kwik Chek as a national franchise are (1) franchiser liability for franchisee actions, and (2) termination of franchise agreement by either the franchiser or the franchisee.

The principal way that the franchiser can be held liable for the actions of a franchisee is if the franchisee represents itself as an agent of the parent company. To avoid this agency issue, all collateral literature published by the franchiser should indicate that all Kwik Chek operations are independently owned and operated. In this way, there can be no mistake on the part of the customer that the local franchisee is working their own business and on their own behalf.

A clear definition of the agency relationship will protect the franchiser from liability related to injury or accidents resulting from improper inspection and also from any financial liabilities that the franchisee may incur.

To address the termination of franchise agreement issue, it should be clearly delineated in the franchise agreement what the required payment procedures and time frames should be from the franchisee to the franchiser. In addition, the level of support that the franchisee can reasonably expect from the franchiser should also be clearly defined. In this way, there is less likelihood of misunderstanding by either party, and the franchiser is protected from having a franchisee that is not performing up to expectations bring down the rest of the organization.

In addition, if the franchiser has agreed to supply credit to the franchisee to start the business, then the franchiser should protect the investment by having strict reporting procedures as to the actions being taken by the franchisee to meet the required revenue goals.

Franchising agreements are being treated more as "relational contracts" that extend over a longer period of time than as individual contracts that have a clearly defined duration and outcome. Many courts are treating franchise agreements as a sort of marriage, and many of the precedents established for divorce law in community property states are being incorporated into termination of franchise agreements. The relationship is treated as a type of partnership, and the parties involved are compensated for their "expected" returns from the venture should it be terminated.

In this way, it should be clearly understood by the franchisee that should the franchisee lose the right to operate under the Kwik Chek name, the business is returned to the franchiser. An equitable settlement for the return can be established at the time of transfer.

Appendix C

Resources

The following list offers you extra resources on a variety of business and entrepreneurial subjects. I included website addresses where possible.

Small Business—General

American Chamber of Commerce Executives
4875 Eisenhower Avenue, Suite 250,
Alexandria, VA 22304
703-998-0072
www.acce.org

The American Institute for Small Business
Educational Materials for Small Business and Entrepreneurship
426 Second Street
Excelsior, MN 55331
1-800-328-2906
www.aisb.biz

American Success Institute
5 North Main Street
Natick, MA 01760
508-651-3303
www.success.org

Business Resource Center
www.morebusiness.com

CCH Business Owner's Toolkit
www.toolkit.cch.com

eWeb: Education for Entrepreneurship
eweb.slu.edu

Small Business Development Centers (SBDC)
www.sbaonline.sba.gov/SBDC

The National Association for the Self-Employed
PO Box 612067
DFW Airport
Dallas, TX 75261-2067
1-800-232-6273
www.nase.org

National Business Incubation Association
20 East Circle Drive, #37198
Athens, OH 45701-3571
740-593-4331
www.nbia.org

Service Core of Retired Executives (SCORE)
www.score.org

Small Business Development Centers
SBDCNET national information clearinghouse
sbdcnet.utsa.edu

U.S. Chamber of Commerce
1615 H Street, NW
Washington, DC 20062-2000
1-800-638-6582
www.uschamber.com

U.S. Department of Commerce
1401 Constitution Avenue NW
Washington, DC 20230
888-324-1551
www.mbda.gov

U.S. Small Business Administration (SBA)
409 3rd Street, SW
Washington, DC 20416
1-800-U-ASK-SBA
www.sba.gov

U.S. Business Advisor (Sponsored by the SBA)
www.business.gov

IRS Small Business/Self Employed Resource
www.irs.gov/businesses/small

SmartBiz.com General Business Information
www.smartbiz.com

Special Topics

The following are specialized resources that may be of use to you in your business.

Census Information

Here is an excellent place to obtain information regarding general population characteristics in your area of question.

U.S. Bureau of the Census
4700 Silver Hill Road
Washington, DC 20233-0001
301-763-4636
www.census.gov

Financing

Here are several locations you can review for information on preparing for financing, or actually obtaining financing for your venture.

SBA Finance Website
www.sba.gov/financing

General and Comprehensive Business Loan Information Link Page
www.smallbusinesscenter.com

LendingTree.com Loan Center
www.lendingtree.com/stm/sblc

Moneycafe.com
www.nfsn.com

American Express Home Page
www.americanexpress.com

Franchises

Don't buy a franchise before talking to these people to determine as much as possible about the parent company of your possible franchise purchase.

American Association of Franchisees & Dealers
PO Box 81887
San Diego, CA 92138-1887
1-800-733-9858
www.aafd.org

International Franchise Association
1501 K Street, N.W., Suite 350
Washington, DC 20005202-628-8000
www.franchise.org

Nettizen.com Franchise Resource
www.nettizen.com

Franchise Solutions
www.franchisesolutions.com/resource

Bison.com Franchise Opportunity Web Page
www.bison1.com

International Business

Business Network International
545 College Commerce Way
Upland, CA 91786
1-800-825-8286 (Outside Southern California)
1-909-608-7575 (Inside Southern California)
www.bni.com

International Chamber of Commerce
1212 Avenue of the Americas
New York, NY 10036-1689
212-703-5060
www.iccwbo.org

International Small Business Consortium
3309 Windjammer Street
Norman, OK 73072
www.isbc.com

U.S. Agency for International Development (USAID)
Public Inquiries
Information Center
U.S. Agency for International Development
Ronald Reagan Building
Washington, D.C. 20523-1000
202-712-0000
www.usaid.gov

U.S. Council for International Business
1212 Avenue of the Americas
New York, NY 10036
212-354-4480
www.uscib.org

Michigan State University GlobalEdge.com Web Page
globaledge.msu.edu/ibrd/ibrd.asp

Import-Export Help General Links Web Page
www.importexporthelp.com

Marketing General

Marketing Resource Center
Concept Marketing Group, Inc.
8655 E Via de Ventura Suite G-200
Scottsdale, AZ 85258
1-800-575-5369
www.marketingsource.com

Software Marketing General Resource Web Page
www.softwaremarketingresource.com/
software-marketing-resource.html

Market Research

Your public library may already subscribe.

InfoTrac General Business Information Source
www.infotrac.com

Specialized Market Research Reports
www.newsletters.com

The Wall Street Journal
www.wsj.com

General Internet Trends and Statistics
www.clickz.com/stats

Minorities in Business

National Minority Business Council
25 West 45th Street, Suite 301
New York, NY 10036
212-997-4753
www.nmbc.org

National Minority Supplier Development Council
1040 Avenue of the Americas, 2nd Floor
New York, NY 10018
212-944-2430
www.nmsdcus.org

Hispanic Business Magazine Website
www.hispanicbusiness.com

Minority Business Entrepreneur Magazine Website
www.mbemag.com

General Entrepreneurship Information for the Black Community
www.einfonews.com

SBA Office of Minority Enterprise and Development
www.sba.gov/8abd

Patents

U.S. Patent and Trademark Office
PO Box 1450
Alexandria, VA 22313-1450
1-800-786-9199
www.uspto.gov

General Patent Information
From a Law Firm: Oppedahl & Larson LLP
www.patents.com

General Intellectual Property Information
From the Franklin Pierce Law School, New Hampshire
www.piercelaw.edu/tfield/ipbasics.htm

Women in Business

Interagency Committee on Women's Business Enterprise
National Economic Council
The White House
Washington, DC 20500
202-456-2174

National Association of Women Business Owners
8405 Greensboro Drive, Suite 800
McLean, VA 22102
703-506-3268
www.nawbo.org

Center for Women's Business Research
1411 K Street, NW, Suite 1350
Washington, DC 20005-3407
202-638-3060
www.nfwbo.org

U.S. Small Business Administration Office of Women's Business Ownership
409 Third Street SW
Washington, DC 20416
202-205-6673
www.sbaonline.sba.gov/womeninbusiness

Women's Business Enterprise National Council
1120 Connecticut Ave. NW, Suite 1000
Washington, DC 20036
202-872-5515 ext.10
www.wbenc.org

Online Women's Business Center
Sponsored by the SBA
www.onlinewbc.gov

Bibliography

General Small Business

Barreca, Hugo and Julia O'Neill. *The Entrepreneur's Internet Handbook: Your Legal and Practical Guide to Starting a Business Website.* Naperville, IL: Sphinx Pub, 2002.

Carlock, Randel and John Ward. *Strategic Planning for the Family Business: Parallel Planning to Unify the Family and Business.* New York, NY: Palgrave Macmillan, 2001.

Entrepreneur Magazine. *Starting an Import/Export Business.* New York, NY: John Wiley and Sons, Inc., 1995.

McQuown, Judith H. *Inc Yourself: How To Profit By Setting Up Your Own Corporation.* Franklin Lakes, NJ: Career Press, Incorporated, 2004.

McWhirter, Darien. *The Personnel Policy Handbook for Growing Companies.* Holbrook, MA: Bob Adams, Inc., 1994.

Paulson, Ed. *The Complete Idiot's Guide to Buying and Selling a Business.* Indianapolis, IN: Macmillan, 1999.

Sutton, Garrett, Ann Blackman, and Robert T. Kiyosaki. *Own Your Own Corporation: Why the Rich Own Their Own Companies and Everyone Else Works for Them.* New York, NY: Warner Books, 2001.

Collections, Accounting, Finance, and Taxes

Carter, Gary. *J.K. Lasser's Taxes Made Easy for Your Home Based Business*. New York, NY: John Wiley & Sons, 2005.

Lasser, J. K. *Your Income Tax*. New York, NY: John Wiley and Sons, updated and published annually.

Magos, Alice. *Small Business Financing: How and Where to Get It. 2nd Edition*, Riverwoods, IL: Commerce Clearing House,2002.

Paulson, Ed. *The Complete Idiot's Guide to Personal Finance with Quicken*. Indianapolis, IN: Macmillan, 1998.

Placencia, Jose, Bruce Weige, and Don Oliver. *Business Owner's Guide to Accounting and Bookkeeping*. Central Point, OR: PSI Research-Oasis Press, 1997.

Troy, Leo. *Almanac of Business and Industrial Financial Ratios, 2006 Edition*. Gaithersburg, MD: Aspen Publishers, Inc.,2006.

Warner, Ralph E. *Everybody's Guide to Small Claims Court, 8th Edition*. Berkeley, CA: Nolo Press, 2005.

Weltman, Barbara. *J.K. Lasser's Small Business Taxes 2006: Your Complete Guide to a Better Bottom Line*. New York, NY: John Wiley & Sons, 2006.

Wilber, W. Kelsea. *Getting Paid in Full*. Naperville, IL: Sourcebooks Inc., 1994.

Marketing, Sales, and Promotion

Barban, Arnold, Steven Cristol, and Frank Kopec. *Essentials of Media Planning, 3rd Edition*. New York, NY: McGraw Hill Trade, 1993.

Levinson, Jay Conrad. *Guerrilla Marketing: Secrets for Making Big Profits from Your Small Business, 3rd Edition*. New York, NY: Mariner Books, 1998.

Additional Reading

Covey, Stephen. *The 7 Habits of Highly Effective People*. New York, NY: Fireside/Simon & Schuster, 1989.

Johnson, Spencer. *One Minute for Myself*. New York, NY: Avon, 1991.

Patsula, Peter J. *Successful Business Planning in 30 Days: A Step-By-Step Guide for Writing a Business Plan and Starting Your Own Business*. Mansfield, OH: Patsula Media, 2004.

Especially for Women

Moore, Dorothy. *Careerpreneurs: Lessons from Leading Women Entrepreneurs on Building a Career Without Boundaries*. Palo Alto, CA: Davies-Black Publishing, 2000.

Moore, Dorothy and Holly Buttner. *Women Entrepreneurs Moving Beyond The Glass Ceiling*. Thousand Oaks, CA: Sage Publications, 1997.

Pollak, Jane. *Soul Proprietor: 100 Lessons from a Lifestyle Entrepreneur*. Berkeley, CA: Publishers Group West, 2001.

Popcorn, Faith and Lys Marigold. *EVEolution: The Eight Truths of Marketing To Women*. New York, NY: Hyperion, 2000.

Shirk, Martha and Anna Wadia. *Kitchen Table Entrepreneurs: How Eleven Women Escaped Poverty and Became Their Own Bosses*. Boulder, CO: Westview Press, 2004.

Silver, A. David. *Enterprising Women: Lessons from 100 of the Greatest Entrepreneurs Of Our Day*. New York, NY: Amacom Books, 1994.

About China

McGregor, James. *One Billion Customers: Lessons from the Front Lines of Doing Business in China*. New York, NY: Free Press, 2005.

Index

J–K–L

Q